THE COMPLETE MARATHONER

Edited by Joe Henderson

World Publications, Inc.

Contents

Part Six: Eating Up the Miles

Part Seven: Hot and Cold Running

Part Eight: Keeping the Sport on Course

Part Nine: The People Up Front

Part Ten: Off to the Races

Part 1
Magic, Meaning, and Myths

1

Lure of the Marathon

Why has the race quadrupled in popularity in the 1970s?

The marathon, like most things worth doing, offers both risks and rewards. Because it gives a chance to go beyond usual boundaries—and at least an equal possibility of failing—the race both attracts and frightens runners. Testing one's limits is risky and frightening, but beating the odds and the fears is a main attraction to this sport.

As the fastest active runner and an Olympic champion, Ian Thompson and Frank Shorter speak with some authority on the marathon.

Thompson, the Briton who has run 2:09:12, said, "In track races, you are against one another. In the marathon, it's the event, the distance, you have to beat."

When you beat it, as Ian did in 1974, the experience is a heady one not matched by beating a mere human rival. Yet Thompson also said, "There are times when the thought of running a marathon quite frightens me."

That common fear undoubtedly sweetens the sense of victory all runners feel when they take on a race the size of the marathon and win by their own definition of that word. The winners may feel a bit superior to non-marathoners for what they've accomplished.

Frank Shorter sees a "superiority complex" developing among marathoners, and wants no part of the thinking which goes: "I run a marathon; you've never run one. Therefore, I'm better than you."

Frank tried in a *Runner's World* interview to take some of the mystique away from this race. "Hell," he said, "anybody who goes out and trains for two months can probably run a marathon." It is, he implied, just another long run—and an over-emphasized, over-romanticized one at that.

However, it was Shorter's win in Munich which helped spur the boom of marathoning in the US. And it was Shorter who pointed out a most attractive mystery of the race.

Tom Jordan of *Track & Field News* said to Frank, "Most people can't even run one five-minute mile, and you're able to string together 26 of them. Does that ever boggle your mind?"

"Yeah," Shorter answered, "I can't just sit here and decide that I'm going to put on my shoes and go out to run even 15 miles at five-minute pace. You just have to be in the race situation. Getting pulled along is the big thing."

This is a paradox of marathoning. More than any other regularly-run race, this is a personal challenge. Success is measured in personal terms. Yet here, perhaps more than in any other event, runners need competition to draw out the best from themselves. They need to lose themselves in the pace of the field to find what they can do. They need others to show them that the "impossible" can happen.

This is true from Frank Shorter's and Ian Thompson's level down through three and four hours. As competition improves, everyone gains.

First, there must be races—lots of full marathons in every part of the country. In 1969, there were fewer than 40 of them in the United States. The *1970 Marathon Handbook* listed one American runner (Kenny Moore with an American best of 2:11:35) under 2:20 for the previous year. The women's world mark then was 3:07, and the number of women who ran this far could be counted on the toes of two feet because they had to break the AAU rules to enter races.

By 1976, the US Olympic qualifying standard had been set at 2:20, and more than 40 men had run it. Bill Rodgers led them with an American record of 2:09:55.

The women made even more incredible strides. Two of them, Chantal Langlace and Christa Vahlensieck, took turns lowering the world record during '77. It ended the year at 2:34:47. The 1969 world mark no longer makes the top 100 times.

There are many ways of explaining the improvement in performance in the 1970s, but no factor weighs so heavily as simple opportunity. US marathoners now have four times more races to enter, and women are always welcome.

New races create new marathoners, and they come together to produce faster races. The speed comes from two directions: First, the

GROWTH OF U.S. MARATHONING

Year	Races	M/2:30	M/3:00	W/3:00	W/4:00
1970	73	50	812	---	---
1971	102	81	1120	3	32
1972	124	115	1428	3	53
1973	127	103	1721	4	91
1974	135	158	2450	10	141
1975	148	226	3060	17	230
1976	166	251	3600	26	430

M/2:30=men under 2:30; W/3:00=women under 3:00, etc.; final 1977 figures not available at time of this book's publication.

crush of runners in the pack drives the winners to better times. And the winners pull everyone along at a stiffer pace.

In this sport, quantity and quality go together. The biggest races usually yield the fastest times. For instance, the 1977 Boston Marathon was both the biggest and fastest in US history. Nearly 900 runners broke three hours.

This growing figure may bother runners who think the weight of numbers cheapens their performance. But there are other, better ways to read the statistics. Remember that each time represents a person who once doubted he or she could go so far, so fast. Think of each new name as someone who helped you go as far and fast as you did.

2

Meaning of the Marathon

It isn't the exercise or the sightseeing that attracts runners

Joe Henderson

On the face of it, it makes no sense to run marathons.

What is a marathon, anyway? Twenty-six miles, 385 yards. Forty-two kilometers, 195 meters. The people who devised this race didn't have the good sense to make it an even distance, in either the mile or the metric system.

What purpose does running a marathon serve? I'm skeptical whenever anyone tells me, "It makes me feel so healthy." Maybe some of the early training makes a runner healthy. But as George Sheehan and others have written, health is a stage you pass through on the way to getting racing fit. Much of the later, more serious training for marathons and the race itself should carry a "Caution: may be hazardous to your health!" warning.

An Eastern podiatrist, a marathoner himself, told me, "I know without looking at the race schedule if there has been a marathon over the weekend. Starting on Monday morning and continuing all week, my office is filled with the casualties of the race."

We can't be going to these lengths because it makes us feel more alive and energetic, either. The hollow-eyed, glazed stare of a runner in the 26th-mile, post-collapse-point "survival shuffle" is proof this can't be true. So are the finishers who hang limply on each other, too weak to stand alone.

It's absurd to think we run marathons because we like to sightsee, because we're running too hard and with too much concentration to know whether we're passing through a park or the city dump. Anyway, most marathon courses don't go anywhere except back to where they started.

Well, then, do we do it for the competition, the chance to be a winner, to earn prizes? Not in the usual meanings of these words. Not one marathoner in a hundred is rewarded for placing well, or runs for that reason, or knows or cares as much about the winner as he does about himself.

Maybe that's the point of marathoning. So many people are running the distance now because it means something to them personally. It's a big athletic goal they can reach with their own sweat, not second-hand through a TV screen. Whether the goal has any purpose is irrelevant so long as it has meaning.

This was Mark Twain's definition of play: any activity which has meaning but no purpose. We forget sometimes that marathoning is just play—a sport, a game. And we waste too much time trying to find the purpose in it and to explain it in purposeful, practical terms.

Maybe it's time to admit that running 26.22 miles is as irrational and illogical as batting a fuzzy ball back and forth across a net, chasing a little white ball around a golf course, or committing assault and battery between two sets of goal posts. None of these games serves any great purpose, none has any great importance to the survival of mankind, but they all have great meaning to the people involved. That's all we should ask of our play.

Marathoning has whatever meaning we runners, by ourselves and as a group, decide to give it. And we've decided to give it more than any other event in long-distance running—perhaps more than all the other races combined.

Some runners object to this. They ask me, "Why give so much emphasis to the marathon? The race is overrated, and you are partly responsible.

I thought this was true myself once, and I said it in print. I thought if we gave as much attention to 15 kilometers as to the marathon, it would take on similar importance. I was wrong. That was as naive as thinking the women's shot put could become as much a glamor event as the mile run.

The marathon is special to long-distance runners, and it will stay that way. Evidence of this is in the mail I read. For every letter telling *Runner's World* to de-emphasize the event, there are 50 asking for details on how to build up to that distance and how to enter races.

The marathon is meaningful because it gives a focus to the long-distance sport in general and to individual running careers in particular. It is the only distance above 10,000 meters with a history going back many centuries, with legends of its own and with an Olympic tradition. It is an "ultimate" toward which an everyday runner can climb. Marathon runners don't just run marathons. They race at shorter and sometimes longer distances, and they train for all of their races.

When promoters create a marathon, they form more than a single race. A full program of races often grows up in the area to supplement the big one, because the marathoners aren't satisfied with one race a year. The shorter races in turn serve as developmental steps for would-be marathoners and as ends for non-marathoners. Runners create races, and racing opportunities create new runners.

The first goal of the new marathoner is finishing. And to finish, he has to train longer than before. This training is a sneaky way of exposing him to other good—but not so obvious—things about running: the positively addicting sensations of runs beyond a half-hour; the habit of maintaining a demanding schedule; the temporary stress and ultimate satisfaction of sub-marathon races; the support of a group on long training runs.

Once the ambition of "I just want to finish" is satisfied, the new goal becomes time—improving one's own best time, running a time which all marathon runners understand and appreciate, a time which has no intrinsic value but has as much meaning as we choose to place upon it.

Times are important because everyone who runs can have one, and because the prospect of improving it is a driving force which keeps many marathoners running.

Boston Marathon officials have caused a brouhaha by applying rigid qualifying standards to the race. The decision was made to limit the size of the race field, and I can find fault with this way of doing it.

But the entry limits have had a good side-effect. Will Cloney and Jock Semple of the sponsoring Boston AA are absolutely right when they say, "Our standards have helped raise the level of marathoning in this country." They have caused marathoners to work harder and aim higher. The marathon itself has that effect on the sport as a whole.

3

Myths of the Marathon

The race isn't the killer the Greeks made it out to be

Manfred Steffny

he origin. The first Greek "marathon" was run on April 10, 1896, as part of the Athens Olympics. This is a fact. Everything that has been reported about the "historical" run of the messenger from the battlefield at Marathon to Athens to announce the victory over the Persians belongs in the realm of legend.

The historians of that time used anecdotes to dress up their pictures of history. The historian Herodotus, a contemporary of the battle of 490 B.C., reported nothing about a messenger's run and subsequent death. Herodotus was an adept storyteller and a conscientious portrayer of historical occurrences. If Pheidippides had made his ill-fated run, Herodotus wouldn't have withheld this fact from the Greeks.

Plutarch brought up the legend of the marathon runner 560 years later. It apparently served him as decoration and as an improved story-telling transition from the battlefield into the cosmopolitan city of Athens and its reaction to the victory. The historians of antiquity were, after all, story-tellers.

The distance. Even the present distance of 26 miles, 385 yards (or 42.195 kilometers) is not correct. From the tiny village of Marathon to the city center of Athens is about 38 kilometers. The present marathon course from Marathon to Athens begins in Marathon, then angles off to the left after about five kilometers to pass the graves of 192 fallen Greeks of 490 B.C. This it must do to cover the distance required today.

The distance of 42.195 kilometers originated by chance. From 1896 to 1908, the distance varied. In 1908, an English princess wanted to watch the start from her window in Windsor Castle, then view the finish from her loge seat in the stadium. Her wish was the Olympic organizers' command. Later, the London course was taken as the standard for future runs. For the lengthened distance—from about 40 to 42.195 kilometers—all marathon runners can thank this princess. Curses during the last couple of kilometers may thus be directed to "Her Royal Highness."

The toughness. Solely the hoopla surrounding marathon running is responsible for the marathon distance being considered the ultimate of all endurance running. Besides the compulsory image of an "historical" messenger's deadly run, there are several factors that contributed to this prejudice.

The early Olympic organizers always irrationally scheduled this long-distance run for mid-day. The participants were often poorly prepared, usually running the marathon as a second event. But this concept of the marathon as the most strenuous race really became a dogma with Dorando Pietri's collapse in 1908, while leading the Olympic marathon just before the finish. This photograph went around the world. It is one of the most published sports photos of all time.

It was not the marathon run that felled Dorando. He was *doped* and therefore collapsed. Only on his death bed did the Italian who was pitied by a whole generation of athletes admit his unfairness.

Certainly more strenuous than marathon runs are stage races in bicycling and singles canoeing races of 10,000 meters. On a similar level are rowing (especially in eight-man and four-man shells, with a high stroke rate) and long-distance swimming. The stress load in marathon running is more distributed—organically immense, to be sure, but muscularly below average.

The training load. Previously, marathon running was the sport of most intensive training, alongside bicycle road racing. Now, the demands of all sports have risen tremendously, and the marathon runner can't keep pace. Three hours a day is enough running even for world-class marathoners. Compared to other sports, this has become less impressive. Six to eight hours daily are demanded of world-class gymnasts; likewise, figure skaters. The best swimmers train 4-5 hours. The list could easily be continued. Because of modern strength training—dispensable, if not damaging, for marathon runners—even middle-distance runners may train more than marathon runners. The martyr's schedules of weight lifters, decathletes, hammer throwers and shot putters are scary for the marathon runner who pleasantly runs 30 kilometers at steady pace.

The "horse's death" to legs. This classic remark of Paavo Nurmi's trainer can likewise be laid to rest. Sufficient preparation and modern running shoes have turned back the danger of injury in marathon running to a considerable degree. Another factor is the turning away from interval training with its untold pounding stress. It's like this today: Many runners who've been injured on the track are turning to road running, where their legs just don't hurt so much. The running invalids of our day and age are reporting from the camp of sprinters and decathletes. Marathon running style is orthopedically healthier than, for example, the triple jump or football.

The automation gap. That marathon runners are wondered at by society lies less in the runner's achievement than in the gigantic distance separating overcivilized man from distance running. To make it clear to himself how far 42.195 kilometers is, the average citizen first calculates how long it would take to drive this distance. Then, he compares this time with that of the marathon runner and finds the difference rather small. The marathoner is "astonishing."

The runner ought not to bask in the aura of this astonishment, but should contribute to the destruction of the myth and try to inspire as many people as he can to run themselves. As long as the general public travels to the mailbox in autos, diseases of civilization will continue to increase rapidly. Where people still live like our grandfathers—as for example in Ethiopia—and where they cover great distances just to go to work, often falling into a run for the sake of simplicity, in those countries the marathon is something natural. Long-distance runs are the true sport of the people there. Here at home, though, the marathon runner must not let himself be stamped "outsider."

The idealists. One meets this opinion at every turn. It is just as far off as calling marathon runners "masochists." People jump, run, swim and climb Mount Everest not because of idealism but to pacify their personal ambition, to still their lust for adventure, to wake up a feeling of happiness, to discover themselves or discover comrades. So much garbage has been pawned off in the name of idealism that a person should defend himself against being called an idealist just because he occasionally covers 42.195 kilometers in competition.

What is marathoning? A very normal sport compared with billiards, bobsledding, sailing and fencing. Being a bit more strenuous than most other sports, marathoning is played up sensationally, false values are propped up for it, and its inner worth is often overlooked. It is a sport with its own laws, demanding a special mentality—like every other sport. That's all.

Part 2
Those Who Ran Before

Where It Started

The event traces its roots and name
to the Plain of Marathon

Jack Galub

I t was 1946, and Europe was a smoking pile. The Berlin airlift was yet to come. For a blessed day, that continent's problems were far away as the Boston Marathon once again was center stage.

From Greece, one of the most battered of the small countries, 36-year-old Stylianos Kyriakides flew into Boston on a lumbering prop plane and went on to win the run in 2:29:27. According to *Life* magazine, he shouted, "For Greece!" as he crossed the finish line.

Now in his 60s, Kyriakides no longer runs. Instead, he works with young athletes and heads the sports committee in the Philothey area of Athens where he lives. I spent a day with Stelios in 1976, driving the length of the historic Marathon to Athens course.

The Plain of Marathon should first be seen not during a race nor with a gaggle of tourists but alone or with one or two runners. In the stillness, it is easy to lose oneself in the history, legend and myth that envelopes the area.

The Plain is much as it was in 490 B.C. when the outnumbered Athenians and Plataeans threw back a Persian army. It still is flanked on the south and west by a crescent of mountains. The Plain itself is flat; 5½ miles long and 1½-2½ miles wide. Gone is the great marsh on its northeast corner along the Bay of Marathon. A number of small, ancient villages also have vanished. Now, there is a two-lane highway leading into the present village of Marathon. There is no industry, and few cars or buses are seen on the road.

Just beyond the southern end of the village is a marble stone on which is emblazoned in gold letters, "Starting Point of the Marathon."The first leg of the run crosses the Plain and goes past the

Tymvos of Marathon—the 39-foot-high tumulus erected over the ashes of the 192 Plataeans killed in the battle—and onto the Marathon-Athens road.

During marathon races, the two-lane portion of the highway is closed to traffic until it links with the four-lane divided artery that cuts across Athens. At that point, one lane is closed off and lined by police to prevent interference with runners by spectators, vehicles and dogs.

At the sixth mile, the road starts an undulating rise topped off at the 10th mile and then easing down for about a mile. The killing segment of the route begins at 11 miles. There the highway climbs almost steadily through the 18th mile, crests sharply at 20 miles, levels off, rises again and then starts down into Athens.

As the runners near the heart of the city, they peel off for the finish inside the glistening Panathinaikos Stadium. Built entirely of white marble, the spectacular landmark was completed in time for revival of the Olympics in 1896. It is now too narrow for modern competition, but is kept for the finish of the National Marathon and as a monument to the Olympics.

The National Marathon is run in April starting at two in the afternoon, an hour when the average Greek is settling down for his afternoon nap. An increasingly popular "open" marathon is run on the course each October. Nowhere else can a runner feel so much a part of the history of his sport.

Bikila's Triumph, Tragedy

He won twice at the Olympics and died in a wheelchair

Dave Prokop

It was only nine years earlier—and seemed like yesterday—that Abebe Bikila, running tirelessly, effortlessly, outclassed the marathon field at the Tokyo Olympics. When Bikila finished, becoming the first man to win back-to-back Olympic gold medals in the marathon (he had won at Rome in 1960, incredibly, running barefooted), he went straight to the infield and, with thousands looking on in awe, started a series of vigorous exercises.

It was not the first time he had done calisthenics after a long race. In 1962, in Sweden, he had done 10 minutes of exercises immediately after bettering Emil Zatopek's old record for the one-hour run, explaining that he stiffened up quickly if he stopped cold after running. But to the fans in Tokyo's Olympic Stadium, Bikila's calisthenics were unprecedented and they spelled out a message about his race that was clear: "See, it was easy."

Indeed, to this superlative endurance runner from Ethiopia, the marathon did seem easy. In the superb slow-motion sequence in Kon Ichigawa's documentary "Tokyo Olympiad," Bikila, who was only 5'10" but gave the appearance of height, seems only bone and sinew. His pencil-thin, long legs carry him lightly, gracefully over the pavement (American writer John Underwood once observed that Bikila's footsteps when he ran were perfectly inaudible). Face totally relaxed, he hardly seems to be breathing. There is not a hint of haste or tension in his running action. Yet he is moving close to five minutes per mile and his competitors are out of sight behind him.

Abebe Bikila, more than any man before him or since, gave the impression of boundless endurance.

On Thursday, Oct. 25, 1973, in Addis Ababa, Abebe Bikila, aged 41, died of a brain hemorrhage after suffering a stroke. He had been paralyzed from the waist down since a tragic car accident 4½ years earlier. He left a wife, three sons and a daughter.

Perhaps fate keeps its own precise balance sheet on us all. Abebe Bikila was gifted with an endurance and a talent for distance running perhaps unparalleled in history. The extent of that endurance was never truly tested, his superiority over his competitors was so great. His victory at Tokyo, for instance, seemed so easy, so controlled—even though he ran 2:12:11.2, fastest in history up to that time—it was obvious he could have gone considerably faster if necessary. How much faster is a question that will never be answered.

But misfortune was also Bikila's fate. Only four weeks before the Tokyo Olympics, in fact, he had to have his appendix removed, an operation that would have dashed the medal hopes of a lesser man. At the Mexico City Olympics, where the altitude seemed to make a *third* marathon victory for Bikila a distinct possibility, he had to drop out of the race after 10 miles with a fractured bone in his left leg. Ironically, it was his friend and longtime training companion, Mamo Wolde, the man Abebe Bikila once said he always knew he could outrun, who won the gold medal. The following year, Abebe Bikila was critically injured in the car accident.

Ethiopia is an ancient, remote land situated in the African high country where the Blue Nile begins. Largely due to Ethiopia's isolation (the country didn't even enter Olympic competition until 1956), Bikila's own natural reserve and his infrequent appearances abroad, the stoic, regal athlete remained a shadowy figure throughout his athletic career. Some were still writing his name backwards, "Bikila Abebe," even after he'd won his second Olympic gold medal!

Born Aug. 7, 1932, he had grown up poor on a farm. At age 19, he joined Emperor Haile Selassie's Imperial Body Guard. In coming from total athletic obscurity to score his barefoot victory in Rome, he was easy to categorize as an untrained but supremely gifted natural athlete.

The truth was that he may have come to Rome unknown, but he hardly came unprepared. He had been running since 1956 and since 1959 had been under the careful direction of Onni Niskanen, a Swede who had come to Ethiopia in 1947 and stayed to become head of the national board of physical education. Niskanen, who also trained Wolde and the other Ethiopian distance runners, prepared Bikila for his glorious Roman victory on a combination of long fast runs (up to 20 miles), hill running and long repetitions (e.g., 1500 meters) on the track—all done at altitudes of 5000 feet or more. Niskanen even had a sauna bath set up for his runners and a marathon course measured out which closely approximated the terrain of the course in Rome.

In training, Bikila had run with shoes and without. But in Rome, all the racing shoes he tried hurt his feet. Besides, on smooth roads he felt both faster and more at ease running barefooted. The historic decision was made and Bikila was apparently well aware of its significance. Several years later, Niskanen recalled how Bikila had said in his native Amharic, "I will win without shoes. I will make some history for Africa."

The Rome marathon was run at night, and for almost the entire distance Bikila ran with Abdesselem Rhadi of Morocco, whose own superb performance in the race now stands largely forgotten and unappreciated. When only a kilometer remained Bikila moved away strongly, reaching the finish line under the floodlit Arch of Constantine in an Olympic and world record time of 2:15:16.2.

In Tokyo four years later, Bikila wore shoes. The results were the same, only infinitely more decisive. The second-place finisher was more than four minutes behind.

After his tragic accident in 1969, much of the mystique surrounding Abebe Bikila seemed to evaporate. It was as if, bound to a wheelchair, this athletic god had finally become a mere mortal, someone ordinary to whom people could relate. He visited England often for therapy. He competed in the World Paraplegic Games. He became an honored elder statesman of Ethiopian athletics.

At the Munich Olympics, Bikila was a guest of honor. After the medal presentation for the marathon, Frank Shorter went straight over to him and shook his hand. It was a gesture easily understood. Every distance runner would have loved to have had the chance to shake Abebe Bikila's hand.

6

Mr. DeMar-athon

Clarence DeMar—seven-time winner
of the Boston Marathon

Jerry Nason

In Boston, Clarence Harrison DeMar is still remembered not merely as a runner, but as an institution. A printer-proofreader by profession, DeMar-athon was no ordinary mortal. He had studied agriculture for three years at University of Vermont and, later, earned his AA degree at Harvard as an extension student. He held a master's degree from Boston University.

He could set type in Greek, German, French and English; he taught a Bible class, led a Boy Scout troop, wrote without literary assistance (*Marathon*, 1937), was the only American medalist in the Olympic Marathon until Frank Shorter at Munich 48 years later, and captured six of his seven Boston Marathon races after the age of 32.

And, despite the fact he last ran in competition at age 69 in 1957—his 1002nd foot race—Clarence's career was stunted early on by a Boston race physician who told him before and after his 1911 victory, "You have a heart murmur. You shouldn't even be going up stairs, let alone run races."

This is why DeMar's smashing triumphs over the Boston course number merely seven and not, logically, 10 or even 12. At the height of his physical prowess, he simply did not run the race because of that warning.

His unequalled string reads: 1911, 1922, 1923, 1924, 1927, 1928, and 1930. Clarence had been two months short of his 22nd birthday and two months shy of his 42nd at the extremities of this remarkable string.

Clarence reappeared on the marathon scene twice, but tentatively, following the false weak-heart warning of 1911: honoring his selection for the 1912 Olympics at Stockholm and, in 1917, finishing third in Boston after an extremely cautious, explorative run in the early miles.

It was at Stockholm that the Portuguese runner Lazaro collapsed during the Olympic struggle and died the following day. This episode, coming hard on the heels of the physician's warning in Boston, alarmed DeMar and accounts for his relative inactivity between the ages of 23 and 32.

It was in the interval that the examining Boston physician (Clarence never revealed his name) died of a heart attack. Later, Clarence was to quip, "I suspect that he had been listening to his own heart, not mine."

DeMar's ultimate Boston comeback brought down the house: three straight from 1922, a one-minute loss to Chuck Mellor in 1925, a third to Canadian Johnny Miles and Finland's Olympic gold medalist Albin Stenroos in '26, and back to back victories in 1927 and '28.

His crowning effort was the 1930 race held on a hot, humid April day. Clarence's superb condition at almost 42 years of age permitted him to keep contact with a near-record pace by Hans Oldag over the first half of the run, then roll out to a 600-yard lead on the Finns Koski and Kyronen on the hills of Newton. Clarence received a tumultuous welcome at the finish. A morning newspaper had referred to him as "DeMar-vel," and the vast crowd picked it up. "DeMar-vel, DeMar-vel," they chanted in unison.

Well, that probably summed him up as well as anything: marvel. He had dominated the event, five of his winning margins ranging from three to more than four minutes.

"Clarence rather intimidates us," rival Fred Ward once revealed. "We show up in Boston worrying about the weather—but Clarence doesn't give a damn whether it's hot or cold, or wet, or windy. It simply doesn't seem to bother him."

Another later recalled, "Clarence knew the Boston course like he knew the contents of his own wallet. He shaved a lot of yards off the distance with his knowledge of the dozens of bends and curves you confront there."

Yet, DeMar-vel's kingdom was not confined to his hometown race course. He captured three National AAU titles out of town and won eight other marathons on courses with which he was unfamiliar. All told, he ran in 100 full marathons in his lifetime, 33 of them in Boston, where he never failed to finish.

In his Boston finale (1954), Clarence was 63 years old. He led 47 of the 133 starters, then showered, dressed and walked 10 blocks to begin the night shift at the composing room of the old *Herald-Traveler.*

Internationally, his most prominent effort was his third in the Paris Olympiad, 1924, although he'd also been on the 1912 and 1928 teams at Stockholm and Amsterdam.

A candid, outspoken champion of individual rights, Clarence could not condone the so-called "coaching" of Olympic teams or the interference by Olympic Committee or AAU officials in the affairs of individual runners. His protests of official sham or incompetence were many and made loud and clear, orally and in print.

"Testy devil," a race official once described Clarence—but they all respected Clarence, even stood somewhat in awe of him.

DeMar constantly urged running on young people. He was a great believer in conditioning. Once, after he finished seventh in Boston at age 50, he remarked to me, "You look young and healthy. You ran track at Newton High, I understand. Yes. Well, why don't you get in shape and run this race instead of sitting in a bus writing about it?"

He was also a "testy" competitor. Clarence twice punched out Boston race spectators on the course—one for interrupting his intense concentration by requesting an autograph en route, another for throwing ice water on Clarence's legs.

Of the latter, DeMar later said, "I wish I could apologize to that man. He probably meant well—but you simply don't throw ice water on a runner's legs. Tightens them right up."

Clarence never inwardly conceded that Albin Stenroos was his better, not even after the Finn beat him in the Paris Olympiad and, two years later, came to Boston to beat Clarence on his home grounds (although both were upset by a 19-year-old unknown from Nova Scotia named Johnny Miles).

DeMar learned that Stenroos was going to run a subsequent marathon in Philadelphia. Clarence hadn't intended to be in the race, but he gained a post-entry. He not only defeated the Olympian but forced Stenroos to abandon the race in exhaustion after attempting to maintain contact with DeMar for 20 miles.

Oh, he was truly DeMar-vel. Witness:

• Once, missing a night train in Harrison, Maine, Clarence ran 32 miles to Portland, satchel in hand, to catch the next train for Boston.

• Another time—he was about 40 years of age—he walked 100 miles with a friend from his home in Reading, Mass., to attend a Bible conference in Northfield. (What makes this interesting is that DeMar, within the week, had competed in two 12-mile races and then a 15-miler the day before his walkathon.)

Not a big man (5'8", 138 pounds), Clarence was well, if inconspicuously, muscled. His sense of pace was uncanny, his self-discipline was rigid, his style superb for distance. Although one Boston columnist persisted in calling Clarence "The Great Shuffler," shuffler he was not.

"His stride fools you," rival Jimmy Henigan once revealed. "He's the most 'economical' runner of us all. His back-kick is never more than eight, 10 inches off the ground. He sort of glides along."

Although he never beat 2:29 for a full marathon (this was in days when 2:34 would probably win you an Olympic gold medal) DeMar had good 10-mile speed in his youth. He originally competed for the old Dorchester Club in Boston at that distance.

Much later in life, he assessed himself at his peak and the speed runners of the modern marathon—candidly, of course:

"They'd have been too much for me in my prime. Oh, I'd beat 'em now and then under certain conditions on certain courses—but I won't say it would happen very often. They are simply too fast.

"I look at it this way: we old fellows set the standards, built up the marathon as an accepted classic run in our generation. The runners coming along picked up confidence from that and went on from there. They have done an amazing job."

Clarence had been a physiologic study, in 1928 and again in 1953 (by heart specialists Paul Dudley White and James H. Currens). They found him to be somewhat of a superman, but it was true that the unnamed Boston Marathon physician 'way back there in 1911 *had* detected something strange with Clarence's motor.

"But it wasn't a heart murmur," they reported. "It was a little 'tick' while his heart was relaxing."

When DeMar died—on June 11, 1958—he was 70 years, four days old, a victim of intestinal cancer. He was running, and working, up to within a fortnight of his death.

An autopsy revealed that his heart was not enlarged but, at 340 grams, on the upper range of "normal." The aortic valve was normal, the coronary arteries were estimated to be two or three times normal size—meaning that the flow of blood to Clarence's heart had been excellent.

What they couldn't determine is whether Clarence had simply been born that way, with large coronary arteries, or if they were the result of his near half-century of running.

Whatever, it should be made clear to another generation that, in all respects, Clarence was truly Mr. DeMar-athon.

7

50 Years of Marathoning

The dean of American marathoners
tells how it was and still is

John A. Kelley

I remember the day my father took me to see my first Boston Marathon. It was April 19, 1921, and I was 13 years old. The winner that day was Frank Zuna and his time was 2:18:57, which was a record at that time for the short course. (In 1927, the course was changed to conform to the international distance of 26 miles, 385 yards, and has been adjusted from time to time since then, because of road reconstruction, etc.)

It was not an immediate love affair between me and the marathon. During my school years, I tried my luck at baseball and spent many happy summers as a caddy in the White Mountains of New Hampshire. Meanwhile, I became mildly interested in track as a miler and cross-country runner in high school days. During that period, I saw Johnny Miles win at Boston in 1926 and became enchanted with the fabulous performance of Clarence DeMar in 1922, '23, '24 and on and on.

By then, I had discovered that I was no Babe Ruth and had begun to concentrate on distance running. In 1928, I ran my first Boston and failed to finish, and for the next four years stayed with the shorter distances. But in 1931, when I saw my friend Jimmy Henigan win at Boston, I became fired with new enthusiasm for the marathon and decided to try again in 1932. I can't imagine why I got hooked, because that day in 1931 was a scorcher and they were dropping out like flies. The winning time was only 2:46:45.

In 1932, I started but dropped out in Wellesley with blistered feet. In those days, we ran in sneakers, or bowling shoes, or what have you, and I learned by experience that year that Vaseline and woolen socks do not make a marathoner. The next year, I ran again and finished

37th. In 1934, I was a surprise second, and in 1935 came my first victory.

My winning time was 2:32:07, which by today's standards would put me back into about 125th place. But training methods today are a far cry from those of my early days. All long-distance runners were warned not to overdo their workout mileage. I never did more than 65 miles a week in my life, usually much less, mostly due to warnings from well-meaning people but partly because I was too lazy. Today, because of improved nutrition and better running shoes, young runners are able to put in many more miles on the roads, and are benefiting from their heavier training program.

In 1935, there were 191 starters out there in Hopkinton, and we thought that was a big field. The race took off at Lucky Rock, the old start near Tebeau Farm race headquarters. That year, when I was coming up to the peak of my career, to the best of my knowledge there were probably fewer than 10 full-distance marathons in the country. Now, there are nearly 200 annually, plus many in other parts of the world.

Improved transportation has made it possible for many of our good runners to compete here and there throughout the world. The sport of marathoning has grown to such enormous proportions that wherever a runner may be, and whatever his qualifications, there is usually a race to be found in which he may compete. This proliferation has created problems. Boston finds it difficult to handle some 2,900 starters, as in 1977, when it took 3½ minutes for the last competitor to cross the *starting* line. I also recall the time in 1975 when I was part of a back-up of cold shivering runners waiting to cross the computerized finish line at the Pru. Officials are still working to improve these conditions.

There was a time, not too long ago, when women were involved only in track and field events. In my Olympic experiences, there were many fine women athletes on our teams, but none in the sport of marathoning. I was born too soon! But even in those days, we had a frolic or two in transit.

In 1936, the US Olympic teams crossed the Atlantic on the steamship Manhattan. Those were happy days at sea when many friendships were established. Training went on as usual, more or less, but there were many other activities. Games, movies, parties and usually a show put on by the athletes, for their teammates and other passengers on the ship, kept us busy. It was a happy time, and not to be compared with today's fast pace.

There were more fringe benefits. That is how I came to know Jesse Owens, to me the greatest sprinter of all time. One day in my stateroom, Jesse insisted on trying on my marathon shoes so he could do a little jogging up on deck. I protested—they were my competition shoes—but to no avail. Before we knew it, one shoe had been ripped! But all was not lost. Johnny Kelley's luck held again, and a maintenance man I found down in the bowels of the ship was able to repair the shoe—for 50 cents. Jesse felt badly to have damaged my tools, but we remained good friends.

That was the year I saw Spiridon Louis, the winner of the marathon in the First Modern Olympiad at Athens, Greece, in 1896. He dressed in his native Greek costume to present an olive branch to Mr. Hitler. What a joke! Another memory of that year in Berlin was the time Hitler's stormtroopers treated me with respect when they learned that I was a marathoner.

In 1940, I qualified again as a marathoner for the Olympic Games to be held in Helsinki, Finland, but those Games were canceled because of World War II. However, in our country there were other marathons and other championships to be sought.

Then came 1945 and my second Boston victory—10 years after the first. It had taken six second places, one third, one fifth and one ninth before I got that win again. Gerald Cote, four-time winner, and Leslie Pawson, three-time winner, provided most of the strong competition. I was disappointed in a second in those days, especially when it was a matter of 13 seconds or seven seconds in time between first and second place.

It was during this era that the consistency of my training paid off with two firsts at the Yonkers Marathon, in 1935 and 1950, 15 years apart.

By this time, the Boston Marathon was really booming. The Greek, Stylianos Kyriakides, won in 1946 in 2:29:27, and it was the last time automobiles were allowed on the race course. Thereafter, three official buses for the press were the only motorized vehicles allowed to follow the runners. Times were changing.

The 1948 Olympic Games were held in London, and I was again a member of the team—at the age of 42. Marty Glickman, an alternate sprinter on the 1936 team, was onboard the S. S. United States in New York Harbor as a sports announcer to interview the departing team. He told me that when he saw my name on the Olympic Team roster, he thought of course it was my son. We had a good laugh over that one! This was the start of a second beautiful voyage across the water.

That was the year when Hildegarde waved to me from the audience as I sang a ballad in the floor show put on by 10 of us from the various teams.

England was just recovering from the war. Food was scarce and times were hard, but the hearts of the British were warm. They really had no one to cheer for. Deprivation had taken its toll. But we had Bob Mathias, who won the decathlon, and everybody had Emil Zatopek. The fabulous Zatopek. This was his first appearance in the Olympic Games, but four years later he won the 5000 meters, the 10,000 meters and the marathon, all in the course of one week—a record which has never been equaled.

One of my most memorable races was on May 30, 1949, from Lawrence, Mass., to Salisbury Beach. I won by two seconds from Lou White of New York. This must be one of the closest finishes ever. I worked too hard to have it forgotten!

By this time, the influx of foreign competitors had changed Boston from an Eastern Seaboard race to an international race, and from then on all winners, until 1957, were from overseas. In 1957, the victory came back to an American. My good friend John J. Kelley, "the younger," established a new record on an accurately-measured course. His time was 2:20:05, and I was 13th. My wife and I were thrilled because John and his wife Jessie were staying with us at our home in Watertown that weekend. Many times, we have been asked if we were father and son. Not so, just good friends.

Since 1957, marathoning has grown in leaps and bounds. Enthusiastic joggers have become competitors, and more and more races are available all over the country. On April 19, 1966, Roberta Gibb jumped out from behind a bush in Hopkinton and became un-officially the first woman to complete the Boston Marathon. Her time was approximately 3½ hours.

The 1977 entry list included more than 100 women and close to 3000 men. It has become a mob scene at the start and presents problems for the future. At one time, the Boston A.A. clubhouse on Exeter Street provided sufficient facilities for those who finished, but in recent years the B.A.A. activities are confined to its track team and the Marathon Committee.

Will Cloney, Jock Semple and a few volunteers have done a tremendous job over the years to keep alive the tradition of the famous Boston Marathon. At one time, funds were generated by the B.A.A. track meet in the Boston Garden, but this affair is no longer being held. The Prudential Insurance Company now provides facilities at the finish, and Mr. Cloney has said, "Without the Prudential, we would be lost."

Even though qualifying standards have been established in an effort to keep the entry list under control, it becomes more and more difficult because of the increasing popularity of long-distance running and competition. The eight-mile Bay-to-Breakers race in California is an example of uncontrolled entry lists. With 12,000 runners, as it had in 1977, how can anyone call this a race? It's a happening and one that I would hate to see "happen" in Boston.

At the moment, American runners Bill Rodgers and Frank Shorter are the best in the world, and they are naturally looking for more than one race during the course of a year to prove their international stature. There are many. However, for those of us who are not in that league, there have been developed a Masters or veterans category and age-group divisions. In the Masters division, I am told that I hold seven records, and I hope to establish more in the future. I still enjoy the shorter races along with an occasional marathon, and don't mind the fact that there may be a little less competition in the over-70 age group, which I entered in September 1977.

However, with two national championships, and any number of marathons in this country and Canada and Europe, after 46 Boston Marathons it's not strange that Boston is still my first love. As I write this, I am training hard for April 17, 1978.

8

The Women's Place

Until 1972, they weren't welcome. Now, they are pushing 2:30

Joan Ullyot, M.D.

Since 1896, the marathon has been an official Olympic event—for men only. Compared to this 82-year history, the involvement of women with the marathon has been very brief—a scant 10 years in practice, less than half that time with "official" AAU approval.

The recent explosion of women's marathoning is all the more impressive in the light of this history of discouragement and obstacles put in the path of women who simply wanted to run distances. Women marathoners have had to overcome prejudice, medical objections, physical disbarment and their own traditions before even setting out on a 26-plus-mile course. Little wonder that, to so many of them, the physical distance does not seem insurmountable. They have already conquered much more potent barriers.

Olympic acceptance is slow in coming. As aloof as any ancient gods of Olympia, the old men of the International Olympic Committee close their eyes to the spectacle of women out running, on the roads, for distances up to 100 kilometers. In 1977, the IOC loftily rejected as "too strenuous" for females the introduction of a 3000-meter track race in the Games. This antediluvian attitude would be cause for hilarity were it not so frustrating to serious women runners who have fought for the right to run as far as men.

Perhaps the IOC should look at the facts of the past few years, as recorded in the *Runner's World* marathon issues. The data for US women alone are as follows:

Year	1972	1973	1974	1975	1976	1977
Sub-3:00	3	4	10	17	27	47
Sub-3:30	15	36	73	102	196	312
Best	2:55:44	2:46:36	2:43:54	2:38:19	2:39:11	2:37:57
	(Bridges)	(Gorman)	(Hansen)	(Hansen)	(Gorman)	(Merritt)

In 1977, the long-standing world record of 2:38:19, set by Jacqueline Hansen in 1975, was lowered twice—first to 2:35:15 by France's Chantal Langlace, then to 2:34:47 by West Germany's Christa Vahlensieck (who incidentally also has the world's best for women at 100 kilometers, 62-plus miles, of 7:50:15). Two other women also dipped under the old mark—Manuella Angenvoorth of West Germany and Kim Merritt of the United States.

Given the rapid improvement of the world record, men and women alike wonder where the record will end up—or, as men frequently inquire in an anxious tone, when will the women "catch up" with the men. Male reporters are especially fond of this question and appear relieved when assured that the marathon distance is probably too short to allow women's endurance an absolute advantage over men's speed.

In the past few years, I have gone out on a limb in making predictions in lectures. World records are only the tip of the iceberg. They reflect the growing numbers of women trying the marathon (in 1977, 600 women entered the Honolulu Marathon—a fifth of the total field, and the entry of young, fast track-trained athletes into long-distance runs. Judging from the growing depth and quality of women marathoners and from the speed demonstrated currently in races of 5-10 kilometers, I am certain that we will see the world record dip under 2:30 by 1979. The main barrier will be mental, as it was for the first sub-3:00 marathoners in 1971. Women are perfectly capable of running in the 2:20 range within the next five years.

These times sound unbelievable to most women who are concerned with finishing their first marathon or at most bettering 3:30 "to qualify for Boston." Even to former national team members like myself who were ecstatic a few years back when we broke three hours, the predictions seem to belong to some different species—not us "ordinary women." But everyone who lowers the record to a new standard makes us, too, realize our potential and run faster or farther than we ever believed we could—until someone older, or heavier, or more awkward than ourselves shows us the way. Then we believe, and do.

From the vantage point of 1978, it may be instructive to look back over the first decade of women's marathoning. The world-record times of the pioneers seem ordinary by our revised standards, and the controversies of the late 1960s and early '70s downright quaint. Yet these early victories shattered generally-accepted views of women's potential and capabilities in sport. A whole new field was opened to us by a handful of unconventional and daring women.

In 1966, everyone "knew that women couldn't run marathons"—in fact, they weren't considered strong enough to run more than a half-mile. The official sports and medical establishments endorsed this myth, and the Boston Marathon was naturally, as always, a men's race. There were rumors that some women jumped out of the bushes and ran along in Boston, but these were discounted or dismissed as publicity stunts and hoaxes. Roberta Gibb, age 23, ran the entire distance in 1966 in about 3½ hours—with plenty of witnesses—but she was "unofficial," therefore regarded as non-existent, merely another unconfirmed rumor.

The following year, Kathrine Switzer slipped past officials after a now-famous confrontation and went the distance wearing a race number. The official strong-arm tactics attracted so much attention to her feat that press and public rallied to the female cause. More women ran Boston in the next few years, loudly cheered by the crowds and tolerated, if not yet recognized, by the officials.

The establishment continued to overlook these few "crazy women" and insisted that women were physically incapable of marathoning—certainly of fast marathoning, anyway. Then in 1967, a 15-year-old Canadian girl named Maureen Wilton ran along in a men's race and finished in 3:15.

Confronted with this obvious impossibility, European reporters turned to a medical maverick, Dr. Ernst van Aaken of West Germany. Van Aaken was an outspoken advocate of long-distance running for everyone—not just champions but children, women, grandparents and patients. As a physician/coach/writer, he developed a unique training system known in the US as LSD—long, slow distance. Runners from his own little town of Waldniel trained this revolutionary way and managed to capture 18 national and European titles, setting records at distances from 100 to 5000 meters.

When asked about Wilton's feat, Dr. van Aaken wasn't surprised. "Any of my 800-meter runners could do the same," he maintained, setting the date for a demonstration for the press a few weeks later. Since his female 800-meter runners had run as far as 30 kilometers in training, van Aaken didn't doubt their ability to go a bit farther—42 kilometers. He used the intervening weeks to round up some men for the event, since German rules didn't permit women to compete in marathons—or indeed any race longer than 800 meters.

A handful of men ran the race in Waldniel, and four women ran along. Eight-hundred-meter champion Anni Pede finished first, in a new world's best time of 3:07:26. Her record stood until 1970, when the new women's sport began to catch on in the US.

Progress thereafter was rapid: Caroline Walker, 3:02:53 (February 1970); Beth Bonner, 3:01:42 (May 1971) and 2:55:22 (September 1971); Cheryl Bridges, 2:49:40 (December 1971).

The second "impossible barrier" (the first having been the distance itself) was broken in dramatic fashion during the New York City Marathon in 1971, when Bonner and Nina Kuscsik raced together and broke through the 3:00 mark. With Cheryl Bridges's 2:49 performance coming only two months later, 2:50 was never the same psychological barrier 3:00 had been.

After 1971, the struggle was more against officialdom than against the clock. Women wanted official recognition and sanction for their increasingly popular sport. Liberal race directors on the East and West Coasts began to overlook AAU regulations and welcome women into their marathons and other road races. Boston took this audacious step in 1972, when seven women (including Ms. K. Switzer) ran with official numbers and approval. All seven had met the same 3:30 standard demanded of the male participants, and Nina Kuscsik won the race with a 3:10 performance.

The AAU finally capitulated in 1972, recognizing a *fait accompli*. Women were given permission to compete at any distance they desired, up to the marathon and beyond. But in one last gasp of regulatory fervor, the AAU decreed that women should start separately from the men.

This rule was immediately assaulted in that year's New York City Marathon, where the women were ordered to start 10 minutes before the men. The women's response was to sit down firmly on the starting line when their gun went off, holding aloft placards with, "Hell, no, we won't go!" and similar rebellious statements. The offending AAU rule was eventually eliminated, though NYC rebels were penalized 10 minutes apiece for their demonstration—their time being measured from the starting gun rather than their actual starting time with the men.

Official AAU sanction was followed by a National AAU Marathon Championship for the women, held yearly since 1974. That first year, in California, about 50 women finished, three of them under 3:00—a record then. By 1977, the ranks of women marathoners had grown to the extent that a separate race for women was considered necessary, in part so the runners could keep track of the competition without hundreds of male bodies blocking their view, as had happened in Boston. The concept proved sound as 15 women (out of 78) raced in under 3:00, a new record. Not even the all-female International Championships held in 1974 and '76 in Waldniel, West Germany, could match this mark for quality and depth of field.

When the third women's International was held in Atlanta in 1978, the race sponsors generously agreed to pay all expenses for the world's top runners—though all women were welcome to run, without time restrictions. Twenty women from nine different countries qualified for the free trip to Atlanta by running faster than 2:50 in a previous marathon.

Now that the sight of women finishing marathons has become commonplace, many onlookers notice a curious contrast between male and female runners. Whereas the men often finish with looks of tremendous pain and exhaustion, the women generally finish smiling and quite fresh. It is the men, not the women, who are photographed afterward, stretched out on the grass in various stages of collapse. The women stand around chatting with great animation, not such dramatic photo subjects. That fearful 20-mile "wall," so devastating to male runners, doesn't appear to exist for the women.

Various explanations have been advanced for the greater ease and freshness with which women conquer the marathon distance. The most controversial theory, originated by Dr. Ernst van Aaken, holds that women naturally metabolize fat as muscle fuel, whereas men have to train their muscles, weaning them away from dependence on ample stores of glycogen. No laboratory evidence exists yet to support or refute this theory, though it is now well established that endurance training (in males) does alter muscle metabolism in favor of fat utilization.

Another theory is basically psychological. I elaborated on this during an interview in Germany, following the 1976 International Championship. The interview took place in a small Rhine village where several of the American runners had journeyed to enjoy the wine festival.

Already well primed with the latest vintage, I explained that women run better marathons because they run realistically, whereas men are great romantics, to the detriment of their racing ability. In other words, the women usually evaluate their own capabilities, based on an analysis of previous races and training, and they pace themselves accordingly. The men tend, instead, to fall for an idealized notion of what they *should* be able to run, given Frank Shorter's performance standards and their own fantastic abilities. Thus, they take off at a pace that feels, romantically, right—and pay for this lack of caution in the second half of the race, when they are passed by many women who run more sensibly.

My German interviewer was distressed by this theory, which struck him as chauvinistic. "Besides," he protested, "women like their men to be romantic."

True, but it doesn't help in the marathon, I replied.

Theories aside, perhaps there should be differences in training between men and women, in view of their different racing capabilities. In simplest terms, a woman's natural ability lies in endurance, a man's in speed. If a man and a woman who have similar times in 6-10-mile races compete in a mile, the man will almost always power his way to a faster finish. Conversely, the woman will leave the man behind in the last miles of the marathon.

So it would be logical, in training to run a *faster* marathon, for women to practice speed a little more, while the men may require more long runs to build up endurance and probably to train their muscle enzymes to use fat efficiently.

Dr. van Aaken, whose pupils include Christa Vahlensieck, Liane Winter and Anni Pede—all world record-holders at one time—notes that Christa seldom runs more than 18 miles in training. She used a combination of relatively low mileage (70 per week), leisurely endurance runs through the woods, fartlek and numerous track workouts to peak for her record performances.

Most of the top American women put in more mileage than the European stars. Kim Merritt, Miki Gorman, Jacqueline Hansen and 1977 AAU champion Leal-Ann Reinhart all run more than 100 miles a week in preparation for a marathon. But they also employ large doses of intervals—the last three of them under the tutelage of former miler Laszlo Tabori who believes in three sessions a week of hard, fast speed workouts. However, one shouldn't conclude from Tabori's obvious success as a coach that this regimen would suit everyone. Gayle Barron, for instance, is self-coached and has run 2:47 off of low mileage (60-80 per week) and little speed work.

My feeling is that men and women can train along virtually indentical lines for the marathon, since the physiological principles that underlie training apply to both sexes. The only difference would be in the speed of various runs. Most men, because of their greater muscularity, can train faster than women in intervals and short workouts, and still be working aerobically. A woman may be running 7:30 per mile and be at 75% of her maximum effort, whereas the same effort for a man would be 6:30 pace. Training should be the same for men and women in terms of *effort*, but effort must be judged individually, not by having all run identical pace.

If one keeps in mind the purpose of various components of training, one can emphasize the parts which need to be developed, according to individual requirements. Long, aerobic runs of 20 miles or more are essential to accustom the legs to enduring long distances without extreme fatigue. For men at least, a second purpose of long training runs is to alter muscle metabolism—to develop the enzymes of a marathoner. Speed work, on or off the track, will develop a mechanical ability to move fast. Hill workouts help to develop leg strength (on the uphills), rhythm and pace (on the downhills).

The aim in marathoning is to run fast for a long distance—an exhausting effort. So as not to get similarly exhausted in training, one should go slow in the long runs and practice running fast only at short distances. The combination of speed and distance should be reserved for the actual race, when it counts.

Women must be especially careful to allow enough time—preferably several months—for a gradual increase in mileage before their first marathon. It is quite possible for women to go the marathon distance after a "crash program" of training and with little experience in long runs. The over-enthusiasm is not advisable, however. The spirit is willing, the muscle enzymes may even be naturally attuned to endurance performance—but the muscles, tendons and joints must be trained slowly. Most women have been relatively inactive for decades by the time they take up running, and the legs need time to adjust. I have seen several unfortunate women tackle a marathon within months of their first hesitant jogging steps, finish in a state of euphoria and then be laid up for months because of leg injuries.

With this one caution, I would like to recall an encouraging statement made by Beth Bonner, first woman to break the three-hour barrier. Asked about that other mythical barrier, the "wall," she shrugged it off with the opinion that "a well-trained woman needn't fear that something mysterious will hit her at the 20-mile mark."

In fact, any properly-trained woman can look forward to finishing all 26-plus miles in relative comfort and with immense self-satisfaction. The first marathon is often easier than the first mile—and an ever greater milestone.

Part 3
Training for Your Marathon

9

Make Your Own Time

Yours is the most important one, and you must work for it

No one plunges into a marathon without a lot of thought and preparation. No one does it successfully, anyway.

In the beginning, the marathon is a free-floating idea: "Hey, wouldn't it be something if I ran one of those things! How far did you say it was again?" The seed of an idea grows into a goal, and from the goal sprouts a plan. The plan blossoms into training and finally matures as racing fitness.

At first, goals are low and vague, and have little to do with time or with outrunning anyone else. The beginner says, "I just want to finish." Finishing is reward enough. Then, he finishes, gets a time and sees where the first race can be improved. A new goal forms, more precise now. A little more training, a little smarter pacing and... "How about that! I'm under 3:30!"

The next jump is down to three hours. By now, the runner is keeping mileage totals and is plotting splits with a compulsion normally reserved for computer scientists. Each improvement in time creates an appetite for even faster times. Faster times require more concentration, more preparation, more exhausting effort. The potential for frustration and injury goes up as times come down.

But the risks are worth courting if they lead to the sub-three marathon. Any time below three is a diploma recognized by every marathoner. It certifies that the runner has graduated from apprentice to journeyman status.

Almost any reasonably healthy individual can, with rather modest training and uncommon persistence, survive a marathon. A large percentage of finishers have the potential, with somewhat more work, to break three hours. But it doesn't follow that the runners who train longest will finish fastest. Somewhere under three hours, this thing called "innate ability" becomes as much a factor as hard work.

The very best marathoners aren't often journeymen who've marched through the usual steps: 3:30, 3:00, 2:45, etc. The best ones have speed, which isn't handed out equally. The race upfront is a fast one. The winners usually average between five and 5½ minutes for each of the 26 miles. A runner who can't break 5:00 for a single mile can't hope to keep up, regardless of training background.

The people who win big marathons seldom come from the ranks of road running specialists. They are track athletes who can race miles of 4:10 or better, and this fact separates them from the bulk of the marathoning crowd. But they can break loose only by doing marathon-type training. Whether the goal is 2:10 or just finishing, training is the dues every runner must pay to join the union of marathoners. No one gets away without paying in this sport. And this makes all the runners a little bit alike.

Nowhere else in running is the racing so closely linked to training investment as in marathoning. The difference between finishing and not finishing, or between a four-hour and a three-hour marathon is most often found in the runner's daily, weekly, and monthly mileage totals.

We're concerned here with minimum mileages—the lowest totals needed to get through 26 miles of *running* (as opposed to "survival shuffling"). Training, of course, reaches a point of diminishing returns at the extremes. Two-hundred-mile training weeks don't necessarily make a runner faster than one who does half that much. But what about someone who's trying to get by on 30-60 miles a week?

Several years ago, researcher Paul Slovic studied the runners in Oregon's Trail's End Marathon, one of the country's largest. He checked their training mileages for two months before the race, and compared it to their marathon times. Those who ran the most generally raced the fastest:

1. Sub-3:00 runners	9 miles a day
2. 3:01 to 3:30 runners	6 miles a day
3. 3:31 to 4:00 runners	5 miles a day
4. 4:01 and up runners	4 miles a day

About this same time, runner Ken Young was working up his "collapse-point" theory. It went like this: Training mileage over the previous 6-8 weeks sets the limit of how far one can hold a fast pace. That limit is about three times the daily average. After that point, the pace slows drastically, and the runner may even have to stop.

Young checked his theory against Slovic's figures. According to Ken, only the sub-three-hour group had adequate training—nine miles a day over the past eight weeks for a collapse-point of 27 miles. Many individuals in that group probably were "undertrained," and this was increasingly so among slower runners. The other groups had collapse-points of 18, 15 and 12 miles, respectively.

If the Young theory was valid, the "undertrained" runners would show a marked slowdown toward the end of the race. This was the case. Group One's average pace dropped by 14% from 20 miles to the finish. The slowdown for Group Two was 22%; for Group Three, 37%; and for Group Four, 58%.

To put these statistics another way, the sub-three-hour runners lost only about 5½ minutes (relative to their 20-mile pace) in that last stretch, while the four-hour-plus runners used up nearly 30 extra minutes on those miles. Their pace by then was a 13-14-minutes-per-mile shuffle.

If Ken Young's collapse-point theory has merit—and there's strong evidence that it does—then most runners who attempt marathons aren't ready to go all the way. Slovic's statistics from Trail's End, a typical US race, show that 80% or more of the marathoners hadn't "collapse-proofed" themselves in the previous eight weeks with 500 or more miles of training. Without that kind of preparation, collapse is likely. Perhaps this explains the "20-mile mystique" that marathoners talk about.

E. C. Frederick, author of *The Running Body* (World Publications, 1973) and editor of the scientific journal *Running*, writes, "It is often said that the halfway point in a marathon is the 20-mile mark. To someone without the experience of running a marathon, that may seem like a bunch of journalistic hogwash. In fact, it is one of the most profound observations I've encountered."

Here's what happens. Say you've training 40-50 miles a week, a common figure among the marathoners. The collapse came between 18 and 20 miles, and the endless miles now stretch out in front of you, the last six seeming longer than the first 20 though you're running two minutes a mile slower than before.

Frederick says, "It's a rare person with the fortitude and mind control to force himself or herself to finish a marathon when not properly trained for it. Even highly trained persons undergo much soul-searching and must dig deeply into their bag of tricks to endure those last six miles. Because they are prepared, most trained marathoners finish. Rarely does an unprepared person make it past 20 miles."

He suggests that a bare minimum of training for surviving a marathon "without endangering your health, without subjecting yourself to undue suffering to finish with a feeling of personal satisfaction and accomplishment" is 40 miles per week for at least eight weeks. The last 6-8 miles won't be a stroll in the park after this preparation, but you can probably grind them out.

Paul Slovic's figures indicate that anyone wanting to break three hours (or its equivalent for women and age groups) should exceed Ken Young's collapse-point standard: 60-plus miles per week for at least eight weeks. This should reduce the chances of drastic slowdowns in the late miles.

Among the runners who break 2:20, slowdowns are seldom a problem. They average 100-plus miles a week, for collapse-points beyond 50 miles!

Total distance is only one of the pieces in the training puzzle. Marathoners also must consider training *pace,* training *progress,* and the *distribution* of training miles through the week.

The problem here is quite different than in a mile track race or six miles of cross-country. Anyone who runs regularly can go 1-6 miles. The "base" to cover these distances is already built in. So training concentrates on pushing up the speed of these short races.

But before a marathoner can think about speed, he has to create the resources to go 26 miles. Most training time goes to gaining and maintaining this basic capacity. Endurance is the first requirement of marathoners, and they need 6-8 hours of running a week to build a minimum amount. That may sound like a frightening figure, but it needn't be. Most runners can build up to it comfortably—if only they let themselves slow down enough to go long. Five-minute mile speed doesn't do you any good if you can't run 10 miles at any speed.

E. C. Frederick advises beginning marathoners that "the concept of *duration* is far more important than that of pace. In other words, it's not a question of how fast you can run a certain distance in each practice run. Instead, the marathon aspirant should concentrate on how much time (or distance) he or she spends running each day. In essence, what you are doing is training your body to run for three or more hours, and teaching it to endure the special discomforts and stresses encouraged in runs of long duration."

"Certainly," Frederick says, "it is an accomplishment to improve your time over, say, six miles in a training run. But it should be more important to gradually increase the *length of time* (or number of miles) you can run."

Distance comes first, speed later, even among the best marathoners.

Statistician Dan Moore learned when he surveyed US sub-2:20 runners that 80% of their running is slower than marathon race pace. In other words, 80 or so miles a week (on the average) is endurance work. They often run slower by a minute or so per mile than they plan to race. The endurance gained this way translates to speed later on.

It should be obvious that marathoners break themselves in gradually to these amounts of running. Either that or they break themselves down. Distance running is a stress, and the human body adapts slowly to all stresses. This process can't be rushed.

It may take months, for instance, to progress from a beginning base of 20 miles a week to the 50-60 or more required of a marathoner. A sensible goal might be to add 10% a week to the mileage total. At this rate, the runner would get into marathon range in about three months, and then should hold the new level for two more months before racing. Runners can climb much quicker than that, of course, just as they can race on half the suggested mileage. But every shortcut has its potential toll of pain.

E. C. Frederick tells would-be marathoners to listen to their inner voices. "The (training) system must not be rigid," he says. "It must be dynamic and responsive to the needs of the individual. If you have a sore knee, you postpone your three-hour run. If you develop a pain during a run, then walk or shorten the run. In the same light, when you feel good, go an extra half-hour."

"In all cases," Frederick says, "be responsive. Develop an awareness of your body, its needs and capacities. Coax a slow, continuous stream of adaptations out of it. If you are diligent and sensitive, training will progress and you will avoid injury."

One way to up the odds of getting hurt (or at least reduce the chances of having a satisfying marathon) is to treat each day equally. You see you need 60 miles a week. That's 8½ miles a day, so you do exactly that much every day. Besides being boring, such a system is inefficient. It gives neither the necessary challenge of longer runs, nor the essential recovery of easy ones.

"Running," writes E. C. Frederick, "is only half of distance training. The other half is repairing the damage incurred by the strain of the training run." This repair process after hard running apparently takes more than 24 hours, so it's wise to alternately push and ease off.

Bill Bowerman, 1972 Olympic US Coach, says the hard-easy cycle of training is basic. "Rest is always necessary for the body to recover and replenish itself. Furthermore, the light days will allow more work in training sessions on the hard days, giving greater progress in the long run."

In *The Conditioning of Long-Distance Runners,* probably the best advice page-for-page ever written on running, Tom Osler gives a plan which puts the hard-easy ideas of Bowerman into a marathoning context. A week's runs:

Day One	5% of week's total
Day Two	15% of week's total
Day Three	30% of week's total
Day Four	5% of week's total
Day Five	15% of week's total
Days 6-7	Remaining 30%

Notice the cycles of easy, medium and hard running, and that Osler intentionally leaves the last two days unplanned. Here, he can fit in a race or time-trial, or more runs of varying distance. For a 60-mile-a-week marathoner, an Osler-type schedule would be: (1) three miles; (2) nine miles; (3) 18 miles; (4) three miles; (5) nine miles; (6-7) total of 18 miles.

For Osler, like most marathoners, the "long one" is a key part of each week's running. This run imitates the marathon in distance and stress, and seems to offer an endurance boost not found in going the same distance every day.

Paul Slovic, the man who studied Trail's End marathoners, discovered that "the more long runs taken and the greater the length of the longest run, the faster the final time—independent of maximum weekly mileage. In other words, longer runs would be associated with faster times even if total or weekly mileage were held constant."

This suggests that a runner might make the best use of training miles by throwing everything into a weekly 20-30 miler, and barely running the other days. Slovic, of course, knows this is impossible because every run would then be like the worst of the races. Every run would feature a dramatic "collapse."

The average runs are necessary to raise the limit for the longest one; the easy days provide recovery from it. Training for the marathon is a blend of all three, taken in balance, in cycles, each contributing in its own way to the final result.

10

Training to Run and Race

What does it take to finish, and then to improve?

Joe Henderson and Brian Maxwell

Marathoning attracts both runners and racers. And the distinction between them is important, because it decides how they approach the event.

Marathon *runners* mainly want to finish. Speed doesn't mean as much to them as simple endurance.

Marathon *racers* want to improve. So their times mean everything because they measure improvement.

Runners and racers train as differently as their aims suggest. Runners need only a certain minimum of distance to assure a safe finish. Racers need both endurance and speed to assure a satisfying time.

Most of us come into marathoning as runners, and only after our first marathon is behind us do we wonder, "How can I go faster?" Once we ask that, we're starting to think as racers. Eventually, as goals are either met or blocked, racers often become runners again.

This chapter is for all types. It advises first-timers, those who are looking at the event more seriously and those who are ready to take it a little less seriously.

TRAINING TO RUN

Too many words have spilled over us telling how grueling marathons are and how those who endure them are a unique breed of athlete.

This might be true for those who link together 5-6-minute miles in marathon *races*. But I don't like to dwell on that part of the sport—because it isn't the part I live in (I *run* marathons), and because it scares away potential recruits. This emphasis on suffering and speed makes marathoning sound impossible, and I'm more concerned with promoting it as a sport of possibilities. The possibilities attract new people.

We decide to run marathons for two equal and seemingly opposite reasons: The distance looks long and hard enough that not just anyone can do it, and yet enough people like ourselves do it that it doesn't look impossible. In short, it's a challenge reserved for somewhat special people, but they aren't so special that they're unlike us.

I ran my first marathon in 1967 because lots of people like me were starting to do it then, but not everyone could. I was a miler and had been one for years. But the challenge of the mile had faded. That was to run the four laps faster than I ever had before, and I'd stopped improving.

One day, I said to myself, "Hell, anyone can run a mile. But not just anyone can keep going for *26* miles, back to back. If I start doing marathons, I can be proud if I only make the distance, no matter how long it takes."

Something else was bringing marathoning within my reach. Among the thousand or so marathoners in the country at the time was a sprinkling of men in their 40s, 50s and 60s, a few kids in their teens and the first of the women long-distance runners. They, much more than the Derek Claytons and Tom Larises (world and American leaders of 1967), drew me into the sport. Clayton and Laris worked in a different world from mine. But as I read the names of the old, young and female—and the slow of every description—I said, "Gee, if they can do it, there's no reason why I can't."

So I became a marathoner. And in the years since I started, thousands of others have taken the same path. The sport is running wild because the positive infection which hit me is at work all over the country. The bigger marathoning gets, the more ex-milers and around-the-neighborhood joggers are exposed to its challenges and possibilities. The more it spreads to the old, young, female and slow, the more people like them are deciding, "If they can, I can."

The sport grows by inspiration and example, coupled with opportunity and education. Give people a reason to run, assurance that it's okay for them to run, and a place and a way to run, and they'll do it.

This is why a book like this is so important. It tells who is running, and why and where they are running. I want to assure you here that you can run with them this year and to tell you how to accomplish it.

Three months from now, you too can be a marathoner. I said in the February 1977 issue of *Runner's World* that it was as simple as this. The magazine printed a three-month training schedule and instructions for following it.

Dozens of runners, including many who were skeptical that marathoning ability could be gained this quickly and easily, tried the program. Some of them wrote later, thanking *RW* for its "coaching." Their results generally were good. I didn't promise anyone fast times, and no one who reported ran much faster than three hours. I did say if they followed the schedule they would finish in comparatively good shape, and most of them did.

Some samples from the mail:

• "After my first marathon seven years ago (finished in 5:19 after a very small running base of 4-5 miles a day), I used your training guide. Finished in 3:56, and was I ever happy to see that finish line!" (H. Green, 56 years old, from Wisconsin)

• "I became apprehensive as race day approached, because I didn't feel like I was building up strength. I had serious doubts whether I could finish. But I completed it. My time (3:34) wasn't great, but I finished. I was very tired and had some pains, but I wasn't totally exhausted as some seemed to be." (Cecil Fry, 48, of Pennsylvania)

• "After suffering periodic breakdowns from exhaustion due to improper training, I had never been able to compete in any event over six miles. I had a lot of apprehension about the training schedule before the race, since I had never gone more than 18 miles in training. However, I trusted you and left the last eight miles unexplored. It worked beautifully. I completed the marathon in 3:45, in good form without too much struggle." (Peter Breyer of New Jersey)

• "It got me to the finish line in four hours, in 90-degree heat and 80% humidity and plenty of hills. It was the greatest feeling of accomplishment I've ever experienced—especially since about one-third of the field of 300 dropped out."

The three-month schedule has no magic in it. As these few experiences show, no training plan wipes away all the hurting of the marathon. These men all had moments of doubt and pain before and during their runs, but following a systematic program made satisfying finishes possible. Finishing a marathon makes the discomfort of getting there worthwhile.

This schedule contained no secrets. Its basis was simply this: If you do enough of any kind of running, if you just stay healthy and interested, you'll finish. The schedule was set up first so that runners could maintain and enjoy it, and then so they'd build up enough background miles to run a full marathon.

Before looking at that schedule more closely and refining it a little, let's look at you and then at some basic training principles.

Start by assessing yourself. Be realistic, because you're the one who'll suffer if you think you can race like Frank Shorter without training like him. Answer these questions:

1. *Where am I now?* I'll assume you're typical of readers. You're already running 3-5 miles a day. The schedule uses that as its starting point. If you're doing less, or nothing, forget about marathon training until you've laid down a better foundation.

2. *What do I need?* You don't ever have to run the full marathon distance in practice. But you must reach the point where you're averaging at least one-fourth of that, or about 6½ miles, daily if you expect to finish the marathon at a run.

3. *How do I get from Point One, my beginning level, to Point Two, marathon level?* The schedule gives specifics, day by day. In general, build gradually and steadily, following training laws which apply to all runners.

Now, plant a few basic notions about training, because they underlie not only the marathon schedule but all good schedules:

• Run longer before running faster. Distance is your most precious commodity, not speed. So forget about pushing your pace until you've pushed up your distance to 26.22 miles for the first time. Remove the temptation to race against yourself by using only distance or only a period of time as a measurement, not combining the two. If you run five miles, don't time it. If you go 40 minutes, don't check the distance. (I use the latter in my schedules, because it seems easier to check.) Just run at a steady, comfortable pace which you feel you can eventually hold for the full marathon.

• Run regularly. Make a habit of running nearly every day. (The three-month program schedules practices six days a week, with the seventh optional.) Even small amounts of everyday running add up to more in the long run than on-again, off-again bursts of effort separated by long breaks.

• Run "hard-easy." While running almost every day, you shouldn't run the same distances or times every day. Improvement comes quicker when you mix long, medium and short runs. This is because recovery doesn't happen overnight but takes 48-72 hours after a hard run. Follow every hard one with an easy one or two. (The schedule has one long run, two medium and four short ones each week.)

• Run longer once a week. A weekend day is a good time for testing yourself, for extending your distance, for simulating the marathon, for stimulating adaptation to prolonged running. Go up to twice your average daily distance or time. Say you're averaging five miles or 40 minutes; push to 8-10 miles or 60-80 minutes. But stop at that, and take two full days of easy running afterward.

• Progress slowly and steadily. The quickest way to get hurt or discouraged is to jump up in distance too quickly. This overwhelms your adaptive powers. Add only about 10% to each day's distance or time each week. That amounts to just a half-mile or four-minute step up for a five-mile/40-minute runner. If a week seems too hard, stay at it and make it easier before stepping up again.

So you're wondering now how much running I'll ask you to do. Don't worry. It isn't much, because you don't need as much as many people try to make us believe, and you don't even need this much for very long. This is my formula:

You only need an hour a day, and you only need that for eight weeks. Oh, you'll run longer than an hour lots of times, sometimes 250% longer, but that's as much as you need to average.

The daily hour is enough for anyone except the best racers, and it's certainly enough for someone only concerned with finishing. The hour self-adjusts for your seriousness.

As I hinted, you need to average about a quarter-marathon a day to *run* the distance, about a third of a marathon to *race* it. I've asked you to train at about your marathon pace. This means, then, that people who are serious about their racing times will go faster in training and cover more distance in their hour. Those of us who won't push so hard in the marathon will run slower every day; we cover less total distance but don't need as much.

Racers who train at 6-7 minute miles meet their one-third requirement by putting in 8½-10 miles a day. Runners who train at 8-9-minute miles get one-quarter, or 6½ miles or so, which they need.

The accompanying schedule won't let you break records or win titles, because it isn't designed for that. It is meant to help you learn to think of yourself as a marathon runner. Once you are that, then you can look at schedules like Brian Maxwell's which tell you how to become a marathon *racer*. But put first things first. Finishing comes before anything else.

SCHEDULE FOR RUNNERS

Day	Week 1	Week 2	Week 3	Week 4
1	25 min.	30 min.	35 min.	35 min.
2	50 min.	55 min.	1:00	1:10
3	25 min.	30 min.	35 min.	35 min.
4	50 min.	55 min.	1:00	1:10
5	25 min.	30 min.	35 min.	35 min.
6	1:10	1:20	1:30	1:45
7	optional	optional	optional	optional
Ave.	*35 min.*	*40 min.*	*45 min.*	*50 min.*

Day	Week 5	Week 6	Week 7	Week 8
1	40 min.	40 min.	40 min.	40 min.
2	1:20	1:30	1:30	1:30
3	40 min.	40 min.	40 min.	40 min.
4	1:20	1:30	1:30	1:30
5	40 min.	40 min.	40 min.	40 min.
6	1:45	2:00	2:00	2:00
7	optional	optional	optional	optional
Ave.	*55 min.*	*1:00*	*1:00*	*1:00*

Day	Week 9	Week 10	Week 11	Week 12
1	40 min.	40 min.	40 min.	40 min.
2	1:30	1:30	1:30	1:30
3	40 min.	40 min.	40 min.	40 min.
4	1:30	1:30	1:30	1:30
5	40 min.	40 min.	40 min.	40 min.
6	2:00	2:00	2:30+	2:00
7	optional	optional	optional	optional
Ave.	*1:00*	*1:00*	*1:05*	*1:00*

NOTES ON USING THE SCHEDULE:

1.   Choose the marathon you want to run, then begin the program exactly three months earlier.

2. The schedule presumes that you're starting from a base of about a half-hour of running a day. If you're significantly below that, don't begin this program until you've reached that basic level.

3. If you're running more than 35 minutes a day, start later and at the appropriate place in the schedule. There is, of course, no reason to back down.

4. Typically, the weeks will run from Monday (Day 1) through Sunday (Day 7), with the longest run on Saturday. But weeks can start and end anywhere you want.

5. One day a week—labeled "optional"—is left open for rest or as a makeup day if you've come up short for the week.

6. The entire schedule has alternating long and short days to allow cycles of work and recovery. They're planned on about a 1-2-3 ratio: a short run is one part, a medium-long run two parts and the longest three parts.

7. The program calls for a five-week buildup, leveling off at an average of an hour a day for seven weeks and then a one-week easing off before the marathon.

8. In the next-to-last (11th) week of full training, you're asked to go at least a half-hour longer than ever before. This is a confidence-builder.

9. You are trying to accumulate an average of an hour a day for an eight-week period (all averages are figured on full seven-day weeks). This theoretically gives you the ability to *run* for four hours or to *race* for three hours.

10. Three months includes 13 weeks, and I give only 12 here. I hope you aren't superstitious because the 13th is race week. "Taper" all week with runs averaging about half of normal—30 minutes a day.

11. Do all your training at about the pace you expect to maintain for the full marathon at the end of the program.

12. You may run a race of 5-10 miles in the first month and one of 10-15 miles in the second month instead of one of the long runs. But this is not a requirement.

TRAINING TO RACE

The preceding article provides an excellent guide for completing your first marathon. But having made the breakthrough of finishing one, the next question is, "How can I go faster?"

When this happens, the most simple of sports can become rather complicated as runners search for the "secrets" that will guarantee faster times and better performances. Runners become concerned not just with running but with times, splits, speed, intervals, fartlek, lactic acid, loading, peaking, pacing and so on.

This is the point where many runners begin to feel the need for a coach to plan longterm training and suggest specific workouts. A coach also can help a runner peak for a specific race, suggest racing strategy, and take the blame for poor performance (and some of the credit for good). But the upsurge in popularity of long-distance running has far outstripped the supply of available coaches, especially for the "average" runner.

However, the near-impossibility of finding a knowledgeable coach with the time and interest to coach you needn't stop you from improving. Indeed, you have the capacity for knowing your own body better than anyone—and the ability to know its strengths and weaknesses is probably 70-80% of coaching. The rest is knowledge of physiology and training methods, and applying them to your needs and abilities.

Just because you don't have a coach, you don't need to be uncoached. I offer this guide on how to plan your running and coach yourself to a better marathon performance.

1. Set a goal. Physiologists have established that we perform better when aiming at a *specific* goal rather than when trying for a generalized improvement. A goal should be carefully considered so that it is both realistic (attainable within a time frame of 3-6 months) and challenging (so that reaching the goal means something special). You can define your goal in terms of improving your best marathon time or perhaps reaching a qualifying standard (like the Boston Marathon standard), or even to win or place well in a certain race.

After choosing the goal and writing it down, put it aside. Focus your attention on your day-to-day running, and let the goal rest in the back of your mind. *Having* a goal is much more important than reaching it. The greatest rewards come from the working toward goals, not in the short-lived exhilaration of achieving them.

2. Keep a training log. This can be as simple or as detailed as you wish, but at least keep a record of the distance and type of workout, and how you felt. When starting the training log, take a page and list three columns: "Where I am now," "Where I want to go," and your specific goal for the 3-6-month time frame. Then fill in the columns with your training load, times for various distances and any other areas that concern your running (such as health, weight and strength).

The log of your actual workouts becomes invaluable in analyzing where you are in your training and what you need to do (or not do) in response to good or bad races or injuries.

3. Personalize your training system. When planning a training system, be aware of how the body reacts to training. All exercise is a form of stress. Running is actually *destructive* to the body through the shock on legs and feet, depletion of energy stores, loss of water and minerals for cooling, and other effects.

However, we have a built-in reaction which allows it to adapt to stresses by rebuilding itself and then "overbuilding" the affected tissues as a protection against the same stress in the future. It is this overbuilding and adaptation that makes training effective, and this can occur only when the stress is no longer present.

Thus, the two components of training are stress and rest. Training is only beneficial when both are present. Finding your own proper balance between the two is the key to maximum, sustained improvement.

The stress. What constitutes a stress will vary according to your ability and conditioning. Running six miles at seven minutes per mile may be extremely stressful for the novice runner. But to a world-class marathoner who has adapted to much higher stress, this might be a recovery run. Stress is necessary for improvement, and as the body adapts to one level of stress, the load must be raised to continue the progress.

Work up gradually, and heed the body's warning systems of pain and fatigue to avoid a "breakdown stress," that causes chronic fatigue, injury or illness. A breakdown stress occurs when the body is depleted of all available energy stores and begins to break down its own muscle tissue for energy.

East German scientists found that it takes six recovery days to attain the previous training level after only three days on an excessive program.

In terms of pure distance, running more than 50% beyond your highest previous total mileage on a given day is likely to cause break-

down, though it can also occur if you dramatically increase your pace
or begin heavy interval training. Mileages should not increase by more
than 10% a week.

However, most injuries among runners are not the result of the
breakdown stress of a single workout but are cumulative—resulting
from a number of subsequent stresses without sufficient time for the
body to recover and adapt to the normal workout stress. This leads us
to the second component of training.

The recovery-adaptation time. Until recently, most athletic training
programs were based on a philosophy of consistent day-to-day intensity and gradually increasing workloads. However, the era of 100-mile-
per-week training schedules brought evidence that maintaining peak
training loads led to deterioration in performance rather than
improvement.

In 1970, Drs. A. K. Chin and E. Evonuk set out to study the
optimum recovery-adaptation times under varying levels of stress.
They found that under moderate training stresses, the body can
rebuild itself within approximately 24 hours.

However, racing involves intensity—being able not only to run far,
but to run far *fast*. Thus, you must increase the intensity of your workouts in order to continue improving. The same study found that under
severe exercise, like that in intense training, it takes *48 hours* for the
body to recover and rebuild. Any stressful training before full recovery
will only delay the adaptation process and will be of no physical
benefit.

Therefore, your training system should incorporate intensity along
with sufficient recovery time for maximum improvement. I suggest
some kind of "hard-easy" system, involving a heavy training load on
one day, followed by one or two days of easy running for recovery.

The intensity can be obtained through various kinds of workouts:
running a longer distance, running at a faster pace, or by doing some
kind of repetition work on the track or hills. In general, your racing
performances will benefit more from a training program of 10-12
miles one day, then 3-4 miles the next, than from running 7-8 miles
every day.

Make the "hard" days as intense as possible (while avoiding breakdown) in order to simulate the intensity of racing—and then merely
jog to boost circulation and aid recovery on the easy days.

Races, even if they are regarded as workouts, should be preceded
and followed by easy days in order to gain maximum benefits from
them.

The knowledge and strict application of this system may be one of the explanations for the rapid improvement in Eastern European athletes over the past few years. East German runners follow this kind of routine, and from their ranks came 1976 Olympic marathon champion Waldemar Cierpinski.

I have found, in my own training, that by maintaining at least four days per week as easy days (5-9 miles at 6-6½ minutes per mile), I have been able to work up to 25-35 total miles of hard distance and track interval sessions on hard days without injury or breakdown.

4. Plan your workouts. If you are interested in improving your racing performances, be aware that the body has two different methods of using energy during running.

The most efficient is the "aerobic" method in which glucose is burned with oxygen (aerobic means "with air") in the muscles, producing carbon dioxide. As long as sufficient oxygen is being supplied to the muscles through the lungs and circulatory system, the aerobic mechanism will supply the needed energy.

However, as the running pace increases, there comes a point where the breathing/circulatory system can no longer supply enough oxygen. At this point, the muscles begin to work "anaerobically." The anaerobic ("without air") method produces lactic acid, which builds up the muscles and will impede performance until neutralized when the "oxygen debt" is paid off during rest.

The main difference between these two methods of using energy is that the aerobic relies on the strength and efficiency of the lungs, heart and circulatory system, while the anaerobic relies on the muscles' ability to work harder and for longer periods of time without oxygen and in spite of the lactic acid buildup.

All races involve varying combinations of aerobic and anaerobic work. This ranges from 17% aerobic/83% anaerobic at 400 meters and 50%/50% at 1500 meters to 99%/1% for the marathon. This suggests a general emphasis for training.

Aerobic conditioning is achieved through running long distances at an easy, sustained pace. The body adapts by making the lungs grow more efficient, the heart stronger and the arteries and veins larger and more numerous. However, while long, slow distance running is purely aerobic, all anaerobic training stresses *both* the breathing/circulatory system and the muscles.

The above percentages are computed for ideal, evenly paced situations which rarely occur in races. The tendency for many runners to train exclusively on aerobic workouts accounts for their sub-par performances on hilly courses or in races which involve a fast early pace. In these situations, they probably lack the anaerobic fitness to be able to handle the temporary stress, then pay off the oxygen debt while maintaining a good pace.

Another system of too little anaerobic conditioning is being stuck at a "plateau" of racing performance, even when your overall mileage has increased. Here, the aerobic fitness may have surpassed the muscles' ability to handle a faster pace. A relatively small amount of anaerobic training may bring a performance breakthrough.

Even marathoners need at least one anaerobic training session per week. This can be done as part of a distance run, employing fast stretches and then jogging, or by doing repeats of hills (sprint up, jog down), or on a track. General rules to follow:

• Make a fast stretch anywhere from 100-440 yards (15-75 seconds). Anything shorter doesn't have much benefit, anything longer becomes a mental strain.

• Include a minimum of 10 fast repeats to make a workout.

• Try to jog the recovery interval in order to get the maximum aerobic benefit.

• Keep the recovery jog as short as possible. Maximum: twice the time length of the repeat.

An excellent anaerobic workout is simply to run on a track, sprinting the straights and jogging the turns. Start by aiming at six continuous laps of this, working up to 10 or 12 laps. Then try sprinting a half-lap, jogging a quarter-lap.

Like all running, anaerobic training involves pain initially. But as you get stronger, the feeling of running fast becomes exhilarating, and the rewards in your racing performances make it well worth the effort.

5. Reach a peak. Lasse Viren's spectacular success at being able to peak at precisely the right time for the 1972 and '76 Olympics was the product of a program called "periodization," originated by a Russian professor, L. P. Matveyev.

Matveyev recommended one or at most two peaks per year for four distinct phases. In a six-month cycle, the periods fall this way:

• *General preparation* lasts 6-8 weeks. It emphasizes general conditioning and a gradual buildup in training volume, with constant, moderate training pace.

• *Intensive preparation*, the next phase, lasts another 6-8 weeks. Here, the total volume of training is kept fairly constant with a gradually increasing intensity involving faster pace and anaerobic training.

• *Competitive phase* again lasts 6-8 weeks and involves a reduction in total training volume, but an increasing proportion of anaerobic and fast distance work along with racing at various distances. The maximum effort comes at the end of the competitive phase and is preceded by a series of hard racing efforts then by a minimum workload during the final few days before competition.

• *Recuperation phase.* During this 2-4 weeks, the emphasis is on physical and emotional relaxation. It involves leisure pursuits but includes daily activity such as easy running at moderate distances.

It is possible to run well throughout the year *and* obtain your best performances in one or two marathons a year by using your stress-recovery system and adapting some of Matveyev's principles as follows:

• Choose your peak. Set your goal for a specific race, 3-6 months in advance, and direct your energy toward it.

• Keep marathon races special. Don't race them indiscriminately and call them "workouts" when you run poorly. Racing when you aren't ready teaches you to make excuses and to take races lightly.

• Race at varying shorter distances for variety and physical conditioning/sharpening.

• Increase the proportion of anaerobic work in your training during the last 6-8 weeks before your peak race. Reach maximum training approximately three weeks before a marathon. Then ease down the training, and relax (easy jogging only) during the last five days, especially if you're using the carbohydrate-loading diet.

• If possible, schedule your workouts at the same time as the race as it approaches. If racing in a different time zone, adjust your eating/sleeping/training schedule at least four days before the race.

• Ignore all concern with luck, chance, etc. It's up to you to go out and make your own luck through training and, ultimately, in the race itself.

SCHEDULE FOR RACERS

Day	Week 1	Week 2	Week 3	Week 4
1	4 miles	4 miles	4 miles	4 miles
2	4 miles	4 miles	4 miles	5 miles
3	7 miles*	8 miles*	9 miles*	10 miles*
4	4 miles	4 miles	4 miles	4 miles
5	7 miles	8 miles	9 miles	10 miles
6	4 miles	4 miles	4 miles	4 miles
7	10 miles	13 miles	16 miles	18 miles
T1.	*40 miles*	*45 miles*	*50 miles*	*55 miles*

Day	Week 5	Week 6	Week 7	Week 8
1	5 miles	5 miles	5 miles	5 miles
2	5 miles	5 miles	5 miles	5 miles
3	10 miles*	10 miles*	10 miles*	10 miles*
4	5 miles	5 miles	5 miles	5 miles
5	10 miles	10 miles	10 miles*	10 miles*
6	5 miles	5 miles	5 miles	5 miles
7	20 miles	20 miles	20 miles	20 miles
T1.	*60 miles*	*60 miles*	*60 miles*	*60 miles*

Day	Week 9	Week 10	Week 11	Week 12
1	5 miles	5 miles	5 miles	5 miles
2	5 miles	5 miles	5 miles	5 miles
3	10 miles*	10 miles*	10 miles*	10 miles*
4	5 miles	5 miles	5 miles	5 miles
5	10 miles*	10 miles*	10 miles*	10 miles*
6	5 miles	5 miles	5 miles	5 miles
7	20 miles	20 miles	20 miles	20 miles
T1.	*60 miles*	*60 miles*	*60 miles*	*60 miles*

NOTES ON USING THE SCHEDULE:

1. Begin the schedule exactly three months before the marathon you want to race.

2. The schedule, based on Brian Maxwell's suggestions, presumes you now are doing 30-40 miles a week. If running less, don't begin this program until you've increased mileage.

3. If you're running more than 40 miles a week, start later, at the appropriate place in the schedule.

4. The three-month buildup includes six weeks of "intensive preparation" (increased distances) and a seven-week "competitive phase" (increased pace).

5. The program calls for building to 60-mile weeks and maintaining that level for eight weeks. Consider this a *minimum* for marathon racing. If you do more, keep the same ratio of mileages listed here.

6. The basic pace of your runs—at least those on the longer-harder days—should be close to what you expect to hold for the full marathon.

7. Observe the hard-easy, long-short, work-recovery pattern throughout the training period.

8. A weekly 20-mile run is scheduled from Week Five on. You need some runs at this distance but may find it too hard to do every week. If so, cut back slightly and make up the difference elsewhere in the week.

9. Recommended "speed days" are marked with an " * ." There is one a week for the first six weeks, then two a week. On these days, add the types of fast training Brian Maxwell recommends in his article, or consider juggling the schedule to fit in 5-15-mile races or time trials.

10. Run easily, no more than five miles a day, in Week 13 which ends with the marathon.

11

Training to Peak

Know how to be ready for the big
event on the day it happens

Ron Daws

The women's marathon record would be 2:24 if it were on par with their world record for 3000 meters. If you think that is an exaggeration, then you might be surprised to learn that the *average* male in his 20s or 30s has the potential to crack 2:30, or if he has a bent for running he could do 2:20. I'm implying that if a good (but not great) time for men is currently 2:20, then a woman of comparable caliber could run 2:36.*

I'm dangling these carrots in front of your noses because with balanced training not only can you race faster, you can eliminate a lot of guesswork in preparing for championships. In other words, if you are one of those who runs well in small races and falls flat in championships, there is something you can do about it.

For women, distance running is wide open. Only recently have they seriously contested the road races. A 2:36 marathon—faster than the American record and only two minutes from the world's best at this writing—is within the grasp of many women once they realize they can train like men can. Most runners gravely underestimate their capabilities and lack incentive to challenge the elite. While the underdog probably cannot beat Bill Rodgers or Lasse Viren (unless they drop out), from experience I have found that by pointing for races that

* Scoring tables rate Lydumila Bragina's 8:27.1 for 3000 meters equivalent to a 2:24:45 marathon. The difference between Derek Clayton's 2:08:36 and a 2:20 marathon is about 11½ minutes. Allowing women the same differential gives them 2:36. (and, given women's recent entry into serious distance running, their 3000-meter record is probably not on par with Clayton's marathon. On that basis, one could argue that the average-class woman marathoner could run in the low 2:30s.)

counted, I was able to make the Pan-American and Olympic Games—
even though on paper I had no chance. The ironic thing is, the other
contenders helped me the most. They made enough mistakes to
eliminate themselves.

But it requires more than just motivation. Thousands are motivated
but don't know how to train. Many who believe they are training
efficiently actually have it all mixed up. The principles of training are
the same for racing all distances; they are the same for women and
men; they apply to those who (presently) plod and to world-class
runners. There are no shortcuts to the top. Even Rodgers and Frank
Shorter have no gimmick up their shorts unless it is their parents'
genes and 130-200 carefully executed miles a week.

THE TRAINING JIGSAW PUZZLE

Experienced runners are familiar with various kinds of training.
They know about long-distance work, fartlek, hill work, sprinting,
interval and repetition running. Additionally, they probably are
familiar with concepts such as aerobic and anaerobic work, and maximal aerobic capacity. Runners understand how to run these workouts
but usually fail to realize that balanced training is not just a matter of
mixing various runs during the week.

Putting together effective training is analogous to assembling a jig-
saw puzzle. You may have all the pieces, but you don't get the picture
until you put them in the right order. Even many world-class runners
do not realize this. The reason various training approaches confuse
runners is because almost any kind of running that places intermittent
moderate-to-heavy stress on the athlete will usually result in fairly fast
races. A coach could train a beginning marathoner on nothing but
220s and 440s, and get him fairly fit. (In fact, Emil Zatopek trained
this way and won gold in the 1952 Olympic 5000 meters, 10,000 and
marathon.) But to make a better weekly program, one could mix distance work, intervals and sprints to balance training. Many runners
condition this way and run fast times.

However, merely racing a fast time is not the ultimate goal. For
example, 17 men had faster 5000-meter times than Lasse Viren going
into the Montreal Olympics, yet no one beat him in the 5000 final (or
in the 10,000, or the 5000 and 10,000 in the previous Olympics). The
reason no one could beat Viren was that his coach balanced his program so that he would peak *during the Games*.

The concept of timing one's optimum condition was popularized in
the early 1960s by New Zealand's Arthur Lydiard after he coached
neighborhood boys to win gold medals and set world records. Lydiard

trained his runners in stages, each built around a specific kind of running. The first phase for all runners was marathon or distance training, which in the early 1960s was highly unorthodox because it put half-milers and milers on the roads to cover 100 or more miles a week. Lydiard's program subsequently became so identified with distance running that many runners and coaches overlooked the ultimate goal.

Several Finnish coaches, however, recognized his goal after Lydiard went there in 1967 to reverse the abysmal state of distance running. Kenny Moore wrote in a June 27, 1977, *Sports Illustrated* article on Lasse Viren titled *An Enigma Wrapped In Glory*, "For his coach, he [Viren] sought out Rolf Haikkola. Haikkola was influenced by New Zealand's Arthur Lydiard, whom he got to come to Finland to advise runners and coaches. Lydiard's ideas of how to bring runners to the best shape at the right time seemed ideal for us with our long winters and short racing seasons,' says Haikkola."

Viren said of his ability to peak for the Olympics, "Some do well in other races, some run fast times, but they cannot do well in the ultimate, the Olympics... The question is not why I run this way, but why so many others cannot."

Viren is not the only world-class runner to use the Lydiard system. The rise of the other Finns and the Mexican runners before the 1968 Olympics was due to Lydiard's stay in these countries. New Zealanders Rod Dixon, Dick Quax and John Walker each use variations of the system, as do most of the East Germans. Canadian Jerome Drayton, 2:10:08 marathoner and three-time winner of Japan's Fukuoka Marathon, uses it also. In a *Runner's World* interview with Drayton after he won the 1977 Boston Marathon, he summarized the key elements of his training so that any aspiring distance runner could adopt them. Without mentioning Lydiard directly, it is obvious where his ideas are rooted:

> Basically, you have all these different types of training and different types of workouts. You've got general distance running, you've got fartlek, you've got hill work, you've got aerobic training sessions, you've got anaerobic training sessions and then you've got the rest phase. You take these phases and you arrange them in the right order. You have to work in time frames. You attach so many weeks to each phase.
>
> What most of the runners do... is try to incorporate any number of these different types of training in a typical week. They will do distance one day, and track another time, and maybe a little hill work. They're sort of fishing in the dark. That's the biggest mistake.
>
> You can get fit no matter what you do, but the idea is to get the best out of yourself. So you should take each of these phases, arrange them in the right

order in degree of difficulty, attach so many weeks to each phase, and stick with it. If you are doing hill work, don't introduce track workouts at all. If you are doing general distance, don't introduce hill work.

What I'm saying, essentially, is that you have to be very organized with your training. You work in time frames; you work in units. The order would be general distance, hill work, aerobic track, anaerobic track and then the rest phase. The rest phase is a drastic taper. This could take anywhere from seven days to three weeks, depending on the event. What you do in the rest phase is a combination of aerobic and anaerobic, high quality and low quality. And the general principle that can be applied to each phase is one rest day followed by one hard day, depending on your state of fitness.

Before Lydiard's system became popular (and even now for many runners), conditioning relied upon interval runs to build endurance and speed by having the runner cover a series of relatively short, fast runs interspersed with enough jogging to provide a partial-to-near recovery. The runner became fit because he ran fast to develop speed, and with the recoveries between fast sections he could repeat these runs many times for stamina. It taught the runner to contend with lactic acid and other waste products he would encounter later in the races because of the anaerobic work load.

However, racing success is not governed primarily by the ability to run anaerobically. Moreover, conditioning runners by using interval work raises other problems to be discussed later. Interval work has a place in the runner's program, but it should not be used to accomplish what can best be done by something else.

The faster one runs relying upon *aerobic* metabolism, the more efficiently he covers the distance. As soon as the runner's pace exceeds his aerobic capacity to produce energy, the additional energy is produced anaerobically. The price paid for this chemical cheating (the runner is burning glycogen in the absence of oxygen) is a rapid buildup of waste products in the muscles which quickly inhibits their ability to function. It stands to reason that the runner who develops his aerobic tolerance on top of an ability to run aerobic 5:30 miles is going to race faster than someone who begins anaerobic training with only a 6:30 per mile aerobic capacity. Furthermore, it has been shown that frequent, intense interval sessions lower the blood pH and the maximal aerobic capacity. The runner then becomes bored, stale and slower.

When Viren said of his ability to win the Olympics, "The question is not why I run this way, but why so many others cannot," he was referring to *the* training enigma that confronts every runner. While I as much as Viren was referring to Olympians and world-record-holders, it is little wonder that to runners of lesser stature extracting one's best in the state meet, the conference, the nationals is often hopeful guessing at best.

Simply stated, the goal of training is to arrive at the important races mentally fresh and at peak fitness. To do this, you must develop endurance and speed, mechanical and biological efficiency, incentive and persistence—and still have the energy to race after training is finished. But the trick is not in listing these attributes; any fool can see what you need. The trick is in figuring out how to acquire them most effectively.

FIVE WAYS TO IMPROVE TRAINING

1. *Use wasted time for training.* Thirty minutes regained a day for training is 30 miles a week. That 30 miles can make the difference between finishing in the middle of the pack or the front.

2. *Innovate to sidestep setbacks.* Successful runners devise ways to train when others give in to excuses. For example, if your schedule calls for hill workouts and you live in Pancakesville, understand that hill training is resistance work and settle for something similar. Run up stairs, in sand or water, into the wind or in snow.

The indomitable Emil Zatopek, who captured the 1952 Olympic triple, ran in place for two hours in a tub of dirty laundry rather than miss a workout when family responsibilities prevented his leaving the house. Dr. Alex Ratelle (American record-holder for marathoners over 50) rides an exercycle to warm up when injured, which usually enables him then to run outside. I built a treadmill or ran the stairs at work to get a morning workout when I couldn't train outside. As 2:09 marathoner Ron Hill said of his never missing a workout in six years, "It's just developing the attitude that nothing can stop you."

3. *Persist through setbacks and mistakes.* Runners such as Ron Clarke, Steve Prefontaine and Bill Rodgers have suffered defeat in Olympic competition and later crushed the opposition. Others such as Peter Snell and Abebe Bikila were seemingly washed up before the Games and then trounced everyone.

In Snell's case, his training which had been spectacular before the '64 Olympics took a downward turn just as he was applying the finishing touches. Times slipped, he pulled a thigh muscles, and for a while cared so little about the Games he avoided making entries in his diary.Yet, within a couple of weeks he was training faster than ever, and eventually was in complete command during the 800 and 1500 meters. Bikila's problem was more straightforward but no less sobering; he had his appendix chopped out four weeks before he spread-eagled the field in the 1964 Olympic Marathon.

Any mistake is painful, especially in the face of high stakes, but nothing ingrains a lesson so deeply. When I developed sciatica 10 days before the 1967 Pan-American Games Marathon, I polished off any chance of recovering because I insisted on running 20 miles two days later. I couldn't see any good in hobbling along the sidelines during what I was sure would be my only chance to represent the USA in competition. Yet, from what I learned there, I was able to survive an identical sciatica attack before the Olympic Trials a year later.

4. *Stick to your schedule.* After you have blocked out your training, stay with it unless something is wrong. Don't inject something you read about from Shorter's program, because it probably won't work for you. Besides, reports are often inaccurate. I realized this for the first time when I told a reporter I ran 30 miles on Sundays, and he wrote that I did it every day!

Don't prematurely begin another phase of training just because the other guys are anxious to try the track. Take a lesson from Snell. He refused a trip to compete for New Zealand during preparation for the '64 Games, even though he was told that unless he went no one else would go. Snell remained adamant even though the others lost the trip.

If your training run is supposed to be easy, don't race after the first mug who passes you, just because your pride is hurt. Similarly, don't water down a difficult run because you think there are lots of other nights. A good schedule balances one workout against another. If you progress from the easy to the difficult as you move from one stage of training to the next, you will discover that your targets are quite immediate. It is much easier to train seriously while thinking that only two weeks of base work remain before the hills than it is to train for a race two or three months down the pike. As Drayton said, "Work in time frames; work in units."

5. *Don't be intimidated by the odds.* To hell with the odds. Caution never did big things. Go for the big ones at some point in your life. Shoot for the stars. Even if you only get to the moon, you will venture into worlds never dreamed of.

SEQUENCING TRAINING

Devising a training program is relatively uncomplicated once one orders his goals and understands the purpose of each kind of training. Training goals should be pursued in this order:*

---

* The program outlined here is discussed in greater detail in my book, *The Self-Made Olympian,* which, despite the autobiographical ring of the title, is a training guide.

1. *Develop aerobic capacity and general endurance.* Maximal aerobic capacity is best developed by long runs—not interval work or sprint work. Initially, the effort is relatively easy, with no "hard-easy" days. The emphasis is on maximal miles without overwork or injury. The runner sets a target mileage he eventually wants to hit and works up to it as quickly as he comfortably can.

Once the target weekly mileage can be covered without overloading, the week's work is structured, setting aside one long run (20 miles minimum for experienced runners) and two or three moderately long runs within a hard-effort-day/recover-day pattern. In other words, after building up to a reasonably high mileage, as the runner becomes more fit, he goes faster and not farther. The fast runs approach but do not exceed the maximal aerobic capacity at the time. For training purposes, one's maximal aerobic capacity at any point can be approximated by guessing the mile pace at which he could run a marathon (allowing for effects of such things as wearing training rather than racing shoes or sweat clothes).

Don't try to accomplish everything at the same time. At this point, you are training to raise your aerobic capacity and general endurance. Your success later will depend upon how well you do it. You don't want or need speed at this time, and there will be plenty of time for it later.

Include one fartlek workout a week, however. The classic fartlek workout is a continuous run on hilly forest paths, interspersed with fast-slow sections. After a couple of easy miles (every workout should begin easily), repeat sections of 5:00-6:00 pace until pleasantly tired. Or run steadily for half the distance, and alternate faster and slower blocks the second half. It is a free and fun run.

As you become more fit, gradually run more at or near your aerobic capacity. This training is not jogging around as some runners have mistakenly thought. You will have to be tough by the time you finish base work, or you will not survive the hill training that comes next. This kind of beginning minimizes injuries and keeps the stress level relatively low, while the runner covers high mileage. Because there is no racing, there are no competitive pressures.

2. *Develop power and stamina.* Power and stamina are developed best by resistance work. Hill running, running in sand, in water, up stairs and into the wind all qualify, but the best are hills. They develop strength, up and downhill technique, and rudimentary speed. They are the first contact with anaerobic running. Whereas it may have taken 1-3 hours of relatively steady work to produce fatigue during base training, the runner now encounters shorter, more intense sections of

resistance running. He moves his body against resistance with a running action, developing the power needed later in racing.

This is a major transition and the demands are strenuous in the extreme. There are various ways to put together hill workouts, but the common elements are fast work up and down 440-880-yard hills and quick sections of striding between hill runs. It is essential to begin easily and gradually pile on the effort. Good downhill technique is letting gravity do the work, but constant practice is necessary to insulate yourself from the slamming. Once learned, you can free-wheel down hills with little effort or risk of injury. Hill-train three days a week, keep the long run, and cut the week's mileage by 10-20%.

3. *Maximize the capacity to tolerate anaerobic work, learn pace, increase efficiency at faster speeds.* Tolerance to anaerobic work is developed by performing difficult anaerobic work, so interval training now becomes of value. It can be performed on the track, but it is usually best to use the track only to check progress.

In Kenny Moore's article on Lasse Viren, he said, "Most of his speed work is not done on the track but on the forest trails or soft roads, and in races. He only went on the track three times all that summer (before the Munich Olympics)."

When beginning interval work, capitalize on what you have most—that is, endurance and stamina. Therefore, *do not* start with fast runs or sprints, no matter how anxious you may be to test yourself after months on the roads. Interval training should begin with high volume, relatively slow work with short rests, and evolve to faster workouts with more rest, and finally move toward fast workouts with little rest. Cutting out all rest from an interval workout makes it a time-trial.

Rarely is more than two or three days of interval work a week needed. Much depends upon the distance races, the runner's innate speed and how long it takes to develop it, and his temperament. It's far better to do too little interval work at this time than too much.

4. *Sharpen.* This is the final stage of training for track and cross-country runners with a regular season of races, and it is the end of training for road racers shooting for a major race. Until now, trackmen and road racers have trained the same. Now, they train according to the demands of their event. Track racers emphasize speed, marathoners emphasize stamina, but trackmen still do distance runs and marathoners sprint.

The idea is to pull everything together for the big race or races, and timing is critical. The tendency is to get ahead of schedule and waste good running in workouts and minor races. Coordinating everything requires skill. Basically, it means that the runner works on his weak spots.

If he doesn't know pace, he learns it. Leg speed is developed by fast striding and sprinting; if he is still short on speed, he does more sprinting. If he is a marathoner, he includes a 30-miler once a week, because he knows it protects him from the kinds of fatigue one encounters after 20 miles in a race. He also probably realizes that if he cannot cover 30 miles at an easy effort, he will probably have trouble racing 26. If he feels tired, he backs off in training so that he enters the races fresh. He practices tactics and studies his competitors. He runs time-trials and uses early-season races as experiments to assess his condition. It is a time of fine-tuning, and this is an art (although it is slowly evolving into a science).

SPEED WORK AND THE MARATHONER

The 1970s opened a new era in marathoning in the United States. Historically, the marathoner was the reject from the shorter distances—a relative plodder who won because attrition eliminated the others after 20 miles. When George Young entered the '68 Olympic Marathon Trial, few considered him a threat. However, my feeling was that the marathon was about to be taken over by the five- and 10-kilometer runners—not the rejects, but top runners who included long runs in their training. In short, the new marathoner would run far, fast. Young fit that description.

He won the Trial. Kenny Moore, then a six-miler, was second. I was the only "true marathoner" of the group to make the team. The 1970s saw the emergence of Frank Shorter—crack two-, three- and six-miler—as a marathoner. Others of the same breed followed. Nowadays, most world-ranked marathoners approach or break four minutes for the mile, and it is this combination of speed and endurance that allows them to clip along for 26 miles at 5:00 pace or under.

This description of the world-class athlete has importance to all marathoners—not only because it puts them farther back in the pack, but because of the implications in training. The days of the plodder are over. Speed is an important factor in training for the marathon, and it will become increasingly important as runners hope to get faster.

By way of illustration, in 1977 at the Catamount Ranch Training Camp in Colorado one of the runners complained that he had not been able to improve his marathon from the 2:37 run three years earlier. Three different days, he went with me to run twice around the camp's hilly 10-kilometer race course with a 250-yard walk between laps (this was at 10,000 feet elevation). Each of the 10 kilometers was at about seven-eighths effort.

Afterward, he said that at home he never trained that fast; it was just Lydiard-type distance training. I suggested that if he introduced interval work into his program, he would be able to race faster with good economy. His problem had been that off of 7:00 pace, the 6:00 pace required for a 2:37 marathon felt like sprinting. A couple of months later, he wrote that he'd cut his time by three minutes.

Many runners preparing for a marathon either do not realize that speed development is important or deliberately keep it out of their programs because of problems with it in the past. It may have led them to injuries or taken the fun out of training.

I would say that most of these runners have used speed work improperly, either doing too much at the wrong time or not working into it properly. There is no doubt that it is more difficult to survive speed work than distance running. There's more mental pressure, and until the runner feels comfortable with it, it produces an unacceptable kind of fatigue.

When first running intervals, one usually feels clumsy and slow. This is because he is not physically and psychologically used to tolerating anaerobic work. When first running a set of, say, 440s or 880s, one does not seem able to drive himself, but feels awkward and tired nevertheless. A month later, he is striding smoothly, his respiration rate is elevated, he can tolerate a heavier load, and he is immensely quicker.

For example, when first coming to the track to sharpen, I find it fairly difficult to run 76-second 440s. I suspect many runners have thrown in the towel at this point, consigned to the belief they have no speed to develop or that the effort is not worth it. I persist because I know I'll get faster quickly.

Even among those who want to do speed work, there is much confusion on how and when to do it. At one of the lectures at Catamount Ranch, I had gone through the phases of training, stressing I thought that one first builds general condition and aerobic capacity with distance runs, moves to hill work and finally introduces speed work to sharpen for races. Afterward, one of the high school runners came over and said that while he realized the base period was a time of aerobic training, couldn't he have just *one* speed workout a week.

This is the kind of thinking that gets runners into trouble. It had, I discovered, messed up this runner's racing in the past. Stressing strict adherence to distance training during the base period may be nitpicking, but it shows that this runner still had no concept either of what he was trying to accomplish during the base period or even his interval work.

Perhaps many readers are still saying, so what if he ran one interval workout a week; it probably wouldn't hurt him. It may be that it wouldn't; one can never say that a particular workout will wreck you, but you can say that the odds go up. More subtly, an improper workout may hurt you *just a little* by not contributing as much as another workout or by draining away the enthusiasm needed later. Small errors add up. The advantage of holding off intervals until later is that you can't wait to start them after months on the roads. You feel like a kid pondering a mysterious Christmas present; the anticipation heightens your drive. The runner who has done intervals all along lacks this feeling.

Runners still argue that the marathon is an aerobic race—blood drawn from marathoners' legs immediately after the race contains no lactic acid, signaling no anaerobic work—so why train anaerobically at all? My answer is that when one performs intervals, he not only develops anaerobic tolerance; he continues to improve biomechanical efficiency. He develops better mechanical coordination. The muscle cells undergo further refinements to enable them to get more out of oxygen. I also suspect that in dealing with anaerobic workloads runners learn to operate at a greater percentage of their maximal aerobic capacity. This last factor appears to be an important ingredient in separating great runners from the rest.

For example, Shorter can consume 71.2 milliliters of oxygen per minute per kilogram of body weight, ranking him low among world-class runners. However, during a marathon Shorter can operate at more than 90% of his maximal oxygen capacity while most other runners cannot.

Further aiding Shorter is a phenomenon common to world-class distance runners. He consumes less oxygen than do middle-distance racers at the same speeds, an advantage perhaps provided by the ratio of fast- to slow-twitch muscle and the effects of relatively greater amounts of aerobic work.

It can be seen, therefore, that the value of anaerobic (fast) running has many facets. If a marathoner can improve his 220 by just two seconds, obviously he is going to run at slower speeds with greater ease. That alone means faster average pace for any race.

This brings the discussion right back to the importance of the aerobic-anaerobic balance. Just as too much distance running eventually brings boredom and undeveloped potential, too much speed work gives added risk of injury, lower blood pH and the rest. Where the balance lies for each athlete is as complex as the psychological and physiological considerations underlying them. It will not be exactly the same for any two runners, or even for the same runner over time. What a runner must recognize is that an equilibrium exists, and that by studying his training diaries, he must gain as much insight into himself as he can over the years.

EVALUATING TRAINING

There are numerous examples of world-class runners such as Peter Snell and Murray Halberg of the 1960s bringing their condition to a peak just before the Olympics. But, again, the example of Viren from Moore's article is as illustrative as any.

Said Viren's coach, "Lasse's problems before the two Olympics were entirely different. Six weeks before Munich, he ran 5000 in 13:19, so he was ready. But was he too early? We had a test run in Stockholm and he broke the world record for two miles with 8:14. He was *ready*. But still the newspapers said the peak won't last. So we employed three tests which put Lasse's mind to ease. Each time, it was the same. He would run 200 meters 20 times, and we would time him and take his pulse right after each 200. In June, he averaged 30 seconds and 190 beats per minute. In July, before the two-mile record, he averaged 29.3 and 186. In August, before the Olympics he did 27.2 and 172. So we had real proof that there was nothing to worry about.

"Before Montreal, we gave Lasse the same test. He averaged 28.2 and 182 beats per minute, not his best. His training had been interrupted by a month-long sinus infection that had to be drained six or seven times. So we did another test to discover what kind of work was needed. He did 5000 meters on grass by sprinting 50 meters and easing 50 meters, sprinting and easing, 50 sprints in all. He finished in a time of 13:32 (better than all but a handful of runners can do while running an even pace). But his pulse was only 186. In perfect condition, he would go over 200 after such a sustained stress-ease exercise. It was obvious that he needed additional speed training, but there were only eight days left before the 10,000-meter heats... Three days later he was quicker; you could see the difference in the action of his ankles. He was reaching his maximum sharpness."

As can be seen, Viren goes on the training track only to gauge his condition. Using time-trials and carefully controlled interval workouts, his coach and he evaluate what needs to be done. For most runners, pre-race time-trials and early-season races will reveal both strengths and weaknesses as well as provide the sharpening work necessary before championship racing.

The difference in the attitude of Viren's coach toward training, and that of many coaches and runners is that it is not enough that Viren trains or time-trials fast. Clues are sought to gauge where he is in his development and what needs to be done. Most runners before the Olympics would have been perfectly content with a world record for two miles or 20 x 200 in 27.2. Viren's coach, however, viewed these performances primarily in terms of the Olympics. Two miles in 8:14 was excellent, but did it mean Viren was sharpening too fast? Twenty 200s in 27.2 was fast, but weighing them against his pulse rate, clues were provided for the remaining training. Of course, the coach needed a working knowledge of physiology and Viren to evaluate these runs as he did. But a degree in work physiology is not required to extract feedback from workouts.

Runners and coaches must understand that a fast workout is valuable only if it contributes to fast racing. No one receives medals for workouts. Many athletes run fast workouts to impress themselves, teammates or the coach without wondering how the effort relates to other workouts and races. If you always outrun your teammates in practice and lose to them in races, something is wrong.

The East Germans and some runners in the US plan upcoming workouts from analyses of periodic blood samples (not to be confused with "blood-doping"). If the blood shows the runner to be tired from a hard track session, for example, the next such session would probably be delayed. Although blood analysis is beyond most runners' means, it not difficult to gain insight in other ways. One soon learns that if during sharpening he feels like avoiding training and is racing slowly, it may be the signal for a rest from the track. Many runners mistakenly try to train harder—especially a week or two before a championship—when they feel they *have* to get in a few last licks.

At the Catamount Ranch in 1977, I had to take inventory during one of my first runs there. Five miles out on a two-hour run run at 10,000 feet, I felt so slow that I wondered if I was getting a workout. I *was* tired, so I decided to see if I was running or fooling around. Twice, I took my pulse. It was 145 each time. That meant a fairly stiff load, despite the speed. With the altitude and terrain I was, if anything, working harder than I had planned. A primitive measure perhaps, but it enabled me to evaluate what I was doing while in unfamiliar circumstances.

Evaluating workouts and understanding what is needed is beautifully illustrated by a story Arthur Lydiard tells. When he was sharpening his runners in the Village before the '64 Olympics, he gave them a difficult 20 x 440 workout. The next day the Canadian prodigy, Bruce Kidd, went to the track, also to run 20 x 440. Lydiard and his boys were there. Kidd, anxioius to impress the New Zealanders, put on a good show, and the faster he went the more the Kiwis shouted and egged him on. Impressed, a reporter came over and asked Lydiard what he thought of Kidd's performance.

Lydiard replied, "I think Kidd just put the nail in his coffin with that workout."

"But your boys ran the same thing yesterday," the reporter said.

"Yes," Lydiard answered, "but my boys *needed* it." Lydiard was aware, of course, that Kidd was interval-trained and already had his fill of track in preparation for the Games. In the Olympic 10,000, Kidd shot out into the lead and then drifted backward as the race progressed. Peter Snell, faced with six world-class races in eight days as he stacked heats, semifinals and finals atop each other, not only won the 800 and 1500; he seemed to get stronger each time he raced.

If training has been timed correctly, there should be no need for more long anaerobic sessions once serious racing begins. Races take the place of training. Hard anaerobic work and constant fast racing will eventually wear the runner down.

When racing, one needs to stay mentally fresh and rested. The runner merely supplements racing with easy recovery runs and short, sharp speed work. Because the emphasis of the fast running done at this time is on redeveloping speed and not upon running a series of difficult intervals with short recoveries, there is no fatigue build-up at the end of the session. (Because there is no lactic acid accumulation, there is no dropping of the blood pH.)

PLANNING A TRAINING SCHEDULE

To a degree, the number of weeks spent on each kind of development depends upon the runner. Novice runners should work longer on aerobic training than runners who have been at it 10 years and possess a good aerobic base. Runners also vary in the amount of work needed to develop their anaerobic tolerance and leg speed. And there is always a finite time available between the beginning of the season and the beginning of important races.

Generally, it takes about 20 weeks to reach top condition, assuming some shape remains from the previous season. Blocking out the workouts on a calendar, one counts backwards from the onset of important racing. Let us say the runner is in college, shooting for the conference meet June 1. His competition begins in April, but important races don't begin until May. Counting back from May 1, he should reserve 4-5 weeks for intervals and sharpening (using early season races as time-trials and difficult anaerobic workouts), schedule the four weeks previous to that for resistance (hill) work, and the remaining 12 weeks for aerobic conditioning.

Lydiard and the East German physiologists say it takes 4-5 weeks to fully develop the anaerobic system. Persisting with difficult interval work beyond that is not only valueless, but as stated previously one risks tearing his condition down. Commonly, these are the runners who look good early, then lose their spark in the championships.

Runners who condition with intervals, especially on the track with a watch, reach their peak faster than aerobically-trained runners. But without the high aerobic capacity, their best will not be as fast. Moreover, once this athlete cannot get his training times faster, he feels he is stagnating. On the other hand, the runner using intervals only for sharpening is eager to see what he can do. The rapid progress in his times over 4-5 weeks makes him eager for races.

Road racers, on the other hand, usually do not have a one- or two-month season with weekly competition like the track men; therefore, they do not curtail training to compete. They probably consider a few of the year's races as special and run the rest as best they can.

When racing once every week or two for several months, road racers must train between competition using minor events as time-trials. During this time, they mix various workouts throughout the week, maintaining a long run, as interval or hill workout, etc. When one has had his fill of racing, he reverts back to aerobic distance work, recharging his batteries until an impending important race requires resharpening.

Though I don't believe in racing year-round, because those who do rarely reach their potential, there will always be those (the majority, perhaps) who want to race for months on end. For you there is a compromise. When you have had your fill of competition, take two or three weeks off. Forget running. Then, without any racing, spend at least six weeks building your mileage and aerobic base, and allot another four weeks to toughening up through resistance work. You can slip in a few races during the hill workouts, so you won't miss many races during a year.

While it may appear easy to ration out a season's work into 10-12 weeks of base conditioning, four weeks of hill work and six weeks of sharpening, it is rarely that simple in practice. A multitude of things can upset the plan: injuries, sickness, studies, work.

But let's forget these interruptions and consider the way one is really confronted with racing. He doesn't just execute 20 or so weeks of tidy training and then race the big one. A month or two later, there may be another major race and perhaps another beyond that. How does one decide whether he should try to maintain a peak between races, or back off after one and then resharpen for the next?

This question confronted me in 1968 when preparing for the Olympic Marathon Trial at Alamosa, Colo., in August. I had run well indoors in February, placed fifth in the Boston Marathon in April and raced the regional marathon trial in May to qualify for the high-altitude training camp in Alamosa.

But from past experience, I knew I never ran well in late-summer races. How would I manage to re-peak this time in August? I had to become something of a sleuth, ferreting out clues from the past to apply to the future. By weighing what I understood about how various kinds of training affected me, by isolating what caused me to slump in the past and by correctly assessing what I would need to race effectively at 7640 feet, I managed to be sharper than ever that August.

In turn, each runner without a coach must become his own detective. The answers will not be the same for two people, and the permutations and combinations of races and circumstances are unlimited.

12

Specifics of Training

Fitness is specific, so practice pace must be close to race pace

Tom Clarke

Picture the sprinter entering the most important competition of the year after six months of weight lifting and overdistance work. Without race-pace training, this runner would be sluggish, uncoordinated and unable to approach his best times. No sprint coach in his right mind would send a sprinter into competition without plenty of technique work.

Marathoners are another story. Most seem to feel that distance running technique is innate and unalterable. Futhermore, although many distance runners pay lip-service to the practice of speed work, few consider its importance as technique practice for the longer events. The marathon runner's rationalization is that his 100 miles per week is more than enough practice for the actual skill involved in stringing 26 miles of 5-7 minutes each.

Perhaps if the marathoner realized how much and to what extent his technique deteriorates throughout the course of the race, he would be more susceptible to suggestions concerning development and practice of his running form.

To serve this end, we conducted a biomechanical study on eight marathoners running in the 1977 Florida Relays Marathon. They were filmed at three, 13 and 23 miles with a high-speed camera, and comparisons of their biomechanical parameters were made from the film data with the help of a computer program.

Of the parameters examined, horizontal velocity, stride rate, stride length and vertical displacement of the body's center of gravity have the most significant applications to the runner.

The group of runners was heterogeneous with final times ranging from 2:23-3:06. They exhibited mean heights and weights of 5'10" and 147 pounds. The mean running experience was 7½ years with a range of 1½-13 years. The previous marathon mean was almost four per runner, and coupled with the overall running experience it indicated that the subjects as a group were familiar with the physiological and psychological stress that would be incurred during the race. The subjects had averaged 86 miles of training per week for the 13 weeks preceding the race.

Race day was warm (68-80 degrees) and humid (86%), yet the subjects performed within two minutes of their personal bests as a group with two runners recording their best times.

From a physiological standpoint, an evenly paced marathon is the most efficient, yet none of the subjects chose to or were able to run such a race. The mean horizontal velocity decreased 26.5% from 3-23 miles. In other words, the runner who started off at six minutes per mile was running 7:30 per mile by the 23rd mile.

The top four subjects decreased less than the overall mean, while the bottom four showed a greater deterioration of horizontal velocity. While common sense would seemingly dictate that those who slow down the most will have the poorest finishing positions in the race, it would not necessarily be true had the slower subjects exhibited more frugal pace judgment early in the race.

The decrease in horizontal velocity observed was by no means atypical. How many times have you heard the marathoners' lament, "I went out too fast!"? Here, we see the importance of practicing race-pace running, preferably over long intervals. This training programs the body to run at a given pace and makes it easier to avoid a kamikaze-like early pace. Long repeats at race pace give one an internal clock to run by, even in the absence of reliable splits.

Horizontal velocity is produced as a result of stride rate times stride length. Which component is more important to the marathoner? It was found that, while both stride rate and stride length decreased significantly between three and 23 miles, stride rate showed a sharper dropoff (21.0%) than stride length (7.1%). This data indicates that stride rate is a greater determinant of horizontal velocity than is stride length.

Some factors which contribute to a decrease in stride rate are: (1) muscular fatigue, particularly in the hip flexor and hamstring muscles; (2) a conscious effort to conserve energy through a slower leg turnover, and (3) a loss of concentration causing the runner to "float."

All three of these problems can be attacked by the marathoner through appropriate physical and mental training. Muscular fatigue will always be present, but specificity in training will optimize the marathoner's ability to hold his desired stride rate. If six minutes per mile is your goal pace, then a substantial portion of your training should be run at or near this pace. Repeat 440s in 65 seconds, although a tough workout with physiological value, do not utilize the same muscle fibers as are used in running 90-second 440 pace. Likewise, long, slow runs used to the exclusion of race pace running will not develop the neuromuscular coordination needed for maximum efficiency.

A slower leg turnover, while striving to maintain a given pace, is actually more costly in terms of energy expenditure, as measured by other researchers in submaximal oxygen uptake tests.

Finally, concentration is a problem for most marathoners. Elite runners are constantly monitoring their bodily responses throughout the race, while the rest of us tend to "flake out" at one point or another. When this happens, you can be sure that your stride cadence will drop and your pace will slow proportionately. Simulating race conditions in practice can improve one's capacity for concentration.

Also remember that when you begin to tire, increasing your stride length without rate is not the answer. Once the foot plant gets too far out in front of the body, a braking action occurs with each step.

An interesting finding concerning stride length was that the stride lengths (right vs. left) for a given runner were different, with the right stride generally being longer than the left. Some of the subjects showed as much as three inches difference between left and right. This asymmetry is probably a common occurrence among marathoners.

When one considers that a marathoner may take approximately 26,000 strides over the course of his race, a difference of two inches in stride length can mean a 3-4-minute difference in overall time. Asymmetrical stride lengths could be the result of muscular imbalance, probably aggravated by the left turns of track running or by different leg lengths. Flexibility work, weight training and/or use of orthotics (foot supports) could improve such a muscular imbalance problem.

If you suspect that you have such a problem, try this test: Run along a track in wet feet (or along a beach) at race pace. Mark the toe of each footprint with chalk and then measure. If your stride lengths are consistently different, work on attaining muscular balance.

The vertical displacement of the body's center of gravity was computed and found to increase throughout the race with a mean increase of one inch. This could be the result of decreased plantar flexion (flexing of the ankle) at pushoff which would cause more force to be directed vertically rather than horizontally.

The negative aspects of this change are: (1) more work done against gravity; (2) less force being applied in the horizontal direction, thus adversely affecting horizontal velocity, and (3) more jarring to the joints at landing contributing to overall fatigue.

This parameter is related to the deterioration in stride rate in that the force is being applied at a different point in the forward-swing phase of the free leg once stride rate slows. Thus, the importance of maintaining stride rate is re-emphasized.

In striving for efficiency, the marathon runner must realize that he, like the sprinter or field-event competitor, must be concerned about technique. Relaxed running at a fast pace requires neuromuscular coordination that can be enhanced through race-pace training.

With this in mind, how should a training schedule be set up?

• First, set a realistic marathon goal and compute the time per mile necessary to achieve it. Include one workout per week of long intervals (1-3 miles), and run at or slightly below your goal pace. Don't be afraid to cover 8-10 miles of intervals in such a workout. After all, you are going to race 26 miles. Jog one-fourth of the interval between repeats.

• Concentrate on your stride rate in these workouts, even if some stride length is lost. Don't cop out by saying long intervals are too boring. Nothing is as boring as the last six miles of a mediocre marathon performance.

• Hill training will strengthen your hip flexors, quadriceps and calf muscles, all of which are important in maintaining stride rate and stride length. Short, fast strides can be emphasized on hills 300-800 yards in length and not overly steep.

• Another "technique" workout is a race-type effort at 3-15 miles. This can be accomplished in an actual race or a time trial. Keep your goal pace in mind, and be satisfied if you hit it, particularly if you are running alone.

That's it—one long interval workout, one hill workout and one race-type effort. Supplement these three weekly workouts as you wish, but relaxed distance will suffice for the remaining four days. Remember, too, that flexibility work can give an additional bonus to stride length.

The next time that you are reeling off 220s in 32 seconds or a 12-mile run at 7:30 per mile pace, ask yourself, "Am I going to race at this pace?" If the answer is no, remember that even the marathon is a technique event.

13

The Young, Old, and Slow

How these new groups might approach running and racing

Hal Higdon

The question sometimes is posed to me, at clinics: should young runners run marathons? By young, the questioner usually means pre-teenagers, but young could include almost anybody not yet 21. After all, running a race of 26 miles, 385 yards involves enormous stress, so it can be argued that placing such physical stress on a still-growing body is unjustified. This does not even take into consideration the psychological stress that training to run such a race imposes, particularly in cases where a Little League Father urges his child on to establish a niche in history —no matter how temporary— by setting an age-group record.

A second related question might involve older runners: Those in the Masters category of 40-plus years, but specifically individuals beyond the retirement age of 65. Should they run marathons?

Finally, what about the very slow? One perhaps presumptuous statement I have sometimes made is that anyone can finish a marathon (the presumption being that by *finishing* I mean covering 26 miles, 385 yards, no matter at what pace, even walking the distance in a dozen hours). "Where we get in trouble," I say, "is when we attempt to finish the distance in progressively faster times." But, of course, this statement is fallacious, since some people are in such poor physical condition that even to walk a fraction of the standard marathon distance might be an impossibility. Still, with training. . . .

But this begs the point, namely: Is there any sense in someone very slow getting into a race of that length and keeping the officials waiting for him or her to finish at a pace two or even three times as slow as that of the winner? In 1977, I ran in at least two marathons (the World Masters Marathon in Gothenburg, Sweden, and the Mayor

Daley Marathon in Chicago) that had finishers officially timed at slower than six hours. And the Honolulu Marathon lists its "records" at both ends of the speed spectrum as 2:17 and seven hours-plus; and invites entrants to attempt to break either record, either by running very fast or running very slowly. Taking more than seven hours to complete a marathon means that you are moving at a pace of around 20 minutes per mile, or three miles per hour. Is that running?

Let us consider the question of whether the young, the old or the very slow (and often a person fits into at least two of those categories) should run marathons.

THE YOUNG

For the record, I attempted my first marathon at the age of 28. It was April 19, 1959, and anyone who glances at that date need not ask where I ran that race: Boston. I had been competing in track and field meets for a full decade with success at the national level, but with faster, younger runners appearing it seemed time to attempt a new event. I went to Boston, my strategy being similar to the one I employed in most track races: run with the leaders as long as possible to either beat them or be beaten. I got about as far as Wellesley, the halfway point, running near the front, but five miles later I was standing on the side of the road. I was stunned, because I never dropped out of track races.

But that was the way marathons were run two decades ago. There were few races and few people to offer advice. *Runner's World* did not exist. First of all, there were only three or four races run at marathon distance in the United States back then, with barely a few hundred competitors (often the same ones) running in them. Hardly anybody finished slower than 3:30, because there were few slow runners in the back of packs. If you could not average close to seven minutes per mile, it got very lonely in marathon races back in the 1950s, which may have helped accelerate the dropout rate. Anyone incapable of doing 3:30 was considered very, very slow.

Today, there are more marathoners who finish slower than 3:30 than who go faster than that pace. We now have hundreds of *marathons* instead of hundreds of marathoners, and had I come along as a youth in this era, imbued with the same interest in running, I undoubtedly would have attempted a 26-mile, 385-yard race at an age much earlier than 28.

How much earlier I can only speculate, but I can relate the experiences of my oldest son, Kevin, who happens to be a reasonably gifted runner. Almost all children run while young, because that is the nature of their play, but Kevin ran more than most partly because he had me as an example. I sometimes would take my children with me to a nearby track for workouts when they were young, because there was playground equipment nearby. He and his younger brother and sister could play in the long jump pit as though it were a sandbox. But Kevin saw me running and, as many children do, decided to imitate his father. (This is the same reason why many children also pick up their parents' negative habits, such as smoking or drinking.)

At the age of about four, Kevin astounded one of the high school runners with whom I trained by running three-quarters of a mile non-stop. Nobody told him to run three laps around the track; he just did it to do it. At age six when I was helping train some older age-group runners, he got in a two-mile race and ran next-to-last in around 16:30, which was an age record simply because hardly anybody that age ran that distance until late in the 1960s. The following year, he ran 7:01 for the mile, also close to the then-current age record.

Eventually, Kevin lost interest in running and applied his athletic talents to team sports such as football, basketball, and baseball. Those sports had better-organized programs he could participate regularly in with his friends. I saw no reason to feed my ego by prodding him to remain a runner, maybe because I still achieved success in that sport myself. I did not need to live vicariously through the deeds of my son, attaining honors I could not achieve myself.

Eventually in high school, he returned to running as the sport most suited to his natural abilities and ran a 4:21 mile and 9:23 two-mile by his senior year, as well as placing fifth in the state cross-country championships. As I write this, Kevin is a freshman at Southwestern Michigan College, a school which, with his help, placed second in the National Junior College Cross-Country Championships in 1977. He placed 22nd, earning All-American honors.

On several occasions during high school, I recall him talking with me about running a marathon. I neither encouraged nor discouraged such an attempt, but my general attitude was: "Don't be in a big hurry to attempt one." Apparently, he got the point. He did some summer road racing—mostly six miles or less, an occasional 10-mile—but confined his competitive efforts mostly to the track and cross-country paths.

At the end of his senior year, however, he announced that he wanted to run a marathon, mainly because another runner on his team, a boy named John Kintzele, wanted to try one. They planned to enter the Tri-Rivers Marathon in Fort Wayne, Ind., in July. Kevin and John had fun together in a 30-kilometer race the previous winter with no ill effects, so moving up to a marathon was not a massive jump in race mileage. Both were reasonably well prepared, since they averaged 70-80 miles per week in their track training. My feeling was: "It is time."

But my advice, using another meaning of that noun, was: "Forget the time." Perhaps mindful of my own early encounters with the marathon (I not only dropped out of that first attempt at Boston, but had two other DNFs before reaching a marathon finish line), I recommended extreme caution. I recommended that Kevin *run* the marathon, not *race* the marathon. His goal should not be to set a fast time (and judging from his training and abilities, I considered 2:30 well within his range), but merely to finish.

"Go to Fort Wayne with the intent merely of completing the course at some comfortable pace," I advised him. "After you get a 'finish' under your belt, then you can consider trying to run faster times." (I only wish that someone had been around to offer that same advice to me back in 1959.)

As to what "some comfortable pace" should be, I suggested seven minutes per mile—at least for the first half of the race. No scientific analysis was involved in this decision; it merely seemed like a good, round number. Since Kevin had run 10 miles in 52:40 the previous winter, I figured that coming by that point in 70:00 should be quite easy for him and permit a reservoir of energy for that most difficult second half of the race.

It did. He passed that distance in 69:50 and the halfway point in 1:29. Then, feeling good, he accelerated gradually and finished in 2:48:20, good enough for 12th place. The entry for his training diary for that day says: "Started off real easy, then picked it up. Was constantly passing people. At halfway point, I was in about 100th place. Felt great and had a pretty good kick."

He also had a good kick at the award ceremony when it came time to receive his trophy. He bounded up onto the platform as though to prove to people: "Look folks, it's not that tough." Ah, the impetuousness of youth. His friend, John Kintzele, did not have quite as good a day. John ran with Kevin past nine miles before a cramp hindered him. He finished slower than 3:30.

As of this writing, Kevin is looking forward to his second marathon: National Junior College Championship race at the end of the school year. Having *run* one marathon, he will attempt to *race* the second. The risk of failure using this second strategy is greater, but having gotten to the finish line once, he now has earned the right to experiment with *how fast* he can get to the finish line.

I was 28 before I ran my first marathon; my son was 18. I feel that had I been born a generation later, as he was, I most certainly would have come to that event sooner. But it is entirely possible that had *he* come along a half-generation later, he too might have been drawn to running and even racing the marathon at an earlier age, maybe even at age eight. My advice, then, would be: "If you want to run it, do it."

I feel, however, that for young runners to get involved in the marathon, the motivation should be mostly internal, not external. This is purely personal prejudice. I still feel uncomfortable about the spectre of the archetypical Little League Parent standing on the sideline, pushing his or her son or daughter toward that parent's definition of success. Maybe it is because I have too great a love for running and the positive benefits my sport can have for a person's health. I hate to think of children turning away from sport, as frequently is the case with age-group swimmers, simply because they have had too much of it at an early age.

As to the possible dangers of permanent injury from running marathons, they probably have been overdramatized by people who have little knowledge of the event. Blisters, sore legs, exhaustion and other debilities that we who do the marathon accept as a price to be paid are generally temporary in nature. Other dangers are possibly less worrisome for the young than the old.

THE OLD

Nothing would indicate that runners over 40 should not run marathons. In fact, all one needs to do is to attend almost any major long-distance race today to discover that increasing numbers of runners past that age, often well beyond, are getting into running. At one time, lawn bowling was considered *the* retirement sport; now a good case could be made for naming the marathon as that sport. Who has more time to put in the necessary mileage for optimum performances than an individual no longer faced with the necessity to work from 9-5 each day? Several individuals in their upper 50s and early 60s, who were with me in Gothenburg for the World Masters Championships in 1977, said they could not wait until they retired in a few years, because it meant they could train full-time.

If there is a danger in older competitors entering marathon races, it is that their arteries, possibly clogged with atherosclerotic deposits, may be inadequate to the demands placed upon them, triggering a heart attack. Particularly this could be a problem with the current generation of old marathoners who have become involved in the sport after several decades of inactivity. Someone like myself, who though now 46, has run dozens of marathons and has been active continously since my youth has much less to fear in this regard.

Older runners can die from heart attacks. They may even do so while competing in marathons. But if the current boom in long-distance running, with people of all ages competing, has proved anything, it is that we are not killing people in wholesale numbers. Occasional incidents occur. In Vancouver, British Columbia, Dr. Leslie Truelove, age 47, who had been running for six years, collapsed at the 21-mile mark during the Lions' Gate International Marathon and died, the result of a burst artery. In my recent book, *Fitness After Forty*, I described in detail the death, from an apparent heart attack, of 43-year-old Jim Shettler, a world-class Masters competitor, who was training to finish his first marathon. But the number of people who die of heart attacks because they *fail* to engage in active physical activity—whether it be running marathons or going for daily walks—is even greater. A million people die in the United States every year from diseases of the cardiovascular system.

Probably the most cogent remark in this respect comes from Ernie Werbel, M.D., a surgeon and distance runner from San Luis Opisbo, Calif. He states: "It's come to the point where we no longer require a physical examination of a person who wants to run—but, instead, of a person who wants to remain sedentary."

I have found that most older marathoners approach their sport with a perspective born of their own maturity. The typical ancient marathoner of today is one who has graduated to the roads from the YMCA jogging track and thus has less likely set his goal, as I once did, on winning the Boston Marathon. That person trains more often on long, slow, continuous running and is also less likely, despite his age, to suffer physical injury than the younger runner bred on doing hard, fast, interval workouts on a track.

Many old runners are performance-oriented; some may equal the 100-plus mileage weeks of those much younger. Yet they often approach their sport from a relaxed point of view. They are more likely to be racing against themselves and their own previous personal records than against others, and are less likely to get in trouble taking this approach. They race within their own limits and enjoy the sport for its rewards in terms of personal satisfaction rather than from a desire to cross the finish line first. Yet, saying this, I know some old-timers who are just as eager for the trophies they win in various age category events as are young runners winning their first ribbon at an age-group meet.

Worth noting are the statements of Thomas Bassler, M.D., president of the American Medical Joggers Association, who claims that if an individual trains for and completes a full-distance marathon that person will be *immune* from a heart attack. He claims that he never—and he emphasizes *never*—has been able to document a death from heart attack in a marathon runner. By documentation, he means that he must see proof by autopsy, because many supposed deaths by heart attack are merely convenient means by which coroners cover their perfunctory examination of people dead from so-called "natural causes." As for the deaths of Dr. Truelove and Jim Shettler, Dr. Bassler correctly points out that they had never *finished* a marathon race, the former having died while running his first marathon, the latter having died while training to finish a marathon after having dropped out of several races that distance because (like me at Boston) he went at them too hard.

Dr. Bassler concedes that the protection an individual gets from finishing the marathon may come not from any mythical process inherent in that event, but rather because of what a person must undergo to put himself in a position to complete 26 miles, 385 yards in a running posture. Most important, thus, is the Marathon Lifestyle, which includes no smoking, moderate drinking, attention to proper diet and regular doses of exercise. People who include that in their lifestyle are less likely to suffer heart attacks whether they run marathons or not.

THE VERY SLOW

As for the very slow, they are increasing in number. In fact, the marathon boom can almost be attributed to these same very slow runners, bless them. But I probably should define what I mean by very slow. During the spring of 1977, I served as a consultant for the First Chicago Distance Classic, a 20-kilometer race that attracted 5300 runners over the Fourth of July weekend.

We planned to computerize results but needed to know in advance at what point we could expect the most runners to cross the finish line so we could anticipate how to handle the crush. To determine this, I analyzed the results of the Revco-Western Reserve Marathon held in Cleveland in May, a race that attracted approximately 500 runners, including myself. I assumed that a plotting of the times of finishers would follow the standard bell-shaped curve, with a few fast runners near the front, a few slow runners near the back, and a graduated slope up to and down from a peak period. To my surprise, when I plotted the Cleveland finish I discovered there was no such bell-shaped curve. The few fast and few slow runners were there, but once in the middle of the field, a plotting of when runners crossed the line produced a plateau rather than a curve. Between the times of 3:00 and 4:30, there was almost no difference between the number of runners finishing per minute. It varied from a minimum of four per minute to a maximum of eight per minute with no surge.

I realized then that marathon running had entered the era of meritorious mediocrity: mediocre being defined as neither very good nor very bad. Very good would be a Bill Rodgers winning the Boston Marathon in 2:09:55; very bad would be anyone who failed to finish. What is left are those of us who are in the middle, reaching our own levels of personal achievement, each one of us competing on separate standards of ability and not caring that much whether we win or lose by some football coach's definition of these terms. Whereas when I first started running marathons, almost nobody finished the race if it meant coming in much slower than 3:30, it is now to the point where the majority of competitors in any race come in after that time. I say Hallelujah!

Years ago, those of us who gave advice to aspiring runners, young and old, thought that a certain amount of preparation was needed to compete in a marathon race. When I wrote *On The Run From Dogs and People* in 1971, I suggested a bottom-line figure of 50 miles per week for anyone wanting to race 26 miles, 385 yards, but I thought that maybe 70 weekly miles were more appropriate. As for how much preparation should go into such an attempt, I suggested taking a full year to merely learn to run, reaching the point where you can do two or three miles per day comfortably. After that, I advised the prospective marathoner to put another full year into preparing to run the full-distance event.

Well, that still is good advice, but the events of the last few years have somewhat changed my mind as to the possible. We now see people attempting marathons on as little as 30 or 40 miles a week training. They do this partly because they use a more efficient blend of mileage: getting that one long run in every weekend, but not worrying if they miss a day, or two, or three during the week—something that marathoners years ago would find disturbing. Missing even a single workout was definitely *infra dig.*

We also see people attempting the marathon after months of preparation rather than years. The Major Daley Marathon in Chicago in September 1977 was attempted by a number of people who never had run seriously before, being attracted to our sport by all the publicity given to the First Chicago Distance Classic only three months before.

A lot of these people failed to finish, but many others made it, even though with times in the 5:00 and 6:00 bracket. Fortunately, the officials waited and recorded every last one of them.

Another facet of the marathon phenomenon today is that many people are going into a marathon as their first race of any distance! This was unheard of years ago when one was expected to undergo a baptism of fire, beginning at one- and two-mile track distances, graduating to four- to six-mile cross-country runs, then 10-20-mile road races, and finally: *voila*, the marathon!

Many purists involved in the sport years ago are offended by these *nouveau* marathoners, and I once was, too. I felt they should pay for their entry with the semi-obligatory regimen of years of preparation and many miles a week. Grudgingly, I have begun to change my mind.

I think the difference is that today people are interested more in *running* the marathon than in *racing* that event. The time is less important than the doing of it. Whether because it is there, or whatever reason, runners persevere. As long as they do so with grace and good humor, perhaps that is all we need ask of either the young, the old or the very slow.

AGE-GROUP EQUIVALENTS

Marathon runners generally have maximum performance potential between ages 25 and 30. This chart, based on statistics provided by Ken Young and Dan Moore, gives approximate equivalent times at other ages.

Age	2:08:33*	2:20	3:00	3:30	4:00
5	3:24	3:43	4:46	5:34	6:22
10	2:50	3:06	3:59	4:39	5:19
15	2:28	2:42	3:28	4:04	4:38
20	2:16	2:28	3:11	3:43	4:14
25	2:09	2:21	3:02	3:32	4:02
30	2:09	2:20	3:00	3:30	4:00
35	2:09	2:21	3:02	3:32	4:02
40	2:13	2:26	3:07	3:38	4:10
45	2:18	2:31	3:14	3:47	4:19
50	2:23	2:37	3:22	3:55	4:29
55	2:31	2:45	3:23	4:08	4:43
60	2:38	2:53	3:45	4:20	4:58
65	2:46	3:02	3:54	4:33	5:12
70	2:55	3:12	4:07	4:48	5:29

*2:08:33 is the current world record for men; 2:20 is considered a "world-class" time; 3:00 is the most common goal of marathoners; 3:30 is the Boston marathon qualifying time for men over 40 and all women; 4:00 is a time 90% of marathon finishers are under.

Part 4
Racing and Pacing Marathons

14

Taking the Plunge

Wanted: marathoners. Experience
not required, but training is

How do you run a marathon? Well, you start at the start, stick to your pace, and finish at the finish. There's not much more to say, because the marathon isn't a technical event. That's not to say it can't get tough sometimes. But the principles of it are fairly simple.

The marathon is like an iceberg. The public part of it is the race. The invisible part, though, makes up most of it, and this private preparation decides what will show. If a would-be marathoner trains well, he'll race well. It's almost that simple.

Little experience is required of marathoners, because there isn't much to learn that hasn't already been learned on training runs. And if it hasn't been practiced there, it's too late to learn it in races.

But despite the fact that marathoners don't really need experience in the practical, learning sense, their first and subsequent marathons provide a lot of experiences in the philosophical, emotional sense.

Emil Zatopek, the Czech who won the 1952 Olympic championship at this distance (as well as the 5000 and 10,000 meters), has said: "If you want to win something, you run 100 meters. But if you want to *experience* something, you run a marathon."

As German runner Manfred Steffny said earlier in this book, "The reason that society holds the marathon runner in awe lies less with his accomplishment than in the giant distance separating over-civilized man from distance running." In other words, to the general public conditioned to driving the car down the driveway to pick up the newspaper, going 26 miles on foot is superhuman. Some of this feeling stays with runners.

The press—even the specialized running press—doesn't help either. Beth Bonner said after running 2:55 in 1971, "I feel too much is written about mediocre marathons. I think something like describing the condition of one's toes mile-by-mile just scares people and puts something in the race that isn't there. Any well-conditioned woman aiming for three hours shouldn't have to worry about attacks from the supernatural at 20 miles."

Any well-conditioned man shouldn't have to worry about such attacks, either.

Probably the hardest thing about the first marathon is thinking about it in advance. It's kind of like standing on the edge of a cold swimming pool on a hot day. Your're anxious to get in but hesitant about experiencing the first shock. So you teeter on the brink. It's best just to fall in without giving it much thought.

This is a high-mileage era. Most runners from high school on up are already marathoners, even if they don't think of themselves that way and have never gone the distance. Marathon training is the norm, even among the non-marathoners.

Today's milers put in more mileage than the marathoners of 20 years ago. Today's teenagers spend more time on the roads than the Olympic marathoners of the 1950s. These are well-conditioned runners. And as Beth Bonner says, they don't have to be overly concerned with attacks from the supernatural after 20 miles.

Arthur Lydiard, the New Zealand coach, has said, "It is a big job building up to 20 miles the first time, but in succeeding years, there will be no difficulty whatever in reaching the distance again, even with comparatively light training. In other words, to operate the marathon training system you have only to do the hard work once. You won't be coasting later, but you'll find it so much easier that it won't seem like work at all."

Lydiard wrote this 15 years ago, when even the marathoners rarely went 20 miles except in races. No wonder the races were hard—especially the first one. Today, runners rarely go into a marathon "cold turkey," without prior long-distance training. They lay the groundwork, do the "hard work" of building up mileage, in their training. They get used to the distances and the pounding of the roads by training long distances on the roads. Then the race takes care of itself—even the first race.

The race can only bring out what has been put in by training and by nature. Within these limits, smart steady pacing and a little old tough-minded, don't-give-in will-power determine how the race will go.

One final word of caution: Just as the race doesn't begin on race day, it doesn't end at 26 miles 385 yards. You can still feel it acutely for hours and days afterward—both the agony and ecstasy of it, and neither of those is too hard to handle. A satisfying race gives the legs a joyous kind of ache. It fades in a couple of days.

A wise old coach has said, however, "Just because you don't feel stiffness in your legs any longer, don't think you're recovered. Subtle things are still getting readjusted inside of you, and you're wise not to push for as much as several weeks."

Two things can happen, one fairly immediate and one a long-term destructive process. As increasing numbers of runners do more training and run more marathons, both become more obvious.

The first phenomenon is the "delayed-action ailment." We'll call this one marathoner Fred. Fred hits it hard, doing upwards of 120 miles a week on an extremely regular basis. He ran a marathon on Sunday. By Tuesday, he was back to regular mileage. By Friday, Fred had a heavy chest cold. By the next Monday, his left knee was so stiff he couldn't run at all. Fred moaned, "Look at me. Just when I start to get in really good shape, every thing goes wrong." Coincidence?

The long-range breakdown works slower but more decisively. A marathoner tastes a bit of success and gets greedy for more. Another runner, we'll call him Ted, ran a promising time in his first try. He immediately doubled his mileage, and started racing a marathon a month. A year later, he wasn't running any more, not a step, and was 20 pounds overweight. Nothing physical happened to him. He just got tired of all that running.

Compare last year's US marathon list with this year's. Notice that close to 50% of the leaders from last year didn't return to that category. That statistic says something.

Addressing himself to these problems, and specifically to the the less-than-championship-level marathoner, Tom Osler (author of *The Conditioning of Distance Runners*) writes:

"I have concluded that the marathon race is a definite form of self-abuse for one who trains as I do (60-80 slow miles a week). That is, to stand on the road and tell yourself that you will run as fast as possible for 26 miles is a most unnatural endeavor, and one which the body was not designed to withstand. I do it, and will continue to do it, because I like to. However, I am aware that as the fatigue progresses, I am likely to become injured and to lower my overall resistance in a most foolish way.

"Thus, I only run an all-out marathon race once, or at most twice, per year. At other times, I give a measured effort, but not a total one. Most marathoners think that racing the marathon does them good. It does not, and only serves to decondition rather than condition the body. I am sure most runners are going to accuse me of babying myself. Believe me, I suffered with the best of them, until I learned to read my body's signs of fatigue and to respect them."

But this is another problem. This refers to the second, and third and later marathons. We started out talking about the first one, and that's a good way to end this piece. Whether you run 100 more or no more, you'll remember the first one. It's like a first romance. It may be pleasurable or it may be painful (most likely it'll be a combination of the two), but there'll never be anything quite like it again.

15

How NOT to Run It

The 10 most common mistakes
made by new marathoners

The most common mistakes made by novice marathoners, and
what to do about them:

1. Run it as a lark.

Myth: If you just want to say you ran a marathon and don't care
about time or place, there's no need for special training. If you're
willing to suffer a little, walk a little and don't care how long this thing
takes, you can finish it.

Fact: Maybe so, but you'll be doing more suffering and more
walking than you thought—or running so slowly it might as well be
walking. The marathon is meant to be *run*, not merely survived. To
run it, you need at least 40 training miles a week for 6-8 weeks. This
also assures you'll want to run again after the marathon.

2. Make up in speed what you lack in distance.

Myth: You can't afford the time to do the minimum of 6-7 miles a
day. So you compensate with effort. You run 3-5 miles daily, but you
do it faster and faster—almost racing it. Or you break it up into
"intervals" and run the fast parts faster yet.

Fact: Training is fairly specific. In other words, you adapt to what
you do. You don't train for tennis by playing badminton, and you
don't train for a marathon by running like a miler. Exclusively fast
training gets you ready for a fast mile but leaves you unprepared for
the stresses of a long, slow run.

3. Run the full marathon in practice.

Myth: How can you know what to expect from the formal event unless you've done the whole thing informally? You want to try a dress rehearsal several weeks before the big performance.

Fact: If you are doing rather light mileage, and you try a marathon in practice, you may never reach the big event. You may hurt yourself and never recover physically. You may drop out or struggle miserably and never recover psychologically. Leave the last several miles of the race unexplored until the proper time and place, when you have other runners to help you and when finishing counts.

4. Keep training hard right up until race day.

Myth: After you've trained this hard for all these weeks, you don't want to let any of it slip away by letting up too much at the end. Allow yourself no chance to be lazy.

Fact: Training has a delayed effect. The reserves you draw on today weren't put there yesterday, but last week. When you stop training completely, it's a week before you notice any physical deterioration. In fact, for several days your potential improves because you're rested. Give yourself a chance to rest before the marathon so you can best draw on last week's reserves. You can't be too lazy in the final week.

5. Choose a marathon in the summer.

Myth: That way, you don't have to worry about feeling cold during those hours on the road. And you can work on your tan as you run. If the day happens to come off cool or rainy, you can dress in long pants and a waterproof windbreaker to hold in body heat.

Fact: A runner in a marathon is like a portable furnace. He generates heat, and his problem is getting rid of it—not holding it in. A good day for running a marathon, then, is a bad day for watching one—and vice versa. You're in for a good day if you feel chilled at the starting line and a bad one if you feel a warming sun on your shoulders. Choose a day when the temperature is likely to be 40-60, then pray for clouds.

6. Eat a hearty meal a couple of hours before race time.

Myth: You'll be burning a couple of thousand calories en route, and you don't want to faint from hunger at the 20-mile mark. Have some protein—meat, eggs, etc.—because your're going to need the kind of strength these "muscle foods" give.

Fact: What you eat on race day (assuming the race starts early in the day, and most do) won't help you much. It's too late to be processed for energy. But it can hurt by leaving you feeling heavy and bloated, and by upsetting a nervous stomach. Eat several hours before the run, eat very lightly, concentrate on easily-digested carbohydrate foods and drinks (*not* proteins or fats), and don't worry about fainting. Your body has plenty of reserve energy, even if you don't eat at all that day.

7. Wear new, light shoes.

Myth: After training all those miles in clunky practice shoes, you'll fly when you switch to racing flats. Think of all the weight you're saving: three ounces per step, times 1000 steps per mile, times....

Fact: Think, too, of how many times an irritating seam in the new shoe is rubbing across a spot which hadn't been toughened by the old one. Think of how much extra shock you absorb from the shoes with soles made thin to shave off three ounces of weight. New shoes are no bargain. For marathons, stick with the old ones you know you can trust.

8. Start quickly.

Myth: Move out smartly so you'll avoid the congestion—and so your friends and family can see you, and so you might get on TV. Also, you're bound to slow later, so make time while you're fresh.

Fact: The first few miles of a marathon are a warmup, and you never sprint before you're warm. Pick a spot in the starting pack corresponding to where you expect to finish. Start cautiously, and ease into your pace. Veteran marathon runners advise dividing the event into equal thirds: (1) the warmup; (2) the best running; (3) the holding on, hoping to finish.

9. Take no drinks along the way.

Myth: You don't want to lose time by stopping to drink, and you haven't yet learned to drink on the run. Besides, drinking while running gives stomach cramps, doesn't it?

Fact: The cost, both in time and discomfort, is likely to be a lot higher if you *don't* drink than if you do. The problems of dehydration are more severe for a runner on the road 3-4 hours or more than for those who run the distance in just over two hours. Sweat losses of 3% of body weight—five pounds in a 150-pound runner—affect performance; those about 6% may affect health. Learn to drink during long practice runs, and take frequent small drinks of water or bland sugar-electrolyte mixtures in the marathon. You aren't likely to have stomach distress at slow pace.

10. Resume full training immediately.

Myth: You're excited about the results of your marathon and already are thinking about how you'll improve in the next one. Traces of muscle and tendon soreness, and lingering fatigue are still there several days later. But there's no time to waste. The next marathon is three weeks away.

Fact: It's never wise to ignore symptoms of pain and fatigue, and particularly not after a marathon. You've given yourself a shock, and you must now allow recovery. Full recovery, as a rule, takes about one day for each mile of an all-out run. This totals almost a month after a marathon. Do no more all-out running in that period.

16

Quickest Ways to Improve

Ten shortcuts for getting faster times in the long run

1 *Have a goal.* You can get better simply by thinking you're better. Raise your sights. Set a realistic target for yourself—like qualifying for Boston with 3½ hours (if you're a man over 40 or a woman) or getting under three hours, which is the average runner's equivalent of a four-minute mile. Then establish a realistic plan for reaching that goal.

2. *Choose an easy course.* Find one that is flat or nearly so, because even when the route has equal amounts of climbing and descending you never make up as much time going downhill as you lose going up. Study the results in *Runner's World*, and find events with a high percentage of sub-three-hour times. Then look for the type of course you prefer (out and back, single loop or laps). Finally, get familiar with the course so you never doubt where you are.

3. *Choose a cool day.* You can't order your weather for race day, but you can go by norms. Keep normal temperature patterns in mind. Look for something in the 40-60-degree range. Temperatures near freezing or below are too chilly. And you can expect to lose about a minute for each degree above 70. Comfortably cool days occur most often in March and April, and again in October and November in the US.

4. *Do a little speedwork.* Sub-three-hour marathon pace is sub-seven-minute miles—fairly fast. So most people who race at this level do some training to get used to it. This can be done any of three ways: (1) regular shorter-than-marathon races (see next tip); (2) a day or two each week reserved for faster-than-marathon training; (3) a little bit of fast running (say, 5%) added to each day's longer, slower run.

5. *Run shorter races.* Don't be a marathon specialist, because you miss both the variety of the sport and the valuable "sharpening" the other races give. Regular races in the 5-15-mile range may be the best form of speedwork, because they mimic the marathon stress so well. Run one every 1-3 weeks, remembering the recovery formula of one non-racing day for every mile raced.

6. *Up your total mileage.* Averaging 6-7 miles a day may be enough for running a marathon, but it isn't enough if you race to your limit. You need to average 8-9—or about 60 miles a week. In studying the times and training of marathoners, Dr. Paul Slovic found that sub-three-hour runners averaged 60 miles, while 3-4-hour finishers fell a shade below 40.

7. *Take longer "long" runs.* The schedules for running a marathon call only for weekly runs of one-half to two-thirds the marathon distance. Even the single 2½-hour run probably won't total 20 miles. This is okay for finishing. But to improve you probably need to top 20 at least once. Dr. Paul Slovic reported that sub-three-hour runners did it three times, those under 3:30 once or twice, and slower runners averaged less than once.

8. *Lose some weight.* This is assuming that you have some fat to shed, and most of us do before reaching the leanness of top marathoners. Lightness gives mechanical advantages; we move easier. But the more important benefit is physiological. For every 1% drop in weight, there is a corresponding 1% gain in the ability to use oxygen.

9. *Load with carbohydrates.* The carbohydrate-loading routine basically involves eating proteins and fats for three days, then switching to carbohydrates for the last three. This gives you an extra energy supply. Dr. Paul Slovic's studies show that, when used properly, carbo-loading can result in a 6-11-minute improvement in marathon times.

10. *Find a pacer.* It's easier to share the work than to carry the load alone. Agree with a friend of similar ability and aims to run together. Or tag along behind a runner with a reputation for wise pacing. In large fields, pacing isn't as difficult, because you always have plenty of company. Fix your gaze on others to take your mind off of your own problems.

17

Going Over the Wall

The man behind the "collapse-point theory" tells how it works

Ken Young

What is the "collapse-point"? In simple terms, it is the maximum distance a runner can expect to go before the urge to slow down overwhelms him. More commonly, the collapse point is called "the wall" (which one runs into) or "the bear" (which jumps on one's back). Ted Corbitt calls it the "quitting" point. The collapse-point is characterized by a sudden decrease in performance, often occurring within a single mile. Pace may drop by two to three minutes per mile or more.

The collapse-point should not be confused with a "fatigue" point, which is considerably more gradual and the performance drop is usually less than one minute per mile. The fatigue point occurs as a result of a progressive imbalance—i.e., salt loss or lactic acid/waste product buildup. "Collapse" occurs as a result of the exhaustion of glycogen stores available for muscular exercise.

What causes this collapse? In terms that I understand, the energy utilized in running comes largely from the oxidation of glucose (glycogen), which produces ATP (adenosine triphosphate), which in turn functions to produce muscular contraction. The exhaustion of glycogen stores available for muscular exercise cuts off this source of energy and results in a rapid drop in energy output or performance.

What determines glycogen storage, and what determines the collapse distance? I'm not a physiologist, so the ideas I present are merely hypotheses, based on my rudimentary understanding of running physiology and on observations of my own running. Glycogen is stored both in the liver and also in muscle tissue. It appears that the glycogen stored in muscle tissue is pertinent to muscular exercise. Studies have shown that the level of glycogen stores in muscle tissue can vary over a fairly wide range in accordance with training and diet. Low-carbohydrate diet and/or heavy mileage loads in training produce low levels of glycogen. Light training and high-carbohydrate diet can produce relatively high levels of muscle glycogen. Utilizing proper training and diet, one can saturate the available sites with glycogen. Then, in a race, one can convert this stored glycogen to energy.

What happens beyond the collapse-point? When stored glycogen is no longer available for oxidation and production of ATP, the body converts fats (and eventually proteins) to glucose. However, this is a relatively slow process. Thus, the sudden drop in performance level is associated with a shift from direct conversion of stored glycogen to a two-step conversion of fat to glucose and glucose to ATP. In this process, the rate-controlling step is the conversion of fat to glucose. Beyond the collapse point, this conversion limits performance levels to probably not faster than 10-12 minutes per mile.

The metabolism of fats at rates commensurate with running produces acetone as a by-product. This acetone can be detected on the breath about 5-10 minutes following extended exercise under conditions of low glycogen storage. "Acetone breath" is a useful indicator as a clue to poor performance or in conjunction with proper carbohydrate-loading.

I've found acetone breath occurs regularly as a result of heavy mileage over a 3-5-day period followed by a hard run of 10-15 miles. After the hard run, I frequently note the odor of acetone, which indicates my glycogen stores are very low. If glycogen storage is purposely low—e.g., in preparation for carbohydrate loading—I try to maintain this low level until two days before the race and then load with carbohydrate. Otherwise, it is an indicator that a high-carbohydrate meal is needed to maintain training performance.

So much for theory. As runners, the pertinent questions are: (1) How can I determine my collapse-point; (2) how can I extend my collapse-point, and (3) what can I do to optimize performance beyond my collapse-point?

The collapse-point appears to be determined almost entirely by training mileage. The simple rule of thumb is to take the maximum mileage for two consecutive months, determine the daily average over these two months and triple it. For example, for November and December 1971, I ran 450 and 470 miles, respectively. The daily average was 15 miles. Tripling this gives a collapse-point of 45 miles. I was able to test this in a 100-mile race and found that I indeed collapsed at 45 miles.

In order to extend one's collapse-point, then, it is clear that the total mileage must be increased over a time span of two or more months. But for some races, such as the 100-mile, it is virtually impossible to run enough mileage to increase the collapse-point beyond the distance to be run. This would mean averaging 33.3 miles per day or 233 miles per week over a period of at least two months. Few people have the time, energy or physical stamina to endure such a volume of training. For such races, then, the object is to increase the collapse distance as much as is feasible according to one's circumstances.

For short races, such as those shorter than 10 miles, minimum mileage based on the collapse-point is of little value since virtually everyone who races has a collapse-point well beyond this distance. Hence, race performance is determined by the type of training and the basic capabilities of the runner rather than his ability to store glycogen.

In races between 10 and 50 miles, extension of the collapse-point beyond the race distance is directly related to race performance. For example, racing a marathon at six minutes per mile through 20 miles and then hitting the collapse-point, dropping to an eight-minute pace, puts you barely under 2:50. By comparison, the runner whose collapse-point is well beyond 26 miles runs six-minute miles for the entire distance, finishing in 2:37.

In training for these types of races, one would like to have a safety factor, and a margin of five miles in the collapse distance should be adequate—*provided* the runner maintains sensible pacing (considering terrain and weather) and employs carbohydrate-loading prior to the race so as to fully utilize the glycogen storage capacity which has been developed through training. Thus, a marathoner should average 10+ miles per day, giving a collapse-point of 30-32 miles. To run a good 50-miler, a daily average of 18 miles is suggested. For a 30-kilometer race, one need average only eight miles per day.

The collapse-point can be extended markedly through proper training. Beyond the collapse-point, the runner is limited by two factors, namely (1) the rate at which energy can be supplied, and (2) electrolyte imbalance/waste product buildup in the muscle tissues. Optimal performance beyond the collapse-point, then, is related to increasing the available energy and minimizing the effects of electrolyte imbalance and waste product buildup.

With proper training, it may be possible to increase the efficiency with which fats are broken down and converted to glucose. This has not been demonstrated, although it would seem likely that the efficiency of this system might be increased by stressing it, in a manner similar to stressing the glycogen storage capacity in order to increase it. This would be accomplished by training under the conditions of low glycogen storage previously outlined—producing acetone breath following some workouts, indicative of the utilization of fats for energy.

During a race, it is also possible to increase the available energy by ingestion of glucose. Since glucose—in the form of dextrose—is readily absorbed into the blood stream, additional glucose can be supplied in this manner. A 25-gram dextrose tablet supplies nearly 100 kilocalories of energy, roughly the energy required to run a mile. From my own experience, the absorption and utilization of 25 grams of dextrose requires roughly 30 minutes. If one can maintain a 10-minute mile pace, this means that roughly 30% of the required energy can be supplied via the ingestion of dextrose.

In order to reduce the effects of electrolyte imbalance, it is suggested that the runner consume isotonic solutions such as Body Punch and ERG at regular intervals. This is essential to maintain a reasonable balance of water and salts such as sodium and potassium. In addition, Kenneth Cooper has shown that magnesium is lost to the intentines during exercise. The loss of magnesium is associated with muscular cramping, and most isotonic solutions mentioned do not contain this mineral. Thus, it is recommended that magnesium (Dolomite) be ingested at regular intervals as well. Muscular cramping frequently occurs beyond the collapse-point—not only leg cramps, but also cramping in the lower back, shoulders and chest area, frequently making breathing difficult. This cramping can be largely eliminated through ingestion of magnesium.

I have outlined a *theory*, advanced on the basis of observation and some knowledge of physiology. I know of no scientific studies of human performance near and beyond the collapse-point, although the potential contribution to race performance by such studies would be great. When we have full understanding of the physiological principles involved with marathon and longer training and racing, I feel certain that truly incredible performance will be achieved.

18

Pacing the Marathon

What is the best way to pace a
marathon to get your best time?

Paul Slovic

Proper pacing in the marathon can make the difference between achieving one's goals and disaster. Yet in this scientific age, the approach to pacing remains at a prescientific level. The runner looking for guidance in pacing must rely on intuition and past experience. Unless his experience is considerable, and unless he has remarkably good knowledge of his present condition, he will likely start out too fast or too slow for optimal performance.

We know that an even pace is the economical way to run, and there are charts available telling us what even pace to run to achieve a particular finishing time. For example, a three-hour marathon requires just under a 6:52 pace per mile which, the charts indicate, will bring the runner to the 10-mile mark in 68:40, the 15-mile mark in 1:43, etc.

But what the runner really wants to know is, "What is the fastest even pace I can hold for the entire distance?" or "Allowing for some slowdown during the latter stages of the run, how fast should I start out in order to finish in three hours?" I provide no definitive answers to these questions, but can describe some first attempts to take a systematic look at pacing in the marathon.

Two types of data were obtained from the 1973 Trail's End Marathon. First was a complete listing of the runner's times at 10, 15 and 20 miles as well as their final times. Second was the responses of runners to a questionnaire concerning personal background and training practices in the two months prior to the run.

Thirty-one runners finished between 2:55 and 3:05 with an average of about three hours. These runners did not hold a steady 6:52 pace throughout the run. Their average time at 10 miles was 64:48, at 15 miles 1:38, and at 20 miles 2:11. All of these times were faster than a 6:52 pace. But these individuals took an average of 49 minutes to go the last 6.2 miles.

Table One shows the intermediate times for nine categories of runners at Trail's End. Runners in each category finished within five minutes of a specific time. It illustrates that the slowdown in the latter stages of the race exhibited by the three-hour and slower finishers is almost universal, and is particularly great in the last 6.2 miles. The runners are surprisingly close together after 10 miles. It is wide differences in slowdown during the later miles that spread them so far apart at the finish. The faster the final time, the closer the runner was to even pace. Runners who finished in excess of four hours had typically slowed by 4-5 minutes per mile.

TABLE 1: INTERMEDIATE TIMES AND AVERAGE PACE

Within 5:00 of	Number of Runners	10 Miles (ave. mile)	15 Miles (ave. mile)	20 Miles (ave. mile)	Final (ave. mile)
2:30	16	55:32 (5:34)	1:24:12 (5:30)	1:52:36 (5:41)	2:29:36 (5:57)
2:45	22	1:00:30 (6:03)	1:31:36 (6:13)	2:02:42 (6:13)	2:45:36 (6:54)
3:00	31	1:04:48 (6:29)	1:38:06 (6:40)	2:11:12 (6:37)	2:58:54 (7:40)
3:15	28	1:08:35 (6:52)	1:44:36 (7:11)	2:20:42 (7:13)	3:14:42 (8:42)
3:30	37	1:14:12 (7:25)	1:52:36 (7:41)	2:32:18 (7:56)	3:30:06 (9:18)
3:45	28	1:16:54 (7:41)	1:57:06 (8:02)	2:40:18 (8:38)	3:36:12 (10:35)
4:00	30	1:17:48 (7:47)	1:59:54 (8:25)	2:47:54 (9:36)	3:59:42 (11:31)
4:15	19	1:18:12 (7:49)	2:00:30 (8:28)	2:52:18 (10:22)	4:15:06 (13:18)
4:30	11	1:20:36 (8:04)	2:06:54 (9:16)	3:04:24 (10:30)	4:30:00 (13:47)

A measure of "slowdown" is calculated by subtracting each runner's average pace per mile (in seconds) during the first 10 miles from his average pace during the final 6.22 miles. Table Two presents some basic descriptive statistics for the slowdown measure for 176 respondents to the survey questionnaire. Included in the table are the maximum and minimum values in the group, the average values, the median, and the 25th and 75th percentile values (denoted P-25 and P-75). The median is the score above and below which half the values are located. The 25th percentile is a value that exceeds 25% of the cases and P-75 exceeds 75% of the cases.

TABLE 2: DESCRIPTIVE STATISTICS FOR SLOWDOWN

Minimum	36 sec./mile	Mean	138 sec./mile
P-25	42 sec./mile	P-75	320 sec./mile
Median	108 sec./mile	Maximum	653 sec./mile

The average slowdown is 138 seconds per mile between early and late pace. More than 25% of the runners slowed by at least five minutes per mile. Only seven out of 176 respondents ran the last six miles at a pace faster than they ran the first 10 miles.

PER-MILE AVERAGES

This chart indicates the per-mile pace of various marathon times. The times on the left are for the marathon (two hours to 4:37 in even minutes). Beside each is the average mile time (to the nearest tenth-second) that it takes to run that fast. To find the pace of marathons slower than 4:37, add approximately 2.3 seconds per mile for each additional minute of marathon time. A 4:38 marathon would equal about 10:40.8 per mile, etc.

2:00 = 4:34.6	**2:10** = 4:57.5	**2:20** = 5:20.4	**2:30** = 5:43.3
2:01 = 4:36.9	2:11 = 4:59.8	2:21 = 5:22.7	2:31 = 5:45.6
2:02 = 4:39.2	2:12 = 5:02.1	2:22 = 5:25.0	2:32 = 5:47.8
2:03 = 4:41.5	2:13 = 5:04.4	2:23 = 5:27.2	2:33 = 5:50.1
2:04 = 4:43.8	2:14 = 5:06.7	2:24 = 5:29.5	2:34 = 5:52.4
2:05 = 4:46.1	2:15 = 5:08.9	2:25 = 5:31.8	2:35 = 5:54.7
2:06 = 4:48.3	2:16 = 5:11.2	2:26 = 5:34.1	2:36 = 5:57.0
2:07 = 4:50.6	2:17 = 5:13.5	2:27 = 5:36.4	2:37 = 5:59.3
2:08 = 4:52.9	2:18 = 5:15.8	2:28 = 5:38.7	2:38 = 6:01.6
2:09 = 4:55.2	2:19 = 5:18.1	2:29 = 5:41.0	2:39 = 6:03.9
2:40 = 6:06.2	**2:50** = 6:29.0	**3:00** = 6:51.9	**3:10** = 7:14.8
2:41 = 6:08.2	2:51 = 6:31.3	3:01 = 6:54.2	3:11 = 7:17.1
2:42 = 6:10.7	2:52 = 6:33.6	3:02 = 6:56.5	3:12 = 7:19.4
2:43 = 6:13.0	2:53 = 6:35.9	3:03 = 6:58.8	3:13 = 7:12.7
2:44 = 6:15.3	2:54 = 6:38.2	3:04 = 7:01.1	3:14 = 7:24.0
2:45 = 6:17.6	2:55 = 6:40.5	3:05 = 7:03.4	3:15 = 7:26.3
2:46 = 6:19.9	2:56 = 6:42.8	3:06 = 7:05.6	3:16 = 7:28.5
2:47 = 6:22.2	2:57 = 6:45.1	3:07 = 7:07.9	3:17 = 7:30.8
2:48 = 6:24.5	2:58 = 6:47.3	3:08 = 7:10.2	3:18 = 7:33.1
2:49 = 6:26.7	2:59 = 6:49.6	3:09 = 7:12.5	3:19 = 7:35.4
3:20 = 7:37.7	**3:30** = 8:00.6	**3:40** = 8:23.5	**3:50** = 8:46.4
3:21 = 7:40.0	3:31 = 8:02.9	3:41 = 8:25.8	3:51 = 8:48.6
3:22 = 7:42.3	3:32 = 8:05.2	3:42 = 8:28.0	3:52 = 8:50.9
3:23 = 7:44.6	3:33 = 8:07.4	3:43 = 8:30.3	3:53 = 8:53.2
3:24 = 7:46.8	3:34 = 8:09.7	3:44 = 8:32.6	3:54 = 8:55.5
3:25 = 7:49.1	3:35 = 8:12.0	3:45 = 8:34.9	3:55 = 8:57.8
3:26 = 7:51.4	3:36 = 8:14.3	3:46 = 8:37.2	3:56 = 9:00.1
3:27 = 7:53.1	3:37 = 8:16.6	3:47 = 8:39.6	3:57 = 9:02.4
3:28 = 7:56.0	3:38 = 8:18.9	3:48 = 8:41.9	3:58 = 9:04.7
3:29 = 7:58.3	3:39 = 8:21.2	3:49 = 8:44.2	3:59 = 9:07.0
4:00 = 9:09.2	**4:10** = 9:32.1	**4:20** = 9:55.0	**4:30** = 10:17.9
4:01 = 9:11.5	4:11 = 9:34.4	4:21 = 9:57.3	4:31 = 10:20.2
4:02 = 9:13.8	4:12 = 9:36.7	4:22 = 9:59.6	4:32 = 10:22.5
4:03 = 9:16.1	4:13 = 9:39.0	4:23 = 10:01.9	4:33 = 10:24.8
4:04 = 9:18.4	4:14 = 9:41.3	4:24 = 10:04.2	4:34 = 10:27.1
4:05 = 9:20.7	4:15 = 9:43.6	4:25 = 10:06.5	4:35 = 10:29.4
4:06 = 9:23 0	4:16 = 9:45.9	4:26 = 10:08.8	4:36 = 10:31.7
4:07 = 9:25.3	4:17 = 9:48.2	4:27 = 10:11.1	4:37 = 10:33.9
4:08 = 9:27.6	4:18 = 9:50.5	4:28 = 10:13.3	4:38 = 10:36.2
4:09 = 9:29.9	4:19 = 9:52.7	4:29 = 10:15.6	4:37 = 10:38.5

19
Realistic Race Pacing

Marathons include the warmup, run, and
"hang-on." Pace varies in the stages

The trouble with most marathon pacing guides you see published (such as the earlier one) is that they're too perfect. They start with an average time per mile and multiply it by five, 10, 15 and so on to give recommended times for the intermediate distances. The result: evenly paced "splits."

This gives a mathematical tidiness. Unfortunately, it doesn't take into account the effects of early race excitement and late-race fatigue. The fact is, very few marathoners hold this steady a pace, and it may not even be right for them to try.

A quick survey of split and final times in runners' best races shows a typical pattern: the first five miles at close to the overall average; speeding up a bit as they warm up between five and 15; slowing somewhat from 15-20; then a rather pronounced drop in pace in the last six-plus miles.

The slowdown after 20 is almost universal. The world-class athletes slow a little, the 3-4 hour people a lot. Even when they don't crash into the dreaded "wall," their pace usually is 5-10% slower in the final miles than in the first 20.

For example, the average pace per mile for a three-hour marathoner is 6:52. But typically, a runner of this level will run about 6:40-45 through 20 miles and then finish at 7:10-15 pace. A 2:30 runner might drop off to 6:00 after doing 5:40s for the first couple of hours. A 4:00 person might go from 9:00 to 10:00.

Since almost everyone slows near the end of marathons, we've put together a pacing table which accounts for this—as well as the related patterns of (1) "warmup" in the first five miles, (2) fastest pace from 5-15, and (3) slight lag from 15-20.

The recommended splits are based on the percentage of total time normally needed to run each segment of the race. The last six-plus miles usually take one-quarter of the time, and a realistic pacing plan

EFFORT-ADJUSTED PACING TABLE

Total Time (Ave./mile)	5 miles (19%)	10 miles (37%)	15 miles (55%)	20 miles (75%)	Last 6+ (25%)
2:30 (5:43)	28 min.	55 min.	1:22	1:52	38 min.
2:35 (5:55)	29 min.	57 min.	1:25	1:56	39 min.
2:40 (6:06)	30 min.	59 min.	1:28	2:00	40 min.
2:45 (6:17)	31 min.	1:01	1:31	2:04	41 min.
2:50 (6:29)	32 min.	1:03	1:33	2:07	43 min.
2:55 (6:40)	33 min.	1:05	1:36	2:11	44 min.
3:00 (6:52)	34 min.	1:07	1:39	2:15	45 min.
3:05 (7:04)	35 min.	1:08	1:42	2:19	46 min.
3:10 (7:15)	36 min.	1:10	1:44	2:22	48 min.
3:15 (7:26)	37 min.	1:12	1:47	2:26	49 min.
3:20 (7:38)	38 min.	1:14	1:50	2:30	50 min.
3:25 (7:49)	39 min.	1:16	1:53	2:34	51 min.
3:30 (8:01)	40 min.	1:18	1:55	2:37	53 min.
3:35 (8:12)	41 min.	1:20	1:58	2:41	54 min.
3:40 (8:23)	42 min.	1:21	2:01	2:45	55 min.
3:45 (8:35)	43 min.	1:23	2:04	2:49	56 min.
3:50 (8:46)	44 min.	1:25	2:06	2:52	58 min.
3:55 (8:58)	45 min.	1:27	2:09	2:56	59 min.
4:00 (9:09)	46 min.	1:29	2:12	3:00	1:00

Select a goal from the total times at left, then attempt to run the corresponding times at each of the checkpoints. The percentages indicate how much of the total time the intermediate distances should occupy. The "splits" are rounded to the nearest minute, so they may vary 30 seconds on either side of the figures indicated.

It doesn't follow, however, that you should race the first half of the marathon as fast as possible—hoping to put time in the bank before the inevitable slowing. The pace still must be relatively even. It just can't be perfectly so.

EVEN-PACED RUNNING

During marathons in the United States, en route times are generally given at five-mile intervals. This chart gives the marathon times which will result if various per-mile paces are maintained throughout the race.

Mile	5 Miles	10 Miles	15 Miles	20 Miles	Marathon
4:50	24:10	48:20	1:12:30	1:36:40	2:07:44
5:00	25:00	50:00	1:15:00	1:40:00	2:11:06
5:10	25:50	51:40	1:17:30	1:43:20	2:15:28
5:20	26:40	53:20	1:20:00	1:46:40	2:19:50
5:30	27:30	55:00	1:22:30	1:50:00	2:24:12
5:40	28:20	56:40	1:25:00	1:53:20	2:28:34
5:50	29:10	58:20	1:27:30	1:56:40	2:32:56
6:00	30:00	1:00:00	1:30:00	2:00:00	2:37:19
6:10	30:50	1:01:40	1:32:30	2:03:20	2:41:41
6:20	31:40	1:03:20	1:35:00	2:06:40	2:46:03
6:30	32:30	1:05:00	1:37:30	2:10:00	2:50:25
6:40	33:20	1:06:40	1:40:00	2:13:20	2:54:47
6:50	34:10	1:08:20	1:42:30	2:16:40	2:59:09
7:00	35:00	1:10:00	1:45:00	2:20:00	3:03:33
7:10	35:50	1:11:40	1:47:30	2:23:20	3:07:55
7:20	36:40	1:13:20	1:50:00	2:26:40	3:12:17
7:30	37:30	1:15:00	1:52:30	2:30:00	3:16:39
7:40	38:20	1:16:40	1:55:00	2:33:20	3:21:01
7:50	39:10	1:18:20	1:57:30	2:36:40	3:25:23
8:00	40:00	1:20:00	2:00:00	2:40:00	3:29:45
8:10	40:50	1:21:40	2:02:30	2:43:20	3:34:07
8:20	41:40	1:23:20	2:05:00	2:46:40	3:38:29
8:30	42:30	1:25:00	2:07:30	2:50:00	3:42:51
8:40	43:20	1:26:40	2:10:00	2:53:20	3:47:13
8:50	44:10	1:28:20	2:12:30	2:56:40	3:51:35
9:00	45:00	1:30:00	2:15:00	3:00:00	3:56:00
9:10	45:50	1:31:40	2:17:30	3:03:20	4:00:22
9:20	46:40	1:33:20	2:20:00	3:06:40	4:04:44
9:30	47:30	1:35:00	2:22:30	3:10:00	4:09:06
9:40	48:20	1:36:40	2:25:00	3:13:20	4:13:28
9:50	49:10	1:38:20	2:27:30	3:16:40	4:17:50
10:00	50:00	1:40:00	2:30:00	3:20:00	4:22:13

20

Marathon Race Tactics

Use the other runners to your advantage during competition

Brian Maxwell

To the uninitiated observer, the marathon is an ultimate physical test. The sheer distance involved creates an image of a mindless struggle to continue in which endurance is the only factor that affects the outcome of the race.

However, running a marathon is more than simply physically traversing the 26-mile, 385-yard distance. It is an intellectual and spiritual experience in which the mind has a role as large or larger than the body. Tactics and strategy do play a role in successful marathon racing, whether that success is measured by breaking through one of the "round-number barriers" (four hours, three hours, 2:30...), personal improvement (running a faster time or getting a higher placing than you have before) or winning an Olympic medal.

Unfortunately, most runners are unwilling or unable to talk about tactics openly, and this has led to a kind of mystique about the subject. One reason for this is that *surprise* is one of the vital elements of strategy.

As one top runner puts it, "Frank Shorter knows that Bill Rodgers reads *Runner's World* too, so he's naturally going to be careful about giving away his secrets!"

Another factor is that the success of a strategy often defies rational explanation. A tactic that may be effective on one day may not work in the next race against the same competition.

However, by being aware of the vital physical and psychological elements of strategy, the observer will be better able to appreciate marathon racing, while the runner will be able to use his body and mind more effectively toward the goal of maximizing performance.

OFFENSE AND DEFENSE

Strategies in distance running can be broken down into "offensive" and "defensive" phases. Though these terms are usually applied to team sports, they also apply to running.

Being "on offense" in a race could be defined as "making things happen"—acting as a stimulus to change the form of the race by accelerating the pace or increasing the effort as an assertive move. Conversely, running defensively involves maintaining the status quo in the race by holding a steady pace and responding to someone else's move. The length of a marathon dictates that you cannot run offensively all the way. Relaxation for a large percentage of the race is vital, and as in the fable of the tortoise and the hare, the best offense is sometimes a strong defense.

The terms offense and defense also seem to imply racing against another person, but the same strategic considerations can be applied against the race distance, or the clock, or even yourself if you wish to look at it that way. By "attacking" certain segments of the race or geographical obstacles and relaxing on others, you can use strategy to explore the race and your personal limitations. An example of this is a senior-age marathoner I know who plans his marathons to run his first mile under six minutes and his first five miles in around 30 minutes, then gradually slows down at least a minute for each succeeding five mile segment (he has a best of 2:51:10). He is on offense during the first few miles of the race, then, as he gets tired, he runs defensively and tries to "hang on" for the rest of the race.

The purpose of any strategy is to use the limited amount of offensive energy that you have in the way that will best enable you to reach your optimum performance goal. The following are some considerations that can influence what strategy you choose in a race and how effective it will be.

PACE

In ideal conditions, *even* pacing—having the time of your first, 10th, 25th miles and all the miles in between the same—is the most efficient way to run. With external factors such as hills or wind, the effort or energy expenditure should remain constant, though the pace may vary.

Most marathoners are aware of this "rule," but many (including my friend described above) steadfastly believe that "I *know* I'm going to tire in the second half of the race, so I try to plan for it. I get some minutes 'in the bank' in the first half of the race, something to fall back on when I die in the second half!"

In order to test the logic of this explanation, we can make a physiological comparison between this strategy and even pace. The ability of the body to absorb and "burn" oxygen is perhaps the most important limiting factor in running a marathon. Oxygen requirements increase approximately as the *cube* of the velocity of the runner ($O = V^3$). Expressed in another way, this means that a runner traveling at five minutes per mile (2:11 marathon) is going *twice* as fast as a 10-minute per mile (4:22 marathon) runner, but requires *eight times* as much oxygen as the slower runner.

I computed the oxygen requirements of two 2:51:10 marathons— one run at exactly even pace, the other with the splits that my friend recorded using his "start fast and hang on" strategy. The calculations show that my friend used 2426 units of oxygen to run his 2:51:10, while another runner of the same size, weight and biomechanical efficiency following an even-pace strategy completes a 2:51:10 using only 2371 units. This represents an energy expenditure of 55 units (2.25% of oxygen consumed) that is "lost" through the inefficiency of uneven pace.

The final calculation shows that using a precisely even pace and the *same* effort and conditioning, my friend would have run approximately 2:49:20 for the race.

The key to running an even-pace strategy is to avoid going out too quickly at the start. It's very easy to get carried along by the excitement of the crowd, and the feeling of strength and elation of *running* when you're rested and "hyped up." But you must concentrate on being controlled in your pacing and patient in your aggressiveness. If you are unsure of how fast you are capable of running, it's best to start conservatively. If you go out too slowly, you can always pick up the pace later, but if you start too quickly, you will have to carry the tiredness of your "oxygen debt" that you incur through the remainder of the race.

Practice pacing by paying attention to your splits and overall times in shorter races. Time your training runs and learn what the rhythms of your racing paces for various distances feel like—then ignore the many runners whom you *know* you can beat who are ahead of you in the early stages of the race. *They're* running inefficiently! If you run your own race at your own pace, they'll soon come back.

FOLLOWING

Following is another tactic which can be used to minimize the amount of energy that you must expend to maintain a given pace. The physics of air turbulence establish that it is easier to follow someone else than to lead a run because of the "slip stream" effect of having the air broken up in front of you. Research has shown that approximately 6-7% of all the energy required for running is used to overcome the resistance of still air.

This can be reduced significantly by allowing another runner to lead and positioning yourself in his turbulence. Ideally, you should be as close as possible—within 2-6 feet—of the person you're following, but you must be careful not to step on the heels or otherwise interfere with the runners around you; this is grounds for disqualification, not to mention dirty looks and insults or worse from the people you interfere with!

Running "on the shoulder" means to be just to the left or right and behind another runner so that your foot plant falls approximately below his arm swing. This is a way to get closer to your leader without interfering and is especially effective when running into a wind that approaches at an angle.

The reduction in energy expenditure that can be obtained will vary according to factors such as wind direction, how close you are to the leader, relative body sizes, etc., but in "average" conditions you can save around 1-2% of the total without interfering with other runners. Again, this seems like a relatively small amount, but over a full marathon this translates into 2-3 minutes. Thus, a 3:02 marathon that you ran by yourself could become a Boston-qualifying 2:59, or a 2:17 could be a 2:15! That kind of improvement is something that most runners would exchange 6-12 months' training for!

LEADING

In spite of the above, many runners like to lead and it is a strategy that can be very effective if used prudently. From a physical standpoint, leading frees you from having to adjust your stride pattern or pace to that of someone else, possibly increasing you biomechanical efficiency and making up for the energy expended in breaking the wind.

There are some situations, such as dense crowds at the start of a race, sharp turns or uneven surfaces, curbs or obstacles on the road where it's safer to either lead or let a gap of at least 6-10 yards open between you and the runner in front. I learned this lesson the hard way in the early stages of the 1977 New York City Marathon.

I wrote in *Runner's World* "As we approach the crest of the Verrazano Narrows Bridge, the view is incredible. The air is crystal clear and far across the harbor, I can discern the Statue of Liberty, while the awesome majesty of the Manhattan skyline rises beyond.... I ease in behind (Jerome) Drayton, relax, let the pack on my left shield the wind that knifes into us. . . . It feels so easy as runners flow around me, the pace increasing as the bridge curves downward, then suddenly I'm off balance, falling forward—but I catch myself, jam my foot down and feel a twinge in my left thigh—almost tripped, stepped into one of the huge expansion joints. . . ." The "twinge" turned out to be a minor muscle pull that hampered me throughout the race.

Approaching an aid station is another time when it is helpful to lead. Being in a pack can sometimes make it difficult to get the drink that you want or to avoid spilling or dropping your refreshment, leaving the choice of going without or having to break your rhythm completely by stopping.

The psychological benefits that come from leading can also be extremely important. One friend of mine takes the lead when he feels the *worst* in a race—and the mental "lift" carries him through to feeling physically better, after which he will again relax behind someone else.

"If I didn't get out there and prove to myself I could lead," he told me, "I know I'd drop off the pace completely."

Of course this, like any other strategy, is best kept secret. If your opponent suspects that you are leading only to overcome depression or tiredness, he will probably try to make you feel worse by pushing the pace himself and fighting you for the lead.

One famous long-distance coach preaches the rule that you should lead a race (or a pack of runners) *only* if you intend to speed up the pace or slow it down. In the former situation, taking the lead should be assertive; you should try to run right *past* rather than just in front of the runner you pass. If you can open up a gap between you, you can deprive your opponent of a wind break and make it easier for him to psychologically "let you go" and accept the space between you as permanent.

An example of the latter strategy occurred in the 1972 Olympic 10,000 meters when Lasse Viren of Finland was tripped and fell to the track midway through the race. He jumped up immediately and amazed all observers by not simply running to catch up to the pack but by moving all the way into the lead! His response was the precisely correct strategy, however, for he then managed to slow the pace from 67-68 seconds per lap to 70-71 seconds for the next few laps, enabling him to rest and recover from the energy expenditure of the fall.

Leading can also be an effective strategy *because* of its inefficiency. The runners who are following you are probably aware that you're doing more work than they are—but if you show no signs of its effects and then maintain or increase the pace, they may become convinced that you are stronger than they are and not try to challenge you.

Occasionally, the situation occurs where none of the runners in a pack wants the chore of leading. Rather than let the pace lag, most marathoners will accept a share of the leading if they know that someone will relieve them after a mile or so. Most will respond to an offer of "I'll take this mile, you take the next." This unwritten rule of running etiquette follows from the philosophy that the marathon is a contest between the *distance* and the individual. Thus, the other competitors are "allies" on your side of the competition. The more runners who are there in your ability range, the easier it is to form groups and share the work of leading, so that everyone can get their best possible performance.

KICKING

"Kicking" or sprinting is one of the most common and effective tactics used in distance racing. It is perhaps the ultimate offensive move—pouring all the available resources that your body can muster into a concentrated burst of speed that will carry you through the finish.

Unfortunately, many distance runners lack confidence in themselves in a close race, because they feel themselves lacking in the basic speed to kick effectively. Physiological research has substantiated the idea that speed is limited by the muscle fibers you are born with, but in the finish of a long-distance race, *endurance strength* and *emotion* weigh much more heavily than all-out sprint speed in determining kicking ability.

Endurance strength means basically how much you have left at the end of the race—the better your conditioning, the more strength you should have left to sprint with at the finish. Emotion has the same root as "motivation"—it's largely how much you *want* to sprint in order to beat an opponent or knock those few seconds off your time that determines how well you can kick. I use the word emotion because this is a mental process that is outside of reason. Logically, your mind registers the pain of the stress your body is under and tells you to ease off, but at the same time, something drives you to "go."

Some runners consider kicking at the end of a long race to be "hotdogging," as if an extra place or a second or two is unimportant. Instead, I prefer to look at it as the icing on the whole emotional experience of a marathon. You've pushed yourself to what you *thought* was your maximum through the 26 miles—but if there's anything left when you reach down inside in those last few yards, use it!

When to kick is something that you must determine by how you feel and your assessment of your opponent. Choosing a landmark before the race and using it as a signal ("I know I can sprint from here!") can be helpful. Being aware of conditions such as mud, wind, sand, etc., can give you an advantage, and accelerating off a turn can enable you to use the centrifugal force to swing up beside and then pass your opponent.

The "how" of kicking starts before you make your move. Shorten your stride slightly in order to get into a faster rhythm and adjust your arm action so that your arms are coming straight through in a forward plane instead of across your body. Lean forward slightly and *drive* with your "back" leg, first quickening your stride cadence and then stretching out your footfall. Again, concentrate on going right past your opponent so that you're not breaking the wind for him, then focus on keeping the arm action smooth and steady. Your legs will be tired, but the arms set the rhythm that the legs will match. Don't look back to see where your opponent is; it may encourage him. Just concentrate on running right *through* the finish. Even if you are re-passed, you never know when your opponent may let up before the finish line, or even if another runner may be approaching from behind.

Like any other skill, kicking is best perfected through practice. It needn't be done all-out or on every run, but occasionally on a training run, try to get a mental image of being near the end of a race. Go through the mechanics of gathering yourself, adjusting your running style and accelerating for a few strides to feel the surge of speed that you can use to "top off" your performance in a race.

Avoid unconsciously practicing negative reactions, like a national-class road racer I know who has a reputation of being "tough as hell," but only during the first seven-eighths of his races. He usually manages to run away from the competition to win most of his races, but when challenged, he seldom wins a close one. Ironically, he has excellent speed, but unless it's a "major" (i.e., national championship) race, he admits that he prefers to "save" his kick and tries to tie or stride through the finish in second or third place rather than testing it. Thus, he never really practices his kick, and in a couple of big-race situations, he has been outsprinted by basically slower runners. The philosophy of "saving something" for a specific goal race is fine, but when it reaches the point of being a learned inhibition against pushing yourself, it's no longer beneficial to top performance.

THE PSYCH-OUT

"Psyching" or mental intimidation is something that can occur on any level of competition. The beginning runner in cut-off jeans, a comfortable old T-shirt and tennis shoes can go to his first race and be "psyched-out" by someone in a flashy sweatsuit and racing uniform, while among more experienced runners, having the latest, difficult to obtain, highly-rated shoes or a race shirt that denotes having finished in the top 10 or 20 or 100 in a particular race can be an intimidating factor. On a higher level, affiliation with a particularly successful club or school can carry intimidation value.

These kinds of subtle devices are designed to plant nagging self-doubts in the mind of the opponent, while more blatant boasts or vocalized performance predictions may be aimed to destroy completely a rival's competitiveness. However, all psych-outs have one thing in common: they rely on a basic lack of confidence in the "psychee" that make him vulnerable to the "psycher."

A simple, bold statement such as, "I'm in this race to win!" can bring about one of two reactions in the person to whom it is said. He can be intimidated, reasoning that "he's so good, he knows he will beat me, what chance do I have?" and not even try to compete. However, a more confident runner can react aggressively, thinking that "he's overconfident or trying to bluff everybody into not trying. Who does he think he is? I'm going to go all-out to beat him!" This "flip-flop" can occur with any psych-out attempt, and while the most blatant statement can be the most devastating, it is also the most vulnerable to reverse psychology and provides the most motivational ammunition for your opponent to use back on you.

This is one reason why most world-class runners almost never make deprecatory remarks about their opponents. However, at this level, word of mouth, stories and time listings in running magazines, and the influence of other media help to build images and reputations that often psych out a runner's opponents. There are many examples of world-class runners actually defeating themselves by being intimidated into trying inefficient strategies because of the reputations of their rivals.

Jim Peters of England was clearly the top marathoner in the world in the early 1950s and was favored to win the 1952 Olympics at Helsinki. However, after winning the 5000- and 10,000-meter double in the Games, the Czech Emil Zatopek announced that he would try for his third gold in the marathon. Zatopek had never run a marathon and Peters was still picked to win. But Peters, obviously nervous, went out at a blistering pace, passing the first three miles in 4:50 per mile, compared to the then Olympic record of 2:34:51, which averaged 5:54 per mile! Zatopek hung back, but gradually moved up when Peters began to fade badly.

At the 11-mile mark, the two were together. The Czech turned to the exhausted Peters and asked calmly, "Ze pace, Jim it is very fast, no?" "No," Peters replied, "It is very slow!" Zatopek nodded, maintained his pace and pulled away to win in a new Olympic record while Peters failed to finish.

Whether Peters' going out too fast cost him the gold medal is debatable. Peters had run much faster than Zatopek's winning time of 2:23:03, and 10 months after the Games, he lowered the world record to an astounding 2:19:22. Zatopek, however, was a ferocious competitor and might have won the race (though perhaps not so easily), no matter what strategy Peters had followed, but most observers agreed that Peters would have surely finished and won some kind of medal had he run his own race.

PUTTING IT TOGETHER

These, then, are the important elements of strategy in the marathon, but how they are employed is up to the runner. Often, being *aware* of them as used by other runners can be more important than using them yourself. There are no formulas for successful races or correct strategies, because no two race situations are precisely the same.

When going into a race, it is important to have a general goal of the time or competitive placing that you would like to achieve, but you should not try to plan your races too thoroughly. Instead, be an artist—respond to your conditioning, your feelings on the day, the course, the weather and the competition using your mind and your intuition. Try different strategies from race to race in order to develop your diversity and adaptability to any race situation. Finally, don't be inhibited about pushing yourself and using any strategy that might expand and enhance the experience of racing and, ultimately, improve your performance as a runner.

21
Racing Etiquette

Don't interfere with each other or
add to the officials' headaches

R unning is a sport of few rules and many customs. This is good for
the sport, because it needs few officials to enforce those few written rules. The runners themselves do most of their own policing by
following their customs, which might confuse a new racer because no
one will announce them; every runner just expects every other to know
and practice them.

These are the rights and wrongs of racing, the glue which holds together the fragile alliance among the three groups who make organized running possible: the participants, the promoters and the people
who control or share the facilities we use. Our dealings with each other
are matters of good manners, which, fortunately, are part of the sport's
tradition.

This might surprise newcomers, as did a Chicago police officer who
said after watching a road race with 5000 entrants, "This is the largest
crowd in the city's history without a harsh word being said. Nobody is
accusing anybody. Nobody is denouncing someone else. Nobody is
mad. It's just a quiet, pleasant event."

Running couldn't operate on the large scale it now does if we
weren't this mannerly. As long as we all follow a simple, unwritten
code toward each other, and the people who help and allow us to race,
the sport runs smoothly. If we let down, it breaks down.

FELLOW RUNNERS

The basic custom is: Don't interfere. Don't intentionally disturb
another runner's pace and concentration.

1. At a crowded starting line, choose a place in the pack that
matches your expected finish. If you're average, start in the middle; if

slow, the back. Don't force faster racers to climb over you to find running room.

2. When someone tries to pass you, give him a fair fight. But the definition of "fair" does not include throwing elbows and veering across his path to hold him off. If you're being lapped, yield the right of way. Move out to let the faster runners through on the inside.

3. Don't start a race unless you intend to finish it, and never jump into one in the middle. This isn't fair to other runners who pace along with you on the assumption that you're going all the way.

OFFICIALS

The key words here are: Be tolerant and patient. Handling races is a big, thankless job usually performed by volunteers or half-hearted recruits. Don't make their work harder than it already is, or they might not show up the next time.

1. Arrive at the race site early, and check in as soon as possible. Don't be part of a last-minute jam-up which delays the start. If you must run unofficially (without entering), don't spoil things for the duly registered runners. Don't get in their way at the start, take their drinks or—most important—cross the finish line and mess up everyone's results.

2. Wait until the race is over before asking officials for your time and place. They can't take their attention off the running until then, and you'll get in the way of people who still are finishing.

3. If you think officials deserve it, thank them for their work. Better yet, tell them you'll help at a future race.

OTHERS

Remember: We share the places where we run. Other people use them; others often control them and can take them away from us if we abuse our privileges.

1. Don't interfere with traffic by running in mid-road, on the right side (which is the *wrong* side for a pedestrian) or zig-zagging back and forth.

2. Respect private property. Don't use someone's front lawn as a dressing room or toilet.

3. Clean up after yourself.

Part 5
The Health of It

22

Work and Rest

Too many runners ignore the second half of the formula: recovery

E. C. Frederick and Jack Welch

His doctors were upset at his determination to race. It appeared pointless. Not even Emil Zatopek could hope to overcome the debilitating effects of his hospitalization in time to compete.

Zatopek had been bedridden for some two weeks with a serious stomach ailment. It seemed impossible that he could be competitive after missing two weeks of training and in such a weakened state. Nevertheless, his determination won out and within an hour of his discharge he was aboard a plane for Brussels and the 1950 European Championships. The rest is history.

Zatopek nearly lapped second placer Alain Mimoun in the 10,000 meters and captured the 5000 by a 23-second margin. Distance running historian Peter Lovesey has termed his victories "the most decisive double long-distance victory in any major international championship." It seems only logical to add that Zatopek's effort was all the more amazing when we remember the two weeks of training that he missed. Or was it?

Most modern coaches and runners would have us believe that everyday training is essential for maximal performances. Equally well touted is the dogma that points to continuous hard work as the only path to high-level running achievement.

We have serious doubts about the supposed truth underlying these ideas. If this training dogma were based on fact, then how could Zatopek, for example, achieve his decisive victories following two weeks of bedrest? A "fluke" would be the answer of the hard trainers. Or perhaps it could be explained away by Zatopek's overwhelming superiority or by speculating poor preparation on the part of his competitors.

These criticisms might be reasonable if the Zatopek story were an exceptional one. The startling thing is that this pattern is not unique. Similar incidents have happened time and again.

Several years ago, Dave Bedford surprised the track world by running a world record for 10,000 meters. The surprise was not that Bedford had run that fast but that he had done it with only minimal training. Bedford had been nursing a hamstring injury, which hampered his running. Instead of his characteristic high-mileage weeks, which sometimes pushed 200 miles, he had been barely averaging 25 miles for a three-month period.

Bedford did have the benefit of three weeks of accelerated training following this light period. But few serious proponents of the hard-training dogma would consider three weeks enough to put the athlete at a world-record peak. The answer has to be in his rest.

Dick Tayler, Commonwealth Games 10,000-meter winner, was in a similar situation. Torn ankle ligaments allowed him only three weeks of hard training before the Games.

Another Commonwealth Games competitor, 800-meter silver medalist Mike Boit, also had little training before the New Zealand competition. After a month's layoff, he trained only two weeks before running 1:44.4 in the final.

Another not so dramatic example is supplied by Craig Virgin. Virgin was unable to train for more than a month due to severe tendonitis. In early February 1975, he began training again, and on February 11 he ran an indoor double. While his times of 4:12.5 and 8:51.0 are not world-class, they were, at that time, strong performances for Virgin.

Emiel Puttemans missed 14 days of training six weeks before the Munich 10,000 final. Yet he ran 27:39 to win the silver medal.

Dave Wottle missed 31 days of training between the Trials and the Munich Olympic Games, averaging only about four miles a day during that period. Yet he had the strength to come from behind in the 800-meter final and win the most exciting race of the Games.

The examples go on and on at all levels of competition. The pattern repeats itself again and again: *Hard work + rest = success.*

We can learn from these examples. They teach us that our ideas of what constitutes an effective training program need some revision. We need to take a closer look at the function of rest in a running program. But, before doing that, we need some perspectives on the use of rest in modern training programs.

Overtrained runners are much more common than undertrained runners. Observing this aspect of the problem, you would think that runners were generally uninformed about the importance of rest. Ironically, this does not seem to be the case.

Engage a group of runners in a conversation about rest, and you'll find that most of them agree that rest is important. Most will also agree that they probably don't get enough of it. Perhaps a number of them will even admit to having given it some serious thought. But in all likelihood, only a very few will have ever done anything about it.

Rest is a lot like stretching exercises in that respect. A lot of lip-service is paid to its importance, even to its *necessity*. But few runners actually incorporate it into their training programs. We are creatures of habit, and our bad habits (or lack of good ones) are firmly entrenched.

Realizing the worth of something, intellectually, does not guarantee that a constructive change will result. Cognition is one phenomenon, application another. Most often, the bad situation will persist, and the new realization will fade into the background.

This seems particularly true when dealing with ideas that relate to the body and health. How many people do you know wish they could lose a few pounds or give up smoking but "just can't"?

The reason so many runners have neither stretching nor rest built into their training programs can only be apathy and/or negligence. The thing that keeps them from caring is largely an attitude we have developed about natural things and their relationship to the will.

What enforces this attitude is a lack of any clear conception of why rest is needed and what rest does. Further, many runners have no idea of how much rest is needed or just how to go about it.

Our Western concept of the path to success doesn't include rest. Instead, the formula contains liberal doses of persistent hard work aimed at overcoming resistance—the resistance supplied by natural physical limits, intellectual capability, financial constraints, etc. It seems like it is always man *against* nature—man overcoming himself. When we get a headache from overstressing, do we stop and rest? No, we take a pill and forge on. The body is just another obstacle on the path to success. All too often, we see it as the object of conquest rather than cooperation.

This brings to mind a story about the first ascent of Mount Everest. There are some enlightening parallels with competitive running.

When Edmund Hilary and Tensing Norgay returned from their successful climb, they had different ideas about what had taken place. New Zealander Hilary spoke triumphantly of conquering the mountain. Norgay, a Sherpa, saw things differently. He stated humbly, "The mountain and I together attained the heights."

More often than not, runners see their bodies as Hilary saw Everest—as another obstacle in their paths. When a runner does well, the impression one gets is that success has come in spite of the body, rather than because of it.

It appears that many (if not most) runners have lost touch with the simplest of realities. They have lost sight of the fact that it is the whole organism which achieves and not just the power of will. Most runners are too busy conquering themselves with high-mileage weeks to see the profound significance of this idea.

If we could only realize that we can gain more (in the largest sense) by cooperating with the body than by trying to conquer it, everything would fall into place. We would begin to see running as a means to develop the body to make maximal performance possible. Words like "nurture, coax and develop" would replace "thrash, push and force". The necessity of rest would become dramatically obvious.

Running is an exercise in destruction. Each time we run, we tear ourselves down. Muscle tissue is torn. Mitochondria, the powerhouses of the cells, swell grotesquely. Metabolic wastes accumulate. Blood-sugar levels drop. Dehydration occurs and, along with it, excessive losses of electrolytes upset the delicate balance required for efficient muscle and nerve function. We become overheated. Muscle glycogen is depleted. And as the intensity and/or duration of the workout increase, this damage becomes more pronounced.

In the period between runs, the body attempts to recover and to rebuild. Torn muscle is repaired. New mitochondria are formed, metabolic wastes are flushed out of the system, blood-sugar levels are restored. We rehydrate and replace lost electrolytes. Any damage to muscles and to the nervous system due to hyperthermia (high body temperature) is repaired. Glycogen is replenished.

These two phases—destruction and regeneration—*together* constitute conditioning. And the two can never be separated if conditioning is to proceed in a positive direction.

In any program of running, then, the body is systematically broken down and rebuilt. And each rebuilding leaves the body a little stronger than before. These incremental increases amount to the development of a progressively stronger body, capable of more and faster running. That is, if it is done right.

If the body is not allowed to complete the rebuilding phase of training for lack of time (rest) or materials (nutrition), then the destruction will eventually exceed the body's ability to repair itself.

Conditioning will proceed at a slower rate or not at all. In extreme cases, conditioning can actually deteriorate.

On the other hand, if the breakdown phase (the stress) is not optimal, then progress is also retarded. Since we have all become experts at the "stress" phase of training, nothing needs to be said about effective training methods. But the rebuilding phase—let's call it "regeneration"—does need some elucidation.

Some aspects of the regenerative phase take longer than others. All depend, to a certain degree, on the intensity and duration of the stress. For example, glycogen depletion, mitochondrial destruction and extensive muscle tissue damage all take about 48 hours to be completely reversed. Eating properly, getting plenty of rest and a little exercise seem to promote regeneration. Still, the time period needed to completely return to the status quo is well over 40 hours.

To understand how this information fits into a running program, we need to juggle different intensities and durations of runs with the frequency of runs.

First of all, no one runs all day every day, so we have, say, 21-23 hours of non-exercise time during each day to recover from the physiological havoc created by a daily run. It should be obvious that the greater the amount of time spent in intensive rest (e.g., sleep), the more effective the rest time is. It should be equally obvious that the more and faster we run, the more there is added to the "regenerative load."

This regenerative load is the product of the speed and distance of workouts, and is also influenced by the quality and quantity of rest during the same time period. We can, therefore, regulate this load by controlling the relationship between our daily dose of destruction and our daily capacity to regenerate.

Let's say we take a hard 20-mile run in the afternoon of day one. If we do nothing on days two and three but rest and recuperate, we should be completely regenerated by the afternoon of day three. But few runners would be willing to do no running for such a period of time. So they are going to contribute to the regenerative load by running during this recovery time. If, however, they do only light workouts, get more rest than usual, and eat a diet rich in carbohydrates, protein and vitamins and minerals, they should regenerate on schedule. Or possibly they will need 72 hours to recover rather than the usual 48-hour period.

By tuning into such subtle body signs as stiffness and soreness, lack of energy, cravings for sweets, etc., it is possible for a runner to determine the period required for rebuilding from a particular workout. Workouts, rest and diet can then be adjusted to promote quick and total regeneration.

However, if runners do the opposite, continue hard workouts and make no concessions in the lifestyle, then they will be delaying recovery from the hard run. Indeed, if high-intensity training is maintained continually, then the body never catches up with the regenerative load, and eventually staleness and overstress symptoms will result.

In this way, workouts can be varied in intensity and duration from day to day to promote regeneration. Running hard or long only every 48 hours seems to be optimal. In between, workouts should be short and/or easy, and one's life should be adjusted to maximize regeneration. Plenty of sleep is certainly important, but what one does with the waking hours is equally so.

This "cycling" of workouts is nothing new. Enlightened students of distance running, like Bill Bowerman and Tom Osler, have been preaching it for years. Its efficiency at producing optimal training effects has been proven time and again by the high proportion of world-class runners who have flourished on this type of program. So there should be little doubt that this type of training schedule is effective.

Much has been written about the structure and application of hard-easy training programs, so in all likelihood we wouldn't be able to contribute anything worthwhile. An area that does need to be developed, however, is the application of rest in this type of program. It is just as important as the running phase, and just as capable of being refined and perfected to produce maximal effects. Let's take a look at some regenerative techniques with an aim to maximizing our gains from this phase of conditioning.

Rest can be divided into two types: "passive rest" and "active rest." Passive rest is what we normally do, or actually *don't* do. In short, passive rest is inactivity. We do nothing in particular to promote rest, but instead give nature time to run its course. Passive rest certainly is important and effective. It has its place in a program of regeneration.

But there are other things we can *do* which will enhance regeneration and will multiply the effectiveness of rest. We would lump these activities under the heading of active rest. In other words, we are doing things to more effectively utilize the regenerative effects of rest.

After a hard run, things like light stretching, meditation, a sauna or a massage will cause regeneration to proceed more quickly than it would if we simply took a nap. These sorts of activities are regeneration promoting. Liberal doses of these activities can quicken and deepen healing, and thereby enhance the rebuilding of the body after a destructive run.

Yoga-type stretching exercises have been shown to stimulate circulation in all areas of the body but particularly in the exercised areas. There is also an enhancement of oxygenation of the tissues, not to mention the physical effects of the stretches on the muscle fibers themselves.

Meditation has been studied by a variety of researchers, and the majority of them have found it to be an intense form of relaxation and rest. The physiological state achieved in meditation is thought to be deeper even than sleep.

Sauna baths and steam baths are cleansing and often produce an intense relaxation, a relief of tension. Swimming and massage have similar relaxing qualities and have the added effect of promoting deep circulation.

These activities also have a soothing effect on the psyche, something which we have neglected so far, but something which is of equal or more importance than the physical factors we've mentioned. We can regenerate a psyche which has been damaged or overworked by a long or hard run using the same positive approach we've taken in healing the body.

Do something unusual. Take a walk somewhere you've never been before, read something different, sit in a bus station and watch the world in action, catch a Walt Disney movie, take a long drive over a back road, walk in the rain, visit the ocean, go to a museum, make love (not necessarily in that order, nor one after another). In short, do something that will increase your awareness, stimulate you, generate new interests and ideas. It is just as important to have a fresh, healthy interest in your running as it is to have a sound body to do it with.

Bedford, Zatopek, et al., have stumbled upon the secret of this relationship. They have all followed long months of intense work with extended rest and then gone on to achieve superlative performances.

Their long months of steady intense work with only minimal regeneration produced a maximal stress load accumulated over time. The result was either sickness or breakdown beginning a period of enforced rest. During this prolonged rest period, their bodies were given the time and materials to completely rebuild—to adapt to the maximal stress which they had accumulated during months of intense training. In short, the body had time to catch up. The results were impressive.

Actually, what they were doing was no more than an expanded version of what every runner should be doing constantly. Using the running-regeneration cycle on a day to day basis is a much more efficient way to accomplish the same goal—maximal adaptation.

Even the most conscientiously designed balance of running and regeneration is bound to produce an accumulation of stress over a long period of time. For this reason, runners should cultivate an awareness of the signs of overstress and be prepared to take extended non-running rest periods from time to time.

For example, world three-mile record-holder Emiel Puttemans at least once a year has a period in which he does no running at all, he overeats, gets a little sloppy, becoming the antithesis of his normal self. Puttemans claims that these "rest" days are the most important part of his annual training pattern.

Ron Hill, a 2:09 marathoner, used to take at least a week's "vacation" during which he ran two daily workouts—two miles in the mornings and two in the afternoons.

Although the idea of not running for even a day can generate tremendous anxiety in certain runners, we don't believe their fears are well founded. After all, look what it did for Zatopek and Bedford.

23

Race and Survive

What do you do to get back to normal after a marathon?

Ted Corbitt

The lure of the marathon has resulted in a record number of such races being held and has produced an unprecedented number of competitors. These runners include the young and the old, male and female, and the well-trained and moderately-trained competitors—a side range in fitness levels. This mixture of athletes shares the same basic competitive conflicts en route to finishing a marathon, but abilities to meet the challenge vary widely.

The wise runner makes adequate preparations to run his own race. Performing and recovering from a marathon may be looked at from three vantage points: things to do before, during and after the race so that the runner reaches the finish line in reasonably good condition and gets back to normal as soon as possible.

PRE-MARATHON RACE PREPARATIONS

1. The marathoner's best friend is thorough training. The runner's goal will dictate his involvement. There is no one best way to train for the marathon, but the novice should spend at least a year training for the race.

2. Adequate training is easily spoiled by badly-fitting shoes. Shoes which serve well for short distances often fail in a long race. Long-distance running shoes should be purchased with extra width and extra length to reduce the blister and friction-burn problems. New shoes should always be worn in training before racing in them.

3. The runner should plan to run at a pace which will allow him to reach the finish line without feeling nearly dead.

4. Train in all kinds of weather, within reason, and get acclimatized to the conditions expected on race day.

5. On a hot day, drink extra fluids beginning early in the day.

6. Try to develop good body posture in daily activities, including running. This elusive quality, once made second nature, will mean less fatigue, and less wear and tear on the body. The head, properly balanced on an extended spine, is the key factor along with good general flexibility and strong belly muscles.

7. A controversial area is nutrition and the use of vitamins and food supplements. A varied diet and the avoidance of "junk foods" should help raise the runner's store of energy.

Popular vitamins in use are A and D (in cod liver oil), B (in liver, brewer's yeast, or in capsule form), C and E (in wheat germ or wheat germ oil). These vitamins help the body in such functions as digestion, circulation, etc. Molasses, nuts and seeds contain minerals and nutrients which affect body functioning and the energy level. Some raw foods in the diet will help the digestive process.

Some authorities would advise the runner to reduce his intake of table salt as an aid to muscle function and to the circulation. It's claimed that most people take in more salt than they need per day even if they don't salt their food.

Avoid experimenting with foods on the day of a race. Cheese or bananas or carob sometimes can help those plagued with pre-race diarrhea.

Learn to stay calm in the days and hours before the race, since tension increases energy expenditure, produces more fatigue from the running effort and results in slower running speed.

Experiments in Sweden showed that what the athlete eats the week of a race can determine how tired he'll get during a long race like the marathon. Suggestion: run to exhaustion (a good long run or a hard run) a week before the race. Eat only proteins and fats (no carbohydrates—sugars and starches) for the next three days. Then resume eating sugars and starches until race time. This can result in less post-race fatigue due to a build up of energy in the body.

ACTIVITIES DURING THE RACE

The marathoner's main concerns en route are to win, to beat his peers or to hit a planned time. He can further help himself by aiding his body to keep within favorable internal temperature ranges: dressing appropriately in cold or wet weather, and in hot weather, using protective covering, running in shade if available and the liberal use of fluids internally and externally.

The runner can replace some of the lost body fluids by drinking water and sweetened drinks, and he can conserve some body fluids by pouring water on the body to evaporate (in place of sweat), thus cooling the body. Dr. David Costill, Ball State University, has suggested that runners drink cool water since it'll lower the internal body temperature as it warms up inside the body.

The novices and the converted track men are in the most dangerous position of all runners in hot weather because they generally don't take advantage of refreshments provided during the race. This fault can be fatal in the summer weather encountered in the United States. Runners should drink and use sponges, etc., at every opportunity during a hot weather race since this will keep them strong longer.

The runner who becomes aware of the fact that he is in trouble from the heat or from extreme fatigue must take care: Change goals and do what has to be done to survive. This could mean slowing down, or walking a while, or walking and running, or dropping out and trying again another day. A hot day is also not the time to go for a personal record.

POST-RACE ACTIVITIES

The runner generally begins his recovery from a race as soon as he slows up to walk after finishing. If he's in trouble as in a "heat incident," he'll need expert attention and possibly hospitalization. The runner shouldn't allow himself to be wrapped up in a blanket after finishing a race on a very hot day, since this could elevate his body temperature to the danger level. Normally, the trained runner who has raced up to his fitness level will not be in serious trouble at the finish even when he feels that he'll never run another marathon race.

The marathoner who has pushed himself will have some post-race problems such as breathlessness (especially if he sprints at the end), fatigue (manifested in a number of ways), dehydration, hunger (hidden or apparent), possibly blisters or skin burns from friction, and sore, strained muscles.

The marathoner can meet these problems by the following means:

1. Walking around immediately after finishing, if possible. After dressing and drinking something, another walk (up to 20 or 30 minutes) will help to keep the circulation more active and help to reduce muscle soreness and stiffness.

2. On warm or hot days, the marathoner should get a lot of fluids into the body at the earliest opportunity. The thirst reflex isn't always a reliable indicator of the need for water. The intake of extra fluids should continue at intervals into the day after the race.

3. While the ordinary hot shower won't aid much in recovery from fatigue, a "contrast shower"—hot and cold water alternating several times—might be helpful. A cold shower can assist in dispersing fatigue products by increasing the oxygen supply.

4. Massage is useful in hastening the removal of some of the fatigue products from the muscles. In most cases, the runner would have to do this himself. The following methods are helpful:

Friction massage of the points where muscles attach to the bone will tend to relax the whole muscle.

Using the whole hand, do soft strokes on the muscles of the legs. Start with the thigh and then do the lower leg. The runner should picture himself pushing blood towards the heart and so it will be done.

Judo Revival Points: To relieve cramps or spasm in any part of the body, take the shoes and socks off, apply deep, firm, steady pressure with the corner of the thumb or a finger on top of the foot between the big toe and the second toes just before the web. Do this on either foot or both feet at the same time for 30-60 seconds. For energy, do either friction massage or do steady pressure with the thumb or a fingertip right on the prominent bone at the lower end of the neck. Stay directly on each point for 30-60 seconds.

Kneading massage of the involved muscle is also effective in handling cramps. (Avoid heat and massage right after soft-tissue injury.)

5. Exercises: Stretch and move the arms and legs to help the circulation and to lengthen the tired muscles which tend to tighten up after a hard effort. A cramping muscle may also be relieved by stretching it. Bouts of deep breathing, such as yawning, which can be learned, will also move fluids toward the heart, facilitating recovery from fatigue.

6. After returning home, lie down and elevate the legs for a few minutes. Occasionally bend and straighten the legs and move the toes and feet in all directions. Repeat this before going to bed.

7. A meal of proteins, fats and a good amount of carbohydrates should be eaten after the race and in the following days. If the runner doesn't feel like eating, he should stick with liquids and eat a solid meal later.

8. If the runner fails to perk up after a reasonable time following the race, an ice bag or cold compress (kept cold) put over the heart and upper abdomen for up to 20 minutes will help to revive him.

THE DAY AFTER A MARATHON

The novice may develop muscle soreness before the race is finished. Most runners have some soreness the day after a hard race, and this soreness reaches a peak the second day afterward. The soreness subsides in the succeeding days. The discomfort is due to muscle strains and especially to fatigue debris in the muscles as a result of running. Anything that promotes an increase in circulation will help to flush the muscles of these fatigue products—e.g., stretching, walking, running, massage, hot soaks. But light running should be the main tool used to come back to normal.

If there are blisters and they don't cause limping or pain when walking or running, they may be left alone. If blisters cause painful walking, they should be opened and drained of fluid, but care is needed to avoid infection.

The day after a marathon and for several succeeding days, the marathoner can speed up recovery by soaking in a tub of hot water (100-106 degrees F) for 10-20 minutes. While soaking, move the legs about occasionally. Self-massage of the leg muscles at that time would also be beneficial.

Ice massage of sore or painful muscles may also be helpful. Make a big ice cube by freezing a paper cupful of water (or use a number of regular ice cubes, one at a time). Wrap the ice cube in a paper or cloth towel to hold it. Put the open end of the ice on the painful area and rub it in a circular manner for up to 8-10 minutes or until the part passes through stages or sensations of cold, pain, burning and numbness. Repeat this daily until better.

If there is extreme or persistent pain in the hip or knee or ankle joints, the runner should see a physician before resuming training. This is the way to avoid unnecessary damage to an injured joint, and this will prevent secondary injuries from developing.

In the post-race days, the runner should stretch his muscles before and after running, and should gradually increase the running, avoiding strain. The novice would be wise to allow himself a month or more before running another marathon.

In summary, the actions taken by the runner before and during a marathon will determine the extent of the problems to be met following the race. Following a marathon, the runner will want to regain lost body fluids; eat muscle-building and energy foods (proteins, fats and carbohydrates); take care of blisters or other injuries before beginning serious training again or racing again; walk, *stretch all muscles* and do easy running in the days following the race; resume real training as soon as convenient; see a doctor if he is suffering from strong local pain in a bone or joint; delay racing until he feels fresh and strong again.

24

First-Aid for Injuries

The ways you can heal yourself
short of visiting a doctor

Too many runners get hurt. This year, as in any year, two in every three of you reading this page will be hurt badly enough to stop or cut back on running, see a doctor or all of the above. As long as we've been checking casualty rates, they've been this high. And, for reasons noted later, they'll probably always stay this high.

Too many of these injured runners react to their problems the way a mechanical incompetent does when his car won't work. He's helpless against any machine more complex than a can opener, so he's confused and scared by breakdowns. He reacts in one of three ways: (1) takes the broken machine to an expensive "expert"; (2) tries to keep it limping along; or (3) quits using it and hopes it gets better by itself.

Injured runners are likewise frustrated and frightened by their own breakdowns and by the technical articles they've read about them. So they either turn their problems over to a specialist, keep running through pain or quit.

Actually, the body is so simple in its operation that you can do most routine maintenance by yourself if you know a few basic rules. Give it the kind of activity it wants, in the amounts and of the intensity it can handle, and it keeps running well. It breaks down when you abuse it.

To treat yourself, first you have to remove the mystique and the mumbo-jumbo language from running medicine, and get rid of the notion that you can do nothing to help yourself. You don't have to be a doctor, or know the names of the bones, muscles and tendons, or know the physiological principles behind the injury to practice effective first-aid and to keep the same thing from happening again.

Next, you have to understand in general how runners get hurt. *Runner's World* has surveyed its readers four times in the last few years. Each sample included about 1000 runners, and a consistent 60-70% of them claimed to be limited by running-related injuries in the past year. Many were hurt more than once (thus, the figures to come add up to more than 100%).

The injuries usually result from the long-term wear and tear of running instead of from sudden trauma. The 10 most common injury sites, averaged from the four surveys are:

Injured Area	% of Runners	Injured Area	% of Runners
1. Knee	25%	6. Arch	8%
2. Achilles	18%	7. Calf	7%
3. Shin	15%	8. Hip	7%
4. Ankle	11%	9. Hamstring	6%
5. Heel	10%	10. Forefoot	6%

This self-help plan tells what happens in these areas and what you can do about it without going to a doctor, spending a lot of money or losing too much running time.

Start with the simplest cures, and work by steps toward the most complicated. Chances are, you'll be healed before you get to the bottom of the list.

A saying among doctors is "if you hear hoofbeats, think first of horses, not of zebras." This means when doing diagnostic detective work, start with the obvious sources of the problem and work toward the exotic ones.

Look first at the obvious information, the most obvious being that you once were healthy and now you're hurt. You want to find the cause of the pain and eliminate it.

Doctors who don't know running are likely to tell you, "If it hurts to run, then stop running. That'll be $20." They're half-right. You should stop doing the *kind* of running that's causing the pain. But rarely do you need to stop all running—or to visit doctors. If you take care of little "horses," you may never need to worry about "zebras" with big names and complex treatments.

HOW MUCH DOES IT HURT?

When first you hurt, find out how serious the pain is by testing what you can and can't do. Define the pain, first in specific terms and then in general ones. There are degrees of pain, determined by how much it limits motion or changes running form:

• *First degree*—no limitation of motion, but low-grade pain at the start of training, decreasing as the run progresses, then reappearing after you stop.

• *Second degree*—pain remains constant or increases as runs go on, but with little effect on running form.

• *Third degree*—mild pain on easy runs, severe pain with disturbance of form on hard ones.

• *Fourth degree*—impossible to run without great pain and a pronounced limp.

Recognize that pain is a little voice inside which is there to remind you that you're pushing yourself too far. Treat pain as a friendly warning that you've somehow crossed the boundary between training and straining.

And heed the words of Dr. Richard Schuster, a noted podiatrist: "Runners should tolerate a little bit of annoyance but no more than that. I think it's a crazy habit some of our runners have, running through pain. I think you should try to run through annoyance, but don't run through pain. Pain is destruction.

WHAT TO DO FIRST?

Throw away your old training schedule and stopwatch for now, because they probably put you in the bad shape you're in. Ignore your usual training partners, because you'll either feel depressed about not being able to keep up with them, or you'll forget yourself, keep up and do further damage.

Tune in completely to your level of pain and the effect it is having on your running form:

• *First degree.* No dramatic changes in routine are required, other than a more thorough warmup. Get rid of the pain before trying anything hard.

• *Second Degree.* Eliminate the runs that cause pain to increase. These usually are races, hard speedwork and the longest training runs.

• *Third degree.* Use jog-walk "intervals." Start very slowly and cautiously. When pain builds to a form-disturbing level, walk and perhaps do some stretching exercises. Run again, walk, run, walk, etc.

• *Fourth degree.* Substitute a related activity such as walking, bicycling or swimming which causes no pain. Do it in amounts about equal to your normal running (2½ miles of walking, five miles of bicycling and a quarter-mile of swimming give about the same Aerobic benefits as a mile of running, according to Dr. Kenneth Cooper).

Work gradually toward lighter degrees of pain—fourth to third, third to second, etc. Do some careful testing once each week to see if you're ready to advance. If you had fourth-degree pain, try some jog-walk intervals. If your pain was second-degree, cautiously try a longer or faster run.

WHY DOES IT HAPPEN?

Nearly all running injuries are self-inflicted. They don't happen by accident but usually are the result of going too long, too fast or a combination of the two.

Once you're recovered enough to go back to your old schedule, look at that schedule. Weigh the stress load it imposes in an attempt to prevent the injury from happening again.

Ask yourself:

1. *How much do I run?* Our surveys indicate that 50-mile-a-week runners are nearly twice as likely to be injured as those who run 25 miles a week. Those who jump suddenly from 25 to 50 miles are prime injury candidates.

2. *How fast do I run?* Those who race are about twice as likely to get hurt as non-racers, both because of the stresses of the race and the intense training to prepare for it.

3. *How often do I run?* Everyday runners are injured more often than those who take days off during the week. Chronic fatigue leads to injuries.

Based on your answers, make permanent adjustments in your training routine if you see obvious weaknesses.

Increase training mileages and paces only gradually, and allow break-in periods when shifting from flats to hills, soft surfaces to roads, training shoes to racing spikes, etc. Mileage, for instance, probably should not climb by more than 10% a week.

Speed builds, but it also can kill. Allow plenty of recovery time after speedwork and races, and don't make a habit of running fast when you're either sore or tired from the previous day's session.

Make rest and recovery days a regular part of your program. Bill Bowerman, developer of the "hard-easy" system, says few runners can work hard more than three days a week. Spread these days out over the full week, and relax between them.

HOW DO YOU START?

You're eager to get into a run, and warming-up exercises seem to stand in the way. But this part of the session becomes more important than ever once you've been injured. Adopt a warmup routine with these features:

1. *Start with stretching and strengthening exercises* (see George Sheehan's "Magic Six" in this section). Give special attention to the weak area where you were injured.

2. *Tiptoe into the run.* There's no way of judging how a run is going to feel before it starts. You may hurt terribly on days when you thought you'd made a miracle recovery overnight, and you may loosen up completely after a crippled start. Therefore, you must learn to withhold judgment on a run until it is 10-15 minutes old. It takes that long for the pattern of the day to announce itself.

Always start, no matter how badly you think the run might go. But beyond simply vowing to start, have only the loosest of plans on what you hope to do that day, subject to change after 10-15 minutes.

Begin at a slow, careful, jogging-on-eggs shuffle. Let the kinks work themselves out without putting any strain on them. Let the day's pace find itself in the first mile or two. At that point, assess the way you feel, and make an honest decision about the run based on those feelings. Be prepared to go faster and farther than planned, to run as planned, cut back or even to abort.

3. *Stop and stretch.* Running tightens the leg muscles, and the tightness may bring pain. Mid-run stretching breaks can reverse this. A convenient, not-too-conspicuous, all-purpose exercise is the "Rodgers Stretch," named for Bill Rodgers who stopped to tie his shoes several times in the 1975 Boston Marathon.

The exercise resembles shoe-tying. Put one foot behind the other as if you're starting a sprint, then rise to straighten the back leg, trying to stretch the heel to the ground. Repeat with the other leg.

WHEN DO YOU RUN?

If you've been hurt, you're advised *not* to get the day off to a running start. Soreness usually is at its peak when you get up. You feel, as Rocky Balboa did, that you need to call a taxi to take you from the bed to the bathroom.

Dr. Richard Schuster says, "People who run in the morning are more apt to get hurt than those who run later in the day. They are physically cold and stiff in the morning. They want to get the day going, so they don't take time to warm up. But it's important for these people to warm up more than they ordinarily would."

If you insist on running early, warm up more and start slower than you normally would. If possible, be out of bed, moving around for an hour before running. This flushes much of the sleep from your head, and the stiffness and soreness from your body.

WHERE DO YOU RUN?

Conventional wisdom is that hard surfaces are bad, soft ones are good. Injuries happen because we pound ourselves too much, most runners believe.

Hard surfaces do give us a pounding. But this in most cases leads only to temporary discomfort, not to injury or the aggravation of injury. Surprisingly, our surveys show no significant difference in injury rates between those who run on hard and soft surfaces.

If injured, some runners prefer to run on a hard surface—not because they enjoy the pounding but because they like the smoothness. Hard surfaces like roads are almost always smooth.

Soft running places like grass produce less shock. But the trade-off is that they also are uneven. The feet constantly are twisting to compensate for it, and the heels sink in more than normal. So the legs get an extra up-and-down and side-to-side workout which they don't need if they're prone to injury.

Dr. Richard Schuster says, "Running on a smooth dirt road would be best. Paths are full of holes. Grass is bad because it hides the irregularities."

Hills can be an injury-producer, too. The three main areas of injury are knees, achilles tendons and shins. Uphill running puts extra stretch and strain on the achilles. Downhills multiply the shock to knees and shins.

WHAT DO YOU WEAR?

Runners share a dream that someday, somewhere, somehow we'll find the perfect shoe. It will make the foot feel like it is swaddled in a protective cocoon which transmits no shock, gives no irritation and yet is as flexible as being barefoot.

The more a runner hurts, the more he chases this dream—from one shoe store to the next. The promise of perfection in the next model is what keeps more than a dozen running shoemakers in business.

Sore runners are brand-jumpers. Manufacturers can't count on our loyalty, because as soon as we find that one shoe doesn't do what we thought it should, we switch. We keep switching, because no shoe can be as perfect as we want it.

The points here are, first, buy best shoes for your needs and, second, throw them away before they hurt you.

Shoe modifications might help, too. Dr. Schuster recommends heel lifts as a preventive for many injuries. These relieve pressure on the backs of the legs, which often are tight in runners. Other running doctors prescribe homemade heel wedges to reduce side-to-side motion. Arch supports help control excessive motion of the forefoot.

WHAT CAN YOU TAKE?

Whenever a runner is hurt enough that he can't run normally, he is prey to all sorts of missionaries and salesmen. He wants a quick cure and is willing to change lifelong habits or to pay for it. The longer he stays hurt, the more of a straw-grabber he becomes, and salesmen have him in their pocket.

Runners generally are not drug-takers. We may even resist taking aspirin. But when we're hurt, we may gobble aspirin to put down inflammation and pain. Dr. Joan Ullyot recommended it in *Women's Running*. And a reader recently commented, "I've discovered that two aspirin taken about an hour before a run does more for me than three visits to a podiatrist. Namely, it allows me to run pain-free." Dr. George Sheehan answered, "I see no reason why you shouldn't do it."

You may have taken perverse pleasure in flaunting your Vitamin J (junkfood) habit but suddenly are looking into vegetarian and natural-foods diets, and exotic supplements in hopes of finding a quick cure.

You hear that achilles tendonitis is related to high uric acid levels, which are related to eating lots of rich, meaty foods. Maybe if you cut out meat.... But you still need plenty of protein to repair the tissues being pounded during your runs. You read of protein supplements. Maybe if you started taking a few of those....

A doctor in southern California says he's found a direct correlation between deterioration of the tendons and a clogging of the arteries. Maybe you need to go on a strict low-cholesterol diet....

If none of this works, maybe you should see a doctor for a cortisone shot. Or maybe you should consider tendon-lengthening surgery....

Whoa! Your imagination is running away. You are hearing the hoofbeats of zebras and setting out on a wild chase after them. There are plenty of horses to track down first, and they're much easier to catch.

25

Magic Six Exercises

Stretch and strengthen the muscles to keep injuries away

George Sheehan, M.D.

I f you want to run a marathon, you must train the Magic Six (miles a day). If you are looking for that natural high distance runners talk about, you must do the same, And if you would prefer to die of something other than a heart attack, the daily six miles is the physiological magic.

But know this: Disaster will pursue you to the very gates of this heaven unless you do another Magic Six. These are the Magic Six exercises designed to counteract the bad effects of this daily training—the muscle imbalance that contributes to the overuse syndromes of the foot, leg, knee and low back. Without this Magic Six, you will soon become an ex-runner, no longer able to accept 5000 footstrikes an hour on a hard, flat surface with a foot constructed for sand or dirt.

Training overdevelops the prime movers—those muscles along the back of the leg and thigh and low back become short and inflexible. The antagonists—the muscles on the front of the leg and thigh and abdomen—become relatively weak. The Magic Six are necessary to correct this strength/flexibility imbalance: three to stretch and three to strengthen.

1. The first stretching exercise is the *wall pushup* for the calf muscles. Stand flat-footed about three feet from the wall. Lean in until it hurts, keeping the knees locked, the legs straight and the feet flat. Count "one elephant, two elephants," etc. Hold for 10 elephants. Relax. Repeat for one minute.

2. The second is the *hamstring stretch.* Put your straight leg with knee locked on a footstool, later a chair, finally a table as you improve. Keep the other leg straight with knee locked. Bring your head toward

the knee of the extended leg until it hurts. Hold for 10 elephants. Relax. Repeat for one minute, then do the same exercise with the other leg.

3. The final stretching exercise is the *backover* for the hamstrings and low back. Lie on the floor. Bring straight legs over your head and try to touch the floor with your toes until it hurts. Hold for 10 elephants. Relax by bringing your knees to your ears for 10 elephants. Repeat stretch and relax periods for one minute.

4. The first strengthening exercise is for the *shin muscles*. Sit on a table with the legs hanging down. Put a 3-5-pound weight over the toes. Flex foot at ankle. Hold for six elephants. Relax. Repeat for one minute with each leg.

5. The second is for the *quadriceps* (*thigh muscles*). Assume the same position with the weight. This time, straighten the leg, locking the knee. Hold for six elephants. Relax. Repeat for one minute then do the same with the other leg.

6. The final exercise is the *bent-leg situp*. Lie on the floor with your knees bent and your feet close to your buttocks. Come to a sitting position. Lie back. Repeat until you can't do any more or have reached 20.

It takes a little over six minutes to do the Magic Six. Done before and after running, this means just 12 minutes a day to keep you in muscle balance.

1

2

3

4

5

6

26

Clayton's Inner Workings

The fastest marathoner goes to the lab to see why he runs so well

David Costill, Ph.D.

What unique physical qualities does Derek Clayton have that enable him to run at less than five minutes per mile for over two hours? Based on our initial research with marathon runners in 1968, we could only estimate the physiological responses during such a performance. Our estimates suggested that Derek would have to possess circulatory and respiratory capabilities greater than any runner we had previously examined.

In 1970, arrangements were made for Derek to undergo an extensive series of clinical and exertional tests in our laboratory at Ball State University, Muncie, Ind. He was not in his world-record form at the time of these tests, as evidenced by his 2:21 marathon in Czechoslovakia four days before his visit. However, our previous research with trained distance runners has shown that there is very little change in one's physiological endurance (maximal oxygen consumption) with variations in performance. Consequently, the results of our tests are probably representative of his physiological limits at the time of his 2:08:33 marathon.

On the first morning of his visit, blood samples were drawn, pulmonary function (respiratory) tests were administered and a series of chest x-rays were taken. All of the 23 analyses made on blood were within normal limits, with the exception that his white blood cell count was abnormally low. After some discussion with Derek, it was concluded that this value was probably a response to the antibiotics administered during a recent pneumonial infection.

His respiratory function tests were superior to the normal 27-year-old male, but not unusual to a distance runner. X-ray examination of his chest revealed an enlarged right ventricle, which is quite common among endurance athletes. Derek's electrocardiogram (EKG) supported the evidence of an enlarged heart. From his EKG, we recorded a resting heart rate of 35 beats per minute. While this value is low even for a distance runner, it is not the lowest rate we have recorded. Hal Higdon had a standing heart rate of 32 beats per minute.

During the next three days, Derek performed numerous submaximal and maximal runs on the treadmill. The purpose of these tests was to assess his physiological responses to varied running speeds and to determine the functional limits of his cardio-respiratory system. Our previous research with marathon runners suggested a direct relationship between one's maximal ability to consume oxygen (aerobic capacity) and distance running performance. In 1968, we measured the aerobic capacity of such runners as Amby Burfoot, Ron Daws, Lou Castagnola, Tom Osler, Hal Higdon and others. The values for these men ranged from 69-76 milliliters of oxygen per kilogram of body weight per minute.

To our surprise, Derek's maximal oxygen consumption was 69.7 ml./kg.-min. Therefore, his running success cannot be explained totally in terms of circulatory or respiratory superiority. However, we should point out that we were amazed at the speed of running he could tolerate with great ease. During the maximal treadmill test, he was able to run an 8:32 two-mile despite being hampered by our respiratory apparatus. We had never examined a runner capable of such a performance.

The physiological explanation for Derek's success seems to be based on his tolerance for exhaustive work and an economical running style. At every running speed, he uses less energy than any other runner we have examined. As an example, at 5:15 per mile Derek requires about 9.5% less energy than the average marathon runner. When magnified by the duration of a marathon race, it is easy to see that he certainly has an advantage.

During a marathon race, most runners utilize about 75% of their oxygen capacity. However, some runners seem to be able to tolerate greater intensity of exertion. Ted Corbitt and Jim McDonagh both employ about 85% of their capacities during marathon competition. During one of our tests, we asked Derek to perform a 30-minute run at 4:56-4:59 per mile, which he did with considerable ease. At that pace, he employed about 85% of his aerobic capacity with a heart rate of 167 beats per minute and very little blood lactic acid accumulation. Derek's maximal heart rate is 188 beats per minute which was recorded during a run to exhaustion. It is logical, therefore, to assume that Derek's 2:08:33 performance was well within his physiological capabilities.

Based on our studies with Derek, it would appear that his success is only moderately dependent upon physiological superiority. It is difficult to explain his ability to utilize a greater part of his aerobic capacity than most other runners, unless we attribute this advantage to his highly intense training program. In the future, we hope to examine more runners of varied abilities to help isolate the factors that determine success and failure among distance runners.

27

Monitoring a Marathoner

Ron Daws wears an electronic backpack
to test a heart under stress

Joan Ullyot, M.D.

Many participants in a California marathon were startled to be lapped by what appeared to be a wind-up runner, wearing on his back a small black box adorned with a large key and numerous wires. Some people grumbled that it was "no fair to be outrun by a robot." Others wondered if this was some device that could be wound up to give an extra kick at 20 miles and wished they could obtain something similar for their own use.

Now that the results are in, the truth can be told. The mysterious-looking black box with its attached wires was actually a miniature electrocardiograph (EKG) recorder, worn by Minnesotan Ron Daws as part of a scientific experiment conducted by the Institute of Health Research at Pacific Medical Center in San Francisco.

In my capacity of doctor-physiologist at the Institute, I supervised the cardiac monitoring and biochemical testing. However, the original impetus for this experiment came from my husband, Dan Ullyot, a heart surgeon and fun-runner. He was impressed by the fast pace maintained by sub-2:30 marathoners and speculated that the load on the heart during an actual competition must be enormous, enough to strain any "normal" heart (as judged by conventional standards).

More specifically, in Dan's words, "My interest was whether the trained runner might show electrocardiographic signs of ischemia (lack of sufficient blood flow to the heart itself) during severe exertion such as marathon running. The EKG changes seen in coronary patients during exercise EKG (treadmill) tests are detected within a few minutes, usually when a near-maximal heart rate is achieved."

This, Dan says, "reflects a situation in which the demand for oxygen by the heart muscle is not met by the blood flow to the heart because of narrowing of the coronary arteries by atherosclerosis. The questions raised is: Can an athlete push himself to the point where the demands of his heart muscle exceed the capacity of his own (presumably normal) coronary circulation?"

Since the Institute of Health Research is involved in defining precisely what constitues "normal" and "super-normal" physiology and body chemistry, we decided to try to measure both the heart rate and the adequacy of blood flow to the heart during a marathon, using recently developed compact EKG equipment. Although exercise physiologists have studied the behavior of the heart during moderately long treadmill runs at sub-2:30 marathon pace, we believed that the stress of competition and the longer run would demand a greater effort than a treadmill experiment. It might therefore give significantly different results.

The guinea pig for this experiment had to be a fast marathoner who would agree to run hard—hopefully at full pace—in the interest of science rather than glory, since he would be handicapped by the monitoring equipment.

We were fortunate enough to enlist the services of 1968 Olympian Daws, who was persuaded to leave the grim and wintry weather of Minnesota to come run in sunny California for a few days. Unfortunately, it didn't work out quite that way in the end, since the Minnesota spring thaw started in February that year, while the San Franciso area suffered an unprecedented rainy spell which made pre-marathon workouts very soggy and chilly.

The unexpected weather was in keeping with the rest of the experiment, no part of which went exactly as planned. Rule number one for researchers should be to remain flexible.

Obtaining suitable monitoring equipment was far more complicated than we had anticipated. The original thought was to use a small, battery-powered, portable EKG broadcasting unit about the size of a cigarette case. This system, called telemetry, has been used fairly successfully to monitor sprinters on a track, but suffers from two drawbacks:

First, the range is very short, only about 100 yards, while the receiving equipment requires a 220-volt outlet and thus cannot be carried along in a car.

Second, the muscular interference with the EKG signals is enormous, even when patients at bedrest are monitored in this way.

So we next considered using a portable "Holter monitor," a self-contained unit which records EKG signals on a 12-hour magnetic tape for later playback. A 10-minute trial run on a treadmill with this bulky contraption (3 x 6 x 8 inches, several pounds) convinced me that to carry it for 26 miles would be idiotic as well as highly uncomfortable. After toying with the idea of carrying it on a bicycle and using special long chest leads to our runner, we were relieved to learn of the existence of a similar but much smaller unit (3 x 5 x 1½ inches, one pound), which could still record continuously for up to four hours.

This was obviously exactly what we needed, but our budget was too small to allow us to purchase the unit ($2500), and we couldn't borrow either of the two which had been sold in northern California. We eventually contacted the manufacturer in Los Angeles, who graciously agreed to loan us a monitor for the race, and promised to send it up by Wednesday before the race so we could try it out in advance.

On Tuesday, Ron Daws arrived right on schedule, but there was no little black box waiting for us at the lab the next day. After many frantic phone calls to the elusive sales representative in L.A. over the next few days, we were told that we could rent the monitor, not borrow it, and would have to fly a technician down to L.A. to pick it up. On these terms, we finally got possession of the crucial EKG recorder on Saturday evening before the race.

Late Saturday night, armed with the monitor and one four-hour reel of tape, we had to figure out the best way to carry it on the run. Ron finally taped it securely onto the back of his web belt, padding both the belt and box with half-inch thick foam rubber to reduce chafing.

My husband was intrigued by the miniature monitoring equipment. Being far more experienced with such devices than I, he was dubious about the ability of the tape to hold the three electrodes (leads) securely for 26 + miles, and suggested using stitched-on or "needle" electrodes for greater security. Ron blanched a bit at this. He was mentally reconciled to giving blood, but had not anticipated minor surgery. Fortunately for him, the only electrodes supplied with the kit are disc type that are taped on, and we had no choice.

Early Sunday morning, we set out for the marathon in Burlingame, a half-hour south of San Francisco. Ron occupied himself during the trip by fashioning a large cardboard key for the black box and labeling the whole sinister-looking apparatus "Vergeltunswaffen," after Hitler's secret World War II weapon. I was far more nervous than he appeared, and I kept mentally reviewing the proper electrode placement, which was color-coded: green for ground, on the upper sternum (breast bone), white on the lower sternum, and red at the apex of the heart, on the left side of the chest. It was this red lead that I feared would be the least stable, since the constant muscular movement is much stronger there than over the sternum. The red lead was necessary to give a good view of the "S-T segments" of the EKG pattern, which would show evidence of any inadequacy in blood flow to the heart.

When we were getting organized in the gym, I fastened this lead on especially hard with two wide strips of tape and kept my fingers crossed. I also prepared the skin under the round, flat leads with abrasive electrode paste and alcohol, and used a generous dab of special conductive jelly in the middle of each lead. The three attached wires were then brought over Ron's left shoulder, taped together, pinned to his shirt, and finally plugged into the little recorder. I flicked the switch on and taped it down in that position 10 minutes before the race started, so we recorded warmup and pre-race excitement as well as the actual racing EKG.

The marathon was run on a flat, five-lap course, on a cool day with only moderate wind and a sprinkle of rain. Despite the extra load of the belt, monitor and wire, Ron finished fourth in 2:26:58, several minutes faster than we had hoped for with that handicap. Afterward, he maintained that the apparatus hadn't really bothered him much— just a little chaffing. The red lead, however, had done just what I had feared, coming loose somewhere around 12 miles. It couldn't be reattached securely with new tape till Ron finished the race.

We left on the recorder to register the recovery period for 1½ hours, and also took several more blood samples at intervals.

Decoding the EKG results took some time. The small magnetic tape in the portable monitor records the electrical activity of the heart on three input channels (one for ground). These signals must then be converted into a readable EKG by a special "scanner," a large machine which incorporates a tape playback device, oscilloscope and conventional EKG machine. Despite my attempt to be selective when scanning, I soon accumulated yards of paper EKG strips all over the floor. When the scanning was finished, I was delighted to find that we had picked up the heart rate continuously during the marathon, despite increasing interference caused by sweating and the subsequent loosening of the red lead.

The results of the experiment were just as interesting as we had hoped. That running a marathon is hard work will come as no surprise to anyone who has tried it. But the magnitude of the effort involved, as determined by the performance of the heart, was quite phenomenal.

At the start of the marathon, Ron's heart rate zipped up immediately to the range of 177-180 and stayed right there for almost 2½ hours. This is close to 95% of his maximum heart rate of 187 (as determined by an exhaustive treadmill run), and represents a much greater prolonged effort than has been considered possible by most physiologists. Heart rate roughly parallels both cardiac output and oxygen consumption, which were thus also about 95% of maximum. In Ron's case, this corresponds to an oxygen consumption of over 70 milliliters per kilogram per minute for the duration of the run.

Recovery from this prolonged hard work was very fast. During the five seconds it took to reattach the red lead after the race, Ron's pulse dropped from 180 to 150. (This illustrates the hazards of trying to estimate heart rate during exercise by taking one's pulse right after stopping.) Two minutes later it was back under 100. However, the rate then persisted between 80 and 100 for the next 1½ hours of monitoring. Since Ron's resting pulse is around 40, this elevation may reflect continued repayment of oxygen debt incurred during the race.

Does the sustained massive effort of a marathon strain the heart? This question cannot be answered fully from our data, since the S-T segments of the EKG were only readable for the first 5-10 miles. However, since Ron's pace and pulse remained steady throughout the marathon, this initial portion is probably representative of the whole. Reassuringly, there was no evidence of heart strain or ischemia (lack of blood supply) despite the extremely high rate and consequent shortened diastole—the phase of the heart cycle when two-thirds of blood flow to the heart muscle occurs. It thus appears that a well-conditioned heart, despite its greater weight, thicker muscular wall and larger stroke volume, must be richly supplied with blood even during strenuous exercise.

Analysis of numerous blood samples showed no significant differences between the baseline and post-marathon values, except for a small decrease in fat content (to be expected four hours after breakfast) and a temporary doubling of the white blood cell count, a well-documented exercise effect which reflects the increased blood flow.

Interestingly, all the samples showed higher values than "normal" for nitrogen and certain serum enzymes. These particular blood tests—like the typical runner's slow pulse, high voltage EKG and (frequently) a soft heart murmur—might alarm any physician unfamiliar with the physiological peculiarities of runners.

Part 6
Eating Up the Miles

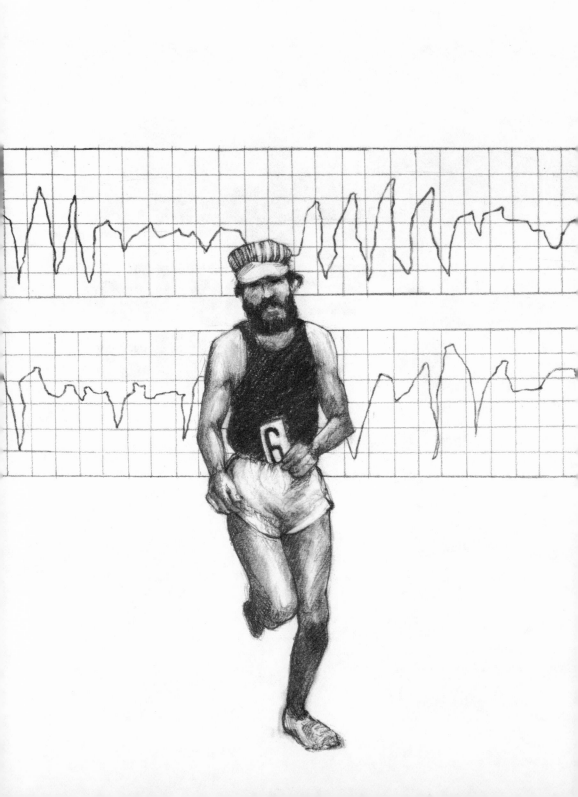

28

Live Like a Marathoner

Run like one, eat like one,
and your heart will thank you

Thomas Bassler, M.D.

True fitness should prolong life. The medical literature contains studies on the Masai warriors, Tarahumara Indians, cross-country skiers and marathon runners which show that immunity to heart disease is associated with physical fitness. But to avoid the criticism of drawing premature conclusions, these scientists write that this protection is "associated" with fitness, not that it is caused by it. However, it probably safe to say that the *life-style* can increase the *life-span*, and the ability to cover 42 kilometers on foot is a good index of one's life-style.

The American Medical Joggers Association (AMJA) continues to review causes of death among marathoners, and no heart attacks have been documented. No cases of coronary heart disease have been observed in the runners while they are active. This does not mean that this protection is permanent, since we have seen some deterioration of the heart when the running is stopped and the life-style includes risk factors such as smoking.

One thing is certain: When a middle-aged sportsman chooses an activity to build up his speed or strength, the AMJA sees no decrease in the numbers of heart attacks in this group. In fact, I consider such activities as weight lifting as a "risk factor," since I feel they actually *increase* the chances of heart attack.

Professor Morris of the London School of Hygiene reported in the journal *Lancet* that vigorous exercise must exceed a "threshold" of 30 minutes to count at all, and it must go beyond an hour to be beneficial. Runners will recognize these times as the "protection of the 10-kilometer men."

The speed and strength events are over in a few seconds or minutes—far below the protective threshold of 30 minutes. And the life-style of these athletes is significantly different from the marathoner's.

"Live like a marathoner so you can run like one." This motto motivates more cardiac patients than the usual admonitions about smoking, diet and exercise from a physician who doesn't follow his own advice. Part of the patient's failure is due to the bad example set by the doctor. AMJA encourages physicians to correct their own life-styles first and then offer fitness advice to their patients. We are seeing effects of this approach now. Cardiac patients are showing up at marathon runs after recovering from heart attacks.

Dr. Jack Scaff designed the Honolulu Marathon for patients who can go the distance. Cardiologists tell each patient how fast to run. Otherwise, these men are sportsmen wearing track uniforms and running 42 kilometers for a special trophy. Several dozen heart patients enter the race each December.

One need not be a cardiac patient to experience tangible benefits from marathoning, of course. I advise everyone to try it. The maximum treadmill stress-test (MTST) will detect those who need the guidance of a cardiologist. Anyone who passes their MTST can join a track club for distance runners. Along with companionship, the beginner picks up advice on the proper running gear, realistic goals, injuries and diet. By copying the habits of successful runners, the beginner gradually adopts what I call the "marathoner's life-style."

All distance runners dislike smoking (and smokers?). They avoid highly refined (processed) foods such as distilled alcohol, sucrose, starch and the saturated (hydrogenated or "hardened") fats. They like fresh fruits and raw vegetables. Fish gradually replaces beef in their diet.

I advise all runners to follow three dietary rules:

1. *One gram of ascorbic acid for each six miles.* Adequate vitamin C is important if the joints and ligaments are going to adjust to heavy mileage. This is most noticeable for runners over 40 years of age who try running over 40 miles per week. Good shoes, proper rest and sensible training schedules are important, too, but with inadequate vitamin C I think runners experience increased collagen injuries (non-traumatic). The "stress syndrome" which strikes three days after a full effort race may also be due to low ascorbic acid. If a runner can eat one orange or the equivalent for each mile, he doesn't need extra vitamin C.

2. *Natural B-complex is necessary for the rapid utilization of carbohydrates during the first six miles.* If the runner complains of fatigue in the early part of the workout, I ask about foods rich in B-complex. Often one week on extra yeast, wheat germ and yogurt puts the spring back in his step. Too much refined carbohydrate can interfere with training.

3. *Unsaturated fat supplies about 75% of the energy during the second hour of running.* Fatigue during this part of the workout suggests that the diet contains too much saturated fat. Beef is often the big problem here. This probably explains the popularity of "soft" peanut butter, wheat germ oil and fish among runners.

Runners can use their training mileage as an index of the safety of their diet when they are cutting calories to lose weight. Even fasting is safe as long as the training runs are enjoyable. Resistant obesity hinders some individuals until they have taken the polyunsaturates long enough to "unsaturate" part of their own body fat. Then the fat is available for energy and they can diet and lose weight without becoming too weak to run. This takes only a few weeks for runners who have reached 12 miles in training but many weeks for those still under six miles.

The health benefits of the marathoning life-style will become evident as larger numbers take up the sport. Diseases which account for two-thirds of the deaths in the average population are not expected to show up in those who are actively marathoning. I do not expect to see distance runners die from heart attack, cancer of the lungs, emphysema, cirrhosis of the liver or stroke due to hardening of the arteries. All of these diseases require a life-style that would interfere with racing performances.

If these diseases are not seen, I would expect the life-span to be longer. That is true "fitness". . . . less disease and a longer life!

29

Fuel for the Long Run

Marathoners burn carbohydrates first, then later rely on fats

Alan Claremont, Ph.D.

Despite well-established findings on the specific role of protein, carbohydrates and fat in supplying energy needs for endurance performance, misconceptions still persist that require further clarification.

Articles in *Runner's World* that are reprinted in this book have described the physiologic effects, advantages and disadvantages of manipulating dietary and fluid intake in efforts to achieve optimal performances. This article complements these reports, and attempts to promote further understanding of how and to what extent food stores in the body are mobilized to meet the energy requirements of distance running.

Athletes can readily identify with energy output in relation to pace and duration of running—e.g., six-minute miles for two hours. Fatigue, and eventual decrease in performance capacity, is also well understood subjectively. Thus, it appeared practical to equate and discuss energy requirements (kilocalories) under the readily appreciated terms of pace and time. The table presents caloric demands for selected events from one through 26.22 miles.

It is necessary here to briefly review the dietary significance of protein, carbohydrates and fats. Traditionally, protein has been considered important to replace "substance" of the muscle used up. However, at rest and during exercise, muscle protein contributes less than 1% of the body's caloric requirements. Increased proportions are not required in a training diet unless an increase in muscle mass is desirable. Since muscle mass, per se, is not central to endurance performance success, the primary "substrates" become carbohydrates and fats. Important considerations for the athlete are:

- What is the extent of carbohydrate and fat utilization?
- What effect does their availability have on performance?

The table lists predicted energy requirements for running specified distances at world-class times by a 70-kilogram (154-pound) runner. Metabolic costs of these runs are expressed both in units of oxygen consumption and in kilocalories. Provided that performance intensities are comparable in percentage of maximal oxygen consumption, similar tables for slower running times would provide the same interpretations of energy interrelationships as this example.

Observe that there is only a 20.5% decrease in running speed (from 4:00 to 5:02 per mile) as the distance increases from one to 26.2 miles. Work intensity remains very high up to and including the marathon. The preferred fuel for maintaining the fastest running speeds is carbohydrates or glycogen.

As distance increases and the event becomes more aerobic, fats are increasingly mobilized and burned. However, world class running requires performance at a high percentage of maximal oxygen uptake. Thus, glycogen *remains* the premium fuel, and available stores become an increasingly important factor influencing the ability to sustain fast pace in excess of 60 minutes.

Measurement of muscle glycogen content from muscle biopsies has indicated that during exercise demanding 75-85% of maximal oxygen uptake, stores are sufficient for approximately 1½-2 hours of activity. An estimated 645-690 grams of available glycogen contained in the muscle, liver, extra-cellular fluid and blood of our runner would last for slightly less than two hours—or less than marathon times.

Fortunately, it is possible to avoid the sudden and marked decrease in performance capacity that occurs when carbohydrates are no longer available. As running continues, fats contribute increasingly to the energy fuel. Better-conditioned athletes are able to derive a larger proportion of their energy requirements from fats, which also extends the time glycogen stores can contribute to the performance. The advantage is in being able to sustain a faster average pace, since it has been shown experimentally that when glycogen concentrations approached zero, running speed was reduced. The sooner this occurred, the sooner running was impaired.

The "premium" fuel for optimum performance in endurance running is derived from combustion of carbohydrates. Fats become an increasingly important energy source with continuing activity, in addition to prolonging the availability of carbohydrates. Energy derived from protein is minimal and can be discarded from practical consideration.

Although it is desirable to enhance muscle glycogen content—especially for distances where depletion of stores can become a major limitation to performance—associated health risks and lack of information concerning long-term effects of repetitive super-compensation ("carbohydrate-loading") underline the necessity for careful personal evaluation of these procedures. In this regard, the value of a safe, uncomplicated, balanced diet with emphasis on carbohydrate intake remains undimished.

PREDICTED ENERGY COSTS

Event (Miles)	Time (/mile)	Speed (m.p.h.)	Total Time	Oxygen Needs (ml/kg * liters)		Kilocalories** (/min. total)		Intensity (%max. VO2)
1	4:00	15.0	4:00	77.8	5.5	27.2	109	105%
3	4:20	13.9	13:00	72.7	5.01	25.4	330	98%
6	4:30	13.3	27:00	70.3	4.9	24.6	664	95%
10	4:41	12.8	46:50	67.6	4.7	23.7	1114	91%
15	4:52	12.3	1:13:00	65.5	4.6	22.9	1674	88.5%
26.2	5:02	11.9	2:11:52	63.5	4.4	22.2	2924	86%

*Runner weighing 70 kilograms (154 pounds); maximal oxygen uptake 74 milliliters per kilogram per minute.

**Assume caloric equivalent of 1.0 liter = 5 kilocalories.

REFERENCES

1. Astrand, P.O. and K. Rodahl. "Nutrition and Physical Performance" in *Textbook of Work Physiology*, Ch. 14, McGraw-Hill Inc., 1970.
2. Bergstrom, J. and E. Hultman. "Nutrition for Maximal Sports Performance," *JAMA* 221 (9): 99-1006, 1972.
3. Lewis, S. and B. Gutin. "Nutrition and Endurance," *Amer. J. Clin. Nutrition*, 26: 1011-1014, Sept. 1973.
4. Londeree, B. "Pre-Event Diet Routine," *Runner's World*, 9: 26-29, July 1974.
5. Van Handel, P. "Drinks for the Road," *Runner's World*, 29-31, July 1974.

30

Eating Away the Minutes

Tests show that carbohydrate-loading may save runners 6-11 minutes

Paul Slovic

For years, discussions about the influence of diet upon athlete performance tended to emphasize the benefits of protein and vitamins. However, few if any of the enthusiastic claims for these substances have been confirmed by scientific tests. Thus, it was rather surprising when highly respected Swedish physiologists described a diet whose proven effect on endurance surpassed even the wildest claims of the health-food huckster.

The Swedish diet originated with the discovery that endurance was directly related to the amount of glycogen stored in the muscles. It was observed that depleting the muscle-glycogen stores by means of exercise and a low-carbohydrate diet would enhance the resynthesis of glycogen and produce stores as much as 100% above normal levels once carbohydrate ingestion was resumed. This increase in stored glycogen was accompanied by a comparable increase in the amount of time an individual could exercise before succumbing to exhaustion during laboratory tests.

The implications of this work for endurance athletes were quickly noted. Physiologist Per-Olof Astrand advised such athletes to exercise to exhaustion one week prior to their event, then keep the glycogen content of the muscles low by consuming a low-carbohydrate diet for three days. Thereafter, a high-carbohydrate diet was recommended until the competition. This diet has come to be known as the "glycogen-overload" or "super-compensation" diet—the latter term arising from the enhanced storage capacity of muscles initially depleted of glycogen.

The basic laboratory work and Astrand's recommendations were published in scientific journals in 1967. This work has since been widely publicized in *Runner's World* and other periodicals devoted to running. As a result, the practice of glycogen loading is increasingly popular among long-distance runners. A survey of runners in the 1974 Trail's End Marathon indicated that 50% of the respondents who finished in three hours or less had followed this diet.

Given the popularity of the glycogen-loading diet, it seems natural to ask what its effect is likely to be upon the performance of the distance runner—particulary the marathoner. In other words, how does increased endurance on the laboratory bicycle translate into minutes saved in the marathon?

To my knowledge, only two studies have addressed this basic question—one by Karlsson and Saltin (*Journal of Applied Physiology,* 1971, Vol. 31, pp. 129-139), the other by myself.

Karlsson and Saltin tested 10 distance runners of varying ability in two 30-kilometer races, three weeks apart. Before the first run, half the subjects ate a normal mixed diet, while the others overloaded with carbohydrates as outlined above, under direct supervision of the researchers. In the second run, the two groups were reversed.

The effects on performance were impressive. Every runner ran faster after the special diet, the mean improvement being 7.7 minutes. The range of improvement was from one minute (two subjects) to 16 minutes (two subjects.) Times for the first third of the run were about equal for both conditions, but thereafter the carbohydrate-loaders maintained their pace while the non-loaders slowed by up to 16 minutes as compared with their other performances.

My own study was based upon questionnaires distributed to participants in the Trail's End Marathons held at Seaside, Ore., in 1973 and '74. One question in the 1974 survey pertained to diet. From responses to this question, runners were grouped into three categor-ies: (a) *non-loaders*, (b) *partial-loaders* who increased their carbohy-drate intake prior to the marathon, but did not follow the full low-car-bohydrate (depletion)/high-carbohydrate sequence and (c) *full glyco-gen-loaders* who followed the complete sequence.

There were 181 survey respondents (out of 322 finishers)—98 were non-loaders, 27 partial-loaders and 56 full-loaders. The fastest re-spondent finished in about 2:16. The slowest spent more than 4½ hours on the course. The average respondent finished in about 3¼ hours.

On the average, the glycogen-loaders finished considerably faster than the non-loaders (2:57:18 compared with 3:23:12). However, the "loaders" also trained harder, had more experience with marathoning and were somewhat faster in the mile. These factors, rather than diet, may have determined their superior performance. Also, the loaders may have been more highly motivated to achieve a fast time.

In order to properly assess the effect of diet, a method for controlling training, ability and motivation had to be employed. This was done by using the 1973 and '74 survey data to develop equations to predict final time. These equations took account of the training, background and ability factors on which the loaders and non-loaders differed. The effects of diet were then estimated by comparing glycogen-loaders with non-loaders who had the same predicted times, according to the equations.

These calculations were used to control training and ability. Despite marked differences between the design of this study and that of Karlsson and Saltin, the 6-11½-minute improvement is close to their 7.7-minute effect over 30 kilometers.

Another similarity between the two studies is that diet made little or no difference over the first half of the run, but was associated with marked changes in performance over the last quarter of the course. The difference between studies is that this "last-quarter" effect began earlier for Karlsson's and Saltin's subjects who were running a shorter race at a faster pace. The marathon runners showed little effects of diet prior to the 20-mile point.

The improvements in performance demonstrated thus far almost guarantee the widespread use of glycogen-loading by endurance athletes. However, the effects of this diet may not be entirely beneficial. Investigation of possible adverse effects certainly seems warranted.

31

Principles of Loading

Diet juggling has benefits, but also be aware of its risks

Ben Londeree, Ph.D.

To super-compensate or not, that is the question. Exercise physiologists have established that performance in long-distance events can be significantly enhanced by storing extra glycogen in the appropriate muscles through diet and activity modification. On the other hand, several comments and letters have appeared in the *Journal of the American Medical Association* and *Runner's World* reporting the deleterious side-effects resulting from indiscriminant glycogen super-compensation.

It is time to clear the air and set the record straight. Can performance be improved by super-compensation? Can reckless tampering with the body chemistry be equated with playing with dynamite? Can glycogen super-compensation be practiced safely? The answer to all three questions is, generally, yes.

There are a number of principles that must be followed to experience success with super-compensation. The adverse results come from violation of one of more of the principles.

Principle 1: During prolonged heavy exercise, the carbohydrate stores are gradually depleted. Energy for exercise is derived almost entirely from fats and carbohydrates. Whereas the supply of fats is virtually inexhaustible, carbohydrates, due to volume requirements, are stored in limited quantities.

Principle 2: Absorption of carbohydrates from the blood in the form of glucose (obtained from the liver and intestines) does not occur at a rate that can sustain high-intensity exercise. Only about 50 grams of glucose can be absorbed from the intestines per hour, so the use of glucose-electrolyte drinks during the race serves only to retard glycogen depletion (50 grams of glucose probably is enough to supply only 20-30% of the carbohydrate needs during one hour of competitive running).

Principle 3: Depletion of carbohydrates leaves only fats available for energy, with the result that the intensity of activity must be reduced considerably (1-3 minutes per mile). Optimal performance requires that the runner avoid depletion during competition. Perhaps related to glycogen utilization is the fact that potassium also is lost from the muscle cells.

Principle 4: The rate of glycogen depletion is a function of the relative intensity (percent of maximal oxygen consumption). Below an intensity representing 50% of maximal oxygen consumption, about 50% of the energy is derived from fat. At higher intensities, an increasing proportion of the energy is obtained from carbohydrates. This means that glycogen depletion can be delayed by reducing the speed.

Principle 5: The time to exhaustion and glycogen depletion is directly related to the initial concentration of glycogen in the muscles. In other words, with higher beginning muscle glycogen levels, an individual can work at a particular intensity of exercise for a longer period of time.

Principle 6: In order to bring about glycogen super-compensation, the body first must be stimulated to synthesize extra glycogen-storing enzyme through depletion of the present supply of glycogen. A high-carbohydrate diet without prior glycogen depletion will not produce super-compensation.

Principle 7: Whereas liver glycogen is readily depleted by starvation, a low-carbohydrate diet and/or prolonged exercise, the only way to deplete muscle glycogen is through exercise. Carbohydrate cannot escape once inside of a muscle fiber.

Principle 8: Depletion of muscle glycogen stores occurs only in the active muscle fibers. Consequently, a significant amount of the depletion activity must be identical with the activity for which the individual is preparing.

Principle 9: The greater the glycogen depletion, the greater the stimulation for the synthesis of glycogen-storing enzyme will be. This, in turn, will increase the potential for super-compensation.

Principle 10: The longer the depletion is maintained, the greater the stimulation for the synthesis of glycogen-storing enzyme will be. As above, this increases the potential for super-compensation.

Principle 11: Depletion can be maintained with a low-carbohydrate diet and continued training. In fact, such an approach will make it less necessary for complete initial depletion via exhaustive exercise and thereby reduce the risk of incurring fatigue injuries. On the other hand, any major modification of the diet will produce considerable stress upon homeostasis, and the hazards may outweigh the advantages. This would be an even more important concern for individuals with health problems. After age 30-35, the ability of the body's metabolism to adjust to dietary changes declines in many persons.

In addition, failure to eat a balanced diet may lead to deficiencies of some vitamins (particularly water-soluble vitamins) and minerals, and may call for some dietary supplementation. While in the glycogen-depleted state, the general weakened condition may make the individual more susceptible to infection and injury.

Principle 12: A small amount of carbohydrate (about 60 grams per day) is essential for adequate functioning of several important systems in the body—e.g., the nervous system, red blood cells and kidneys. Reliance upon fats for energy leads to a condition know as ketosis—i.e., accumulation of ketone bodies which produces metabolic acidosis. Excess ketone bodies are excreted by the kidneys, but in the process other key substances are excreted as well. These lost substances include sodium bicarbonate (thereby reducing the acid buffering capacity of the body fluids), electrolytes (e.g. sodium, potassium and chloride) and water.

In addition, some proteins are broken down to supplant the carbohydrates. Low blood glucose leads to depression of the central nervous system. Symptoms of glycogen depletion, low blood-sugar and impending ketosis include, first, a general muscular weakness upon exertion (similar to the weakness that is associated with intestinal flu) and, subsequently, central nervous system impairment as evidenced by dizziness, headache and inability to concentrate.

The central nervous system depression can be avoided and alleviated by an intake of a small amount of carbohydrates, particularly at the first meal after exercise. A booklet, *Brand-Name Carbohydrate Gram Counter,* which lists the carbohydrate content of many brand name foods is available at many supermarkets and can help you plan your dietary compostion. Drinking of large quantities of water will help to protect against dehydration.

Principle 13: Before commencing the high-carbohydrate diet, redeplete through appropriate physical activity. This is to make sure that you are depleting as much as possible and probably will require only 5-10 miles, depending upon the carbohydrate content of your diet

since the previous depletion run. If you have not used the low-carbohydrate diet, then this depletion run must be much longer (15-20
miles). This latter approach, of course, exposes the individual to an
injury very close to the time of competition.

Principle 14: Glycogen super-compensation (following depletion)
will occur only to the extent that carbohydrates are made available in
the diet. The greater the percent of carbohydrates in the diet, the
greater the super-compensation will be. Adequate proteins (2-3
ounces per day), minerals, vitamins and lots of water should be included in the diet.

Principle 15: *Do not overeat* when on the high-carbohydrate diet,
Although you will need a positive caloric balance in order to store
energy in the form of glycogen, the reduced activity will more than
take care of this if you eat your normal amount of food. The important
point is to increase the dietary carbohydrate percent. The modified
diet is enough stress without the added problem of handling excess
food.

Actually, it is best to eat small meals and include a couple of snacks
between the meals. In this manner, glucose from the intestines will be
available for storing in the muscles and liver most of the time, thereby
enhancing super-compensation.

Principle 16: Drink a large excess of fluids while on the high-carbohydrate diet. About 3-4 grams of water are stored with every gram
of glycogen. If an inadequate supply of water is drunk, the extra water
is withdrawn from other body sources and a relative dehydration will
occur. It is not uncommon for infections to result from such
dehydration. A good indicator of proper water intake is clear urine.
An amber urine means that you need more water.

The water associated with stored glycogen will be released as the
glycogen is consumed during activity, and this water will be available
for other vital processes—e.g., temperature regulation. For example,
it is possible to store two pounds of glycogen along with 6-8 pounds
(3-4 quarts) of water during super-compensation. These figures are
twice the values normally found. Very few runners will consume this
much water (the extra 1½-2 quarts) from external sources during a
long race. However, even when super-compensated the runner should
drink fluids during the race.

Principle 17: Activity will tend to reduce super-compensation and
should be avoided while on the high-carbohydrate diet. Stay off of
your feet as much as possible.

Principle 18: Once super-compensation occurs, the excess glyco-gen-storing enzyme is inactivated and the muscles will tend to burn off the excess glycogen during normal activities. Therefore, timing of the peak super-compensation is rather critical and varies among indivi-duals—typically 2-4 days on the high-carbohydrate diet. The time will depend on individual genetic differences, and will tend to be shorter for those persons who regularly deplete and super-compensate during their normal training and diet regime. Some symptoms that the peak super-compensation has passed include: bloated feeling, loose bowels and excessive urination.

Principle 19: Reduce the quantity of carbohydrates as well as other foods in the diet during the several hours before the event. There is evidence that a large amount of carbohydrates at this time may impair performance.

Principle 20: It is not necessary to full super-compensate for all competitions. For short activities, it probably would be beneficial to increase the percent of carbohydrates in the diet for 1-2 days only for the purpose of insuring that glycogen stores are not low. For events lasting 30-60 minutes, moderate super-compensation would suffice (e.g., 10-mile run 48 hours before competition followed by a high-carbohydrate diet and rest). For longer periods of competition, moderate super-compensation would be beneficial, but utilization of the full protocol would produce better results. Consumption of a dilute glucose-electrolyte solution during the event would help also.

Principle 21: If, after weighing all of the pros and cons, you decide to super-compensate, try it in stages during your training. For example, start with a long run followed by a high-carbohydrate diet (start with Principle 13). Keep a detailed log of what you do and what happens. Notice how you feel when running at the increased weights associated with super-compensation. If satisfied, then try the entire series (depletion, low-carbohydrate diet, redepletion, high-carbohy-drate diet), but stay on the low-carbohydrate diet for only one day. If there are no adverse effects, then extend the low-carbohydrate diet gradually to a maximum of 3-4 days. Do not take shortcuts. Remember, you are playing with biochemical dynamite.

Another use of a modified form of super-compensation occurs when long runs on successive days are taken. On a regular diet, recovery from depletion will not take place in one day, and consequently the runner will experience greater fatigue each day until he finds it impossible to perform properly or an injury occurs. However, a rela-tively high-carbohydrate diet permits use of the quantity programs without exhaustion.

At this stage you should be fully cognizant of the potential benefits and hazards of practicing glycogen super-compensation. One reason for the adverse experiences reported in the literature is due to the large number of principles to consider and the resulting confusion among naive users.

In the March 26, 1973 issue of the *Journal of the American Medical Association* (also in the March 1973 *Runner's World*), Gabe Mirkin, M.D., reported a case in which a 40-year-old runner experienced angina and EKG modifications while super-compensating.

The term used in Dr. Mirkin's report was "carbohydrate-loading" and, as you will see, was very appropriate. After three days of a diet consisting of cheese (which, by the way, contains carbohydrates), meat and turkey, the subject switched to a diet that included as much bread as he could eat for three days. He ate almost two loaves of bread at one meal; this represents the equivalent of one day's energy needs, and I assume that his other meals were comparable. As a flagrant violation of Principle 15 (overeating), I feel certain that gluttonous quantities of fats and/or proteins would have produced adverse results also.

The second case strikes closer to home and was in the "News and Views" column of the March 1974 issue of *Runner's World*. Dr. Richard Hessler sought my counsel regarding super-compensation procedures prior to a marathon. He drank lots of water while on the low-carbohydrate diet, but apparently due to a misunderstanding he restricted his water intake when he converted to the high-carbohy-drate diet (violation of Principle 16) and suffered an infected prostate. Although Dick suffered a great deal of discomfort and was unable to compete in the race, he confided that the daily physical therapy was like a second honeymoon. Therefore, our friendship remains intact.

Upon reading Dr. Mirkin's report, I felt that the case was so ridiculous that most observers would recognize the problem. However, Dr. Hessler's experience suggested that a written set of guidelines with appropriate commentary would help to prevent such misunderstandings and warn potential super-compensators of the hazards. In addition, even though Dr. Hessler and others have argued against tampering with the body chemistry on moral and/or ethical grounds, I am not so naive to think that athletes would refrain from using legal but also hazardous procedures that would improve their performance.

Also appearing in the March 1974 issue of *Runner's World* ("Medical Advice") was a letter from Ralph Nelson, M.D., Head of Clinical Nutrition Section at Mayo Clinic. Dr. Nelson referred to Dr. Mirkin's report, to angina-like leg pains in Swedish runners using super-compensation, the disadvantage of increased weight due to glycogen hydration and to the fact that excess stored glycogen can

destroy muscle fibers. Unable to find support in the research literature for some of these claims, I had an interesting telephone
conversation with Dr. Nelson in order to gain insight into his written
comments.

The label "angina-like symptoms...in the leg muscles" was Dr.
Nelson's interpretation of Bergstrom and Hultman's (*JAMA*
221:1005, 1972) warning of heaviness and stiffness in the muscles of
sprinters who need only limited amounts of glycogen. Conversely,
in distance races the increased weight due to glycogen hydration
cannot be considered significant when times under normal and
super-compensated conditions are compared. Either the small
increase in weight has little or no effect on performance, or the
benefits of large stores of glycogen and endogenous water far outweigh
the disadvantage of glycogen weight. Perhaps the extra weight would
hamper performance in which glycogen needs are minimal.

The potential hazard of excess stored glycogen upon muscle fibers
has been substantiated in certain disease states where key glycogen-
storing or breakdown enzymes misfunction or are lacking. However,
in these diseases the glycogen may accumulate to six times normal,
remain in the tissues unused and may be defective. Conversely, in
super-compensation the glycogen concentration seldom exceeds 2-2½
times normal. If unused through physical exertion within about two
days, the body's metabolism adjusts to use the excess glycogen in
normal daily activities within another 2-4 days. Heart muscle, in
contrast to skeletal muscle, responds much more transiently to dietary
modification. Myocardial super-compensation occurs within four
hours and returns to normal within 8-48 hours.

There are two points where Dr. Nelson and I agree. First,
super-compensation is potentially hazardous, particularly for
individuals who may have underlying health problems. Secondly, a
point not mentioned before is that there is no evidence available about
the long-term effects of repeated super-compensation. Therefore, the
person using these procedures may be trading future health stock for
improved performance now.

My recommendation as an exercise physiologist familiar with the
research and as a competitive runner with personal super-compensation experience is to use moderation. Make sure you understand all of
the principles and hazards discussed here before attempting the
procedures. Use caution at all times. Although minor alterations in
the diet probably pose little danger, the use of the whole set of
procedures (deplete, low-carbohydrate diet, redeplete and high-carbohydrate diet) should be attempted only after gradually leading up to
them and then only 2-4 times per year.

32

The Modified Diet

Skip the high-protein phase, and go right to carbohydrates

Bob Fitts

I t has become apparent to me that the widely used dietary practice of carbohydrate super-compensation is poorly understood and hence misused. Dr. Ben Londeree presented a good description of the principles. After reading his article, one should be able to use the overload technique in the correct way and hence limit the chance of undesirable side-effects. My purpose is to emphasize one point Ben made, and then present facts supporting a *modified* version of the generally used dietary procedure.

Dr. Londeree's Principle 15: "Do not overeat when on the high-carbohydrate diet." The diet should be high in carbohydrates but normal in terms of total caloric intake. After muscle glycogen reaches levels 2½-3 times normal testing levels, the production of it is inhibited regardless of how much carbohydrate is consumed. There-fore, it does no good to multiply many-fold your normal total caloric intake per day. Such dietary procedures will not further increase muscle glycogen, but will produce undesirable effects.

In my opinion, the major risk of the glycogen super-compensation procedure is the severe hypoglycemia (low blood glucose) that may result if one continues to run hard while on the low-carbohydrate phase of the diet. The generally used procedure involves a long run of 1½-2 hours to deplete muscle glycogen, three days on a low-carbo-hydrate diet, three days on a high-carbohydrate diet, and then the race.

Examination of the original literature reveals that the final level of muscle glycogen super-compensation reached is not affected by the low-carbohydrate phase of the diet. The main purpose of this phase is to lengthen the amount of time between the depletion run and the race. Following the depletion run blood glucose and muscle glucose are lower than normal.

If one continues hard training during the low-carbohydrate phase of the diet, blood glucose may fall to critically low levels. Even if you take small amounts of carbohydrate as Dr. Londeree recommends (Principle 11), continued regular training may still produce hypoglycemia.

Alternatively, you can reduce your training, but this would mean six easy days before the race. This rest should not hurt your performance (you might even run better), but you may feel uncomfortable with such a long inactive period.

Since the final level of muscle glycogen super-compensation is the same with or without the low-carbohydrate phase of the diet (2½-3 times normal levels), I avoid the potential dangers of this phase by taking my long run on Tuesday (15 miles), followed by a high-carbohydrate diet Tuesday night through Friday, with the race on Saturday morning. If four days of rest are desired, one can do the long run on Monday, eat a low-carbohydate diet on Tuesday, a high-carbohydrate diet on Wednesday through Friday, and race Saturday.

33

Drinks for the Road

What runners should drink, how much and how often

Peter Van Handel

The previous chapters have discussed the importance of stored carbohydrate (glycogen) for endurance running and have presented protocols that runners may follow in an attempt to "carbohydrate-pack." It has also been emphasized that this technique does not benefit everyone and, indeed, may not be advisable for certain individuals.

As would be expected, there is a large group of runners who, for various reasons, cannot or do not wish to "pack." However, based on the available experimental and practical evidence, we have to concede that *all* runners need to maintain adequate carbohydrate levels during endurance exercise. This article is directed to these athletes—the ones who are asking themselves, "How do I insure that adequate carbohydrate is available to the muscles if I can't carbohydrate-pack?"

The answer is obvious. You take sugar or some other form of carbohydrate while "on the road." Hundreds of runners answer the gun with dextrose tablets tucked away someplace in their uniforms, while the most common form of carbohydrate ingestion occurs in the form of a cup of Gatorade, Body Punch, ERG or some other drink every few miles. However, there are problems with taking carbohydrates on the run, and for all practical purposes these cannot be separated from the problems associated with fluid intake. Therefore, this discussion centers on the drinking of carbohydrate solutions.

Basically, most runners drink the various commercially available "ades" or other homemade solutions to provide quick energy. I've seen national caliber endurance athletes take honey on a spoon in an attempt to delay fatigue during a long race. Others drink both for the energy supplies and to help delay or prevent dehydration and the symptoms of heat stress when the runs are held in hot weather.

But a nagging question remains: "Does the substance you are taking during the run to provide energy really do the job?" Unfortunately, there is not a simple "yes" or "no" answer since there are several complicating factors.

Generally speaking, the following are true: (1) the greater the volume of fluid in the stomach, the faster it tends to leave the stomach, but (2) the more sugar or carbohydrate the fluid has, the longer it takes to leave the stomach, and these factors interact in an athlete drinking carbohydrate solutions during a race. The importance of this is that if the fluid is in your stomach, the carbohydrate present can't get to your muscles.

Let's examine these factors in greater detail.

• *Effects of Volume of Fluid in the Stomach:* The falling off of pace and the fatigue felt as the carbohydrate stores become depleted isn't due to a sudden drop in energy supplies. Rather, the evidence indicates a gradual and continuous depletion of carbohydrate stores. At the same time, large sweat losses may occur. Present distance running rules regulate fluid intake during an event to certain intervals. This combined with the sweat losses, carbohydrate depletion and the problems of "voluntary dehydration" usually means that by the time fluid is available to the athlete, it is too late to solve the immediate problems. The dehydration and fatigue have already started to set in and drinking a large volume of fluid loaded with "energy" can't bring the body back to a normal state, since it takes a relatively long time for the material to leave the stomach.

Indeed, Dr. David Costill has reported that national-class runners attempting to consume large volumes of a sugar solution during runs at competitive pace complained of stomach discomfort (fullness) and an inability to consume fluids after the first few feedings. This was in spite of the fluid need as evidenced by subjective reports of muscle and nervous system fatigue, and by the sweat losses.

While volume is the least important of the three factors mentioned, it does have some effects on performance, especially when combined with the next two factors. Therefore, based on our experience with distance runners, we suggest that drinking approximately one pint 10 minutes *before* the run, and then supplementing with frequent (every 10-15 minutes) drinks of small volume, is the best procedure to follow.

• *Effects of Sugar Concentration:* The next question is, "What do we drink?" I've already mentioned that in general the more carbohydrate in the drink, the longer it takes the solution to get out of the stomach. The energy available in the drink *cannot* be used until the carbohydrate leaves the stomach and enters the blood from the small intestine. Numerous studies have shown that salt solutions leave the stomach very rapidly, and the addition of even small amounts of sugar can drastically slow down the rate of emptying. This slowing delays the movement of water into the circulation.

During endurance running in the heat, the prevention of dehydration and heat stress is of utmost importance, carbohydrate supplementation is secondary. Therefore, under these conditions the sugar content of the drink should be minimal so that water can rapidly enter the circulating blood.

Various commercially available drinks claim to have everything you need to take during an endurance run. Unfortunately, there is little hard data to back up these claims. In fact, the evidence seems to indicate that champion distance runners are able to complete a marathon with little or no fluid intake. However, in the process they sustain water losses of 6-10% of their body weight and rectal temperatures in excess of 105 degrees (F). This obviously places severe demands on the runner and exposes him to the hazards of muscle cramps, heat exhaustion and heat stroke.

All in all, the research studies on the effects of drinking a carbohydrate solution during an endurance event on the body's energy-producing mechanisms are contradictory. Costill reports that the carbohydrate taken during severe endurance exercise does not reach the muscles in significant amount, and the little that is used to produce energy takes 20-30 minutes to reach the muscles from the time it enters the stomach. This tends to support the idea of drinking *before* the run and then supplementing at frequent intervals.

Costill's data also indicates that while the contribution of the ingested carbohydrate to muscle metabolism is minimal, it does seem to conserve liver carbohydrate stores by maintaining blood sugar. The blood sugar and liver stores are seemingly used to prevent brain and nervous system fatigue.

While Costill's data points to insignificant use of carbohydrate by the muscles, another research study estimated that 60-80% of the carbohydrate used after the feeding came from the drink. Here again, though, the time from intake until utilization was rather long. Factors such as intensity and type of work play a role in these studies so that comparisons between the two are difficult.

Other supportive evidence for fluid intake before the event comes from the 1968 Olympic 50-kilometer cross-country ski champion who was reported to have drunk more than a quart of 40% sugar water before the start of the race. This fact seems to indicate a wide variability in tolerance to drinking carbohydrate solutions, as most people could not swallow a 40% sugar solution (commercially available drinks are about 5-10% carbohydrate).

One last comment on sugar concentration: There seems to be no reason for eating dextrose tablets, honey, etc., as fatigue sets in during a race. The material remains in the stomach too long to be of any practical value in supplying immediate energy. The benefits of dextrose would not be felt until 30 minutes after consumption, and dextrose also tends to keep water in the stomach.

• *Effects of Exercise Severity:* Research has shown that exercise tasks which exceed approximately 70% of the individual's maximal ability to use oxygen inhibit the emptying of the stomach. Champion distance men can run an entire marathon in excess of 80% of this capacity. For example, in tests on Derek Clayton (see Part Five) in our laboratory it was shown that the pace for his 2:08 marathon was in excess of 86% of his maximal ability.

Obviously, not all of us can function at this level. The point is that many runners can exceed the level where stomach emptying becomes affected by the work intensity. The carbohydrate (and water) tends to stay in the stomach longer.

Let's tie things together at this point. I've already stated that the factors of volume of fluid in the stomach, the sugar content of the fluid and the severity of exercise all interact in the athlete who drinks on the run. This interaction is more complex than I've made it seem, so that research data on the topic of fluid intake during exercise is hard to evaluate. In turn, no specific recommendations can be made at this time concerning how much, when and what a runner takes to provide energy and prevent dehydration during a long run.

However, based on the evidence to date and our own experience with distance runners, the following suggestions are made:

1. In order to minimize dehydration, a pint of fluid should be consumed 10 minutes *before* competition.

2. In order to prevent stomach distress (fullness) and to promote maximal entry of the fluid into the blood, the drink should contain

very little carbohydrate (less than 2.5%). This amount is adequate for energy production and use by the nervous system.

3. The fluid should be taken at 10-15-minute intervals during the run in amounts of about one-half pint.

4. Runners should be vocal in emphasizing to the governing body the need for rules changes regarding fluid intake during distance races. (The current rule allows no drink in the first seven miles of long-distance races.)

In addition, scheduling should be such that these races are held during the cool hours of the day to minimize heat stress problems. The present situation seems to benefit the officials, sponsors and spectators, and is not in the best interests of the athlete.

34

Eating After It's Over

How to replace foods and fluids lost in the marathon

Donald Monkerud

Legend tells of an Athenian named Pheidippides who, in 490 B.C., ran from the battlefield at Marathon to Athens, telling of the victory over the Persians. Shouting the news that Athens would be spared pillage and fire, the Athenian dropped dead.

Although scholars attempt to correct the story, the myth lives on. For anyone who has run the marathon, the story of Pheidippides dying after his run is believable. Some runners claim they "die" after *every* marathon. If Pheidippides had known then what we know today about diet and fluid replacement, he might have lived to run another day. By the same token, modern marathoners might recover faster from their races by understanding nutrition.

Diet plays an important role in recovery from a marathon. Proper nutrition can help the runner quickly return to his or her running program, feeling better both physically and mentally. But what kind of diet promotes this? We don't get many hints from running literature.

There has been lots of discussion on what to eat *before* the big race. For instance, carbohydrate-loading has been popular. But what about the next days? Life doesn't suddenly stop once the marathon is finished.

The question of what to eat afterward can't be separated from the rest of the runner's diet and training program. But because so much has been said about the pre-race diet, attention here will focus on the first drinks and foods afterward, and the diet in the following days. In order to discuss this, something must be understood about what happens to the body during the marathon.

Most marathoners are aware of the advantages of running. But when questioned closely, many don't know specifically how their bodies are affected. For one thing, the ability of the muscle tissues to burn food fuels for energy is greatly enhanced. Well-trained runners need less energy for a given performance than do untrained persons or unexperienced runners. The efficiency of the working muscle is much improved, the metabolism is more economical, heart-lung efficiency is much greater, psychological confidence is greater, and coordination and technique are much improved. Not only does the well-trained runner store more glycogen for energy, but the muscles are trained to metabolize fat more effectively.

Glycogen, which is a carbohydrate made from the sugar glucose, is stored in the muscles and liver. Most runners are aware of the need to store maximum amounts of glycogen provided by such foods as spaghetti, fruits, milk, and cereals and grains.

According to G. Cahill in "Carbohydrate Metabolism and its Disorders," the average person can store only around 200 grams of glycogen with 120 of that in the muscles. But muscle glycogen storage can be increased markedly by dietary manipulations. This is the rationale of the carbohydrate-loading practice. For the average runner who "loads," glycogen storage is about twice normal levels.

The body of a trained individual also turns to another source of energy. The most marked difference between trained and untrained runners is their metabolic response in the proportions of fat and carbohydrate used for fuel.

Dr. Joan Ullyot, an exercise physiologist, explains, "During training in distance running, the muscles are using fat as fuel. They are burning fatty acids and lactic acid. Most of the time, the distance runner is running on a mixture of fat and carbohydrates, but the longer you run, the higher the proportion of fat.

"A male who is untrained isn't going to be very good if the muscles fail. And his muscles won't be really accustomed to burning fat without training. He will burn a higher proportion of glycogen and be unable to continue after around 18 miles."

Training is the key difference in the muscles' ability to use fat. Running places a stress on the muscles which changes their chemical and enzymic action. The adaptation of the muscles to the oxidation of fats has an extremely important "glycogen-sparing" effect. This effect plays a major role in accounting for increases in capacity for prolonged strenuous exercise which occurs in response to endurance training. If it were not for this "glycogen-sparing" effect, most marathoners maintaining 75% of their maximum pace would probably deplete their glycogen stores after only about three-quarters of the race and have a hard time finishing.

By using fat for fuel and metering out the glycogen to last the entire race, the runner is able to finish the marathon. The increased oxidation of fat in the trained runner appears to be due entirely to the adaptive increase in muscle mitochondria, or the energy-producing center of the cell, and the increase in mitochondrial enzymes involved in the oxidation of fatty acids. The more trained the runner, the more fat and less carbohydrates are used for energy in the marathon.

In the search for the proper diet after the marathon, however, fat is not recommended to get one feeling better and back on a training schedule. Unlike glycogen supplies which are depleted and need to be replenished, the fat supplies are plentiful in the body even after a long, hard race. Most marathoners are quite lean and may think they need to eat more fat to build up their body reserves. But researchers feel it's not fat stores which limit performance. The limiting factor seems to be the ability of the muscle to *use* available fats.

For a runner, therefore, fats are not recommended for the post-race meal nor the days following a hard marathon. The average American diet contains from 40 - 60% fat, which is the leading cause of heart disease. If the runner eats large amounts of cholesterol, which is commonly found in high-fat diets, there is no guarantee his arteries won't clog with atherosclerosis. Runners are urged to cut down on fats so they provide no more than 10 - 30% of total calories. Even with this reduction, there will still be plenty of fat to be metabolized.

Considering what is depleted from the runner's body will determine what to eat afterward. We've seen that glycogen is depleted almost completely, and that fat needs are met in the daily diet and from body stores.

"In order to recover as rapidly as possible, the obvious thing is to consume considerable carbohydrates," says Dr. David Costill of the Human Performance Lab at Ball State University. "Probably the first meal after the marathon should be like the last big meal before. If the night before you have spaghetti or some other heavy carbohydrate, the meal after competition should be very much the same. You want to recover as much of that used up glycogen as possible.

"It takes 3-5 days to recover the glycogen. That's part of the problem of recovering from a marathon. A lot of people don't go after the carbohydrate hard enough, and that is part of the cause for the fatigue and difficulties in getting back to running form again."

For older marathoners, three ingredients must be in the diet before they will be able even to finish a marathon, according to Dr. Tom

Bassler, who is a member of the American Medical Joggers Association. It is especially necessary that these ingredients be replaced after a marathon so the running program can be continued.

"We have found that after 18 months of running if older people lack any of these three ingredients they will have to stop running," says Dr. Bassler. "One of them is vitamin C, another is linoleic acid which is an essential fatty acid, and the third is silicon which is in food fiber. If you are deficient in any one of these things, you just cannot finish a marathon."

Without these essential nutrients, running will be stopped due to a lack of energy or an injury. Silicon in food fiber helps the intestinal tract to function efficiently and keeps the energy stores functioning properly. Vitamin C is essential for the bones and joints to help prevent and heal injuries. Linoleic acid, a polyunsaturated fat, is a fuel used by the marathoner after 18 miles and is essential for the "glycogen-sparing" effect mentioned earlier. Fresh fruits and vegetables will supply these essential needs.

In addition to the three essential ingredients, Bassler believes anyone running more than one or two marathons a year should be on a special diet. But when questioned about the contents of that special diet, he responds, "anything that helps you run." Even more important are the foods that should be avoided, he contends.

Many people believe the body will tell you what to eat and what it needs after a marathon. This is partly due to the way the trained body uses fat stores, the fact that the runner knows the body needs to replenish glycogen stores and the fact that most marathoners are more aware of their nutritional needs than most non-runners. Immediately after running, most people crave fruits, vegetables or juices. Later, their usual diet will fill the depleted stores. But the body can be fooled if one only listens to what it craves.

"The only problem with listening to what your body craves," explains Dr. Tom Bassler, "is that society has refined so many foods. You may crave them, eat them and not get what you need. You have to think and avoid anything that is refined. For example, canned fruit. You might crave fruit and eat a can of peaches. This won't fill your body needs. You would be better off eating raw peaches. The only way your craving will protect you is if you stay away from refined foods."

For nutrition before, during and after the marathon, no single factor is as important as fluids. Certainly no single factor poses a greater threat to a marathoner's health and performance than does becoming overheated. Advice on drinking during a marathon is given elsewhere in this section of the book. Here, our concern is with what to drink afterward.

"During the marathon, you can't even come close to replacing the fluids you lose," emphasizes David Costill. "Drinking at aid stations may replace only one-tenth of the fluids you lose. You are going to be markedly dehydrated. Immediately afterward, you should consume fluids to get rehydrated. You could incorporate some sugars in that drink so you could either drink fruit juices or some commercial athlete drinks that are available."

"The human thirst mechanism is quite slow," he explains. "As a result, you may be eight pounds dehydrated and have a couple of glasses of fluid and feel satisfied. But an hour later, you will be thirsty again. It's a delayed reaction. Other animals are different. They rehydrate 100% at the first watering. But humans don't respond that way. You have to force yourself to drink some extra. Watch your body weight for the next 24 hours. Generally, this is enough time to get your fluids back."

Proper rehydration after the marathon can be facilitated by weighing yourself on a regular basis, like before and after training every day. This will give you an idea of how much water you lose in your training and allow you to replace it daily. At the same time, it will give you an idea of your proper weight. After a marathon on a particularily warm day, you will want to replace lost body weight with an equal or greater weight of water.

One gallon of water weighs about eight pounds. If you lost eight pounds during a marathon, most of the loss is water. You would need to drink an extra gallon of water within the next 24 hours to bring your body to it's normal functioning.

Unfortunately for Pheidippides, he didn't have the knowledge which we have. If only he had known to carry a canteen, his life might have been spared. But then, that's the stuff legends are made of.

Part 7
Hot and Cold Running

35

Living with the Elements

We can't change them, but we can make important adjustments

Ken Young

Few persons in our modern society spend more time out of doors than does the typical marathon runner. The necessary training requires the runner to experience mother nature first-hand for 1-2 hours a day, year round. Missing a run is often considered as a sign of character weakness. Hence, we often face the extremes of heat, cold, wind, rain or snow, pollution and, on occasion, altitude.

When dealing with the elements, a little advice and some common sense go a long way. With this in mind, I'll present some do's and don'ts (along with tables and graphs) and give you some tips that I've had to learn through trial and error.

COLD AND WIND

Running in cold weather generates heat, which allows a runner to dress quite lightly, even when the temperatures are below freezing. A distance runner will experience chilling only if he loses heat more rapidly than it is being generated by running. This heat balance may be expressed as:

heat generated = heat loss due to heating breath
evaporative heat loss from lungs
heat loss by radiation to surroundings
heat loss by conduction/convection to air.

This equation may be used to determine the air temperature below which a runner, running at a specified rate, wearing specified clothing and experiencing a given relative wind, will become chilled. The faster a runner runs, the more heat is generated, and the runner can get by with lighter clothing. Running into a headwind will cause the runner to lose heat much more rapidly than when running with the wind.

Using the heat-balance equation, one can determine how much protection a runner will require for given combinations of temperature, wind and pace.

These relationships are quantified in the accompanying figures. Each figure pertains to a particular pace, from five minutes per mile to 10 minutes per mile. Each figure then relates the degree of protection required for various combinations of temperature and wind speed. A description of the clothing recommended for each of the five regions is given toward the end of this section.

You can use these figures in the following manner. Let's consider a runner who expects to run at six minutes per mile. The temperature close to race time is 25 degrees F (-4 C), and there is no wind. However, the runner effectively "creates" a wind of 10 miles per hour (six minutes per mile). This is indicated by the horizontal dotted line. The combinatioin of 25 degrees F and a 10-m.p.h. relative wind indicates that the runner should be "moderately clothed." This suggests that the runner should wear sweat top, mittens and head protection, but that he will feel comfortable running bare-legged.

Now let's suppose there is a 15-mile-per-hour wind. If the course is out-and-back or is a loop course, the runner will experience this wind both as a headwind and as a tailwind. The headwind represents a relative wind of 10 plus 15 or 25 m.p.h. With a temperature of 25 degrees F, this is well into the region where protective clothing is recommended—for instance, the runner should protect the legs and face, and wear a heavier sweat top, perhaps one with a hood.

While running with the wind, the runner experiences a relative wind of five miles per hour (the absolute value of the quality 10 minus 15 m.p.h. per hour). The graph indicates the runner can get by only lightly clad. This would be fine if the race were entirely with the wind, but the runner usually needs to be prepared to run into the wind as well. This illustrates the dangers of starting a winter workout running with the wind. You may feel quite comfortable going out, but you could go so far that you might not be able to make it back.

The same procedures can be followed for any combination of wind, temperature and pace. You may need to interpolate for in-between paces such as for seven minutes per mile. For longer races, you should consider the slowest pace you may run (toward the end of the race) and the worst conditions that are likely to occur.

Direct sunshine effectively raises the temperature by about 12 degrees F (7 C). This suggests that these charts can be entered at a temperature above the actual air temperature (by about 12 degress F) if the sun is relatively high in the sky and is shining. Since light-

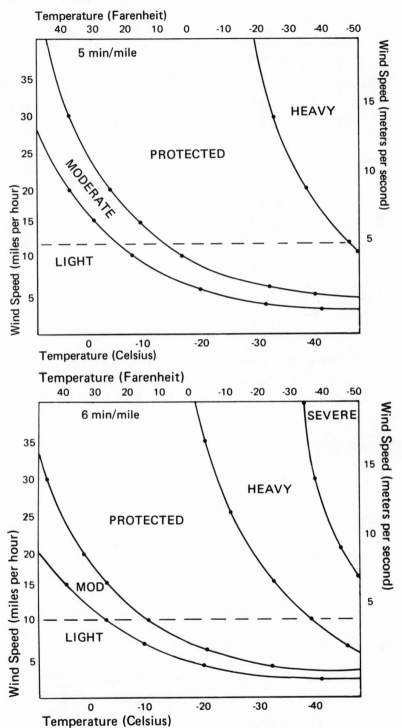

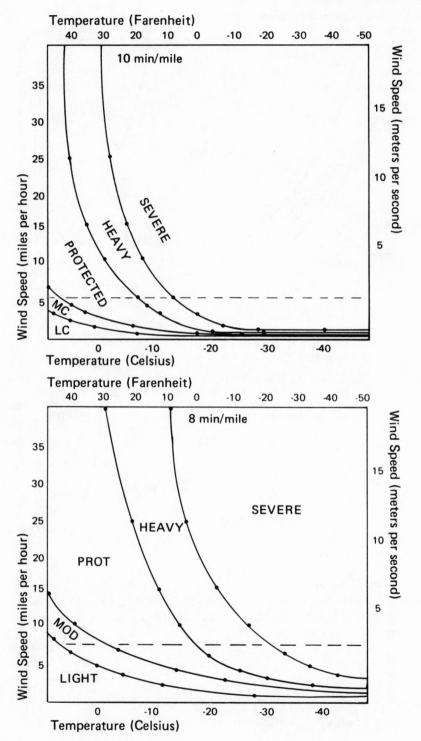

colored clothing reflects sunlight more than dark clothing, wearing darker colors in the colder weather will make you feel somewhat warmer.

The clothing worn by the runner for protection against cold and wind is governed by several factors. The major heat loss experienced is due to the air motion around the runner, suggesting that one needs to protect the more exposed extremities (ears, hands, etc.). The major sources of heat are the legs and torso, while the upper extremities generate or receive relatively little heat. Finally, the clothing worn should not restrict the running motion.

In general, several layers of light clothing provide better insulation against cold and wind than a single layer of much heavier clothing. Multiple layers of clothing also allow the runner to strip layers while running with the wind in order to avoid excessive sweating. Wet or damp clothing cannot insulate as well as dry clothing.

The hands in particular require protection. The supply of blood to the hands is significantly reduced while running, which means that the hands will chill more rapidly while running than they would walking. If the skin temperature drops below a certain value, the blood vessels near the surface constrict, further reducing the blood supply and increasing the likelihood of frostbite. Once frostbitten, the

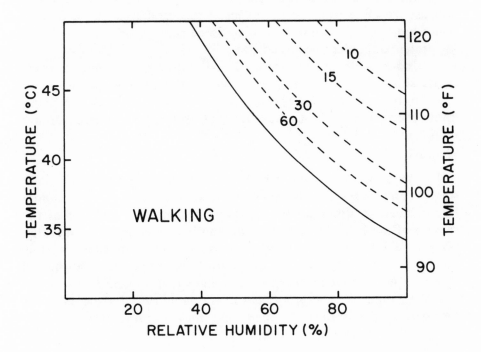

tissues are more susceptible to chilling and frostbite on subsequent exposure to cold.

Once your hands start to go, you will need to take immediate pre-
cautions to prevent frostbite. One simple but awkward method is to
place your hands under the opposite armpits. Placing your hands
directly on the bare skin of you abdomen (underneath your sweats)
also provides a measure of relief. The best procedure, however, is to
get back indoors and place the hands in a pan of tepid water until the
pain ceases.

Even under conditions when runners may go lightly clad, the hands
(and ears) often need protection. This is particularly true under all-
out or race conditions when the blood supply is greatly reduced by the
exercise. Socks make handy mittens; mittens are preferable to gloves.
If the temperature is below 10 degrees F, I usually wear ski mittens.
To protect the ears, I prefer a ski-band, although many runners like
knit stocking caps. This serves to protect the forehead as well as the
ears. A hooded sweatshirt by itself is generally not adequate.

I have four categories for my winter gear:

1. Under "lightly clothed" conditions, I will run with my arms and
legs bare, with a T-shirt and running shorts, but may use light mittens
(socks) and a ski band.

2. When "moderate clothing" is indicated, I will wear a light
sweat-top but remain bare-legged. If more protection is indicated, I
will use Vaseline to cover my exposed face and legs and a heavier
sweat-top, perhaps one with a hood. Some runners use pantyhose for
leg protection under these conditions.

3. Under conditions requiring "heavy clothing," face masks, sweat
pants, ski-mittens and multiple layers of clothing are indicated.

4. In the "severe" region, you should use great caution. Let a friend
know your route and estimated time of return, just in case you are
unable to make it back.

HEAT

The generating of heat which greatly aids the runner in cold
weather creates serious problems in hot weather. One bodily response
to this need to dissipate heat is perspiration. This helps cool the
surface of the body by evaporation. Another response is an elevated
body core temperature which increases the rate at which heat is
conducted to the skin and then to the air. Core temperatures above 104
degrees F (40 C) have been reported in marathon runners.

If the runner is generating heat at the same rate that he or she is
losing heat, then in principle the runner may continue to run indefin-

itely without experiencing symptoms of heat stroke. The heat balance equation describing this condition may be expressed as

heat generated =	heat loss due to heating breath
	evaporative heat loss from lungs
	heat lost by conduction/convection to air
	heat lost by evaporation from skin.

Certain of these terms may be negative, representing a gain of heat. For example, if the air temperature is higher than the skin temperature, the third term representing heat lost by conduction and convection to the air will be negative.

The heat balance equation can also be used to determine the rate at which the body accumulates excess heat which it cannot dissipate. This puts a limit on the duration of exercise, since body core temperatures in excess of 104 degrees F will soon lead to heat stroke. The accompanying charts give the recommended maximum duration of exercise for different running paces as a function of temperature and relative humidity. The area lying to the left and below the lowermost curve represents the condition where a "well-watered" runner will be able to dissipate all the heat generated.

These charts may be used as follows. Let's consider a runner who intends to race at six minutes per mile. The temperature at race time is 100 degrees F (38 C), and the relative humidity is 40%. The chart for six minutes per mile gives a recommended maximum time of exercise of 15 minutes for this combination of temperature and humidity. This corresponds to a distance of 2½ miles—i.e., the runner should not try races longer than two miles under such conditions unless he curtails the pace. If the pace is cut to eight minutes per mile (see the appropriate chart), the length of exercise is unlimited.

Race directors should assume that the runner will run as fast as possible, regardless of the conditions. To avoid the dangers of heat stroke, one should consider the top runners in the race (who are in the greatest danger) and limit the distance of the race accordingly. For example, the race director has scheduled a 15-kilometer race. However, at race time, the temperature is 90 degrees F, and the humidity is 40%. The recommended maximum duration of exercise is 20 minutes (using the chart for five minutes per mile and interpolating between the plotted curves). Thus, the race distance should not be longer than four miles (the distance a runner can run in 20 minutes at five minutes per mile). The race director should make the race five kilometers in length rather than risk the possibility that some of the runners may suffer heat stroke.

These charts assume that the skin is wet—i.e., that the body continues to supply water to the skin for evaporation. The rate at which the body loses water can be calculated from the heat balance equation. It turns out that the water loss is not dependent on the relative humidity; it is dependent only on the rate of exercise and the air temperature. If there is no water replacement, the distance a runner can travel before experiencing dehydration may be calculated. These distance are given in the accompanying table for different running paces and temperatures. The first value represents a weight loss of 1%—the distance at which the runner should begin ingesting fluids, according to David Costill. The second figure represents a weight loss of 3% and is the level of dehydration considered by Costill to impair running performance. The last figure is for a weight loss of 8% and represents a level beyond which dehydration can have serious consequences. The middle column may be considered to be a distance that the runner can cover without needing to replenish liquids and still not be adversely affected by dehydration. In general, the runner should either limit the distance run or should replace the lost water.

These charts and tables illustrate the twin problems a runner faces while running in hot weather. The maximum duration of exercise according to the charts assumes that the skin is completely wet. In other words, spraying the runners with water during the race will not alter this recommended maximum time. It will, however, serve to replace water for evaporation that otherwise would be supplied by sweating. This can reduce the rate at which the runner becomes dehydrated and extend his running distance, *provided* this distance does not exceed the maximum duratioin of exercise recommended for that combination of pace, temperature and humidity.

The body will acclimate itself to hot weather if one exercises under conditions of mild heat stress for at least three days. The most important physiological change is an increase in the perspiration rate, which allows the evaporative cooling mechanism to operate more effectively. Runners not acclimated to heat stress should be on the conservative side when applying these charts.

The most important piece of advice to avoid the dangers of heat stroke is to *slow down*. What may be hazardous conditions at six minutes per mile may be fairly comfortable at eight minutes per mile. A slower pace serves to lessen the generation of heat, reducing the heat stress and the rate of water loss.

The clothing worn should be light and porous, allowing evaporation without insulating the body. If the sun is shining, light-colored clothing will have a slight advantage over darker clothing in reflecting some of the heat.

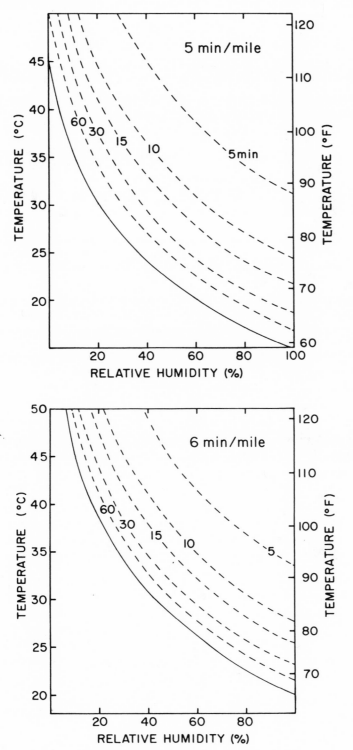

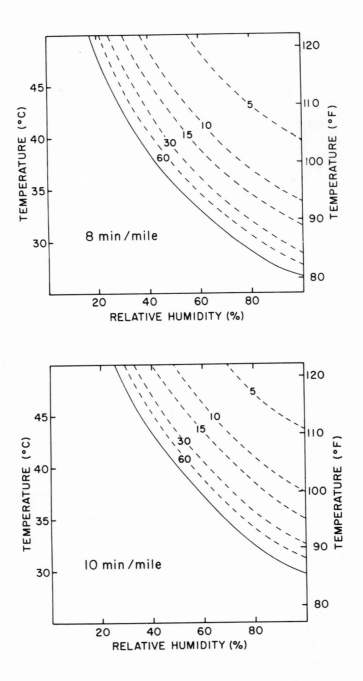

Spraying the runners with water during the race generally serves to reduce sweating, which helps conserve the body's supply of water and to retard dehydration. Dumping cups of water over the head and neck serves a similar purpose. More than 90% of the water lost during hot weather exercise is by sweating.

Ice can be very useful in helping cool the runner. For example, a 128-pound person, running at six minutes per mile at an air temperature of 104 degrees F will generate about 275 calories per second by conduction from the air. The ingestion of one ounce (30 grams) of ice will reduce this required heat loss by 10% over a period of 80 seconds. (I usually hold the ice in my mouth until it is small enough to chew.) Other pieces of ice can be rubbed on the back of the neck and on the face and forehead to help cool the runner.

A handy method to delay the effects of dehydration is to ingest an electrolyte solution immediately prior to the start of the race. I prefer Body Punch and usually consume between a pint and a quart within 15 minutes of race time, ending at least five minutes prior to the gun. This allows the fluid to exit the stomach to avoid stitches but is too short a time to allow the fluid to reach the bladder (with obvious consequences). Once the race starts, the fluid generally remains in the intestines and is gradually taken up by the bloodstream as water is lost through sweating.

Using these methods, I completed the 1976 Boston (Inferno) Marathon comfortably in 2:38 without drinking any liquids *per se*. The only fluid I had during the race was the melt water from the 20 or so ice cubes that I ingested.

RAIN AND SNOW

Rain usually presents many more problems for the runner than does snow. Snow is usually dry in the sense that it can be brushed off before melting and soaking into one's clothing. Rain under warm (and humid) conditions can be a blessing, reducing the need for perspiration as well as generally cooling the air. Rain at temperatures in the 30s or low 40s can be exceedingly unpleasant.

Protection against rain really depends on how much the runner values his comfort. Under the worst conditions of cold, wind and rain, the runner can get by with protecting just the exposed skin such as the forehead, ears and hands. Here, a ski-band and mittens suffice. During a workout, you may wish to use a water-proofed windbreaker or a plastic garment bag, cutting holes for the head and arms. However, you should be well aware that such water-proofed garments tend to retain the body's heat, resulting in heat stress if the runner dresses too warmly.

My own preference is to dress lightly and accept the discomfort. In a race, I will wear shorts and a T-shirt, using a ski-band and mittens if it is fairly cold and windy, and the race is fairly long. Wearing even a light sweatshirt does little to keep the runner warm (in the absence of a windbreaker or garment bag), and the sweatshirt usually becomes rather heavy with the water it picks up.

DEHYDRATION DISTANCES

Temp.	5 min./mile			6 min./mile			8 min./mile			10 min./mile		
50°F	6	17	45	9	26	60+	30	60+	60+	36	60+	60+
55	5	14	38	7	20	55	17	50	60+	36	60+	60+
60	4	13	35	6	17	45	11	32	60+	36	60+	60+
65	4	11	30	5	14	38	8	24	60+	18	55	60+
70	3	10	27	4	13	34	6	19	50	11	33	60+
75	3	9	25	4	11	30	5	16	42	8	24	60+
80	3	9	23	3	10	27	5	14	37	7	20	50
85	3	8	21	3	9	25	4	12	32	5	15	41
90	2	7	20	3	9	23	4	11	28	5	13	36
95	2	7	18	3	8	21	3	10	26	4	12	31
100	2	6	17	2	7	19	3	9	23	4	10	28
105	2	6	16	2	7	18	3	8	21	3	9	25
110	2	6	15	2	6	17	2	7	20	3	8	22
115	--	--	--	2	6	16	2	7	18	3	8	21
120	--	--	--	2	6	15	2	6	17	2	7	19

The figures in the three columns represent the distances covered by a runner without fluid replacement, which will result in weight losses of 1%, 3% and 8%. A weight loss of 1% represents the distance at which Dr. David Costill recommends the runner should have started fluid replacement. A weight loss of 3% represents the distance at which the running performance may be impaired if fluid replacement has not been utilized. A weight loss of 8% represents extreme dehydration and one should not anticipate exceeding these distances without fluid replacement.

Socks and shoes will become soaked as well. Wearing shoes with nylon uppers and light socks serves to minimize the water-logging. The runner usually generates enough heat to keep the legs and feet warm, even when soaked. Some runners use plastic bags over the socks for protection.

Running while it is snowing presents relatively few problems. Running through deep snow, however, will not only get your feet quite wet and cold, but is also quite exhausting (a good workout if you're up to it). Again, in lieu of hiking boots, the runner is better off with nylon uppers and a moderately heavy pair of socks. You may wish to use the plastic bags mentioned above.

The cautions which apply for running in wind and cold apply here as well. Make sure that your proposed workout is not too ambitious for the conditions and that you are not so far from home that you will have difficulty getting back. Running into the wind mixed with rain can chill the runner very quickly.

Footing on ice and snow can be quite treacherous. Rule number one is don't make sudden, sharp turns or stops. Beware of snow covering ice. The type of tread on your running shoes has relatively little to do with traction, regardless of what manufacturers may claim. Waffle soles may, in fact, be more treacherous on ice than no tread at all. The important thing to remember is to run as flat-footed as possible. This will serve to maximize what little traction you can get and will maintain your balance better. This technique is helpful for snow and mud as well.

POLLUTION

Air pollution can be a problem in large urban areas. Whether the offending pollutant is ozone, sulfur dioxide, various nitrogen oxides, unburned hydrocarbons or particulates, our main concern is to avoid it. Short of wearing a gas mask, little can be done to alleviate the conditions.

In order to minimize the affect air pollution will have on one's training, the runner needs to be flexible. Long runs or intensive workouts should be done when the air is relatively clean. When the air quality is poor, the runner should do recuperative-type workouts.

The air quality is largely governed by the meteorological conditions and to a lesser extent by human controlled factors such as automobile traffic and factories. The air is most likely to be clean following a cold frontal passage which serves to sweep out the polluted air and replace it with air from the surrounding countryside or nearby ocean. Frontal passages occur with a fair degree of regularity in the colder part of the year. Thus, episodes of air pollution generally do not last more than a few days in winter, and the runner is advised to schedule long runs to coincide with such frontal passages when the air is most likely to be clean.

In the summer months, the air is relatively stagnant, allowing the pollutants to build up gradually over several days. The severity of air pollution episodes tends to be worst during the summer months for this reason. Again, taking advantage of the occasional frontal passages to schedule longer runs is a good idea. Taking longer runs on the weekends when the levels of pollution are usually lower corresponds to the common practice of most runners and helps avoid the worst of the pollution.

Daily variations in pollution levels are quite local, depending on both the meteorological conditions and the type of pollutant. If ozone is the main offender, running at night or early in the morning before the sunlight can generate much ozone is best. If you live near a large body of water (oceans or larger lakes), you can take advantage of the land-sea breezes. Running at mid-day when the sea breeze is best developed will minimize the concentration of pollutants you encounter. If you live in a hilly area and can choose running courses higher up, running in the morning will tend to avoid the pollutants which are trapped near the surface, and in the valleys and basins. Avoiding traffic and industrial pollution is common sense. Avoid major traffic arteries and your local steel mill if you can.

ALTITUDE

Running at high altitudes affects the runner in several ways. The most obvious change is the lack of oxygen. At 10,000 feet elevation, the partial pressure of oxygen is 70% of that at sea level; at 14,000 feet, it is 60%. No directly calculable relation exists to determine how much of a slowdown effect this has on running performance, but it may be estimated to be roughly 30 seconds per mile for an acclimated runner at 10,000 feet elevation.

The effects of altitude for sea-level-conditioned persons begin to be felt above 3000 feet elevation, becoming more and more pronounced with increased altitude change. These may result in shortness of breath, headaches, feelings of tiredness and inability to sleep. Above 10,000 feet, the unacclimated runner may hyperventilate (very rapid and shallow breathing) during exercise. This occurs as a result of changes in the partial pressure of carbon dioxide in the bloodstream (which regulates the breathing rate) as the total air pressure changes.

The acclimatization process generally takes at least two weeks and may require as much as four weeks. Typically, running performance will decline and symptoms worsen for the first 5-7 days. After the first week, things gradually improve until after 2-3 weeks the runner is quite acclimated. This suggests that the runner who doesn't have adequate time to properly acclimatize to the altitude for a given race should time his arrival to immediately precede the race.

Two significant changes occur during the acclimatization process. Almost immediately, one begins to breathe more deeply in an attempt to make up for the decreased oxygen pressure. The stress imposed by this oxygen deficiency stimulates the body to produce more red blood cells in order to transport the available oxygen to the muscles more effectively. Once the concentration of red blood cells has leveled off at its higher value (about two weeks), the runner generally feels "acclimated."

Acclimatization to extremely high altitudes (above 10,000 feet) is little understood. It is known to occur over a much longer period of time (years) and does not appear to require continuous exposure. For example, the first two times I ran the Pike's Peak Marathon were nearly identical in regard to the duration and intensity of prior training at moderate altitude (5500-7500 feet near Boulder, Colo.). My sea-level conditioning was basically the same. The first year, I ran the ascent in 2:47; the second year, I ran it in 2:29. The first year, I experienced disorientation and hallucinated above 10,000 feet; the second year, I observed no such symptoms. In successive years, I've managed to lower my ascent time by another 18 minutes (adjusting for the new, longer course) with much of this improvement coming above timberline. Talking to other runners, I've found this is not an isolated experience.

In addition to proper acclimatization, there are two pieces of advice I would give to runners who insist on running at high altitudes:

First, if you do begin to hyperventilate, stop and force yourself to take deep, slow breaths. This will serve to put the breathing regulatory mechanism back in order.

Second, beware of dehydration. Despite relatively cool temperatures, the ability of the air to carry heat away from the runner is reduced the evaporation rate is increased. The increase in evaporation rate results from an increase in water vapor diffusivity with decreased pressure. The runner will tend to dehydrate 30-50% faster at altitudes about 10,000 feet than at sea level, given the same temperature. Tips for dealing with dehydration presented for hot weather may be applied at high altitudes as well.

36

Dealing with the Heat

Hot, humid weather is the biggest threat to health that runners face

Tim Noakes, M.D.

The history of the marathon, more than any other sport has been etched with the tragedy of heat stoke. The marathon race itself commemorates the mythical run of a soldier, fully armored and "hot from battle," to Athens to inform the Greek capital that the invading Persians had been defeated on the plain of Marathon. Within seconds of delivering his news, "Rejoice, rejoice, Victory is ours!", the messenger reportedly died suddenly from what was probably heat-stroke.

More modern examples are as well remembered. The hero of the 1908 Olympics in London, the diminutive Italian Dorando Pietri lay in a semi-coma, desperately close to death, for the two days following his collapse in the final meters of the marathon. In the 1912 Olympic Games in Stockholm, the Portuguese runner, Lazaro, collapsed from heat stroke after running 19 miles and died the next day. Jim Peters, one of the first marathon runners to break the two-hour and 20-minute barrier, entered the Vancouver Stadium 15 minutes ahead of his nearest rival in the 1954 Commonwealth Games Marathon, only to collapse, like Pietri, before reaching the finishing line.

At present, with the improved awareness of runners and marathon race organizers, the dangers of heat injury have been almost totally eliminated from racing with the important exception of the Comrades Marathon, a 90-kilometer road race run annually between Durban and Pietermaritzburg, South Africa. However, athletes involved in any sport should be aware of the physiological stress imposed by heat, so that they can not only protect themselves from heat injury but can also improve their performance in heat.

Man is a homeotherm. That is, he keeps his temperature constant despite wide variations in environmental temperatures and differences in levels of physical activity. During exercise, the body acts as a machine converting chemical energy into mechanical energy in the muscles. As in a machine, this conversion is inefficient, and as much as 70% of the total energy used is released as heat rather than as athletic endeavor.

In order to maintain a constant body temperature, the athlete must dissipate all this heat so as to stay in thermal equilibrium with his environment. When all this heat is not lost, heat retention occurs and the body temperature begins to rise. If it is allowed to exceed 107 degrees F (42 degrees C), certain of the body's regulatory mechanisms break down. Blood forms pools in the arms and legs, and heart function drops precipitously, causing collapse. Because of both the resulting inadequate blood supply and a direct effect of the very high body temperature, the major organs of the body (brain, heart, liver, kidney and muscle) are severly damaged. In its full-blown presentation, this would be the classical picture of heat-stroke.

The less severe form of heat injury, acute kidney failure, may constitute a lesser degree of temperature elevation, causing kidney damage in persons predisposed by individual susceptibility.

To control the heat rise associated with exercise, the body can call upon a number of mechanisms. As exercise begins, the blood flow to the muscles is increased. Not only does the heart pump more blood, but blood is preferentially diverted away from non-essential organs toward the working muscles and skin. As it passes through the muscles, this blood is heated up and distributes this heat throughout the body, but particularly to the skin.

In this manner, as well as by a direct transfer from muscles lying close to the skin, heat is conducted to the skin surface. Here, circulating air currents convect this heat away, while any nearby objects whose surface temperature is lower than the skin temperature attracts this heat, which travels by electomagnetic waves in a form of energy transfer known as radiation. In the final method of heat loss, surface heat is used to evaporate the sweat lying on the skin. It is important to appreciate that "sweating" itself does not lose heat, but only when that sweat actually evaporates is heat lost.

The efficiency of all these mechanisms depends on a variety of factors, most of which are open to modification by the athlete. This is one area in sport where the intelligent application of knowledge will supply a competitive advantage.

1. The Exercise Intensity (Speed of Running). As the intensity of exercise increases, the body must decide whether to pump more blood to the muscles so as to maintain their increased energy requirements, or to increase its skin blood flow, thereby assisting with heat dissipation. Faced with conflicting demands, this regulation *always* favors an increased blood flow to the muscles. The result is that, while body heat production is increased, the ability to lose that heat is decreased.

It is now known that athletes running at world-class speeds develop a marked limitation to skin blood flow and therefore a limited ability to lose heat. They thus run in a "micro-environment" in which their ability to maintain heat equilibrium depends entirely on the prevailing environmental conditions. If these are unfavorable, the athlete being unable to increase his heat loss adequately will continually accumulate heat until his body temperature reaches the critical level at which heat stroke occurs.

This physiological "quirk" is the prime reason why among marathon runners, the problems of heat stroke have largely been confined to the highly-trained competitive athletes such as Pietri and Peters who are able to maintain high running speeds for prolonged periods despite adverse environmental conditions.

2. The Environmental Temperature and Windspeed. The air temperature and wind speed determine the amount of heat that can be lost from the skin by convection (that is, the heating of the surrounding air by the skin).

High wind speeds cause a larger volume of unwarmed air to cross the skin in unit time, and therefore allow for greater heat loss. Running itself produces an effective wind speed which aids heat loss. However, in severe environmental conditions, this is not sufficient to adequately increase heat loss. In contrast, the wind speed developed by long-distance cyclists appears to be sufficient to compensate even for severe conditions and explains why heat is not as great a problem for endurance cyclists as it is for marathon runners.

3. The Humidity of the Air. At rest, the skin body temperature is about 99 degrees F (33 degrees C). If exercise is undertaken in environmental temperatures greater than 99 degrees, then heat cannot be lost by convection, because the air temperature is higher than that of the body surface. Therefore, the direction of heat transfer is reversed, and the superficial tissues gain heat from the environment. In these conditions, the only avenue for heat loss is by sweating. However, as the air humidity increases, the ability to lose heat by this mechanism decreases until the evaporation of sweat practically stops.

4. Dehydration. With sweating, fluid is removed from the body, causing dehydration which may be compounded by vomiting and diarrhea. It is of some historical interest that Professors Wyndham and Strydom of the Human Sciences Laboratory in Johannesburg were the first to draw attention to the dangers of dehydration in predisposing to heat stroke. They studied runners in a 20-mile road race and showed that the body temperatures of athletes, who became dehydrated by more than 3% of their body weight, approached values previously only recorded in victims of heat stroke. In addition, they found that athletes of 155 pounds or more, who did not drink during the race, had incurred a 5% water deficit at the end of the race.

The result of their work was to emphasize the importance of adequate fluid ingestion during exercise in the heat and, in particular, for those involved in prolonged high intensity exercise such as marathon running. This work was clearly in conflict with the International Amateur Athletic Federation Rule Number 165:5, which stipulated that marathon runners could drink no fluids before the seven-mile mark of the standard marathon and thereafter could drink only every three miles. This ruling had the direct result of discouraging marathon runners from drinking during races and promoted the idea that drinking during running was a sign of "weakness."

Fortunately, science has prevailed, allowing the 1976 Montreal Olympic Marathon to be the first run without restriction on the amount of fluid that athletes could drink during the race.

5. Clothing. Besides aesthetic reasons, the rationale for wearing clothing is to trap a thin layer of air next to the body. As air is a poor conductor of heat, this thin layer rapidly heats to body temperature and acts as an insulator, preventing heat loss. Clearly, during exercise in the heat, any clothing that is worn must be designed for the opposite reason, so that it can promote air heat loss.

Marathon runners have learned that light, porous clothing such as "fishnet" vests best achieve this. In contrast, T-shirts or heavy rugby jerseys, particularly when soggy with sweat, become very good insulators, preventing adequate heat loss.

One often observes beginning runners, particularly those who might be a little overweight, training in full sweatsuits in the heat. Besides the aesthetic explanation, it is probable that many neophyte athletes believe that the more they sweat, the more exercise they must be doing, and therefore the greater the weight they stand to lose. The unfortunate truth is that in running at least the energy cost is related *only* to the distance run. Thus, to lose more weight, one needs to run farther.

Excessive sweating, by dehydrating the body, will effect a sudden loss of weight. This is the procedure used by boxers, jockeys and wrestlers in "making the weight." By exercising in the heat for as little as half an hour, it is possible to "lose" as much as a kilogram, but this is a fluid loss that will be rapidly replaced if the athlete rehydrates himself by drinking. In contrast, to lose a *real* kilogram of body weight requires the expenditure of about 65,000 calories, the equivalent of running 65 miles!

The insulating qualities of different clothes is expressed in Clo units. One Clo unit is equivalent to the amount of insulation provided by that ordinary business apparel, which provides comfort at temperatures of 70 degrees F when both wind speed and humidity are low. The clothing of the Eskimo provides 10-12 Clo units and is essential for life in Arctic conditions. However, because of the considerable heat production during exercise, clothing that will provide one Clo unit of insulation is all that is required when running in temperatures well below zero (provided the wind speed is low). Thus with one exception discussed below, there is seldom, if ever, the need for runners from warm weather areas to train for any period in a sweatsuit. By doing so, he merely increases his own discomfort and promotes conditions favorable for heat stroke.

Fatal cases of heat stroke have been recorded in American high school football players who thought they would lose weight more quickly if, while training in summer heat, they wore a neoprene diving suit (wet suit) under their normal football uniforms.

6. Heat Acclimatization. It is a well established observation that when sportsmen who have trained exclusively in cool weather, are suddenly confronted with hot, humid condition, they suffer an immediate and dramatic fall-off in performance. However, with perseverance and continued training in the heat, performance soon recovers, returning rapidly to normal.

The process underlying this adaptation is termed heat acclimatization. It begins after the first exposure to exercise in the heat; it progresses rapidly and is fully developed after 7-10 days. Only by *exercising* in the heat can one become heat acclimatized. The optimum method of achieving this is to train daily in the heat, for periods of 2-4 hours, for 10 days. Once established, heat acclimatization is fully retained for about two weeks. Thereafter, it is lost at rates that vary among individuals. It is best retained by those who stay in good physical condition and who re-expose themselves to exercise in the heat on at least a fortnightly basis.

The importance of heat acclimatization is that it confers considerable protection from heat injury. Competitively, when running in the heat, the heat-acclimatized athlete will always have the "edge" over his equally fit, but unacclimatized, opponent. This was particularly apparent at the 1960 Olympic Games in Rome when the afternoon temperatures were frequently over 88 degrees F and the humidity was high. It is said that at those Games, the endurance races went to the fittest, only if they were also heat acclimatized.

FLUID REPLACEMENT

During exercise in the heat, athletes lose 1-2 liters (about 1-2 quarts) of sweat every hour, with the heavier athletes losing the greater amounts. Progressive dehydration occurs when this fluid loss is not replaced. If it is allowed to exceed 3% of body weight, the risk of heat injury becomes considerable.

Since the pioneering work of Professors Wyndham and Strydom, it has become common practice for marathon runners to drink about 300 milliliters of fluid every 15 minutes while competing in races. While the fluid requirements of long-distance canoeists and road cyclist are somewhat less, both these sporting groups are aware of the importance of fluid replacement during exercise.

If it is accepted that fluid ingestion is important during prolonged exercise, what is the theoretical composition of the ideal drink? This is an area bedevilled by so much mystique, malpractice and, more recently, by commercial interests and their attendant pressures, that it deserves careful attention.

The greatest source of fluid loss during exercise is obviously sweat, but it may be compounded by vomiting or diarrhea. What people seem unwilling to comprehend is that the really important constituent of sweat is *water*. It is the loss of water that poses the threat to life. The attendant loss of small quantities of the compounds dissolved in sweat (sodium, potassium and magnesium) are of trivial significance compared to that of water. This can best be exemplified by considering the sweat losses of an average runner during a marathon race.

Besides water, the important chemical contained in sweat is sodium chloride (common table salt). Its concentration in the sweat of a heat acclimatized athlete is about 0.3%; that is three grams of salt (equal to a teaspoonful) in one liter of sweat. To develop symptoms of salt depletion, an athlete's body must be depleted by at least 35 grams. At this level of depletion, the athlete begins to feel lazy, his blood pressure is low, causing him to feel faint and giddy, particularly if he stands up suddenly. If this deficit exceeds 50 grams, the athlete becomes apathetic, his level of consciousness is reduced, leading ultimately to collapse.

How easy is it for a marathon runner to become depleted by 35 grams of salt? During a three-hour marathon race, a 70-kilogram (145-pound) athlete who drank nothing and who was sweating at a rate of 1.5 liters every hour, would lose a total of 4.5 liters of sweat; corresponding to an overall body weight loss of 6½%. The salt content of this sweat would be 13.5 grams, far less than the 35 grams required to produce even mild symptoms of salt depletion. Yet, the loss of 4.5 liters of water would raise the body temperature to heat-stroke levels and would represent an extreme risk of heat injury.

Thus, for practical purposes, this small loss of sodium chloride during marathon running is of minor importance compared to the need for adequate water replacement. If the athlete wishes to ingest salt during exercise, it should be in as dilute a form as that found in sweat; namely a teaspoonful of salt dissolved in a liter of fluid. The practice by some runners of taking large amounts of salt tablets (each containing one half gram of sodium chloride) without adequate water is to be condemned as dangerous.

Potassium chloride, the third important constituent of sweat, has only recently achieved any real status in the marathon runner's drink. This followed the work of an American marathon-running biochemist who analyzed his sweat, rationalizing that if that was what he was losing, then the ideal fluid should replace these losses. As he found potassium chloride in his sweat, it became an important constituent of his "recipe," which subsequently became so popular that it was bought by a commercial firm and made available on a large scale. But was his original rationale correct?

The important feature of potassium is that it is stored in muscle cells in combination with muscle glycogen (the term for stored glucose or sugars). Marathon runners store large amounts of glycogen in preparation for marathon races, and during the race a large percentage of their energy comes from the breakdown of this glycogen. As this glycogen is burned, it releases large amounts of potassium, which must be lost from the body. The easiest way to lose this is in sweat; thus, the potassium found in sweat represents that which the body is trying to lose. Clearly, there is no need to compound this by drinking potassium-containing fluids during exercise. However, *after* exercise when the body starts to restore glycogen and with it potassium, there is a clear indication to drink potassium-containing fluids.

When running in adverse conditions, regular sponging with a cool fluid seems to offer considerable psychological relief. The physiological effects of sponging on overall heat loss are ill-understood, largely because it has received little scientific attention. However, recent research suggests that the skin temperature plays an extremely important role in controlling some of the physiological responses to heat, and as it is unlikely that sponging itself effects a large heat loss, its major advantage may be to prevent the skin temperature from rising.

The best place to sponge is the legs, particularly the thighs. Because they are the active muscles, they have a large surface area and they are exposed to the greatest air movement.

The problems of exercise in the heat are magnified in an event such as the Comrades Marathon. Fortunately, the organizers are acutely aware of the problems it poses, and they have done everything in their power to alleviate these.

The magnitude of the problem is such that at the end of every race, a large number of athletes are treated for severe dehydration and varying degrees of heat exhaustion. From among this group, a small number have had to undergo intensive hospital treatment for heat-induced kidney failure. While the numbers in this latter group are small and all these athletes have subsequently recovered, the Comrades Marathon is the only sporting event in the world that is plagued by this condition.

An alarming feature of the 1976 Comrades was the condition at the finish of some of the top runners. Descriptions of these athletes suggest that they were in advanced states of dehydration, with high body temperatures probably approaching the heat-stroke range.

An overall view of athletes who develop heat-related problems in the Comrades Marathon clearly delineates two groups. For the average runner, heat is only a problem if he does not carefully follow the guidelines prescribed in this article. The athlete who is not heat-acclimatized, who does not drink and sponge regularly and who wears inappropriate clothing has only himself to blame should he develop problems.

However, the highly-trained competitive athletes can develop heat injury despite meticulous attention to all these details and through no fault of their own.

For an athlete to be "competitive" in the Comrades Marathon, it is estimated that he must run at close to 80% of his maximum oxygen uptake capacity for the entire race. At this level of intensity, it is likely that the athlete develops a limitation on the amoung of blood that he can afford to divert from his working muscles to the skin.

A restriction on the amount of heat that can be lost by convection (through the skin blood flow) places increased demands on sweating as the important method of heat loss. It also means that the athlete can no longer depend on his body to lose all the heat that he is producing. Instead, he is at the mercy of the elements.

If the surrounding air is cool, windy and of low humidity, then heat loss may be adequate. In contrast, in hot, humid conditions with little wind speed, both convection and maximal sweating may be inadequate to lose all the heat produced by a high running speed.

Under these conditions, not only will there be a gradual progressive rise in body temperature, but the process of sweating, by removing fluid from the body, will cause progressive dehydration.

A fluid loss of 3% or less of the total body weight has little measureable effect on body function. However, above this level of dehydration, the body begins to make short-term adaptations, each of which becomes progressively less able to prevent a final dramatic rise in body temperature—the hyperthermic spiral.

The first adaptation to dehydration is to raise the body temperature. By this, the temperature gradient between the body center and the skin surface is increased so that the transfer of heat to the skin surface is facilitated without requiring a diversion of blood from the muscles. However, when dehydration becomes more advanced (greater than 5%), there is no longer sufficient fluid in the body to waste it either as sweat or as a "luxurious" blood flow to the skin.

The body then takes the potentially drastic decision of shutting off the skin blood flow and diverting all the remaining blood to keep the muscles working. From this point, the athlete is locked into the hyperthermic spiral, from which only a voluntary reduction in the rate of energy production (i.e., running speed) or the finishing line, will effect release.

During the 1976 Comrades Marathon, the environmental conditions, from the beginning, were unfavorable. For the top competitors, this would mean that to maintain adequate heat loss, they would have to sweat maximally right from the start of the race. Even with perfect assistance, it is almost impossible for an athlete who is sweating maximally to prevent himself from becoming gradually and progressively dehydrated.

In a race as long as the Comrades, the point must be reached when dehydration exceeds the level at which both the skin blood flow and the sweat rate fall, and the body temperature begins to rise. Fortunately, most athletes seldom reach this point because, due to fatigue caused by factors other than heat, they hit "the wall" after about 30 miles and start to slow down. By slowing down, the athlete immediately reduces his rate of energy production and is released from the hyperthermic spiral. Thus, "relative" unfitness is paradoxically the safety factor that protects against heat stroke.

In contrast, the fitness of the competitive runner carries him beyond this point, and unless the environmental conditions alter favorably, his race becomes literally one of reaching the finish before the spiral in body temperature catches him. In practice, environmental conditions are almost certain to deteriorate as the race progresses. The air temperature and humidity inevitably increase during the day, while the transfer to the runner of radiant energy from the sun further compounds his heat balance problems.

The problems of the 1976 Comrades Marathon were caused by its being one of the fastest-ever ultra-distance races run in severe environmental conditions. As even the most superbly conditioned athlete cannot cope with every combination of fast running speeds and severe environmental conditions, competitive Comrades runners must accept philosopically that they are at the mercy of the elements and if they choose to *race* in adverse environmental conditions, they run a small risk of developing heat injury. More than any sportsmen, they need, therefore, to be fully conversant with every possible method of reducing their risk.

A way in which the organizers might assist runners in making this decision intelligently would be to inform them regularly during the race of the environmental conditions and indicate, on a scale of "heat stress," what exactly this means.

37

Dealing with the Cold

The secret of staying warm is to dress lightly but wisely

Alan Claremont, Ph.D.

Cold, windy and slippery conditions may appear to be good reasons for avoiding or severely restricting running activity during winter months. However, appropriate adjustments for prevailing climatic conditions can result in much beneficial and enjoyable training during this season.

Adequately protected, man can tolerate environmental temperature ranges between 58 degrees below zero and 212 above, but only a seven-degree variation in "core temperature" without impairment to physical working capacity. The most important physiologic adjustment in the cold then, is the maintenance of body temperature. Fortunately, even the slowest running speeds (11-12 minutes per mile) result in energy expenditures approximately 9-10 times the resting metabolic rate and are adequate to maintain desirable body temperature levels in sub-zero weather without the need of heavy, restrictive clothing.

In addition to an increase in metabolic rate, another protective mechanism to maintain heat balance is the constriction of surface blood vessels. This can greatly increase the insulating capacity of the skin and adjacent tissues. Reduction in blood flow to the body surface and gradual cooling of the skin results in less heat being lost to the environment.

Adequate protection from the cold is obtained when the athlete brings his preferred semitropical microclimate with him. Appropriate clothing is of extreme importance to avoid sudden changes in body temperature (chilling), for even a small drop in internal temperature will initiate shivering which can interfere with coordinated muscular activity. Further, lowered tissue temperatures appear to be associated with common respiratory ailments and muscle-tendon injuries.

Clothing should be selected to provide, as much as possible, protection against chilling at low levels of activity and yet sweat evaporation at higher levels of activity to keep the body temperature from going too high.

Lightweight, porous materials of an absorbent nature will provide sufficient protection under most cold conditions. During the initial, cooler stages of running, a thin layer of trapped air helps prevent loss of body heat. With the onset and increase in sweating as body temperature rises, a "wicking" action of porous clothing promotes sweat transfer to the outer garment where maximum evaporation can occur.

The term "lightweight clothing" requires defining in standardized units in order to determine what constitutes "adequate" protective covering for various training intensities and environmental temperatures. The "Clo" unit is generally used. A Clo unit is equal to the amount of insulation provided by ordinary apparel which will maintain comfort at room temperature (about 70 degrees F).

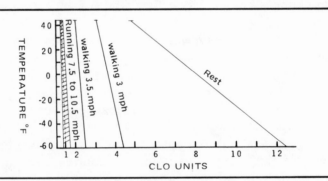

The figure illustrates how little protective covering is required while running at 7½-10½ miles per hour. From the observed decrease in Clo unit requirements with increasing metabolic rates, it appears reasonable to extrapolate insulative needs of 0.75-1.25 Clo units at temperatures decreasing to as low as 30 below zero.

This agrees reasonably well with my training experiences, in which comfort was maintained at temperatures down to 20 below by wearing leather ski mitts, cotton underwear, running shorts, heavy cotton T-shirt, standard cotton sweat suit with hooded top, ski goggles, wool socks and leather training shoes. The total weight of these garments (4½ pounds exclusive of shoes) does not impose appreciable restrictions on faster running.

Up to this point, the degree of cold stress has been related only to absolute temperature, without consideration of the "wind-chill" factor which is critical at low temperatures. Wind-chill expresses the discomfort associated with the combined effects of absolute temperature and wind velocity. "Effective temperature," the degree of cold perceived, is a more appropriate guideline from which to determine appropriate Clo units. For example, a 10 m.p.h. wind at zero degrees (F) would produce an effective temperature of minus-40 —a severe cold stress.

However, wind velocity is usually a varying factor that can cause the chill factor effect to fluctuate considerably within a given training session. Additionally, windbreaks such as trees, buildings, gullies, etc., can considerably modify the wind speeds to the extent that one may be substantially overdressed at times within a given training session. Under these conditions, the following personal approach has been satisfactory in compensating for the variable chill factor of fluctuating winds.

I wear a light nylon top in addition to the previously described clothing. Admittedly, sweat evaporation is impeded with nylon, but the top can easily be removed and tied around the waist if the heat load builds up excessively. The major advantage of nylon is the excellent wind-proofing and anti-chill properties, in addition to its negligible weight. When starting out, I run with or diagonal to the prevailing wind, mainly to minimize initial cold sensations on the face. After running a short while and warming up, direct wind and cold are much less noticeable on the relatively unprotected face. Finally, I select courses which maximize shelter from the wind.

Proper selection of lightweight, insulative clothing can enable an athlete to continue running within a warm and comfortable microclimate during winter months. In addition to the physiologic benefits of continued training, there are also many aesthetic qualities of this season which are better experienced than described.

REFERENCES

Astrand, P.O. and K. Rodahl.—"Temperature Regulation," *Textbook of Work Physiology.* McGraw-Hill Book Co., 1970.

DeVries, H.A.—"Environment and Exercise," *Physiology of Exercise*, Wm. C. Brown and Co., 1966.

Consolazio, C.F., R.E. Johnson, L.J. Pecora. *Physiologic Measurements and Metabolic Functions in Man*, McGraw-Hill Book Co., 1963.

Henschel, A.—"The Environment and Performance," *Physiology of Work Capacity and Fatigue*, Charles C. Thomas, 1971.

Pugh, L.G.C.E. "Cold Stress and Muscular Exercise with Special Reference to Accidental Hypothermia," *Brit. Med. J.* 2:333-337, 1967.

Part 8
Keeping the Sport on Course

38

Races with Growing Pains

Officials wonder what to do with all the new marathoners

M. Dean Hill

T he 10th Annual Palos Verdes Marathon passed a milestone when it went over the 1000 entrant mark for the first time in the race's history. The field totaled 1204.

That was in 1976, and 1977 was something else entirely. The 11th PV Marathon drew 2040 entrants, and 1706 of them finished.

Such sharp growth in just a year might seem surprising because Palos Verdes is a scenic but terribly difficult course that produces somewhat slow times, attracts few big-name runners and gets little national or even local publicity.

But it should not be surprising in light of what's happening to other marathons around the country. The post-Bicentennial year featured unprecedented growth in marathoning.

The New York City Marathon in October 1976, run for the first time through the city's five boroughs, drew a record 2000-plus. In 1977, entries were cut off at 5000.

Mission Bay in San Diego, 120 miles down the California coast from Palos Verdes, had about 800 marathoners and 420 half-marathoners in 1976. The total field in 1977 ballooned to 2300 runners, 1400 of them in the marathon.

It was also not unusual for younger, smaller and lesser-known marathons to double and triple in size in one year, and for first-time races to draw far more runners than their surprised sponsors envisioned.

Just about everyone involved in running and racing, or simply watching and wishing, can supply reasons why there is a boom in marathoning. But whatever the reasons are, this boom raises perhaps a more important question: What effect will this mercurial growth have on the sport? The answer is unclear as yet, but it is clear some sharp growing pains lie ahead.

The Los Alamitos Marathon is one of the younger and smaller events on the marathon calendar, and in 1977 it grew substantially but without bad pains.

Run through Los Alamitos, Calif., and three other northwest Orange County communities, the race was born in 1976 as part of a city-sponsored community festival. There was no festival in 1977, but the race lived on and the marathon had 117 runners, 107 of whom finished.

"That's about double the first year," said Mitch Lansdell, race director and the city's director of community services. "We had anticipated with better coverage we would get that many." Thus prepared and because of the still-small number of runners, Lansdell had few problems.

"Next year, though, if it goes to 500, I could have a problem," he said.

The race, however, is usually in early March, and Lansdell has time to get some idea of what may happen by watching other events between now and then.

Los Alamitos has a pleasant course, flat and fairly fast, and is run through residential areas, by the Los Alamitos Naval Air Station and several golf courses. But it also has something like 98 turns, and that factor may keep its growth within manageable limits.

At 13 years old, with a good runners' course and an established following, Mission Bay, on the other hand, suffered some of the sharpest growing pains of 1977, pains that are in the offing for other unprepared races.

"We used to have about a 30% increase each year, and usually it's been very predictable," said race director Bill Gookin of the San Diego Track Club. Based upon this predictability, he said, they figure a "fudge factor" into preparations.

"This time, it was just more people than we expected," Gookin said after the overall field nearly doubled in size from 1976.

"That means we used up all the registration forms," he said. "That means that the race start had to be delayed, and that's something we don't like to do. It also means, if you're not prepared for it, there are problems at aid stations."

There was also a parking crunch, and the start was not only delayed, Gookin said, "we had traffic backed up on the freeway, and that is not good. . . . We're having to move the start and finish."

Gookin takes pride in the race because "Mission Bay, and Palos Verdes for that matter, are designed to try to do things for the runners."

That, however, may become more of a problem as the number of entrants continues to grow.

Les Woodson was luckier, and he was able to keep to a minimum the growing pains for Palos Verdes despite the 67% increase in entrants. Almost as soon as entry forms began arriving in mid-April, Woodson knew his early predictions might be too conservative.

"I had been shooting for 1500 until the applications started coming in," he said.

Based on the large number of early entries and what he'd seen happen elsewhere, Woodson was ready for the 2040 entrants. This meant extra work lining up volunteers, carefully preparing check-in and finish-line procedures, and close liaison with the local police who patrol the four cities through which the race is run.

"I would say we had about 250 people working the day of the marathon, and that's a lot of bodies," Woodson said. "We had 50 people working at aid stations, 20 timers and recorders, probably 40-50 people handling check-in, 54 (Los Angeles County) sheriff's and 26 Palos Verdes Estates police personnel and reserves."

The race through expensive communities on a rural-like peninsula jutting from the middle of the otherwise densely populated Los Angeles coastal section is sponsored by the Palos Verdes Kiwanis Club, whose members also help race day.

The consensus afterward was that, despite the largest field ever, it may have been the best Palos Verdes Marathon yet. Runners thought so, the cops thought so, and a tired Les Woodson was pleased with the outcome.

"Palso Verdes was probably one of the most well organized in the country for that many runners," 1977 winner Ron Kurrle said. "Boston wasn't that well organized."

Kurrle, who was coming off a victory at the World Masters Marathon and a 21st-place finish at Boston, ran 2:23:10. It was his second win at Palos Verdes. Kurrle's only "problem" really came after the race when he picked up his car near the start and returned to the finish area to pick up his award.

"I drove around for about 35 minutes looking for a place to park," he laughed.

There was also some runner-vehicle congestion along several of the two-lane roads.

"Because of the high number of runners and their physical abilities, they stayed relatively bunched up longer than we expected," said Lt. Walt Thurner of the Los Angeles County Sheriff's Department, which patrols three of the four race cities.

"We anticipated they would stretch out to single file around the eight- or nine-mile mark. Some stayed four abreast clear into 15 and 16 miles."

But that was only a minor problem. Overall, Thurner said, "It went just fantastic, just really out of sight. It's the only event I've ever worked where the cops have a good time."

That is evidenced by the fact that all 54 sheriff's personnel were volunteers and on their own time. The only cost to the taxpayer, Thurner said, was gas for the patrol cars and the sheriff's helicopter, which was on duty anyway. Nine Sheriff's Department members, including Thurner's boss, a couple of narcotics officers and a 50-year-old secretary, also ran the race.

Woodson, a Kiwanis Club member, has directed the race the past three years and, in effect, has shepherded it to its present spot as one of the four biggest marathons in the country.

'Yet," he said, "with a 67% increase in the number of entries, we had fewer problems in terms of runner satisfaction, in terms of community satisfaction and awareness. We had fewer problems this year than last."

And he is proud of this for both himself and everyone else involved with Palos Verdes.

"I think I have a right to be proud of this race," he said. "The people that run in Palos Verdes and the people who work in PV really make it the race that it is."

But what will Palos Verdes and other events be in years to come? The indication is that changes are coming—that they have to for some events to survive.

The changes, in some cases, may be small, like a few course alterations, more aid stations and better coordination with local police to insure conflicts are kept at a minimum.

At Mission Bay, the San Diego Police have been very cooperative, particularly Sgt. Gordie Clausen, race director Gookin said.

"After this year's race, he (Clausen) went over the course and timing very carefully, (and) he came up with suggestions where we could start and finish with a minimum of changes," Gookin said. "Most people would say, 'You change this or no race!' He went to all that trouble to make it possible for us to continue the event."

Other changes, though, may be more drastic, like limiting entries, imposing qualifying times or various types of split starts. None of these yet has won much popularity.

"I personally don't see any way to limit entries that's equitable," Woodson said, "The runners are going to run anyway."

And some race directors like Woodson also have philosophical problems with trying to cut off potential entrants.

"I hate to set a limit," Woodson said. "Philosophically, the Palos Verdes Marathon is not an elite race. It's a race for people who in many cases are running their first marathon."

By imposing some type limit, he said, "I think we'd be cutting out the very type person who has supported us so well in the past. We're not Boston."

Woodson was quick to add, though, that he and the club will have to take a hard look at what to do in the future.

"I think we may have reached our limit," he said. But he added that 3000 entries at Palos Verdes is easily within the realm of possibility for 1978.

Some shorter events, such as the Bay to Breakers in San Francisco and the Peachtree Road Race in Atlanta, whose thundering hordes totaled 12,000 and 6000 respectively, already have become major running and media "events" like Boston.

Though this probably won't happen to most marathons, most will continue to grow, small races will become large ones and large ones much larger.

And one thing is clear: Unprecedented jumps in race size, if not adequately prepparred for, may overstretch the limited resources of some sponsors, place severe strains on the cadres of race volunteers and officials, and most important, may irreparably harm the community goodwill so vital to the success of most larger marathons.

39

Course Measurement

Driving a car over the route won't do.
Runners expect precision

Ted Corbitt

T he United States long-distance running course certification prog-
gram was started in 1964, first by the Road Runners Club of
America (RRCA) and months later by the Amateur Athletic Union of
the US. Originally, the AAU was concerned with requiring accurate
courses for its national championship long-distance events. In 1966,
the RRCA and the AAU, via the Sub-Committee on Standards of the
National AAU Long Distance and Road Running Committee, agreed
that the AAU Standards Committee would take over all course certification. The RRCA has continued to keep a list of certified courses in
this country, in cooperation with the AAU Standards Committee.

To certify a marathon course, the course must be measured accurately, using an acceptable measuring technique such as
"chaining," the use of a steel tape, the "calibrated bicycle method" or
the "calibrated measuring wheel method." The recommended method
of measuring is the calibrated bicycle method, which will be described
later.

COURSE PLANNING

The International Amateur Athletic Federation defines the marathon race as being 42,195 meters, or 26 miles, 385 yards. The course
should be on paved highways, but it may be on paved bike paths, on
pedestrian walkways, on closed roads in parklands, on city or country
roads with limited traffic, where the roads can be closed during the
race or where traffic can be controlled by the police.

There are numerous marathon course configurations. Some
generally-used course layouts include:

1. "Point-to-point" Course (e.g., Hopkinton-to-Boston Marathon
and the Fiesta Bowl Marathon, Scottsdale, Ariz.).

2. "Big loop" Course (e.g., Yonkers Marathon, wherein the start and finish are near each other.).

3. "Out-and-back" Course (e.g., Culver City Marathon and the San Francisco Marathon.

4. "Out and Back, with a Loop " (e.g., Holyoke Marathon and Observer Marathon, Charlotte, N.C.).

5. "Lap course" (e.g., Atlantic City—out and back three times: Detroit Marathon, Belle Isle, five laps).

6. "Figure-of-eight loop" (e.g., Atlantic Avon Marathon and Land-O-Lakes Marathon, Minneapolis, Minn.).

7. "Out-and-back in two directions" (e.g., Rotary Shamrock Marathon, Virginia Beach, Va.).

Generally, the race promoter should plan to use the most favorable course in his area, in terms of safety, ease of staying on the course and so forth. Sometimes, the location of the sponsor or of dressing facilities dictates the site of the course, especially as to the start and finish points. Some courses have been set up out of town for special effects, such as to race at higher altitude, or to take advantage of parklands which are relatively free of vehicular traffic and air pollutants.

In striving for personal best times and to qualify for the US marathon tryouts for the Pan-American Games and the Olympic Games marathon teams, runners want some courses which will help them make fast times. The hardest courses are the hilly ones, with the emphasis on hill climbing. These courses are easier to run in cold weather, and they are harder and "slower" in hot weather. The easy courses are the more or less flat ones. It is possible to make fast times on such courses, provided other factors are favorable. The fastest courses are those that are gently rolling, featuring mild to moderate hill climbing, interspersed with many long gentle to moderately steep downhill sections. There are courses of various mixtures of these types of layouts. Most courses are capable of producing fast times with fit, determined runners, striving under favorable running conditions. (The Boston Marathon course, for instance, is moderately hard, and features a lot of hill climbing, rewarded with many long down sweeps, which helps fit, courageous runners to generate fast times.)

It is claimed that "following winds" don't actually push the runner along, but they reduce the air resistance which impedes his moving ahead. Courses with prevailing winds which create tailwinds will generally produce faster times. Headwinds cause slower times. These factors may be considered in laying out a marathon course, especially where weather patterns are consistent.

Running over a scenic course can add to the runner's enjoyment of the challenge and can stimulate him to tolerate a harder effort over the course. While selecting a scenic route should take a second place to course safety, frequently the two factors merge, with planning.

Safety usually refers to the absence of danger from automobile traffic and air borne pollutants. Hostile neighborhoods and poor footing may be problems occasionally. Weather also is a common safety factor; snow and ice are sometimes ignored but such footing is a big danger to older competitors, and hilly courses under these conditions are a danger to all runners. Shady lanes for summer races make such racing safer.

The race promoter should select a course that the runners can stay on without getting lost while racing. With plenty of police protection, almost any route can be used. If police protection is likely to be non-existent or skimpy, the selected course should present the minimum number of encounters with traffic. Ideally, the course would be cleared of traffic, or perhaps one lane would be closed to traffic. Some of the mass-participation races effectively close entire roads to traffic as the runners take up every bit of free road space. Traffic-free loops of 5-6 miles inside parks are good racing sites, except for the marathons with extra large fields where the slower runners get lapped, complicating the lap-recording job.

Once the course is selected, the promoter should check with the police departments concerned along the route and make certain that the race will be permitted as planned. Police have in some cases demanded changes in race routes as late as the day of a race. Route problems should be resolved before the final selection and measurement of the race course.

The race promoter must monitor the marathon course with people and with signs to keep the runners on course. If personnel are to turn the runners onto new roads, they should be in place before the race starts, especially at turns as well as at forked roads where a decision must be made by the runners as to which way to run. Guide signs are useful, although there have been cases in which they have been removed or replaced to lead runners off-course.

Many races have been spoiled after the gun went off by having the lead runners or others run off course. In some cases, police escorts have led runners down wrong roads. The sponsor should make certain that lead vehicles actually know the course route. When runners go off-course, all releases of race results should mention this fact. Such incidents usually result when the courses are too complicated, winding, or leave apparent main roads without adequate guidance or signaling to the runners. Such courses need a lot of people on duty to keep the runners on the measured route.

A few marathon sponsors have, at some expense, followed the lead of the Munich and the Montreal Olympic marathon courses and painted blue lines on the road to point the way. These painted lines are solid at points but mostly broken lines, as at the New York Marathon's point-to-point loop and at the Ocean State Marathon with its three lap course. Painted signs on the road and other use of paint can also aid in keeping runners on-course, if permission can be gotten from the police department to put them down.

Courses which serve well for less than 200 runners, give or take a hundred, can suddenly become obsolete as racing sites when the entry lists explode to upwards of 1000 starters. The start area and the first few miles of the Boston Marathon course used in the 1970s is a good example of an obsolete racing start. Courses which use sidewalks, bikeways or similar small paths become unmanageable when several hundred starters show up to race.

Race starts on stadium tracks also become impractical with several hundred starters, since running even a half-mile on the track could result in the runners in the back of the pack getting lapped. It then becomes more sensible to start the race outside of the stadium and, if desired, to have the race finish on the stadium track. Also, loop courses of more than three repeated laps for a marathon present problems with slower runners getting lapped, complicating lap recording, especially in those races with no qualifying entry times. In some cases, race sites have been changed for established races to meet the demands of larger fields. Others should be changed, or perhaps the sponsors should break some of these races into several separate races to make racing fairer for all of the runners.

There are marathon fans who will travel around to see marathon "shootouts" among the stars. The circular, out-and-back and figure-of-eight loop courses favor spectators to varying degrees. Spectator welfare is often considered in laying out courses. Fans have resorted to walking or jogging around loop courses during races, and to riding such vehicles as bicycle, automobiles, buses, subways and even helicopters to scoot from place to place to watch a marathon battle unfold.

PREPARING TO MEASURE

A prospective marathon course may be roughly and quickly surveyed by automobile to check out possible routes. The course may be more closely inspected by walking over it, or preferably running over it. It may also be checked or plotted out on large-scale maps from local sources—for instance, maps with a scale of one inch on the map to 150 feet on the ground, or US Department of Interior Geological

Survey topographic maps of the area, purchased from a map store. Measure the proposed route by scaling of the road with an adjustable divider, with a ruler or a string calibrated on the map's scale.

Course measuring should not be done in extreme weather conditions such as rain, snow, windy days or very hot weather. Measuring should not be done when a wide variation in the temperature of the atmosphere will develop during the measurement.

The names of all streets and roads making up the marathon course should be written up and kept for reference. A map should be made of the course. A profile of the terrain may also be made by referring to maps of the area.

The race course must be measured at least twice, using proper, acceptable procedures. A written report of what was done, when and how the course was measured, must be sent to the AAU Standards Committee for review. This committee studies the report and determines if the measurement techniques are acceptable, and if the course appears to have been measured with "reasonable accuracy." If all is correct, the course is added to the list of certified courses being kept by the RRCA. If the measurement is not acceptable, the race promoter is informed of this fact, with suggestions as to the needed corrective actions.

Re-certification of marathon courses has become common. Many road changes still occur. Each promoter of annual races should arrange for an inspection of the course before race day each year, to determine that the measured route is still intact. If road changes have been made, the course must be brought back to the 26-mile, 385-yard (42-kilometer, 195-meter) distance, and the results of the alterations sent to the AAU Standards Committee for study and re-certification of the course. For information on road course measurements or course certification, contact the AAU Standards Committee, through the AAU of the US national office, or the RRC of America. It is wise to study acceptable procedures before measuring a race course so as to avoid wasted efforts. Professional measurers also need to know the special needs of road course measuring before measuring a race course.

The standard mile: It is necessary to lay out a road calibration course with a good steel tape, in order to calibrate a bicycle wheel or a surveyor's measuring wheel. Accuracy of the calibration course is essential to get course accuracy. This standard length should be one mile for best results, but it may be one kilometer or one-half mile as the minimum length. Select a straight, level, paved, lightly-traveled road for the road calibration course. It should be carefully measured at least twice, if an experienced measuring crew does the job; if they lack much experience, the calibration course should be measured four times. The average of these measurements is used as the calibration distance, and the start and finish lines are permanently marked (drive nails in asphalt/macadam surfaces, or chisel cross-cuts in concrete, and use paint to identify lines/points).

Tape-measuring equipment needed to lay out a road calibration course includes: a calibrated *steel tape*, preferably 100 feet long. Inspect the tape for splices, kinks or evidence of repairs. Such a tape shouldn't be used unless it has been re-calibrated and the "corrected" length known for use. The exact starting and ending points of the tape should be located. A *spring balance* (or by a spring scale from a hardware store) is attached to the forward end of the tape. Also, have a *notebook* and 4H *pencil* to record everything that is done; a *red pencil* to mark distances on the road, and *keel or lumber crayon* to mark a circle around the red penciled mark to make it easier for the rear tapeman to find the red mark (the number of tape-length increments may be written on the road), or *chaining pins* may be used to mark the red line by laying them on the road mark; and a *hammer*, cold *chisel*, *nails* and *paint* to put permanent marks at the start and finish of the calibration course.

A minimum of two persons, at least one of whom has experience, can lay out a road calibration course, but it is best to get at least three persons to form the measuring team. The chief of the measuring party should have had experience and should supervise the measurement. He might act as the *rear-tape* man and serve to keep the *lead tapeman* in proper alignment as they travel over the calibration course, and he may keep written records unless another person is on hand to do it. The lead tapeman carries a red pencil to mark tape increments on the road. He handles the spring balance or scale with which the tape is stretched for a 10-pound pull with a 100-foot tape. A *recorder* writes notes of tape increments, and so forth (the rear tapeman may do this if no recorder is on hand). He may also assist the lead tapeman by marking tape lengths. If there is another person to serve as an *assistant*, he can direct traffic and assist in other ways.

An electronic distance meter or measurer may be used to lay out a road calibration course on a level, straight, paved road. The accuracy of the electronic distance meter is greater than that for measurements with a steel tape.

Running tracks are not acceptable for calibrating either a measuring wheel or a bicycle fitted with a special counter.

CALIBRATED BICYCLE METHOD

It is difficult to accurately measure road race courses, but the easiest and most practical means of measuring a road course accurately is to use the calibrated bicycle method of measuring. It permits measuring at about 10-12 miles an hour. A bicycle fitted with a special counter is calibrated and then ridden over the route to be measured.

A road calibration course must be measured with a steel tape before measuring the race course with the bicycle. Instructions on setting up a calibration course have been described previously.

Equipment: (1) bicycle, with good tires, pumped up but not too hard; (2) bicycle counter: there are several counter systems in use, none of which can be purchased in stores; contact the AAU Standards Committee for information on acceptable counters which are available; (3) marking materials: hammer, chisel, nails, paint to mark the roads at checkpoints, etc., and for field notes: notebook, pen/pencil; (4) steel tape: to fix the start/finish and checkpoint marks to permanent landmarks; marks put on the road often get wiped out due to road repairs or to re-paving of roads.

Method: Before calibrating the bicycle, ride it several miles to warm it up. Then ride over the road calibration course at least four times, recording the counter readings (e.g., "counts," or "revolutions and spokes," or "odometer and wheel units," depending on the counter used). The readings are averaged and this result is taken as the "constant," with which the race course is then measured. The bicycle is then either carried or ridden to the race course site.

The bicycle is ridden over the race course. The front-wheel axle is placed on the starting line, and the bicycle is ridden along the path the runners will take, including all possible shortcuts. The latter is especially important in measuring around turns. Unless barriers will be set up to channel runners onto a specific path, the shortest route lies about one meter from curbs or painted boundary lines, fences, vehicles and so forth.

Meter readings should be taken and recorded periodically at intersections. Checkpoints or intermediate distances, preferably in metric increments of 1-5- kilometer intervals, should be set up along the course. The latter should be identified (by tape measurements), with nearby permanent landmarks for future reference and marked. These marks can be useful if part of the course must be re-measured due to road changes or if the start/finish points must be changed later on.

After the bicycle has been ridden from the starting line to the finish line (or vice versa), it is recalibrated by riding it over the calibration course again at least twice. These figures are averaged. Next, the original constant from the calibration rides is averaged with the post-course-measuring calibration rides average for the final "constant" for the day. The latter is used to compute the distance of the measured course. In most instances, no adjustment of the race course is needed. However, the arithmetic should be done. Modest adjustments will need to be made at the start or finish line, when there is a sizeable change in atmosphere temperature between the original calibration rides and in completing the course measurement.

The race course must be measured a second time to confirm the distance. The remeasurement may be done the same day or on another day. Or, two bicycles, each fitted with a special counter, may be ridden over the course at the same time. The results should be very close. The average of the two measurements is taken as the race course distance.

The calibration of the bicycle, the course measurement and re-calibration of the bicycle must be done the same day, for each measuring occasion. The person who calibrates the bicycle should do all of the riding, including the race-course measurement and the recalibration of the bicycle.

CALIBRATED MEASURING WHEEL METHOD

The measuring wheel is inferior to the calibrated bicycle method as a measuring tool. It is slower and less accurate for measuring distances on paved surfaces. It is not the precision instrument that the advertisements suggest. However, it is possible to get acceptable results with careful use of a measuring wheel. Otherwise, measuring wheels tend to produce short course, but a given wheel could produce a long course, or the result could be close to accurate, depending on the wheel and how it is used. Select a wheel that has a circumference of about 36 inches or a diameter of about 15 inches.

Equipment: Measuring wheel; steel tape; marking materials: hammer, chisel, nails, paint; notebook, pen/pencil.

If a partner can be taken along as the wheel is walked over the race course, he can serve as a recorder and helper. A steel tape and marking materials will be needed in special situations—e.g., to pinpoint checkpoint stations and start/finish marks to nearby permanent landmarks. Any unpaved sections of the course should be measured twice with the steel tape, and cross checked with the wheel. If an unpaved course is to be measured with a wheel, the wheel should be calibrated on a special calibration course measured on the same type of surface, is possible. Ideally, such surfaces should be measured with a steel tape.

Method: To measure a race course, the measuring wheel is calibrated by walking it at about two miles an hour over a road calibration three or four times, averaging the meter readings and comparing this to the known ground distance of the road calibration course, which has been previously established with a steel tape. The latter has been described previously. The average number of feet per mile as found by the calibration walks over the road calibration course may be used directly to measure the race course, or a "correction factor" may be used.

For example, if the measuring wheel has been pushed over a one-mile road calibration course several times and produced an average reading of 5290 feet for the taped 5280 feet, then divide the wheel recorded readings into the actual ground distance: 5280 ÷ 5290 = 0.9981 which becomes the "correction factor." To use the latter, the wheel reading for the race course, obtained by slowly walking the wheel over the course, is multiplied by the correction factor to get the actual (corrected) measured distance of the race course.

Avoid jogging with the wheel or towing it with a vehicle, as this produces inaccurate results. It must be walked at less than three miles an hour. Place the axle of the measuring wheel over the starting line and walk the wheel over the race course, generally keeping one meter from the curb or from parked vehicles, lines, fences and so forth, going in the running direction. A second guide is to measure where the runners will run, including all shortcuts. Runners tend to take all shortcuts possible, and this should be considered in laying out the course. In measuring around turns, measure where the runners will run.

Wheel meter readings should be taken at various intersections, and intermediate or checkpoint distances (preferably in meters) may be marked en route. A final counter reading is taken as the wheel reaches the proposed finish line. The course must be measured a second time. The average of the two measurements is taken as the course distance. Then permanently mark the start and finish points. Finally, walk the wheel over the calibration course once to determine that it is functioning properly as compared to pre-course measurement calibration figures.

CHAINING

Chaining or measuring with a steel tape will give the most accurate measurement for road courses, provided experienced personnel is available. (The inexperienced measuring team will get a more accurate course measurement by using the calibrated bicycle method of measuring.) A marathon promoter might be able to get the services of a surveyor who also runs and who might donate his time to such a measurement; otherwise, it might be relatively expensive. The surveyor must be thoroughly informed by the promoter as to the standards of measurement needed for race courses. The race course must be measured twice for certification consideration. The course might be measured with a steel tape, and the second measurement to confirm the distance might be done by the calibrated bicycle method.

If professional help is not available, the race promoter should find at least one person who has had experience measuring distances with a steel tape, to be part of a three (or more)-person measuring team.

It is a good idea to make a rough survey of the route by automobile, or to lay out the course by means of large scale maps.

Equipment: (1) calibrated steel tape, 100 feet long, free kinks, splices or repairs; other lengths may be used; (2) spring balance or a spring scale, registering up to 15-30 pounds, attached to the front end of the tape; (3) marking and note-making materials: a hammer and chisel to mark points on concrete, nails to mark asphalt paved roads, and paint or make visible lines or circles; adhesive tape, masking tape or a flagging tape may be used to make marks; a red pencil to mark taped increments on the road surface, and keel or lumber crayon to mark a circle around the red penciled mark, or use chaining arrows to point to the tape increment marks; and a notebook and pencils or ball point pens; a tape thermometer may or may not be used to make temperature corrections for the tape.

Steel tapes should be handled with care, and they should be protected from vehicles. When the tape is lying on the ground, it should be kept straight. For measurements less than a full tape length, reel out as much tape as needed, and keep the rest on the reel. When the tape is on the ground, it should be moved by dragging it from the front end only. If the tape is raised off the ground, the tapemen should lift it up together and keep it stretched out. The tape should be cleaned and greased lightly with Vaseline before storing it. Steel tapes can be calibrated by the National Bureau of Standards, Washington, D.C.

Method: Measure the race course one meter from curbs, marking lines and so forth in the running direction, generally along the path that the runners will take, including all shortcuts, and using care in measuring around turns to measure where the runners are likely to run.

A measuring team should include a minimum of two persons to tape measure a race course. The taping team should have 3-7 persons, plus the use of an automobile to travel with the group. One person will be at each end of the tape, and specific duties will be assigned to each member of the party, for example:

1. Chief: Supervises the measurement. He may serve as the rear tapeman and he might keep records. He helps to keep the lead tapeman in proper alignment.

2. Lead tapeman: Carries a red pencil (and possibly keel) to mark tape increment lines spots on the road. He keeps the measurement aligned properly, and he operates the spring balance attached to his end of the steel tape.

3. Recorder: Keeps notes and figures for the measurement and makes sketches of the route.

4. Tension man: Handles the spring balance (relieving the lead tapeman of this job).

5. Assistant: Assists the measuring party and controls traffic.

To measure the course, locate the zero and end points of the steel tape. Lay the tape flat on the road surface. The rear tapeman holds his end of the tape on the starting line, while the lead tapeman applies 10 pounds of pull/stretch on the tape and then marks the spot with a red pencil or equivalent. The rear tapeman has a difficult job keeping his end of the tape fixed furing the 10-pound stretch by the lead tapeman, and this is a key to accuracy. Chaining arrows may be used to mark the spot on paved roads as a supplement to the red mark, and they are a must if taping on dirt or grass. The rear tapeman helps to keep the lead tapeman in alignment on the course. After marking the tape length, the lead tapeman drags the tape forward for the next increment, and the rear tapeman carries his end which may have the reel attached. To measure around turns or curves, the course should be measured in tape increments of 5-10 feet instead of full tape lengths. At the end of the measurement or at the end of a section, the lead tapeman may carry the end of the tape past the end point, lay it on the ground and walk back to mark the point, or the tape may be reeled in to make the measurement.

The taping team should be alert to the dangers of measuring in traffic. It is helpful to have a person on hand to control traffic. Measurements should not be done in extreme weather conditions which affect the length of the tape, and measurements should not be done on very windy days. The race course must be measured twice and the average of the measurements taken as the distance.

40

Planning and Executing

Organizing marathons, like running
them, requires a detailed plan

Len Wallach

The satisfaction of organizing a marathon race can be likened to
that of a maestro of a symphony orchestra leading the musicians
through a complex composition with ease and grace to the thundering
applause and calls for encores from an adoring audience. Or it can be
destroyed by the hisses and boos of the same audience because the
chubby tuba player oomp-pah-pahed at the wrong spot in the musical
score.

Putting on a race can be a joyous, deeply satisfying creative experience, or it can be a path through a bewildering administrative and
logistical maze, depending on the amount of preparation and the insight of its organizers. The joys or horrors are directly proportional to
the leadership and ability of the race planner. Unfortunately, many of
the efforts of well-meaning people are confused and fall well short of
the mark.

Certain basic principles can be applied to most human endeavors to
insure success, whether the effort is in race administration, medical
science, automobile sales or basket-weaving. Without a grasp of these
concepts, the race director will wind up with gray hair as well as the
permanent dislike of (and from) the running community, the very
people he has chosen to serve. A command of these principles and
their correct application are the key to a successful race. Without
them, there may be a few accidental successes, but there are sure to be
many failures.

Paramount in the race director's personality are two characteristics.
The first is the ability to *contemplate,* the capacity to perform willful
thought. Somehow, it is presumed that the necessary reasoning and
logic are automatically possessed and applied by race directors. This

leads to viewing race administration as the mere completion of a long series of checklists of things to do or obtain. Race direction is just the opposite of chronicling a litany of "need-to-get" and "need-to-do." Listings can be delegated or at least delayed until after the person who heads the race organization has had sufficient time to contemplate the race theme, components, problems and mechanics. Unless an orderly process of willful thought occurs, focusing on these four areas, a race can be doomed to mediocrity.

The second characteristic of a capable race director is the ability to take a *calm, deliberate attitude* and approach to his work. With this seasoned and mature manner, he can bring order and a connective process to the event, insuring that the theme is carried out by utilizing a system of interlocking components, each with a separate but inter-dependent mechanics, all of which anticipate, identify and resolve problems.

It seems to be the common denominator of modern race directors to rush about, clipboard in hand, extinquishing small crisis after crisis, correcting errors, dramatically interpreting rules, making profound decisions. This type of race director adds immeasurably to the confusion, stress and turmoil when a quiet, well-measured, and calm approach is so vital to successful race operations.

The four previously mentioned items—theme, components, problems and mechanics—are one method of looking at race direction. These four divisions of effort are merely a means to separate a race into natural areas for an analysis of the task. The simplistic and orderly separation works.

THE THEME

The theme is the essence of a successful race. Like a good play, novel or song, there must be some central purpose, readily identifiable and easily explained. It is the road map on the journey to success.

It is inexcusable for a race director to skip the theme-identification step. Merely labeling a race as a "marathon" is not sufficient and will not produce the effort within subordinates or the athletes to put forth their best. The race director must determine the theme and see that it is communicated to all levels, particularly the athletes.

If it is a national or international event, especially a championship, there may be sub-themes which need to be identified. In California, the West Valley Track Club, College of San Mateo, the Pacific Association of the AAU, and the San Mateo Park and Recreation Department have frequently combined their efforts to put on such events. Before the planning even begins, each of the key people involved generally has a different view of what the purpose or theme is to be. But by the time a decision is made to bid for the event, everyone is fully conscious of the theme. The AAU National Marathon Championship, for instance, has the natural theme of "who is the best on the road?" Consequently, it is almost understood that this is a race for the swiftest of the swift rather than some special traditional occurrence such as the Patriot's Day classic in Boston where the tradition is the theme, kind of a "daddy of them all" concept.

The National Marathon Championship for women, when first born in 1974, had the sponsors working with the news media to avoid having the race labeled as "just a bunch of women's libbers finally getting their way." What the race sponsors wanted and what they got was coverage which emphasized a theme of "gifted athletes, who happened to be women, pitted against the clock in a significant historical development in running."

When the women Masters finally got their AAU status, it was tempting to try to grab media coverage with the theme of the "female geriatric set defying the aging process." Instead, a theme was developed of "the emerging older athlete running for the first time in a women's national championship." The sponsors elected to separate the race from the Masters men's championship held on the same course on the same day. The men's theme was much different: "the seasoned older athlete in friendly but serious national competition over the toughest course in the United States."

Only by going through this deliberate process of theme determination can a race director constantly be in control, and expect staff and athletes to behave in a predictable fashion, thus orchestrating a successful race.

Frequently, races are held in commemoration of a community's anniversary or the founding birthday of an institution. These races are usually an adjunct, sometimes the opener, to a larger extravaganza. San Francisco used road races to signal the opening of the Golden Gate Bridge in 1937 as well as the Treasure Island's World's Fair in 1939. Another community, Redwood City, has a foot race to draw and warm up the crowd for its annual Fourth of July parade. These themes are hoopla and fun. They are approached lightheartedly, without the usual preoccupation for splits, prizes and all the other niceties that go with the keener competition.

Sometimes, almost unconsciously, race directors develop an unwritten theme of using their race as a living memorial to their unfulfilled egos. They want to make their race "Boston West" or counter the notoriety of the Alley Oop Five-Miler put on by a fellow coach in a neighboring city.

"Boston West" or the "Junior Chamber of Commerce Ego Special" are good ideas and certainly should be used, but the race director has to be clear in his own mind that the central objective in this kind of undertaking is simply notoriety, frequently his own. If, on the other hand, it is a sincere effort to attract people to a charitable event, and notoriety is the means, so be it—but that sets the mood and the theme for the race.

Pax Beale, super-promoter of several great running events in San Francisco, puts on a race which starts at an ancient military post on one side of the Golden Gate Bridge and finishes near the San Francisco Yacht Club on the other. The race is held to raise money for Big Brothers, a non-profit charitable agency; consequently numbers count. Pax secures a band consisting of a banjo, trombone and tuba to play the theme from the Lone Ranger at the start of the race and gets lions and tigers from Marine World-Africa USA at the finish. Pax knows clearly what his theme is and so does everyone else, so the race is popular, reasonably well administered and gets lots of publicity, thus raising the necessary money for Big Brothers as planned.

THE COMPONENTS

As part of the race director's planning, the second segment of race organization and administration is determining the components needed for a successful event. The segmenting of work is usually done haphazardly without an appreciation of its full impact on the race.

Take, for example, the promotion of a race. This is generally reduced to a very shallow effort to try to hustle the local press and television people to run a pre-race story and cover the competition. Some race directors even develop press packets as handouts and provide printed results at the finish. But in most cases, they give little thought to the entire gamut of information and media relationships which need to be a well planned and major component, not delegated lightly or organized by a volunteer whose other promotional experience is limited to the church bulletin on the scout cookie sale.

The component system establishes a thoughtful process of how to approach the work properly. Promotion might be broken into all kinds of sub-components such as press packets, planned feature stories, biographical data sheets, pre-race press luncheons with top competitors, and race-day isolation of the winners for press interviews. The plan for getting the results quickly into the hands of the media is but one small item of this component.

When the AAU's Senior Men's Cross-Country Championship was held at the Crystal Springs course in Belmont, Calif., the pre-race promotion component was well planned and executed. Frank Shorter was the key figure the press wanted to focus on, but as he would not have arrived on the day convenient for the press conference luncheon, race director Jack Leydig arranged a luncheon anyway and got Shorter hooked up by a long-distance telephone call for a two-way amplified conversation for the press. A series of predetermined thought-provoking questions fed to the unknowing Shorter made the interview more colorful. A similar well-thought-out post-race interview system was developed.

Component thinking requires that the director determine the major parts and sub-parts of the operation. By identifying these, the actual delivery of the product is relatively hazard free.

Officiating is certainly a major component—intricate and unnecessarily difficult only when not organized in an orderly fashion. The race director usually approaches the task by looking at the people available and then deciding that Joe will be the starter, and Mary the clerk of the course, and the high school cross-country team will serve as course guides. The formula for failure, or at least a major problem, is borne in this type of approach.

One must determine the unit of work, officiating, break it into its natural division, and delegate the task of organizing and recruiting to someone else or leave it vacant until the entire event is finally categorized, sub-categorized and refined. All too often, precious energy and time of the race director is spent in trying to find a celebrity to start the race or handle the scoring table rather than directing his talents to analyzing and assigning the major work units. Whether "Miss Sweatsock" or "Mayor Hot Air" is the starter is of no consequence, but the time and system it takes to get from application to awards, from bidding to the results, can only come from careful use of the race director's resources.

Bidding for the race is another important component. Planning this effort, working with the calendar of the jurisdictional bodies, both athletic and governmental, is an improtant and sizeable task. It requires an analysis of other races to be held about the same time, planning the presentation and knowing how to get the necessary votes ahead of time, whether they be the AAU delegates at the national convention, or getting the chief of police and his sergeants to concur in your effort to mess up local traffic. It also requires getting a suitable site which meets the event's needs. Frequently, planning on dates and locations are so fixed that the inflexibility causes the award to go elsewhere.

Racing logistics, while appearing to require the talents of the superman, are usually relatively easy to assign. There are certain types of people who get enormous joy from putting together the complex and difficult physical work of race logistics. This overall component's boss is usually a very capable individual who would be as comfortable setting up a marathon with 25 water stops, 200 directional signs, a tightly controlled finish chute, and all the other support details needed, as he would providing the same back-breaking work for a stage play, dinner banquet or the Republican National Convention. In California, one such human dynamo is Dave Schrock, who not only has a healthy appetite for work, but also the capacity for seeing the big picture as well as the detail. During a race, this athlete-logistician gets double pleasure from watching the competitors and from seeing his own handiwork control the event.

One failing of a race director is to assume this task for himself, thinking that no one else would be foolish enough to take the assignment. On the contrary, many dedicated volunteers like Schrock get a genuine delight from the physical planning and execution of the support role. Many people prefer this type of assignment to working directly with people.

A separate component might be scoring. But a race director, in his analysis of the event planning, may place this either under officiating or race logistics. It doesn't make any difference. Any of these three would be satisfactory, but the act of willfully planning the division and subdivisions pinpoints the responsibility and determines the flow of both authority and administration.

Race timing has to be part of the scoring, but it might not be linked to it until the clocking task is completed and the time sheets are handed over to the people counting up the results. Generally, there are far too many people involved in the timing and scoring drama, and seldom is there a clear hierarchy arranged. Consequently, the finish area becomes something a little short of a comic movement of the Keystone Cops trying to arrest Buster Keaton.

The final part of the process of the component systematizing is a simple series of boxes on a sheet of paper labeling the major work units on the top of each square and a listing of sub-components on the inside, each with a name alongside the task. On the flip-side of the sheet is an exact and easily read organizational chart, showing who reports to whom as well as listing each individual's telephone number. As the pre-race planning develops, additions, modifications and deletions can be made. Everyone connected with the race receives a copy of the original sheet and any changes.

Only after the components have been decided upon and the sub-components selected does one begin the task of developing checklists of duties for each individual assigned to a particular piece of work. Race directors should stay out of this part of it except to check regularly with the responsible individual to insure himself that the list of things to do and things to get are complete and progress is being made. To insure that this is done, the race director—either by calendar, chart or checklist of his own sets up dates and times to get formal feedback on progress and problems.

THE PROBLEMS

The ability to anticipate problems is the hallmark of the successful race director. It is not the ability to solve them once they come up in the middle of an event; it is clearly the ability to foresee and be ahead of them with predetermined solutions that separates the good and the bad director.

Certain traditional problems crop up, catching even the most experienced race director breathless while he frantically tries to stop impending doom after he overlooked a small but essential detail.

In the 1977 Christmas Relays, almost 2000 athletes ran portions of the 50 miles from the University of California in Santa Cruz to Half Moon Bay. The university logistics were smooth, well organized as was the administration of the six hand-off points along the beautiful California coast. The crowds at the checkpoints were anticipated and, but for a few irritating moments, motorists could move down the highway easily during the seven or more hours of the race.

The race was to end with an awards ceremony in the school gymnasium which was also to be utilized for shower facilities. The custodian, being paid overtime to open the building a couple of hours before the first finisher crossed the line, showed up, didn't see anyone and left.

Almost 2000 athletes and about the same number of other interested folks began to mill around restlessly while the race director frantically tried to locate the missing custodian and the key to the gym. Fortunately, the small town detective system found the janitor, and the day was saved. This close call was not caused by the janitor, but rather by depending solely on one individual who wasn't aware of the magnitude of the event, as well as by a race director who did not have an alternate plan. As the race had been run four straight years, a certain complacency crept into his mentality and he let his guard down for one dangerous moment. If something can go wrong, it will. Consequently, the race director must anticipate the problem and have the solution to plug in automatically.

Hassles with police are becoming more frequent. Thus,

considerable effort must be directed to prepare for the uncooperative patrolman who decides that runners in a marathon must stop at signal lights or run on the sidewalks. Several contacts must be made with the law enforcement offices ahead of time, and race directors should only assign this task to their most trusted subordinate.

In working with the police, race directors must develop the psychology that cops are never wrong. Never! With this kind of anticipatory attitude, the race director should arm himself with a bundle of commemorative race T-shirts to give to the uniformed police as "just a little token of our appreciation, officer." Many a resistant cop, mouth hanging open, has been turned into a permanent ally, for a $2 bit of colored fabric.

With the development of liability sensitivities on the part of local, regional and state governments, race directors are sorely pressed to get approval for a public site unless they are saddled with huge insurance coverage requirements. Most of these problems can be solved by getting the jurisdiction's park and recreation department to co-sponsor the event and asking the mayor to be the starter. But failing that, get a letter requesting the site reservation through the AAU or some other equally suitable organization which might be better received than one from the "Gentle Souls Track Club."

If a race director does not have almost a lawyer's grasp of insurance data and doesn't take the necessary overt steps to meet "reasonable and prudent" behavior requirements, then indeed he will have an almost unsolvable problem. Generally, the relationship of a race director to an athlete is like a parent to a child. There is an implied duty to provide for the runner's well-being and safety during the competition. Government jurisdictions are frequent targets for liability claims and suits, and themselves have difficulty getting insurance, so many have taken the view that "high-risk sports" are to be avoided as they add to their own problems.

Regardless of whether runners and race directors feel the sport is not in the high-risk category, we have become our own worst enemy by the exaggeration of the stresses of athletes and by placing too much emphasis on the super-human effort it takes to run rather than the fun of it. Even insurance companies view running with something less than eagerness as they remember a handful of deaths and injuries rather than the millions of safe miles run by thousands of Americans.

The race director who tries to keep out unofficial runners, requires sanctions, athletic and race registration, and insists on more than the minimum requirements for aid stations, traffic control and emergency procedures has nothing to fear—except for the economics of insurance. But one who doesn't see his responsibility to the runner can create serious problems for them and himself.

Fire departments and the Red Cross will generally provide temporary care for the injured and ill during a race and will frequently set up first-aid stations at the site of the competition if they are asked well in advance and particularly if they know that a gift of the commemorative T-shirts is part of the deal. It is an interesting commentary on public servants, be they civil or volunteers, that the T-shirt is usually a bigger attraction than being paid a salary.

Other than cops, insurance and the usual bickering over timing, the other frequently encountered problem is from runners going astray by the direction of a well-meaning but thoroughly confused course guide. In Sonoma, Calif., one race director sent an entire marathon crowd off in the wrong direction at the beginning of the race and could find no solution in time to salvage the event. He made a public apology and promptly scheduled the race the following year as the "Wrong-Way Marathon" which delighted the runners and enriched tradition.

The race director must anticipate, wherever possible, where the probable blowout will occur and have a spare tire and jack ready to make the change. He should have backup timers, chalked and coned turns as well as human course guides, thorough knowledge of the rules and protest procedures, extra trophies for ties, and solutions for an endless list of things that can and will go wrong.

THE MECHANICS

The final item of the four in the race director's bag of tricks is the one which invariably is placed first when it should really be last. Race mechanics are those inner working procedures and processes which provide continuity to the event. From the moment of the birth of the race idea to the final payment for the trophies, the event is like some huge interlocking assembly line with each part dependent on the other.

Most race directors are excessively and prematurely preoccupied with the mechanics of the event rather than taking an overview. Race detail is a safe and understandable task, an easy refuge for the unenlightened and inexperienced. Once the theme, components, problems are thought through, then the minute-by-minute process of the race will follow easily.

There are all kinds of tricks of the trade from having the runners address their own envelopes for results to the use of electronic timers. It's the little-known shortcuts which appear to be the cause of good administration; however, they are actually the result.

Take, for instance, the envelope addressing: Having the good sense to use pre-printed, postage-paid envelopes with a rubber-stamped return address is a miniscule expense but saves hours of stamp licking and address writing. Give out one at a time at registration, then direct runners to a table with a large cardboard box stuck on all four sides with a half-a-dozen ballpoint pens. This provides a stress-free, economic and smooth communication process.

The vertical system of laying out a couple of long tables with stacks of race applications stapled to pieces of heavy cardboard with a ballpoint pen tied by a string, moves the runners quickly and happily through the first step of the registration procedures. One table can handle four people on each side, which means that two tables can take 16 applications simultaneously. It doesn't take a mathematician to calculate the anticipated number of runners divided by the time set aside for each registration, to determine how many tables and how many pieces of cardboard needed to avoid long, irritating lines.

The next step in the shortcutting process is a set of tables perpendicular to the first set of application stations where a battery of volunteers accept the runner's money, provide him with a race number or finish tag and an envelope, and send him to the table in the rear to address it. There are many variations of this technique, but it is a simple matter to determine how many people have to be at this spot to avoid the bottlenecks.

Some race directors like to require huge numbers on each runner, but other than making the athlete feel good and providing the media with the obvious mark of an athlete, the number does little to make the race mechanics flow. If race numbers are used, small stick-on addressing labels, with their waxed backing sheets still intact, are pinned onto one of the corners. This little tag with the athlete's name can also be pinned to the athlete's clothing separately. By insisting that all runners wear the numbers with tags in the same spot, the finish chute mechanics can go swiftly. Tags are removed, the waxed backing pulled and the tags are stuck on a large sheet of pre-numbered cardboard. Quickly calculating the length of this process provides a determination of how many people you need at the finish.

Frequently, you can use the same people who handle registration to monitor all aspects of the finish line. The Times Nine Relays, a combination of a three-person, nine-mile relay, a 9.99-kilometer individual race and three other smaller races, was all handled by only four people. The race director avoided much of the usual volume of work by having each of his staff double up on assignments, in addition pulling willing volunteers from his friends in the crowd to serve as a starter and to make the presentation of awards. Others were asked to give up but five minutes of their day to monitor hands off points, knowing full well that this is a seldom-violated aspect of running.

The science of timing has taken a lesson from swimming. The first known race use of the huge swimming pace clock in solving an acute race problem was the San Francisco's Bay to Breakers. The event had an insoluble finish line backup after the first 500 of several thousand runners came across the white line at the beach. In the country's biggest footrace, the backup was solved by borrowing a swim clock and letting the runners read their own finish time as they crossed the line. As the race grows in the future, it will probably be necessary for a second clock to be stationed 500 yards from the finish line to guarantee each runner that a time is available.

The latest timing solution is electronics devices. "Cronomix," an offshoot of a company which manufactures swimming timing devices, came to the attention of the College of San Mateo's track and cross-country coach, Bob Rush, who has been plagued with race timing problems all of his career. With some modifications, he had developed a device which prints time and position just as fast as the human thumb can operate the gadget. It makes an instant and easily readable printout available at the score table and the bulletin board for both the press and the runners to view.

Finally, there is the mechanical problem of what to do about unofficial runners. There are many solutions, but the simplest means is to force everyone into the chute, including them in the results and later listing some as "unofficial." It keeps records straight, provides a written record for statistical and insurance purposes, and identifies culprits to the rest of the running community. Social pressure has a big impact on each of us, and no one wants to be singled out as either being cheap or uncooperative.

Race directors, in preparing for the decision to put on an event, need to approach their task as couples might when deciding to adopt a child. Each runner, whether slow or fast, needs a guarantee that he or she will be well cared for. The runner's only obligation during a race is to do well. A runner is not there as a guest but as one who contracts for services. Having attracted a runner to an event, the race director must fulfill his portion of the agreement with the same excellence that is expected of the athlete.

41

Help from a Computer

How the Boston Marathon deals with its numbers dilemma

Jerry Kanter

I n this day and age, the only way American business has been able to maintain its pace is by adapting data processing to its operations. Otherwise it could have been stopped in its tracks years ago by an avalanche of paperwork and record-keeping.

It's the same for the Boston Marathon. The pace gets faster every year, not only on the course, but also in terms of the numbers of runners who want to compete. Only two ways exist for responding to the demands—cut off the runners or find ways of accommodating them.

Over the past several years at the Boston Marathon, the only workable alternative seems to have been limiting the field. A qualifying time of 3½ hours was instituted in the early 1970s. Then, after a record of 2365 qualified entries were received in 1975, the standard was lowered to three hours for the next year's race.

It is virtually impossible to handle thousands of runners with the same manual techniques once used to handle hundreds. So officials of the Boston Athletic Association have had little choice but to narrow the field by imposing qualifying standards.

That was, however, before the full potential of the computer as an aid to athletic competition had been realized. We've seen computers used most recently in the Olympics to handle the scoring and processing of diverse events. In Sweden, the performances of some 6000 skiers have been determined by a computerized time clock which requires all competitors to check in at the end of their runs. This type of finish line procedure also has been tested by more than 6000 runners in San Francisco, although the results fell short of expectations.

Up to now, computer services for the Boston Marathon have been restricted to pre- and post-race procedures. Honeywell has donated equipment, programming and staff to handle entries, registration and posting of results.

The system has been described by Will Cloney, president of the Boston AA, as a "sensational" aid to pre-race preparations. Honeywell compiles the official list of entries, mails entry acknowledgements and instructions to competitors, and organizes registration procedures in Hopkinton, where the race begins. Information fed into the computer also is used to prepare entry kits containing runners' numbers, instruction sheets and baggage claim tags.

The Honeywell system is an invaluable aid after the race, too. It produces lists of finishers, speeds the verification of results by officials and provides the raw material for a souvenir publication called *Racer's Recordbook*, which is distributed to all participants. (The Honeywell system for computerizing the Boston Marathon has been dubbed "Racer"—short for Runners Administration and Computerized Entry Routine.)

As long as the computer is restricted to working before and after the race, however, its potential will go unfulfilled. The key to improving race administration is using the computer *at the finish line.*

Steps in that direction were taken in 1976. Honeywell designed an experimental computer program that, in effect, provided its minicomputer with a built-in time clock. The clock was synchronized to the official Boston Marathon stopwatch at the starting line in Hopkinton and the computer was set up at the finish line in Boston. Each time a runner completed the course, the computer recorded a finishing time.

These times were matched with the order of finish, which was recorded manually at the line and at a series of check-out stations beyond the finishing line. Times also were recorded manually as a backup to the computer.

The system worked smoothly as long as runners crossed the line in single file. But as soon as they began finishing in bunches, the credibility of both the computerized and manual systems was stretched to the limit (and sometimes beyond). Problems also occurred in matching times to the order of finish, because runners did not always stay in line. Some collapsed, others lost their numbers and occasionally recorders wrote down the wrong numbers. Most of the mistakes were ironed out by tedious manual examination and double checking of the records. But no one can vouch for all the results, even to this day.

The administration of marathon races must get better before the events can get bigger. It must be organized and administered and controlled just the way production lines, traffic systems and even space ventures are directed these days—with the aid of sophisticated computers.

The objective of applying data-processing techniques to marathon races would be to provide an automatic, instantaneous record of the finish. In other words, as soon as Jack Fultz crosses the finish line, the computer—at the very least—would print his name, number and time. When Gerald Faucher finishes—even though it's an hour later—the computer would deal with him just as rapidly and accurately. Such a system would eliminate errors occurring under the present system during the manual matching of separate lists of times and places. It also would speed up the processing of complete race results.

Objectives, however, must be tempered by the human condition. One thing we learn very rapidly in the computer business is that our systems are only as good as the people who use them. If the system requires people to do something they can't do (or don't want to do), the system will fail. Planning the computerization of a race like the Boston Marathon is something that must take into account what runners can and will do when they finish the race.

Will runners be willing to wear wristbands which could be scanned electronically at the finish line? Would they carry ID cards from their necks and plug them into time clocks at the end of the run? How would they react to having part of their numbers (electronically coded) ripped off by an official and put into a scanner? In fact, how many would even have a number by the time they reach the finish line? (It is estimated that 15% of the finishers either lost their numbers or carried them by hand to the finish line in the 1976 race.)

Perhaps the most critical problem is that no means of automation exists which could provide instant and simultaneous recording of both time and place—at least not with 40 runners crossing the finish line in one minute, as occurred at several stages of the 1975 Boston Marathon. If time clocks are installed at the finish line, runners would have to stand in line to get them. Hence, the recorded times would be slower than the actual finish. On the other hand, if times were recorded as runners finished ("four men at 3:17:30") and they lined up afterwards, the order would likely be imperfect.

In other words, I don't think we can have it both ways. My colleagues at Honeywell would say that we "can't reconcile all the objectives"—guaranteeing accuracy of both time and place, providing immediacy of response, doing it at a reasonable cost and accounting for the proper sytem reliability and backup. We must make some tradeoffs.

My tradeoff is time. I think a system can be designed to do every-thing we want except provide split-second accuracy at the finish line. But how important are precise times in a marathon, anyway? Except for the winner (who can be clocked accurately by hand), will a few seconds make much difference to the average marathoner? I doubt it.

Here's a proposal for automating large marathons that satisfies my professional pride (as a computer official) as well as my fancy (as a marathon runner):

• Let the computer assign starting positions by putting all runners in order of their qualifying times. A section-by-section list could be es-tablished automatically for as many runners as wish to enter. Each succeeding section would require slower times so that no one would be unfairly impeded by slow-moving crowds in front.

• Provide each runner with a wristband electronically coded with his or her assigned number. Like a hospital wristband, it would be removable only by cutting. The band would not be lost, detached or defaced as runner numbers sometimes are, and it would not distract or impede competitors as much as a neckband might.

• Design the finish line like the main entrance to a big turnpike. Several electronic check-in stations would be the "toll booths" and runners simply would have their wristbands scanned by an attendant using a hand-held electronic scanner which would simultaneously record the finish time. Ahead of the finish line would be a special corridor lining up runners the way some banks queue their customers in single file. The head runner would always go to the first open station.

Each check-in point would have a built-in time clock. When a wristband was scanned, time and place would be automatically recorded along with the finisher's number. The computer system would then match the number with all data on file about a runner and add his name to a continually updated list of finishers.

• Use videotape at the finish line as a backup to the automatic system and to resolve disputes. (Runners would still wear numbers on their chests for identification along the course and on tape.) Cameras could scan the finish line for as long as it takes everyone to finish or up to a pre-determined cutoff point (such as four hours). Yet the cameras would need to be activated only when runners were finishing so as to conserve tape.

A digital timing device would run as an inset in the picture to indicate precise finishing times and help make necessary adjustments. This was tested at the Buffalo-to-Niagara Skylon Marathon.

- Adjust times according to delays at the finish. If the line stacked up at 3:20, for example, and it took finishers 20 seconds to reach the check-in station, the computer could be programmed to make corrections. This wouldn't insure split-second accuracy, but would bring most times within seconds of the actual finish.

- Test the system with high school or collect students. A Boston Marathon promotional trial could be staged weeks ahead of the race in which students would flood the finish line, the queues and the check-in stations. Any bugs in the system would be discovered and there would be time to make adjustments before the race.

It's no easy task to design a system to handle marathon races. In fact, I've used the situation as a problem for students in a computer course I teach at Northeastern University. In three years, no one has been able to solve the riddle.

My own solution has evolved over years of observing and running marathons and through many opportunities to apply computer technology to the problems of business and industry. Added impetus has been provided by the success Honeywell had since 1975 with its experimental data-processing work on the Boston Marathon.

Part 9
The People Up Front

42

Men of Marathoning

A survey of what makes the sub-2:20 runners so effective

Jim Lilliefors

Throughout history, we have assumed that excellence contains a secret, and our inclination always has been to probe at the factors surrounding it, trying at least to unearth some hints at that secret.

In November 1976, I sent out questionnaires to all of the nation's active sub-2:20 marathon runners to try to determine some of the factors responsible for this particular type of excellence. Areas covered were: personal information, racing history, training history, training specifically for their fastest marathon and motivation.

America's most famous marathoner, Frank Shorter, once said of this sort of study, "You get writers who think there's some sort of magic formula, and they want to be the first to tell the world how to do it. What's the secret? I don't know. But I'll tell you one thing. You don't run 26 miles at five minutes a mile on good looks and a secret recipe."

First of all, it's much more than just the writers who want to know. Writers fill the reader's needs. And from the questionnaires, it was plain that even those who seem to have a grasp on excellence are still looking for a secret. When asked what he thought made him run his best race on the day he did, one respondent said, "If I knew that, I'd be Olympic champ and world record holder." He has run a 2:12, and yet he senses a gap between that and his ultimate potential that stems from some secret not yet within his grasp.

Some respondents teased that they knew the secret but were not going to divulge it. One runner, who has a 2:14 to his credit, described his training as 40% slower than race pace, 30% faster and 10% the same, and then added, "leaving me with 20% of 'Secret Stuff.'" Next to this was drawn a face with a mocking smile.

But the questionnaires revealed an inconsistency that illustrates how the sub-2:20 runners actually don't have such a reign over their powers. In reply to one question, 50% claimed that they were able to tell beforehand when they were going to run a personal best. But in another section of the questionnaire, they were asked specifically at what point in their fastest marathon they realized it was a PR, and the answers were somewhat different.

Most reported they couldn't tell it was their fastest until the final five miles. A full 35% didn't realize until it was all over. Only 22% said they could tell from early on. Only one runner said he could tell beforehand.

So the search for a secret to sub-2:20 running is relevant not only to writers, readers and lesser runners, but also to the very subjects being probed.

"The marathon is a very boring race," Emil Zatopek, who was bored enough to win a gold medal in the 1952 Olympic Marathon, once said. Seventy-two percent of America's sub-2:20 marathoners report that the marathon is not their favorite race. And this figure isn't culled just from the lower part of that group. It comes from people like Bill Rodgers, Don Kardong and Tom Fleming. Nearly 50% say that the marathon isn't even their best racing distance. And yet one-half of their training is thought of specifically as "marathon training."

Whereas the marathon lacks the tension and concentrated excitement of the mile, it makes up for it in terms of longevity. And here lies much of its lure. There are few things people enjoy enough to say definitely they plan to do for the rest of their lives, and yet not a single sub-2:20 marathoner answered "no" to the question "Do you think you will run for the rest of your life?" Many emphasized the point with a series of exclamation marks. When asked whether they would *race* the rest of their lives, though, the overwhelming response was not "yes" or "no," but "maybe."

Don Kardong wrote on his questionnaire a statement that was puzzling at first, but which soon became something of a focus for the other responses. He said, "Adversity is the mother of marathoning." If the marathon is indeed a very boring race, as Zatopek says, then that is the adversity, the challenge. In fact, those words, "The Challenge," popped up frequently in response to the question, "What motivates you now?"

Another finding to support Kardong's theory was a surprising one. More than 50% of the runners reported being injured at some time during the eight weeks prior to their fastest marathon. The most extreme case was that of 1972 Olympian Jeff Galloway, who ran his best marathon at the 1976 Olympic Trials. What made his feat so extraordinary was the fact that he had bronchitis and only was able to put in a total of 100 miles in the eight weeks before the race. This is an average of 12.5 miles a week, or 1.8 miles a day. Jeff ran 2:18:35.

In *Runner's World*, Frances Knowles reported on extensive research done into the make-up of the "average" runner. By far the most popular reason for starting running was to get in or to keep in shape. When asked what got *them* started, the sub-2:20 runners overwhelmingly replied it was the desire to excel. Only one said it was to keep physically fit. With this pursuit at the very root of their motivation, and the average age they started being 15-16, it becomes understandable why they excel so much more than the "average" runner.

A culture has grown up around the marathon like no other event. There's always a place for the three-hour marathoner, but there is really little place for a 12-second 100-yard dasher or a 27-second 220 sprinter. The sub-2:20 runners reported much more often that the thing that drives them is the desire to reach their potential, rather than just the fact that they enjoy it. In this sense, they are a separate species from those who run for the fun of it.

Another finding that separates the 2:20 from the 3:00 marathoner and indicates a change in the last 5-10 years concerns pacing. In the '60s, America's first sub-2:20 runner, Buddy Edelen said, "The fastest times in the marathon have invariably been achieved by athletes covering the latter part of the race faster than the first part."

Today, just under 80% of the fastest marathoners say their best race was achieved with even pacing. Data compiled several years ago at the Trail's End Marathon in Oregon and reported in Part Four supported the importance of even pacing. It found that those runners between 2:55 and 3:05 held a much less even pace than those within five minutes of 2:30.

So the 2:20 runners are on the whole very familiar with their event, in terms of pacing, training and—perhaps most importantly—its adversity.

Experience seems to be the prime source of this familiarity. In a *RW* survey taken four years ago, the sub-2:20 runner had run an average of 4.55 marathons prior to his fastest. This time, the average was 10.2, with several reporting having run more than 20 before their best. The high was 35.

And although three became sub-2:20 runners in their first try

(Shorter, Kardong and Tony Sandoval), for most it was a long process of perseverance. The average time for the sub-2:20 man's first marathon was 2:48.

The American sub-2:20 marathoner, 1977, is a different physical specimen than that of the early 1970s, and different from the champion marathoner of different parts of the world today. In a survey reported in the *1972 Marathon Handbook*, the average sub-2:20 man was 5'11", 143 pounds. Since then, he has steadily shrunk. In a survey reported in the June '74 *RW*, he was down to 5'10½", the average weight 138.

Yet even as the American runner grows smaller, he still carries more bulk than his counterpart in other regions of the world. The median height of the 1976 Olympic marathoner was 5'7" and the median weight 130. The American median (as opposed to average) for sub-2:20 runners is 5'9½" and 137. If we look at the average of our three Olympians at Montreal, we come up with 5'11½" and 137. And if we took their median, we have Frank Shorter, 5'10¾", 135 pounds.

Not only are the US's best marathoners larger and heavier than the rest of the world's, they are also younger. The median Olympian age was 29. Of our three Olympians, two were 28, one 27. But even this is several years older than the average. The age, like the size, has been growing steadily smaller. In 1972, the average age was 26.2. In 1974, it was reported as 25.4. It is now down to 25.2 (age taken at the time of their fastest marathon). Perhaps experience again becomes relevant in explaining the seniority of our Olympians over our almost-Olympians.

But the most significant change has been one of sheer bulk. The 1972 survey (actually taken in 1971) included only 12 runners, because that was the total number who had bettered 2:20. At the time of the 1974 accounting, exactly twice that number had done it. In November, 1976, I mailed out more than 40 questionnaires. The number has almost doubled again.

Why? Could it be training? Let's take a look. In 1974, the average number of miles run in the eight weeks prior to their fastest marathon was 877. In those handful of years when the total number of below-2:20 marathoners practically doubled, and the best single time plunged 35 seconds, training mileage has surprisingly gone down. The average is now 805. The number of runs more than 20 miles has dropped even more markedly, from 5.47 to 3.8. The maximum number of miles in one week has fallen from 126 to 121. The distance of their longest single run has gone from 26.6 to the present 23.6.

Could the explanation be that they are running their miles harder? Seventy-four percent of training is done slower than race pace. In 1974, that figure was 80%. This is not a significant difference.

What other explanation could there be? Are they just better, faster runners? Apparently not. They are, in fact, *slower* runners—this despite the fact that 88% include track intervals in their training. In 1972, the average sub-2:20 marathoner had a mile best of 4:10.6, a three-mile best of 13:41 and a six-mile best of 28:31. By 1974, these times had dropped to 4:11.3, 13:44 and 28:37.1. They've now slowed even more, to 4:13, 13:52 and 29:00. The time decline has been steady and consistent. In shorter distances, many wouldn't even place in a high school track meet. The average best 100 was 11.7 and 440 was 54.1.

All of these figures undoubtedly indicate a trend, but what the trend indicates is not so clear. Identifying a trend is always more attention-getting than understanding it. These statistics explain what is happening but they don't explain why. They are merely statistics, numbers on a page.

In 1971, Marty Liquori, a mile (and now 5000-meter) specialist said, "Someday I'd like to go up to altitude for two months and then come down and try to break the world record. I think that's (Kip) Keino's secret—altitude." A couple of years later, Frank Shorter, who still trains at altitude, urged the late Steve Prefontaine to join him in the mountains so he could break the world 5000 record.

That the secret could be something as simple as altitude, or number of miles run, or carbohydrate-loading, or any of the several other things that have been candidates in the past, perhaps reveals why it is still a secret. It's not that simple. You can't just go to a certain place where the air is thinner, and then come back and run a world record.

The reason past possibilities for "the secret" have fallen short was because they were externally and primarily physically based. No matter what is done to the body, the runner still has to deal with the act of running the race.

Britain's Ian Thompson, who was almost eight minutes below 2:20 in his first marathon, who later ran the fastest race of this decade, but who failed to qualify for the Olympics, said it best: "It's what you do on the day that counts."

Although he did train harder for the faster time, nothing physical can explain why Bill Rodgers ran a full 15 minutes faster at New York City than at Montreal in 1976. The real reason, as Rodgers said, was "I was psyched up just because I got nailed at Montreal." Being psyched up usually has a lot to do with high-mileage training, anyway, and probably has a lot to do with the secret we're after. But being psyched up is not something that shows up in the statistics. It is not something that has been studied.

I asked the runners why *they* thought they ran their best marathon on the day they did. One response was "Divine intervention and/or presence in a cosmic vortex at that moment." Another was "flat course, cool temperature." The secret probably lies somewhere betweeen the two.

Nothing in their personal lives reveals that the sub-2:20 marathoner is anyone but an average person. In 1972, Dave Wottle was criticized by some for getting married right before the Olympics. Dave had quite a honeymoon. He won a gold medal in the 800 meters.

Almost 70% of the nation's sub-2:20 marathon runners are married, and when asked how their personal living situation affected their racing, just about all answered positively, many adding that they couldn't do it without the support of their wives. Although this can't be measured, it is probably just as significant as number of miles or type of diet in determining how fast they run. Of those married, 80% are childless, so marathon running is probably a very important part of both of their lives. Some runners report that their wives also run.

In the 1974 survey, all of the runners were either students or teachers. In the earlier survey, all but two were. Although these two occupations still feed better than half of the sub-2:20 runners, it's a much lower percentage today than ever before. Only 23% are teachers and 30% students. A new occupation has made a tremendous gain in the past few years—13% report they own a sporting goods store. Other jobs include such divergent things as steelworker and shoe salesman (both by the same runner), corrective therapist, helicopter pilot, waiter and policeman.

While the student-teacher dominance probably exists because it allows the most time for training and racing, the growth of other occupations reflects the role of adversity once again, and the ability to overcome it. Returning to the first-ever member of the sub-2:20 group, Buddy Edelen once said, "To become a good marathoner, one of the most valuable prerequisites is tremendous determination. One cannot attach too much importance to it."

One of the more determined respondents I came across was 2:18 marathoner Phil Camp. Phil is in the Navy, stationed on a ship in the Mediterranean. But this hasn't stopped him from running. He still manages 30-60 miles per week, most of it around the deck of his ship.

Says Phil, "Running on a flight deck is a real drag and requires maximum motivation to keep it up at times."

And that's one of the keys in our search: tolerance. Frank Shorter called that his main strength when he said, "I imagine there are a lot of people who, if they were to go out and do it all the time the way I do, might be better than I am. But maybe that's where I had the advantage. For some reason, I don't see it as that much of a burden to go out and train every day."

Bill Rodgers: "We have all had our perfect race or have come close to having them. Mine came at Boston" (1975, where he set an American record of 2:09:55).

When asked what caused their fastest races, many of the runners spoke of a "coming together" of their mental and physical faculties. "My mind and body finally came together on that particular day," says Ed Bingham of his best race. Though the physical proficiency can be gauged in terms of miles run or quality of workouts, nothing can be done to determine when an equivalent level of mental prowess will develop. Bill Rodgers sees this as an essential aspect of improving running standards, but does not expect US runners to be the ones to develop it. He thinks probably the East Germans will lead the way.

East German chief medic, Dr. Manfred Hoppner, talked about the training of Olympic Marathon champion Waldemar Cierpinski: "He also kept himself fit psychologically, as instructed, and avoided getting caught up in the feverish atmosphere of the Olympic Village."

The term "fit psychologically" is an almost foreign phrase to US running. This country, more than others, seems to have a history of runners who hit their peaks in non-Olympic competition, and then are unable to reach it again in the Games (or who don't even make it to the Games). And we've certainly never had an Olympic distance phenomenon to match the feats of Paavo Nurmi, Emil Zatopek or Lasse Viren.

That "coming together" was described by Don Kardong as a "magical transformation." Two responses on the questionnnaire go a long way toward supporting this idea. After their *fastest* marathon race, 86% of the runners say they were less exhausted than after previous races; 71% found it easier to recover. Logic says that if they ran harder, they would be more tired and would find it less easy to recover. But for some reason, this isn't so.

The apparent transformation seems magical only in that the runners are not accustomed to this coming together, to having their mind function so perfectly in tune with their bodies. For someone like Cierpinski, the word "magical" probably wouldn't come into play, since the East Germans already have the more sound term—"Fit psychologically."

The secret would seem to lie here. The sub-2:20 runners have a deep-rooted motivation based on drive, on desire to excel. They seem to feel that consistency is the major factor in their success. Doug Schmenk, a 2:15 runner, said, "I'm pretty much convinced that I don't have any more talent than anyone else. I think that my success is due mostly to the fact that I train consistently. I haven't missed a workout in over a year."

But there are 2:40 runners who haven't missed a workout in more than a year and three-hour runners and probably plenty a lot slower. Consistency, which seems so important to these runners (it was the most popular response to the question, "What aspect of your preparation has been most successful in your racing success?") must be measured in more than just not missing a day. What about mental consistency? What about consistency of attitude?

We know about the adaptation syndrome, how ". . . a stress is applied which is within the organism's current capabilities of adaptation, a suitable recovery period is allowed for the adaptation to take place, followed by another stress and recovery, etc., gradually increasing the stress as the organism's adaptation increases. . . . With properly applied and individualized measures of stress, the human organism shows remarkable adaptive powers." (Dr. Henry T. Uhrig, M.D. in *New Guide To Distance Running*). But are these adaptive powers solely physical? What about the mental adaptive powers?

If the answer we seek is rooted here, it would help explain a few of the statistics. Olympic marathoners are nearly 30 years old, an average higher than that for any of the other track events. This might be explained by the need for maturity to cope with an event that a former Olympic champion termed "a very boring race."

The fact that the US has increased emphasis on the marathon during the past half-decade could explain why the age of sub-2:20s has shrunk and the number grown. As for the fact that marathoners are growing smaller, keep in mind that the average American is now 5'10", which is just what the average marathoner is.

Poring over questionnaires for several weeks has revealed a missing element in marathon running. Don Kardong wrote on his questionnaire, "Hey, all these questions imply a scientific, rather than artistic approach to running."

I don't know if it's artistic, or just mental, but there is plainly a whole dimension to marathon running that has yet to be explored, and it may be the most important aspect of all.

The "average" sub-2:20 marathoner measures up this way:

- *Age*—25.2 years; height—5'10"; weight—138.1 pounds.

- *Training in the eight weeks prior to the fastest marathon:*
  Total number of miles—805 (range 100-1090)
  Longest single run—23.6 miles (16-48)
  Number of runs longer than 20 miles—3.8 (0-8)
  Maximum number of miles in a week—121.1 (40-165)
  Minimum number of miles in a week—73.8 (0-120)
  Training slower than race pace—74%; faster—17%; same 9%
  Injured at some time during this period—52%

- *Racing:*
  First marathon time—2:48:43 (2:17-4:30)
  Other times: 100—11.7; 440—54.1; mile—4:13.7; three-mile—13:52.4; six-mile—29:00

- *"What aspect in your preparation do you feel has been most essential in your racing success?"*
  1. Consistency.
  2. Hard training.
  3. Mental attitude.
  4. Long runs.
  5. Combination of types of workouts.

In a sense, everyone who returned the questionnaire was participating in the search for a secret that may be too involved ever to be fully revealed.

And, of course, there are those who feel that the secret is that there is no secret. Frank Shorter said, "There's no secret. You just go out and do it all the time."

Maybe he meant for him there was no secret. Maybe he meant he knew the secret all along. There's really no way of telling. But we do know he was sincere about the statement. Frank didn't return his questionnaire.

43

Waldemar Cierpinski

East Germany's Olympic marathon champion talks of his victory

Ivan Berenyi

O n the night of July 31, a lonely figure ran stealthily along the tree-lined paths of the Olympic Park in Montreal, moving like a well-oiled clock. It was Waldemar Cierpinski, surprise winner of the marathon in only his fifth start over the distance earlier in the day.

"I suddenly woke up, after only an hour of sleep, and something simply pulled me out of bed," the newly-crowned Olympic champion later explained. "Unable to relax, I went out for a run and moved around at a fair clip for an hour or so."

Was it the shock of finding himself, contrary to expectations, the best marathon runner in the world? Was it a sudden need to release all the pent-up excitement or the joy of having been able to match the incredible performances of his East German teammates? Or was it an inner call to subject himself to physical strain, to do what he had been so meticulously programmed and prepared to do for months by his country's sport scientists?

His comments in post-victory interviews showed him to be an un-assuming and by no means overtly self-confident person who tends to give more credit to his helpers for the glory that befell him than to himself.

"True enough, I was up front alone and ran by myself for some one-sixth of the race," he said. "But I do realize that my win was no soli-tary achievement. It was success borne out of collective effort. The exacting preparation of the whole team, the work of our team doctors and masseurs, of my coach Walter Schmidt, of my fellow marathon runners—it all played an organic part. And so did the phenomenal performance of the East German Olympic squad as a whole. One victory generates another. It spurs you on if your teammates do so well."

He confessed to having been "very nervous" on arrival in Montreal, but gradually finding his cool as the East German golds were piling up.

"By the time I had to run, our athletes had already collected an avalanche of medals," he said. "This made me think: 'They could do it—why couldn't I?' And conversely, I feel certain that my win provided a measure of inspiration to our soccer squad, which was to play in the final in the Stadium immediately afterward and, of course, won the gold.

"I felt very happy, and grateful, that so many unknown people sent me congratulatory telegrams, and out of my depth at receiving my first ever messages from members of the government," he said. "But I do hope that people won't see me as a different person at home. I don't want to be pointed out as someone special at every turn.

"What did I think of first, after the victory? My family. They are the most important for me, and I thought of them, hoping that they were all healthy. The Games? They were perfect. First, I felt a bit apprehensive about what I had considered excessive security measures. But the trouble-free staging of the whole Games proved the organizers right. The spectators were terrific. They cheered me on and gave me lots of encouragement."

The chief medic of the East German squad, Dr. Manfred Hoppner, without hesitation put his finger on Waldemar's prime asset.

"I would praise his attitude to discipline above all," he said. "He never balked at doing exactly what he had been told in training, and strictly followed all dietary advice, subjected himself to all the prescribed massage and other treatment. He also kept himself fit psychologically, as instructed, and avoided getting caught up in the feverish atmosphere of the Olympic Village. In his leisure time, he stayed in and quietly listened to records. He followed the daily routine as outlined to the dot. It helped, of course, that it rained on the day of the race. Otherwise, the 75% humidity would have made his tempo excessive."

What was most notable about Cierpinski's winning 2:09:55 run in the Montreal marathon was his unprecedentedly even pace. An analysis of the time at each five-kilometer interval shows that the differential between the fastest and slowest five kilometers was a mere 38 seconds—something that leaves it without parallel if compared to other sub-2:12 performances. The fastest five-kilometer split was between 10 and 15 kilometers (15:10), and slowest between 35 and 40 kilometers (15:48).

Furthermore, Cierpinski—though he failed to better Derek Clayton's 1969 world mark (2:08:33) and Ian Thompson's European best (2:09:12)—still had enough left to run an extra lap. Whether this was really a *"fur all falle"* (to be on the safe side) addition, as he claimed (because apparently the lap board still indicated the figure one when he finished the course) or because of an attempt to emulate the incomparable Abebe Bikila's Tokyo showmanship remains open to conjecture.

The East German's strategic plan was less than impressive. "I was told to stick with the leaders," he said, "and this is precisely what I did. I was really happy to see that Frank Shorter's early bursts thinned out the leading group, but I found no real difficulty in staying with him. At 34 kilometers, I started to break, because that's where I went away from the field once before (in Wittenberg eight weeks previously). It worked there, so I thought, "Why shouldn't it work in Montreal?' "

Cierpinski's instructions reportedly included one thing that helped him—an order to stay very close to the favorite, Shorter, "almost to the point of body contact." The East Germans knew full-well that this is something Shorter dislikes, and told their man to play it awkward. This did lead to some mid-race skirmishes but afterwards Waldemar was all innocence and sweetness when questioned on the subject.

"It was the first time I competed against Shorter. He is a great sportsman, and good, fair man," he said.

Shorter, asked by *Sportecho* (the East German sports daily) reporter if he was angry for being unable to retain his title, replied, "On the contrary. I am happy that I won the silver. This was a bigger and faster race than the one in Munich, and I did my best. On this day Cierpinski could do better, and justifiably won."

Innocence continued to color Cierpinski's comments on a host of other subjects, too, giving a strong impression that he had been schooled in what he was to say. On being asked about his diet, he said he had a substantial breakfast the day before the race, and "fowl" for lunch, but nothing very much on the day of the race.

"Of course, I do eat a lot of sweets before marathon races," he volunteered, much to the consternation of all present (who came to the probably wrong conclusion that he, and his helpers, had no idea of the carbohydrate-loading diet). "Cakes, chocolates, ice cream—anything sweet I like."

Did he feel the strain at any time during the race?

"Well, one tends to forget the hardships after a race and remember only the good things. This is especially true after such a successful race. But nonetheless, it was hard, very hard. When? Well, I could not exactly say. Here and there. It always is."

It would also be hard to imagine comments of this kind from the likes of an Emil Zatopek or Abebe Bikila, to mention just a couple of the all-time greats of the marathon event. But to be fair to Cierpinski, the conscious clouding of issues may not be entirely his idea. In East Germany, revealing "sports secrets" contravenes the local version of the official secrets act.

It does happen on occasion that a virtually unknown athlete emerges from an undistinguished field. But this rarely happens in the marathon, and the Montreal collection of marathon men was anything but undistinguished.

Cierpinski was little known prior to the Games, though he had been an active competitor for a decade. Born in Neugattersleben on Aug. 3, 1950, he was transferred to the industrial town of Halle to realize his potential. Described as a sports student, he competes in the colors of the SC Chemie Halle club. Prior to the Games, his career had been somewhat undistinguished. He campaigned as a steeplechaser to start with, was national champion in that event and switched to the marathon 2½ years ago.

He says there were two reasons for the switch from the steeplechase. "One was that I felt that my 8:32 personal record was close to the very limit. The other was that I was injury-prone, due to my risky hurdling technique. And then I simply love running, especially long distances. That's what I like doing best."

Subsequently, he competed at 10,000 meters, achieving a best of 28:28 (not that impressive compared to Shorter's proven sub-28 ability) and his results over the marathon distance were to improve. He ran once each in the 1974 and 1975 seasons (2:20:28 and 2:17:30, respectively), and his '76 results were, prior to the Games, 2:13:58 and 2:12:22. The first 1976 run in Karl Marx-Stadt put him into the top 10 on the world list, and the second (which was to decide Olympic nomination) in Wittenberg at the end of May, reflected the even tempo of his Montreal performance.

Is the 5'7", 128-pound athlete one of the genuine greats? Or is he just someone to have emerged momentarily from the welter of East Germany's athletic industry, only to disappear into oblivion soon? We shall see.

44

Frank Shorter

His Olympic performances helped set off the U.S. marathoning boom

Jim Lilliefors

If nothing else, the running career of Frank Shorter has demonstrated how fulfilled ambition can be easily transformed into subtle, unintentional, even unwanted leadership. Shorter, whose ambition at the start of the '70s was exceptional, never anticipated the position it would assume for him by the middle of the decade.

Once, he was simply a good college runner at Yale, uncertain if he should pursue a vocation, or run, or do both. Whichever it was, he would do well; he just had to make the choice.

In 1970, after trying medical school for eight weeks and dropping out, Frank chose running. Restless and working at odd jobs, he moved across the country. Finally, he settled in Gainesville, Fla., to run with Jack Bacheler, "because I didn't have anywhere else to go."

Once committed to running, Shorter quickly tripled his mileage. In 1970, he won the AAU six-mile.

"He surprised me a little," Jack Bacheler said in 1970. Bacheler was then ranked as one of the nation's top 10,000-meter runners. "I didn't expect Frank to come quite that far."

Talking of his potential, Shorter then said, "It all depends on the importance you give to running...It's coupling being able to sleep that much with being able to run that much—and wanting to run that much...It's the compulsion to get out there and do it."

With his compulsion for greater mileage, Shorter was improving so fast he had no time to consider concrete goals. He wasn't striving, yet, for the Olympics; in fact, he spoke of the futility of aiming for a single long-term goal: "How long do you stand up there on that victory stand? It seems inconceivable to me to say it's got to be this or nothing."

319

Indeed, until the 1971 AAU Championship, Frank Shorter had never run a marathon. His forte seemed more at the shorter distances. He was the American indoor record-holder in the two-mile, and talked of trying to break four minutes for the mile. In 1970, he had run several fast 10,000-meter races, including a victory at the AAU Cross-Country Championship.

His style though—fluid, buoyant, almost imponderable at times—seemed to favor longer races, and after the 1971 indoor season he finally decided to try a marathon.

Preparing for that first marathon, his ambition was dizzying: "If I could run 2:15 my first time out, I wouldn't be disappointed."

He ran 2:17:44 at the AAU Championship, second place behind Kenny Moore. "I have a feeling I'll do much better next time," Shorter said shortly afterward. Later that summer, he began a string of marathon victories, winning the Pan-American Games race at Cali, Colombia, with 2:22:40. Between that race and the 1976 Olympics, Shorter won all of the marathons he entered except for the 1976 Honolulu race which he "ran through" after Fukuoka, and a European race which he was forced to drop out of, while leading, with an injury.

Late in 1971, Frank traveled to Japan with Kenny Moore to run the prestigious Fukuoka Marathon. "Whoever wins this will have to be a favorite at Munich," he told Moore before the race, showing an initial sign of crystalizing a goal.

His victory in Japan with 2:12:50 surprised many, and further fueled Shorter's drive.

John Parker, who shared a house with Shorter in Gainesville, Fla., during the fall and winter of 1971, witnessed the transformation.

"It was during that time that I began to realize that Frank Shorter was really serious," Parker said. "He had always been thoughtful (and occasionally downright spacey), but during that fall he seemed to shift gears. He became a mass of total concentration on an impossible goal. But I suppose that's how one accomplishes such goals."

His aim seemingly firm, Shorter worked hard all winter and spring, running 170-mile weeks at high altitude in Taos, N.M. At the Trials, he tied with Moore at 2:15:57 to lead the US marathoners. He also won the 10,000.

At Munich, the town in which he was born, Frank Shorter started with the leaders—imposing talents such as Ron Hill, Derek Clayton, Karel Lismont—and ran with them until 15 kilometers, when he sped up.

"It is a little scary to throw your cards on the table so early," he admitted afterward, "but if no one chases me I feel fine—I ran a little harder and no one came with me. I pushed a little more and still no one. So I said, okay, I guess this will be it."

It was. "At 41 kilometers, I think I said to myself, 'My God, I've really done it.'"

Not since 1908 had an American won the Olympic marathon. Consequently, it was never considered an American specialty. This changed drastically after Shorter's victory. In 1971, Frank was the lone US representative among the world's 15 fastest marathoners. In 1976, three of the five fastest were Americans.

There was also a dramatic marathon "boom" in the US after Munich, and although it's not simple to isolate a single greatest contributing factor, Shorter's victory is surely a candidate. And, in the years between the 1972 and '76 Olympics, Shorter became what few runners, especially marathoners, ever have—a household name. He was a nationally-recognized sports figure, featured on the cover of magazines such as *Life* and *Sports Illustrated*. Shorter was deluged with requests for interviews, training schedules, advice. In two hours, 12 minutes and 19.8 seconds, he had become the best-known American marathoner in history.

The intense concentration, developed a year earlier, finally let up. "I can do it now because I like it," he said.

To date, 1972 was Frank Shorter's most effective year. Besides his marathon win, he placed fifth in the 10,000 meters, behind such greats as Lasse Viren, Emiel Puttemans, Miruts Yifter, setting an American record of 27:51.4. After Munich, he won the classy Springbank 11.6-mile race, and repeated as AAU Cross-Country champion. In December, he returned to Japan and ran the fastest marathon of his career, 2:10:30, an American record until 1975.

In the post-Olympic year, Frank still led the US in marathoning, with 2:11:45, second best in the world. In 1974, he ran a US-leading 2:11:45. In 1975, though Shorter's spirit and past accomplishments were still leading thousands into the sport, in actual performance his leadership was threatened.

It began late in 1974, when Shorter's four-year winning streak at the AAU Cross-Country meet was snapped by John Ngeno. Shorter didn't just finish second or third; he placed an oddly distant 11th. In 1975, another streak was broken. It was the first year since 1970 that he wasn't the US leader in the marathon. Bill Rodgers ran his amazing 2:09:55 at Boston that year, beating Shorter's American record by more than half a minute. Shorter was far from the top of the US list, with 2:16:29. Seven runners in the country ran faster than he

did. In shorter-distance races, a close rivalry developed between
Rodgers and Shorter, but Rodgers seemed to be gaining an edge.

Evidence of a faltering motivation was blatantly revealed in a
March 1975 interview with *Track & Field News*: "If I decide that I
want to go back and run another Olympics, then everything is
going to have to be right and I'm really going to have to *want* to do it,"
he said. "Everyone says, 'Well, are you going back to another
Olympics?' and the answer is a definite 'maybe.' Right now, it's
probably 'no.' "

Yet by early 1976, Shorter's thinking, and motivation, had again
turned to the Olympics. His previous victory had dimmed, and he
seemed anxious again. "I don't think about it any more," he said of
1972, at the start of his 1976 quest. "It's something you do, then it's
done, it's gone."

By the Trials, he was in top shape again, mentally and physically,
and won in 2:11:51, seven seconds ahead of Bill Rodgers.

"It was just a good hard 20-mile run and then a nice jog home," was
his description of the effort.

Attention was on him at Montreal unlike it had been at Munich.
The pressure he spoke of in 1972 was much more profound in 1976;
this time, he was the favorite. Rodgers, who had run faster, was still
less known.

Of course, few anticipated Waldemar Cierpinski's superb race, not
even Cierpinski. "I expected to finish 10th," he said recently.

As in 1972, Shorter employed surging tactics, but this time he
couldn't shake the field. He began his surges at 20 kilometers, but the
lead group stuck. Gradually, they began to drop behind—Rodgers
and Viren—but Cierpinski kept up. At 34 kilometers, Cierpinski
broke away. Shorter never caught him.

Besides the East German, a problem for Shorter was the rain. "I
don't run in the rain very well," he said. "I get tight." Frank ended up
with another medal, this time silver.

Sports writers immediately recorded the tale of his "defeat," but
Shorter was hardly bitter. He had said, after all, back in 1971, "I don't
consider coming in second losing. It's just not winning."

After the Games, Shorter's uncertainty returned. He was quoted in
People magazine as saying he intended to turn to cross-country skiing
instead of running. He told a *Runner's World* interviewer, "I'm going
to start practicing law pretty soon and not train very hard for about
2½ years." Meanwhile, he had opened a lucrative sporting goods store
in his hometown of Boulder, Colo., and was marketing a line of
apparel bearing his name.

However, in the 1977 indoor season, Shorter ran an 8:27 two-mile, his best time in six years. In the final stretch of that race, he threw up his arms in obvious elation. Afterward, he told Bruce Jenner, "The marathon is still primary." Later that year, he discounted the rumors about skiing, claiming he'd been misinterpreted.

His great ambition seemed intact in 1977, though minus the innocence that had characterized it six years earlier. He entered big money races—too many—across the country, sometimes even two races in different cities within a single weekend, and ended up injured. At the New York City Marathon, he dropped out at 17 miles.

With his various interests—business, law, running—still in conflict, Shorter's ambition seems as splintered as it's ever been. And though he expresses uncertainty over which channel it will take in the future, it has an uncanny ability to return, if sometimes inconsistently, to running.

45

Bill Rodgers

His 2:09:55 is the fastest time ever run by an American

Jim Lilliefors

Much as the style and attitude of Marlon Brando ushered in a new breed of actors in the 1950s, Bill Rodgers's non-traditional approach to marathoning symbolized, perhaps even created, a new breed of marathoners in the mid- to late-1970s.

Just four years before running the fastest marathon ever by an American, Rodgers was smoking a half-pack of cigarettes a day and not running at all. He feared he would soon have to flee the country because of his concientious objector status.

But in 1975, at the Boston Marathon, little-known Bill Rodgers did much what Marty Liquori had done in 1969 in the mile: he challenged a legend. It was his year of ascension and a turbulent one for Frank Shorter, much as 1969 was for mile great Jim Ryun. Shorter spoke of quitting in 1975; Ryun quit in 1969.

Bill Rodgers, like Liquori, exuded a refreshing exuberance that sometimes translated to brashness. In the minds of many, he would never surpass Shorter.

The record at Boston, 2:09:55, was among the most unexpected sports records in history.

"It was a combination of several factors that combined over a period of perhaps three years," was Bill's simple explanation. "These factors were training techniques, luck, emotion and several people who helped me."

His explanation starkly contrasts the more analytical approach Shorter has often taken in describing his efforts. Improving one's time by nearly 10 minutes in 12 months invites a need for more analytical explanation, but it is not a matter Bill Rodgers has mulled over publicly.

One explanation is simply the frame of mind he was able to assume on that day, for Bill Roders is a runner whose intensity often wavers. He admitted he thought of quitting during that 1975 Boston race. "The noise was incredible. It kept me going when I felt like quitting."

Bill Rodgers is an emotional runner, and this accounts for his often surprising success, as well as for his inconsistency. He is a runner who sometimes puts too much pressure on himself, such as at the Montreal Olympics and at Boston, 1977, and then wilts beneath it. It's a problem that has affected many great runners, most notably Ron Clarke.

It can usually be traced back to a runner's earliest races. When Bill Rodgers was in high school, he ran a 9:36 two-mile, yet at the New England Regional Championships, the most prestigious race of the season, he only managed 9:56.

At college, Wesleyan University in Connecticut, where he schooled and ran with Amby Burfoot, also a Boston winner, was really where Bill Rodgers developed what became his influential approach to marathoning. Perhaps influenced himself by Burfoot, he quit doing interval work entirely and ran mostly long-distance workouts at a 6:00-6:30 pace.

Burfoot noticed something innovative in his style: "It is his relaxation that most amazes me. He seems to be able to run with almost complete detachment from the mental and physical effort involved."

At Wesleyan, he didn't have the chance to develop as a marathoner, even though his training was geared for the long race. He competed in the two-mile, an event in which his time fell slightly, from a 9:32 as a freshman to a 9:23 as a sophomore.

As in high school, and later in his marathoning, surprising success and inconsistency were also characteristic in college. As a junior, for example, he failed to improve at all on his 9:23; in his senior year, he ran an 8:58 indoors, then quit running entirely.

"I was worried because of the draft situation," he said. "I wanted to apply myself to some school work, which had really piled up."

He stopped running "for a long time" and only resumed after his motorcycle was stolen and he was forced to run the 1½ miles to and from his work. It rekindled his interest. He started running at the local YMCA track and found himself enjoying it again.

Steadily, he decreased his smoking and increased his mileage. By October 1972, he was doing 100 miles a week.

His first competition, after the hibernation, was a 20-miler in February 1973. He ran 1:44. When asked to explain how he was able to run so well after his long layoff, Bill replied, "Well, psychologically, I was really high to be racing again after such a long layoff."

In October 1973, he ran the Framingham Marathon in Massachussets in 2:28 and set his sights on the next year's Boston race.

His preparation involved running 100-140 miles each week, and racing in several class competitions. At the highly-regarded Coamo, Puerto Rico half-marathon, Rodgers took off in the lead, in front of a number of Olympic runners. He led for 4-5 miles before a pack, headed by Lasse Viren, burst past. Still, he finished seventh.

At Boston, Bill started ambitiously—2:13 pace—but was ruined by leg cramps at 18 miles. Despite having to stop several times to stretch and massage his leg muscles during the remaining miles, he improved his marathon best dramatically, to 2:19:34.

During the 12 months before the next Boston race, Rodgers's training became more varied and, at times, much more voluminous. One week, he ran 201 miles.

At the International Cross-Country Championship in Morocco, he surprised many with his third-place finish, after having led for more than two miles.

Before Boston, 1975, Bill Rodgers said modestly, "I just want to improve upon my 2:19:34 of last year. If I have a good day, I may be able to hit 2:16 or something around there." It was a far cry from Frank Shorter saying he wanted to run 2:15 his first time out.

As the runners passed through Framingham, 6.8 miles into the run, Bill was with the leaders. Shortly afterward, Jerome Drayton and Mario Cuevas took a 20-yard lead. Rodgers pursued, caught them. By Natick, the 10.5-mile mark, Rodgers and Drayton were running stride for stride, just two seconds behind Ron Hill's 1970 course record pace. At Wellesley, three miles laters, Bill was alone, 11 seconds faster than the record pace.

"I kept thinking, 'Too fast, I'll crack just like last year,'" Rodgers recalled. "I don't know what made me go to the front. Sometimes, I think I have a suicidal instinct."

At Heartbreak Hill, he lost 20 seconds tying a shoelace; before the finish, he stopped completely several times at the aid stations to drink fluids. He was never challenged.

His final time of 2:09:55 broke Frank Shorter's American record by 35 seconds.

Bill Rodgers is not a calculating runner. The suicidal instinct, which he credits with carrying him to the front and setting such a fast pace, obviously paid off at Boston. But if a runner takes that sort of chance, there will be days when it won't work so well.

Less than a year and a half later, after finishing 40th at the

Olympics, having run with the leaders for much of the race, Bill admitted, "The pace I set for myself was suicidal."

Rodgers has always been a gambler, and a bit of a rebel. He has said, "One hardly has to be in the Olympic Stadium as a competitor to run the race of his life."

Many sportswriters picked Rodgers to win the Olympic race. He had, after all, the fastest time of anyone in the field. The great irony of Montreal is that Waldemar Cierpinski's winning time was the identical time, 2:09:55, that Rodgers had surprised so many with at Boston in 1975. He had no excuses for his 2:25, but clearly a connection could be drawn to that 9:56 two-mile he had run in high school many years earlier. If Shorter's problem was the rain, Rodgers' was the pressure.

Bill's explanation was basic, if a bit cryptic: "When one loses one's focus on aim, the results are understandable."

Still, time-wise at least, Rodgers was the greatest American marathoner in history, and the urge to redeem himself was great after Montreal. His chance came just 11 weeks later, when he met most of the world's top marathoners, though not Cierpinski, at the New York City Marathon.

This time, the pressure was different. He didn't *have* to prove himself so much as he *wanted* to.

His victory at New York, with 2:10:10, beat second-place Frank Shorter by more than three full minutes. Bill's time was the number two clocking ever by an American, second only to himself.

It was clearly an emotional race. "I was psyched up just because I got nailed at Montreal," he said.

Emotion very plainly drives Bill Rodgers. "Emotion as a stimulating factor is a quality scientists and researchers cannot analyze effectively," he said. "The physiological results induced by a highly-charged emotional frame of mind can be devastating. A good example of a runner exceeding himself in a superlative effort is Billy Mills's tremendous 10,000-meter victory in the 1964 Olympics." Or Bill Rodgers' 1975 Boston and 1976 New York.

Jerome Drayton has said of Rodgers: "He has his moments, and then he has his downfalls, whereas a guy like Shorter is very consistent."

At Boston, 1977, Rodgers was reportedly as fit as he'd ever been. Friends indicated he was planning a world-record attempt. But Jerome Drayton won in 2:14:46 and Bill Rodgers dropped out.

Much as after Montreal, Rodgers came away from Boston in need of redemption, and found it. He turned the rest of 1977 into one of the best years of his career. He won the New York City Marathon, over Drayton, and ran faster, 2:10:55, in wining the Fukuoka race. He was virtually unbeaten in the last half of 1977, recording the world's two fastest marathon times of the year.

Also in 1977, following the trend of Frank Shorter, Gary Tuttle and others, Bill Rodgers opened his own sporting goods store, the Bill Rodgers Running Center in Boston.

The pendulum of success for Bill Rodgers seems, early in 1978, almost due to swing into more negative times. Perhaps it won't; perhaps he has found a means of avoiding that pitfall again. But even if it does happen, it will probably only charge him up to hasten the swing back to even greater success.

Rodgers said, after he rose to national prominence with his performance at the International Cross-Country Championships, "It was the race of my life. I'll probably never run that well again." This was before Boston, 1975.

Then, after Boston, he said, "We have all had our perfect races or have come close to having them. Mine came at Boston."

Yet Rodgers's running has demonstrated that those who have the strongest faith in him are those who take his predictions and analyses with a grain of salt. One senses his perfect race may not have come at all.

He might not be able to predict it, but he will probably find it. As Marlon Brando once said, "It's the hardest thing in the world to accept a pinch of success and leave it that way."

46

Women of Marathoning

A collective profile of the first generation of female runners

Gail Campbell

Most of us will never be world-class marathon runners or even race against them. We do compete with the top women, however, and are often curious about them—about how they train, what motivates them and sometimes even how they beat us in a race."

This statement, made by a male running companion, coincided with the publication of Jim Lilliefors' survey of the nation's active sub-2:20 marathon runners (see preceding chapter).

My friend and I were curious to see how world-class women would match up with these men in terms of mileage and motivation. We debated whether the gap between the record times for men and women distance runners could be partially explained by a comparison of training methods or psychological characteristics rather than blaming the lag solely on hormones.

In February 1977, I mailed questionnaires to the top 50 female marathon runners in this country. Sections of the survey, patterned on Lilliefors' article, were: personal information, racing history, training during the eight weeks prior to their fastest marathon, analysis of the fastest marathon, and a motivational and psychological profile.

Although many responses and statistical averages were similar to the men's, the motivational section of the survey was the most revealing. When asked why they started running, 27% replied, "for fun." "To get in shape" and "to lose weight" were also common answers, and one woman admitted her efforts were to "fight middle-age spread." Although this correlates well with a *RW* survey of the *average* runner, it differs dramatically from the responses to Lilliefors' questionnaire. The nation's fastest men were motivated almost exclusively by the desire to excel.

Every woman surveyed had a unique motive for entering racing and marathoning. Marilyn Paul said, "My then husband wanted me to help him train for his first marathon. Having trained, I entered the race and found I could do well."

Judy Ikenberry similarly explained, "My husband started to coach me, and I was willing to try what he suggested. (A marathon) was something to try. Most people were impressed with the idea."

Vicky Bray, who at 15 ran a 2:53 marathon, wrote that she started racing because she "enjoyed doing it, and it was easy." She became a marathoner "because it was there."

Joan Ullyot wrote that she "just drifted into it." As a footnote, she added, "Walt Stack, president of Dolphin-South End Runners, thinks *everyone* should run marathons!"

Jacqueline Hansen, former world record-holder, responded, "To race long distance was an inner desire, thus I became a marathoner. From that point, I looked to my coach for advice and assistance which is always there."

When asked what motivated her to become a marathon runner, Doris Brown-Heritage, who ran the 1976 Lion's Gate International Marathon in 2:47, answered, "I'm not. I believe I could have been a good one if it had been available earlier. I may still be one yet! I always ran what was longest and available (800 meters in the 1968 Mexico Olympics, 1500 meters in the 1972 Munich Olympics)."

Sixteen-year-old Diane Barrett admitted that her father, *Runner's World* and "seeing the 1973 Fiesta Bowl Marathon" motivated her to become a marathon runner.

Several women were inspired by well-known male runners. Marilyn Taylor was impressed by fellow Humboldt State University classmates Chuck Smead, Gary Tuttle and Bill Scobey. She explained, "I wanted to show that HSU could also produce good female marathoners."

Penny DeMoss was motivated by Frank Shorter's performance in the 1972 Munich Olympics.

Once involved in racing, the women surveyed became as achievement-oriented as the top men. When explaining what one factor in their character contributed most to their success as a marathoner, they answered, "competitive nature," "mental desire," "determination," "stubbornness," "mental toughness and self-confidence," and "willingness to put up with the pain."

When asked what they thought made a great runner, 71% wrote "self-discipline," 64%—"desire to excel," 64%—"training," 64%—"mental approach to the sport," 29%—"genes" and 7%—"desire for awards." (Many obviously answered more than one way.)

Judy Ikenberry answered, "It's really a complex puzzle," while Doris Brown-Heritage added philosophically, "Using what God made to one's best potential for the good of others as well as for self-fulfillment."

When questioned about their goals in this sport, 79% wanted to improve their best in the marathon, 79% desired to compete in the Olympics if or when they open more events to women, 71% hoped to fulfill their potential, and 57% wished to compete in other international events. Only two women said they had no goals and raced for fun, but even they checked off several other options as well.

Although most of these athletes entered the sport as fun-runners, eventually both their personalities and life goals reflected their competitive **nature.** Doris Brown-Heritage continued, "Distance running is a lifestyle of friends, interests, use of time and values. (Competitive running) has totally directed my life—along with Christianity."

All of the women surveyed thought that they might run for the rest of their lives, and all but one predicted that they might race forever. Not a single woman wrote that she would stop racing when she stopped improving.

When asked what made them run their best marathon on the day they did, most of the women displayed self-confidence and command of the situation. Typical responses were, "I was properly trained for it —deliberately—and knew I could run that pace," "I was well prepared and knew it; had a plan and stuck to it," and "I had prepared to peak for that race for six months."

A comparison of the top men and women's training methods during the eight weeks prior to their fastest marathon raised many questions. During this time period, the women averaged a total of 533 miles (range, 340-760) while the men logged 805 miles. The minimum and maximum number of miles run in a week was 46 and 87 for the women and 74 and 121 for the men. The average distance of the women's longest single run was 20 miles while the men's was 23.6 miles. The number of runs greater than 20 miles was 2.29 for the women and 3.8 for the men.

Clearly, the female marathoners were not logging as high mileage as their male counterparts. The one significant advantage was that only 36% of the women reported being injured during the eight weeks whereas 52% of the men were.

It would be interesting to compare the women's training statistics with those of men running equivalent best marathon times (2:38-3:00). It appears that, in terms of mileage, the women have more in common with these men than with the world-class male marathon runners.

A second area where this becomes apparent is in pacing. According to Lilliefors, "Just under 80% of the fastest marathoners say their best pace was achieved with even pacing. . . . Those runners between 2:55 and 3:05 held a much less even pace than those within five minutes of 2:30." In the survey of the fastest women, only 38% said they ran their best marathon with even pacing.

When asked what one aspect of their preparation had been the most essential in their racing success, the women differed dramatically from the men in one area. Although both groups rated "consistency" as being most important, the men ranked "hard training" next while the women placed it last. The women felt that "mental attitude" and "long runs" were more crucial.

This opposition to hard training was emphasized throughout several questionnaires. One woman ranked it ninth, although there were only five choices, and then wrote, "I don't train hard." Another echoed her with, "I don't push hard." The most surprising disbeliever was a successful marathon runner who ran every training distance at an eight-minute-per-mile pace. She logged only 45 miles each week and covered merely 14 miles in her weekly "long run."

Although the women de-emphasized hard training and high mileage, on the average they ran more of their mileage as fast or faster than race pace than the men did. While the women ran 20% of their miles faster, 15% the same and 65% slower than race pace, the men logged only 17% of their miles faster, 9% the same and 74% slower than race pace. Apparently, the men surveyed were running more long, slow distance miles in spite of the fact that more of the women (64%) than the men (50%) considered the marathon their favorite race and that more of the women's training mileage (59%) than the men's (50%) was specifically marathon-oriented.

A comparison of their best times for various distances revealed surprising consistency among the men and women surveyed. It is generally agreed that women record-holders are 10% slower than men at shorter distances but 20% slower in the marathon. The average speed for the top women was one minute to 1:08 per mile slower than the fastest men. The women marathoners had an average best 100 of 12.5 seconds (men, 11.7), best 440 of 64 seconds (men, 54.1), best mile of 5:13 (men, 4:13.7), best three miles of 16:56 (men, 13:52.4), and best six miles of 35:26 (men, 29:00).

In analyzing the women's fastest marathons, it became evident that although they were prepared and determined, they were less familiar with the race than the top men. On the average, the females had already run 5.57 marathons before completing their best, whereas the men had finished 10.2 each.

A total of 43% of the women felt mentally and physically strong prior to the start of the race. Mary Etta Boitano, 10 years old at the time, admitted that she "just felt giddy and excited" prior to running 3:01:15. Although they thought that they would do well, only 25% of the women predicted a personal best. Lilliefors survey revealed that at least 50% of the men forecast a PR.

Two women entered the ranks of the top 50 US marathoners on their first try in spite of being sick or injured. Vicky Bray ran the 1976 Livermore Marathon in 2:53 in spite of a cold, while Doris Brown-Heritage completed her first marathon (1976 Lion's Gate International) in 2:47 in spite of "a sore leg, a cold, a fever and being too busy."

Heritage elaborated, "I had to slow down with leg cramps the last five miles and limp the whole way on a sore leg.... I ran it with my students who wanted to do one before graduation (the next day) but could never do one before because it interfered with track and cross-country. It was finals week, the end of school and the day after a big track meet. I had not run much that week because of a cold. I just wanted to try for a six-minute pace (2:37 marathon) anyway. I actually believe I was capable under better circumstances. Maybe I won't be in such good shape in the future."

When asked what single incident in the race was the turning point for them, the runners replied, "the start," "the 20-mile split," "when I passed Jacki Hansen," and "when I saw Joan Ullyot up there ahead of me at 20 miles, I had to pass her." One youngster wrote, "passing my brother and finishing" while a 16-year-old replied, "At 20 miles, I zoomed past a bunch of guys and they about passed out."

In commenting on how they felt after their best race, 43% said they were less exhausted than after previous races, and 64% recovered easier.

Further comparison of women's and men's vital statistics and racing history reveals intriguing similarities and differences. The top women began running and racing between 17 and 18 years of age, while the men started on the average of two years younger. The female runners completed their best marathon at 26 while men scored a PR at 25.2 years. Only 36% of the women were married and 29% had children, while 70% of the men were married and only 20% had children. Of the remaining women, 50% were single and 14% divorced.

When asked what is women's greatest barrier to developing their full potential as an athlete, Marilyn Paul wrote, "lack of belief in herself (and not having a wife to cook and do the laundry!)" Although 71% of the women have a boyfriend or husband who runs (43% race), it is not clear that marriage is an asset for a female runner as seems to be asserted about men in Lilliefors' article.

Although 64% of the women agreed that their personal living situation affected their racing positively, over 43% emphatically said the opposite. One replied that racing "had been the center, the vehicle (toward my goals in life) until my marriage one and a half years ago. . . . My husband approves and my job sort of allows (racing), *but* being married does not allow the kind of commitment I used to devote. It's frustrating at times now that distance running is acceptable."

Another wrote, "A married working woman must still keep a clean house and get dinners ready. A working mother: add child care. Societal demands can become a tremendous obstacle."

An answer with a different twist was, "My husband and I are almost too close, too perfectionist, to really relax and accept my races."

One marathoner cheerfully answered, "Now that I'm divorced, I can adjust my own schedule better!"

Marilyn Paul, who ran 2:49 in the 1976 Lion's Gate International Marathon, elaborated on the problems of being a competitive athlete in modern society: "It's in close relationships that the pressure develops. Men are attracted by success (and enthusiasm and a firm body), but when it dawns on them that you're not going to give up your workout 'just this once,' or stay late at a party the night before a long run, or have nice hot dinners ready and waiting each evening, some find they're not independent enough to handle that.

"Once in a marathon I passed a man and said, 'Hi.' 'Hey,' he called, 'Will you marry me?' 'Thanks,' I said, 'but I'm not crazy. I wouldn't marry a long-distance runner.'

"Those words have since been repeated to me. A friend of mine, a competing athlete, told me he was torn between his attraction for an athletic, achieving woman and one who was an overweight, dependent homebody. He thought, but regretfully, that he'd end up with the homebody, because he said he needed somebody who'd put his needs first, take care of things at home, and *be there* when he returned home from a hard workout. 'Ah,' I said, 'don't we all!' "

Another common source of stress mentioned in the questionnaires was unemployment. One woman explained succinctly, "I graduated from college and am broke, unemployed, and . . . depressed. I don't run well when I'm depressed."

A total of 21% of the women were jobless, another 21% were teachers and 29% students. These figures correlated well with the men's since 53% of them were students and teachers. Other careers ranged from physician and medical research technician to commercial artist.

One woman replied, "I won't take work that inhibits my training." Jacqueline Hansen apparently agrees. Presently self-employed, in the past she has sacrificed jobs as an insurance underwriter, cardiography technician and manager of a sporting goods store.

The sacrifice has been worth it, however, for she wrote, "[Being a competitive athlete] definitely enhances my life! My great love in life is to run and to travel, and I've been fortunate enough to do a lot of each." She elaborated on how she overcomes adversity: "The self-discipline I've learned in training has taught me I can achieve my goals, whether they're in races or other situations."

While composing my questionnaire, I became curious as to whether anyone supplemented the physical training with mental conditioning. In his article, Jim Lilliefors stated that "the term 'fit psychologically' is an almost foreign phrase to US running." I, therefore, asked the women if they did anything to keep psychologically fit.

Marilyn Paul responded, "Before a big race, I set things up so I'll have successes and no failures. I don't do anything hard." Several women mentioned "keeping the workouts enjoyable" or "staying calm and relaxed about races," but the most common answers were "setting realistic goals."

In a related question, I asked, "Is your mental attitude toward training and racing consistent?" A total of 42% admitted it was not. If racing is 80% brain power as is commonly asserted, maybe mental consistency should be a racer's primary goal. Perhaps in the future, sport psychologists will help runners achieve this by revealing how the *mind* can be trained and controlled, and how mental conditioning can be integrated into the athlete's training program.

In the meantime, women are running faster than ever and seem to be overcoming the various hurdles keeping them from reaching their potential in distance racing. Although the results from this questionnaire may provide theories to account for the gap between the record times for men and women distance runners, it was in no way a scientific investigation. It may appear that women will set new records merely by increasing their weekly mileage, pacing their races more evenly or increasing the amount of hard training, but long-term improvement will probably depend on experience, greater racing opportunities and attracting more women to the sport.

Caroline Walker spoke for all female marathoners when she wrote, "Women runners aren't going to improve any faster and get people interested at a faster rate if the opportunities to race, and the opportunities to be recognized, encouraged and satisfied aren't available."

Penny DeMoss wrote on her questionnaire, "I hear comments from men like 'women don't run marathons, they run *at* them,' and I want to scream. I'm totally convinced that, if there were as many women marathoners as there are men, the women would be running as fast as the men. The talent is there, I just know it is; it just hasn't come forward yet."

Until recently, there was no external incentive for women to enter this sport. It was not until 1972 that the AAU allowed women to officially enter their sanctioned marathons and all other distance races, and the longest event for women in the 1980 Olympic Games will be only 1500 meters!

It is amazing that women are shattering the time barriers as fast as they are when female distance runners are still banned from official competition in most countries and in the most prestigious events, the Olympic Games. It appears that training methods, mental attitude and hormones only partially explain the gap between men and women's running speeds. More and more racing enthusiasts are concluding that equal records will only come with equal opportunity and recognition.

47

Kim Merritt

The quiet young woman
who holds the American record

Dennis McBride

Kim Merritt is not nasty, conceited or masochistic. She is shy and exceedingly complex. She is also extremely hard to beat, opponents have discovered time and again.

Perhaps every introverted distance runner finds bewildering the attention success attracts, and especially so the talented woman marathoner. Because people find women runners fascinating, Kim has been the subject of many stories.

"I'm so sick of reading articles about me I could die," she groaned, and no wonder. She has had no hiding place since she beat the heat and dozens of women runners (and hundreds of men) to win her division of the 1976 Boston Marathon.

Her time of 2:47:10 was only a bit slower than her winning 2:46:14 at the 1975 Women's National AAU Marathon Championship in New York, an amazing performance in the 90-degree hell that was the '76 Boston. Characteristically, the intense Kim was not satisfied.

"I wish I could have run faster," she said. "I wasn't pleased with my time. I don't know how fast I could have run without the heat. But I went out at 2:38 (world-record) pace, which wasn't too unrealistic."

Her first five miles were run in 29:12; her first 10 in 61:00.

"I didn't do anything differently for the heat. But I wish I would have run more slowly in the beginning," she lamented. "Before the race, though, I just decided I'd run as hard as I could."

Kim knows no other way. To her, a race to be run is a race to be run hard. She is amazed—and more than a little disgruntled—at how reporters view her performance. Story after story stressed her triumph over pain. "Parkside Star Never Quit: Kim Ran and Ran, Despite

Pain," "Sickening Experience for Runner," and so on. Her coach Vic Godfrey explained:

"She really took off on some of the reporters when they came around. She thinks they overplayed it, but it's true—three weeks before Boston it was doubtful she was going to run. Her ankle was really bothering her. All she was able to do after that was run straight ahead and slow, although she never really runs slow. She's always moving at a pretty good pace.

"Boston almost became an obsession with her. She said, 'If I can't run Boston, I'm going to give up running any more races this season.' The whole thing almost blew her mind. She even told a local reporter that on the Friday before the race, and his paper printed a story saying that she wasn't going to run. The last three weeks were really an ordeal for her. It wasn't until that Friday she made up her mind to run."

Her feet were also badly blistered by her Boston effort, but Kim does not consider her "triumph over pain" unusual. She ran not less than 100 miles a week all year in preparation, pushing it up to 125 miles the month before.

"I had trained for so long that I just couldn't say I wasn't going to run," she said. It's the kind of statement one would expect from any runner who had worked so hard for one race.

She did do well in the heat, however, displaying a sturdiness in the warm air that would make Frank Shorter envious.

"I never felt hot because spectators kept spraying me with water," she said. "I also drank a lot of water, but I didn't eat oranges or anything like that. If I wanted a sideache, I would have."

A cold front came through late in the race to drop the temperature by 20 degrees, but too late to help her.

She admitted, "If you've run 18 miles in 90-degree heat, it's already done its damage."

Stories of her stoicism notwithstanding, she did entertain the typical occasional doubts about finishing. She ran without socks, not uncommon but something unknowing reporters blew out of proportion when they saw her feet being treated after the race.

Godfrey said, "The thing about the socks really blew her mind. She really got mad about everyone writing about her as if she were a masochist or something."

It took Kim a week to sufficiently recover from the race, a new experience for her. In her two previous marathons, she had no such trouble, but then the 1976 Boston race was more demanding for everyone.

"I don't know if I want you to write that it took me so long to recover," she said. "People will probably say that women can't take marathons then, and that isn't right." Quick assurances that most men took longer to recover were still not enough to ease her doubts that she should have been so tired.

In a track meet two weeks later, she ran an 880 trial and won the two-mile (11:06.9) one day, and won an exhibition three-mile and the mile (5:06.3) the next before dropping out of the 880 from weariness. She had run much faster previously in all of these events.

How does she do all of this racing?

"I'm used to it by now," she said. "Last year, the coach had me tripling every weekend, but this year I'm only doubling. I feel funny if I go to a track meet and only run one race." So much for the myth of the weak female.

Considering her success (dating from her Wisconsin state high school mile championship days as Kim Piper) it is surprising that she professes little love for *any* competition. She will always run, she says, but how much longer she'll compete she cannot predict. She prefers to train endlessly, without restraints. If she doesn't pour it on, she feels restless.

Godfrey said, "The biggest thing I tried to do for her is to get her to run less. The more she runs, though, the more confident she feels."

"You really can't train hard for long without finding out what kind of condition you're in," she explained. "Races now are getting to be like rewards for me, a way of finding out."

Ideally, she would race about once every three weeks. She would prefer to concentrate on her workouts: eight miles in the morning (often rising with husband Keith at 4:30 a.m. to see him off to work) and 8-14 in the afternoon. Twice a week she runs intervals.

Godfrey predicts a future 2:35 or 2:36 marathon for Kim. She has the confidence for it but won't say so. The "Greta Garbo of distance running" does want to be alone.

Her coach said, "She's always been like this—bashful, shy, retiring or whatever. She couldn't stand it in the last two marathons when she's had people swarming all over her. She's like any other girl, though, when you get her going. She's real talkative with friends."

As the final question was asked, Kim simply said, "I'm so glad this is almost all over with." But she's wrong. She's only beginning to have the times of her life.

(Eighteen months after her victory at Boston, Kim Merritt set an American record of 2:37:57 at Eugene, Ore.)

48

Jacqueline Hansen

A personal account of the world's first sub-2:40 marathon

Jacqueline Hansen

Since marathon running has evolved as my "specialty," my training is basically geared toward the longer distances—although I do compete in track and cross-country as well. Speaking very generally, my workouts can be outlined as three days of intervals per week and three days of moderate running, plus one day for racing or a long run (15-20 miles).

Whenever I'm asked what a typical interval workout might be, I am at a loss for an answer. With my coach, Laszlo Tabori, there is no "typical" workout. Under his expert direction, each runner is given no more, no less than he determines that runner is capable of doing. And though I'm quite sure Tabori methodically outlines the workouts in his "little black book" the night before, I'm also quite sure he never hesitates to modify the workout according to circumstances of the moment.

For several months prior to the Nike-Oregon Track Club Marathon in October 1975, I had been prospecting a race with potentially the best conditions. This one seemed to fulfill all the requirements: an AAU-certified course, flat roads and bike paths, probable cool and accommodating weather, pleasant environment, etc. I felt the timing was good.

In the previous 14 weeks of training, I had averaged about 100 miles each week and taken 10 Sunday morning runs of 20 miles each. In addition, I'd run seven or eight different races of between three and 16 miles, and had maintained an uninterrupted schedule of Tabori's interval workouts. So the decision, reached only a couple weeks prior to the race, seemed a sound one.

Regarding my preparation for the race, one friend wrote me, "You must have found the perfect formula." And maybe I did for the moment. All I know is what has worked for me in the past, and experience has been a good teacher. One week before race day, I ran 19-20 miles slowly to deplete my carbohydrate reserves in preparation for a carbohydrate-loading diet. With that completed, I began a four-day diet of meat, fish, natural cheeses, cottage cheese, tomatoes, lettuce, butter, eggs. Other foods, negligible in calories, included small amounts of mushrooms, parsley, spinach, celery, onions and spices to make the meals more delectable.

Now that I've worked with this diet for three marathons, I'm becoming a gourmet of such dishes as egg-and-cheese omelets altered with mushrooms, chives, baco-bits or parsley; poached or lightly fried fish; salads of lettuce or spinach and tomatoes with homemade dressings of oil, vinegar and spices only; boiled chicken in broth with celery, onions and spices. Snacks are pretty much limited to cheese and celery. The only possible beverages, of course, are coffee, tea, water or those awful diet sodas. I limited myself to water and occasionally tea.

I should mention that my primarily vegetarian-oriented regular diet only slightly reduces the variety of dishes possible under this diet. If one is given to eating meat, the possibilities are unlimited. The main thing to remember is *no* sugars, in any form (fructose in fruit, lactose in milk. and so on). My only exception is tomatoes, with their fractional amount of carbohydrate.

My protein diet ended Thursday morning, when I consumed a normal breakfast, relishing every morsel of grapefruit and granola. Without overdoing the loading aspect, I simply supplemented my regular diet with high-carbohydrate foods, especially the last pre-race meal which I prefer to be rice with chicken and green beans. I had no problems other than overcoming my lack of desire to eat, since I had lost five pounds and my stomach had shrunk. However, arriving in Eugene two days before the meet, my appetite was stimulated by Joy Ledbetter's great zucchini bread.

During tne final week, workouts remained basically the same as always, with some tapering off: Monday—an easy 11-mile run; Tuesday—a regular interval workout; Wednesday—nine miles easy; Thursday—a brief interval workout; Friday—a scenic five-mile run with a noon-running group at Oregon University; Saturday—only 3-4 miles easy running in the Ledbetter's neighborhood.

The morning of the race, I knew it was to be a good day. The clouds overhead were threatening rain, but they only provided an overcast that shut out the sun. Temperatures remained in the 50s, and there was no wind. Everyone checked in at Nike's Athletic Department store for their numbers and last-minute instructions.

I met Jon Anderson and silently wished it to be a good omen. The last time we ran a marathon together was our duo-win at Boston in 1973. Janet Heinonen, marathoner and writer, came prepared to assist with dispersing drinks or leading the way on her bike. We had met once before in Charleston's 15-mile extravaganza, but neither of us was sure the other remembered.

Personally, I was much relieved at Janet's presence. The thought of going off course while fixated on my running tempo was frightening. As every marathoner knows, to navigate is no easy task after 20 miles of running. (Unfortunately, two of my friends from California found this to be true that day, ruining their chances for a good marathon time.)

The race began smoothly with the relatively small field of runners leaving the downtown area of Eugene for the Willamette River and adjoining woods. Nowhere to be seen were the runners who earlier offered to pace me. As I discovered later, all had gone out too fast and typically fell behind in the latter stages of the race. Fortunately for me, I fell into a comfortable pace of about six minutes per mile. In the company of several of the runners, the time flew by, and I felt secure about staying on the course.

Conversation was at a minimum, but relaxed. At times, I found this distracting and lapsed into a panicky feeling, losing concentration. But here, a little mental discipline carried a long way. Zeroing my thoughts in on my pace and the rhythm of my breathing, I was able to regain a calm mood and close out any distractions. Like meditation, it made the time sail by and really eased my efforts. I was able to concentrate on my running, drink my ERG, converse coherently, appreciate the surrounding natural beauty, feeling in total control of the entire situation. This "in-control" feeling was really a new and exciting experience.

Before long, we reached 20 miles in 2:01, and the last I heard from accompanying runners was, "Gee, you must be feeling pretty good." Indeed I was, knowing the same pace would match the record. Every second faster would better it that much more. And with that thought in mind, I emerged from the woods to the finish in a park clearing where my friends were waiting.

As I crossed the line, hearing 2:38:19, I was greeted by numerous hugs from Lili Ledbetter (a world-class marathoner in her own right) and Doug Schwab, who was capturing the joyous event on film. How lucky I considered myself to be, that I could have such a splendid experience shared with special friends. I could not have asked for more.

Part 10
Off to
the Races

BOSTON MARAT

FINISH LI

PRUDENTIAL CEN

49

Boston

How to run the historic course from Hopkinton to the Prudential

Marshall Childs

The Boston Marathon owes its fame partly to the fact that it is a point-to-point course. No running in circles here. You really get somewhere—from the 17th century farming village of Hopkinton to the shadow of old South Church in Boston. You could be mesmerized by the American history you are passing.

But the biggest hazard of a point-to-point course is disorientation. In Boston, the disorientation is almost complete. There are no official mile markers. Such markers as there are (portable orange signs) are removed before most runners get to them—and that's a blessing because they contain messages like "19.6 miles to go" that are incapable of enlightening an oxygen-poor brain.

Thus, most runners in Boston fall prey to one or both of two dangers: the "super-runner fantasy" in which you flirt with elation over the prospect of knocking a minute per mile off your best time, and the "why-am-I-doing-this" routine in which you plod through the fog of depression or quit altogether. The first fantasy typically lasts into Wellesley or Newton. The second usually takes over during the last 10 miles.

(*Note:* In rare cases the super-runner fantasy lasts for the whole trip. This is an experience enjoyed by almost all Boston winners and very few others. Don't count on it. Rely, instead, on what I am going to tell you now.)

The Boston Marathon is a happening that no qualified runner should miss. But the benefits generally do not come in the form of statistics. In fact, the benefits are difficult to describe. It has something to do with the group experience.

In general, don't expect to run your best time at Boston. There is a delay at the start, the hills slow you down a bit and pacing is fiendishly difficult. Sometimes, it is true, there are conditions like those in 1974 and 1975—50 degress and a tailwind—that makes champions of us all. But more frequent are precipitation, headwinds and extremes of heat and cold.

Some of my friends tell me that trying to optimize one's time at Boston is a distraction, if not downright gauche. Better, they say, just to run as you feel. Express yourself through the free-form medium of running. Store up sensations. Enjoy the crowds.

I try to do these things, too, but I cannot resist trying to make the numbers come out right. So I'll try to tell you some things to do and not to do, hoping that the information will improve your overall experience.

PERSONAL CHECKPOINTS

Part of the trick is knowing what to ignore. Sad to say, the list includes official checkpoints, all mile markers and all timers. The official checkpoints migrate from year to year. The mile markers you sometimes see are do-it-yourself efforts, usually measured with automobile odometers and probably not corrected for odometer error, which can amount to plus or minus 5%. I have not had good luck with the timers who sometimes shout times at the approximate checkpoints and at purported 10-, 15- and 20-mile marks. Most often, these times do not jibe with my watch, and the distances that they represent are often badly in error.

What, then, do I recommend? Be self-sufficient. Wear your own watch. Rely on immovable landmarks for segmenting the race. Carry a schedule either in your head or written down (I carry a 3 x 5 card showing seven checkpoints and the time that I should arrive at each).

A supplemental chart included here gives a list of good checkpoints. For the most part, they are significant crossroads boasting street signs and highway route signs that in Massachusetts are clearly visible from a distance. The table also shows the approximate distance to each checkpoint, correct to the nearest .05 mile as well as I can gauge it. Total mileage is 26.25 rather than 26.22, because the course is a trifle long.

The last column in the table shows the percent of time that you should spend in each segment. The percentages are not strictly proportional to distances but instead are based on the topography of the course and on your natural tendency to slow down as you go along.

Estimate your total marathon time in view of your condition. Then

BOSTON MARATHON CHECKPOINTS

	Approx. Total	Mileage Split	Time in Segment
Start—Hayden Row, Hopkinton	---	---	---
Ashland—Main Street & Route 135	3.85	3.85	13.3%
Framingham—Routes 126 & 135	6.80	2.95	11.0%
Natick—Routes 27 & 135	10.50	3.70	13.8%
Wellesley—West Junction of Routes 16 & 135	13.50	3.00	11.4%
Newton Lower Falls—Routes 16 & 30	17.80	4.30	16.3%
Boston College—College Rd. & Commonwealth Ave.	21.25	3.45	14.7%
Railroad Overpass—Beacon St. near Fenway Park	25.25	4.00	15.7%
Finish—Boylston Street, Boston	26.25	1.00	3.8%

multiply the total time by each segment percentage to arrive at the time for each segment.

BEFORE THE START

If you can, wear your racing outfit to Hopkinton under your clothes rather than changing in the high school gymnasium. You'll save time and you'll stand less of a chance of forgetting things. With thousands of runners, there is so much bustling activity in the gymnasium that it is hard to concentrate on those little details of equipment and preparation that protect you against heat, cold, blisters, chafing and the like.

The baggage service from Hopkinton to the Prudential Center is remarkably efficient. I have never heard of a theft or a lost bag. So when you have stripped for action, you can confidently entrust your clothing to the volunteers who load it on the buses.

Waiting in line for a toilet is something to do to kill time and for conviviality. But if you don't have the time for it, visit the woods behind the high school athletic fields. Do this before you set off for the starting line. Do not mess up people's lawns, flowers and shrubs. For last-minute emergencies, some homeowners will let you use their bathrooms if you ask politely.

Unless you are a seeded runner, you won't see the starting line before the race. You can find its approximate location, because it attracts hordes of photographers who occupy every tree and promontory and half a dozen helicopters. Hayden Row is not a wide street, and the runners form a crowd a hundred yards deep behind the starting line.

Select your place in this crowd with an eye to your finishing place. If you are slow, select a spot near the back. If you are fast, go toward the front. By doing this, you will help avoid trampling others or being trampled in the hectic first mile.

HOPKINTON TO ASHLAND

After the start, the racket of helicopters and the cheers of the crowd are left behind as you plunge down out of Hopkinton. The surroundings are suburban and rural. The spectators are quiet little family groups, too awed by the flood of runners to applaud them, much less identify them. On this first part of the course there are few water hoses and no other aids. The runners talk to each other easily and frequently, and at length the press truck, honking loudly, forces its way through the crowd and on ahead. Photographers snap pictures of the cheerful mob.

The pace for that first segment may look terribly fast on paper. Maybe it's that 300-foot drop that does it, maybe it's the old Boston madness, or maybe I'm wrong about the distance. But the pace is right. The only modification you should make to it—and this is a must—is to estimate how much time you lost at the start. You may lose as much as three minutes.

ASHLAND TO FRAMINGHAM

This stretch is the least memorable of any segment of the Boston course. Here, your attention is likely to be drawn inward as you sort out aches and pains and think about your pace. By this time, you should be settling into a pace that you can hold, with a little slowing, for the next 14 miles.

You must start seeking water here, and you've got to be a bit clever about it, for there are no official stations and traffic is still heavy. Try not to stand in line for water hoses unless the day is very hot. There will be more water later, but if you can just put a little on your stomach now it will come in handy.

FRAMINGHAM TO NATICK

Leaving Framingham, at first you pass a commercial area with service stations, ice cream stands and the like. Then the course leads up over a couple of small hills.

For half a mile, you run along the shore of Fisk Pond where on hot days runners have succumbed to the temptation to dive in for a good cooling-off. Up a little slope and you are in Natick. Here Route 135 is called Central Street, and it is wide and empty of cars, with both sides shaded by great elm trees. The local folks are fond of handing out orange slices, but there is little water. What you really want is a cooling spray and a drink.

NATICK TO WELLESLEY

Beyond the checkpoint in Natick, there is an official refreshment station. Drink!

Now the spectators are two and three deep. You run the gauntlet. Never mind the curious architecture of the Wellesley dormitories; the pressure is more immediate. The crowds are choking off the course. For the first (but not the last) time in this race, you may not have room to pass.

The mood of the crowd is like that of a prize-fight, except that here the spectators are women, now strident, now silent, looking for action. Most of all, watching for women runners. Running close to a woman in 1975 when I passed Wellesley, I had the impression that I was in on the finish of the Olympic 1500. The excitement of the crowd penetrated even my rational bones and my stride lengthened and my chest protruded. What a trip it must be to be a woman marathoner!

In terms of mileage, the halfway point is at Wellesley approximately at the end of the Wellesley campus, but don't waste your time looking for any markers. After a few blocks of some of the most fashionable shops in Massachusetts, Route 135 runs into Route 16 (Washington Street). Here is your 13.5-mile checkpoint.

WELLESLEY TO NEWTON

You soon find a large athletic field on your right, called Hunnewell Playground. Here is another official refreshment station. Beyond that is the community of Wellesley Hills, where the spectators are in the habit of passing out ice cubes. I prefer not to put ice cubes in my mouth for fear of choking on them, but they are good for external use such as rubbing on your face and arms or wearing under your hat.

You pass over Route 9, which is a good rendezvous point if you are attended by someone in a car. Then there is a 100-foot descent over half a mile, to the Charles River. This is the lowest elevation you will see for a while. The next five miles are generally up.

"THE HILLS"

When you make the right turn onto Route 30 (Commonwealth Avenue) you have gone more than two-thirds of the distance and you have used up not quite two-thirds of your marathon time. Do some thinking. You can predict your total time by adding half again to the elapsed time, plus a little more.

If you're a hill runner, these famous hills of Newton won't impress you. The slopes are very gradual, and only their length and the fact that they come when you are already tired make them at all formidable. The avenue is wide and curving, divided by islands of grass upon which the residents lounge on a good day. The scene is as pastoral as anywhere on the course.

Take it easy on the hills. Your schedule calls for you to do so, and you can slow down a bit with an easy conscience. Your strength will be better spent in the last five miles.

BOSTON COLLEGE TO OVERPASS

It is hard to identify the exact summit of Heartbreak Hill. There is Hammond Street, after which you run along a plateau for a quarter-mile. Then there is a clear drop-off beginning at Boston College (College Road), and from this point there are five miles to go.

As you go down the hill, try out your legs to see what kind of speed they'll give you. You're going to want to pay out your remaining strength as wisely as you can.

You turn left at Cleveland Circle and run east on Beacon Street for a seemingly endless time. You actually descend 80 feet in three miles along Beacon Street, but it is a gradual slope and you hardly notice it. For most of its length, Beacon Street is a wide thoroughfare divided by trolley tracks and hedged with large apartment houses. Most of the citizens appear not to know that there is a race in progress. Little water or other aid is given, and slower runners may have a problem avoiding cars.

In all likelihood, you will have a morale problem on Beacon Street. You will be tempted to slow down greatly or walk. Your head will tell you all kinds of reasons for giving up. Now is the time to bring out your personal defenses against depression. My own defense is to concentrate on passing runners who are walking or jogging.

THE LAST MILE

At length, you arrive at a slight climb where Beacon Street passes over the railroad tracks. Fenway Park is to the right. From here, there is one mile to go.

It is the mile that you have come all this way to experience. Almost immediately, you find yourself in Kenmore Square amid a hysterical crowd that barely manages to keep a funnel open for the runners. You are conducted on waves of adulation. You pick up your pace just a little, make a quick right for two blocks along Hereford Street, and a quick left on to Boylston.

Suddenly, there it is, a block away: that most gratifying of all checkpoints, the finish line of the Boston Marathon. And it's all downhill.

50

New York City

The country's largest city
now has the largest marathon

Hal Higdon

T he real hero of the 1977 New York Marathon—now we can reveal it—was Jay Wendt! *The New York Times, Sports Illustrated*, and CBS News somehow missed the significance of Jay's achievement, but let it be recorded here. The sons of Jay Wendt were leaving the finish line in Manhattan's Central Park, about 3 p.m. on Oct. 23, 1977, wearing baby blue t-shirts saying "Jay Wendt Fan Club," carrying signs bearing the same message, and they numbered only slightly less than does Franco's Italian Army in Pittsburgh.

Judging from the smiles on their faces, Jay did not let them down. Since the start of the marathon occurred at 10:30 a.m. that morning on Staten Island, Jay Wendt probably completed the 26-mile, 385-yard course that wound through five boroughs in (at risk of committed libel) four hours, give or take a few thousand flashes of the digital clock over the finish line. May God bless Jay's future steps. May the wind be always behind Wendt's back. Jay Wendt is what the race was all about that year.

But can we accurately call the New York City Marathon a race? A "run" seems a more accurate term. Or maybe an "event." Even a "happening." Certainly an "experience." A few dozen up front were *racing*, among them Bill Rodgers, the first native, male ex-butterfly collector across the line, who did 2:11:28. Miki Gorman finished first female in 2:43:10. Fritz Mueller won a National AAU title by being the first over-40 athlete. He ran 2:27:25, a national Masters record.

Others in the field of approximately 5000 undoubtedly waged individual races of varying intensity with themselves, seeking to better previous personal records, but most came merely to be where it was happening that weekend. They sought the excitement like a moth seeks the searing light from a candle. And they particularly came to run New York, which, in a matter of a few years, has attained a stature that nears, if not equals, that of Boston.

Why run the New York City Marathon '77? It was not merely to run in a race that bills itself as the biggest and the best. As for being the "biggest," New York probably was that, marginally, since the Mayor Daley Marathon held in Chicago four weeks earlier also attracted more than 5000 entrants. As for being the "best," what signifies best? There are flatter, faster, hillier, prettier courses than New York, as well as races equaling New York in organization (which nevertheless was superb) and hoopla.

It probably matters little to the average runner—say, Jay Wendt—that his passage through the city is monitored by "the largest non-emergency ham network ever formed" or that he can cross the Queensboro Bridge over the world's longest carpet. Even the presence of 36 sub-2:20 marathoners, including four of the top six in the 1976 Olympic Marathon, does not touch the life of Jay Wendt greatly. It's nice to be out there with Frank and Bill and Lasse and the boys, but would he trade them for another aid station at 24 miles?

No, if New York was great—and the 1977 race certainly deserves that designation—it was not because of any press agent's gee-whiz statistics, but because it was a race with texture. It had rough edges and smooth spots. There was the magnificent view of the harbor from the crest of the Verrazano-Narrows Bridge and all those heads bobbing before and behind you like some massive, pulsating worm. There were burned-out, graffiti-covered buildings in Bedford-Stuyvesant and the crowd pinching in so close on the runners along the singles-bar row on First Avenue that it became nearly impossible to pass.

The run touched almost every type of neighborhood within the city, except 42nd Street's porno-film strip. If King Kong had come to town on Oct. 23 and stared down from the World Trade towers (or Empire State Building) at what was passing beneath him, what would he have made of it?

There was a theme from "Rocky" blaring from stereo loud speakers at a half-dozen places along the way. Black kids reached out of the crowds lining the course for hand slaps. One woman, wrapped in a window curtain, stared down from an upper floor. Hasidic Jews stood on the corners, bearded, wearing black cassocks and capes. Smiles on faces. Cheers from many, although more often than at Boston, awed silence. New Yorkers do not yet know exactly what to make of these people winding in a long parade through the streets. Signs. The crackling of a radio from a police car annoucing someone collapsed with a heroin reaction, hopefully not a runner. Finally, the sunlight gleaming off the autumn-tinted leaves as the parade passed through Central Park—and the smell of horse manure.

There was all that, and more, as the course traversed all five of the city's boroughs, crossed four bridges, and blocked 218 intersections. Many among the 5000 runners probably came for the same reason as expressed last year by Frank Shorter: "I just wanted to show up and see how the police would clear the streets." Clear them the police did (those who were not running, one competitor having "New York's Finest" on the back of his shirt), although many drivers jammed in midtown Manhattan traffic leaned heavily on their horns with pent-up frustration, sending a wave of marathon-induced anger echoing up the canyons between skyscrapers. Those are the same people who complain about the Concorde landing at JFK. Of course, the sound of angry horns is not foreign to the New York environment, being merely one facet of America's biggest city. The marathon now is one more facet: big, noisy and beautiful. More than one out-of-town competitor was tempted to comment: "It's a good place to run, but I wouldn't want to live there."

One other aspect of the 1977 New York Marathon was that it took endurance not merely to finish the race, but even to *enter*! The sponsoring New York Road Runner's Club established a set of barriers a prospective entrant needed to hurdle before receiving a number. If you wanted to enter, perhaps after having picked up one of the two-page fliers the race committee distributed at their hospitality suite in Boston, you first had to write for an entry blank. Several months likely passed, particularly if you wrote in late spring, because RRC members were busy planning and staging the Bonne Bell Mini-Marathon in June. What you received in mid-summer, however, was not the official entry blank, but rather a four-page brochure describing the glories of "NEW YORK CITY MARATHON '77," including a map of the course and a history of the event listing past winners (men and women), the top finishers from 1976, and leaders at various points along the course. But no form to fill out. That had to be requested a second time!

Eventually, after perhaps another month passed and the form finally appeared in your mailbox, you might be tempted to duplicate copies for distribution to friends and neighbors. Forget it. "Only official entry forms will be accepted—no Xeroxes or copies," said the instructions. Also: "You must fill in *all* blanks (except those which are optional). The Games Committee reserves the right to reject any entries."

One reason for rejection was failure to list a currently valid number indicating your membership in the AAU. That failing, your entry blank came bouncing back and you were rejected. New York seemed determined to become the first race to spend more money keeping people *out* of its field than getting them *in.*

"We added the AAU requirement as simply one more barrier," admitted race director Fred Lebow. "We didn't want to impose a time standard on the field like Boston, but we wanted to make certain that only serious runners, who had prepared thoughtfully for the event, went to the line."

Even serious runners might have begun to experience feelings of paranoia, particularly since organizers of the race had announced in their four-page brochure that entries would close Aug. 23 (two months prior to the start), with "no applications...accepted after the first 4000, even if this number is received before Aug. 23."

That number had be a modification of a lower number quoted in earlier literature, but Fred Lebow was telling friends privately that the limits were not firm. "We're saying 3000, but we plan to accept 4000," he commented in Boston. By July, however, when he appeared as observer at the First Chicago Distance Classic, he admitted: "We've been telling people 4000, but we'll probably allow 5000." By August, at one of the monthly pre-marathon clinics designed, ostensibly, to prepare people for The Event, he commented: "We'll probably not hold the line at 5000." By then, he had abandoned one plan to take out a full-page ad in *Runner's World* telling people *not* to come to the race.

Even while marathoners throughout the country, like homecoming queen candidates, nervously worried whether they would be issued invitations to participate (entry became easier after 5000 showed at Chicago), the organizers were producing 100,000 copies of a four-color, 96-page official program for the marathon that rivaled in quality, and certainly surpassed in intensity, anything done previously for such mundane non-participant events as the Super Bowl, World Series or Indy 500.

Peter M. Lincoln traced the history of the New York City Marathon at least partway back to Pheidippides, namely to 1896. "Which brings us to a more pertinent bit of mythology," wrote Lincoln, "the notion that American marathoning began in Boston. There is no question that Boston sustained the sport through the first seventy years of this century, but the very first "marathon" was run here in New York, seven months before the Boston inauguration."

This first American marathon in 1896 went from Stamford, Conn., to Columbus Circle in midtown Manhattan (through which the current race passes only a quarter-mile from the finish). It was organized by a group of New Yorkers who watched the first Olympic marathon in Athens, Greece, that summer. Another group of Olympic spectators from Boston, meanwhile, organized a race in that city the following year, April 19, 1897.

This second race persisted; the New York event was not repeated. This proved fortunate for those who deplete their glycogen stores between 20 and 24 miles, since the distance from Stamford to Columbus Circle supposedly was 35 miles, the winner covering the distance in 3:25:55. (Considering the quality of running in that era, the time seems suspiciously fast.) Among 30 entrants, only nine finished. *The New York Times* reported spectator reaction: "There was a pandemonium of joy...and women who knew only that the first race of its kind ever held in this country was nearing a finish waved their handkerchiefs and fairly screamed with excitement."

One of the announcements for the 1977 race also includes some historical information, not all of it totally accurate: "New York City did not see another marathon until 1970," states the blank, "when the first annual New York City Marathon was held in Central Park."

Actually, a very important marathon race had been held in suburban Yonkers for years. At a time during the 1950s, when you could count the number of American marathons on one hand, the Yonkers Marathon was second only to Boston in its traditions and appeal to runners. For many years it was near-permanent site of the National AAU Championship and also frequently served as a qualifying event for the Olympic team.

Even if you disqualify Yonkers for its suburban location, New York had another 26-mile, 385-yard event in the Cherry Tree Marathon, held in March, usually the Sunday after the National AAU Indoor Track and Field Championships on a multi-repeat course that started in the shadow of Yankee Stadium and paralleled the Major Deegan Expressway.

But to be technical, the Cherry Tree Marathon occurred in the Bronx, not Manhattan (which most people throughout the world equate with the term "New York"). Then in 1969 a newly-converted jogger, Fred Lebow, ran the Cherry Tree Marathon in 4:20 and, having spent all those hours and minutes on the course, had ample time for reflection on the race's flaws.

"It wasn't supported by any city agencies," recalled Lebow. "Traffic was a problem, and the course went through some desolate areas. I remember kids throwing rocks at us along the route. And there was no reception for the hundred or so entrants after the race."

Coincidentally, Mayor John V. Lindsay had recently closed Central Park to automobile traffic on weekends to permit joggers, walkers and cyclists freedom of movement. Lebow reasoned that the relatively idyllic setting (at least during the daytime) of Central Park with its trees and lakes and lawns punctuated by rock outcrops would be an ideal marathon setting.

The first New York City Marathon, on Sept. 13, 1970, attracted 126 runners, 72 of whom finished, a bare hint of what would occur within a half-dozen years.

By 1976, when 2090 jammed the starting line, the race had been moved out of Central Park to Staten Island in front of the Verrazano-Narrows Bridge spanning the Upper Bay as it flowed into the Atlantic Ocean. The event now could be said to be a *true* New York City Marathon since it spanned all five of that city's boroughs: from Staten Island, across Brooklyn, into Queens, then over the Queensboro Bridge into Manhattan with a touchdown in the Bronx, Lebow was among those originally opposing this route.

"I thought it would involve too many problems," he recalls. "Traffic would hassle the runners. I worried about their safety. I never dreamed the city would support the plan."

But support it they did: in 1976, 1977, and presumably for many years to come. The New York City Marathon, because of its size, entrants, and particularly because of its texture, has established itself as one of the significant distance running events (not races) of the world. How significant? Its sponsors now boast that New York is the "Great American Marathon," and that, "The Big Apple has reclaimed its status vacated since 1896 as American's top marathon city."

Well, not quite. Boston cannot be that easily shoved aside. The Boston Marathon, because of tradition, still retains its mystique, its unique appeal. Claims as to who is number one are best left to football fans. It is enough to say that New York City—as Jay Wendt, Bill Rodgers, Miki Gorman and 5197 assorted others discovered—is simply a good place to run.

OFFICIAL
JOGGER'S
WATER HOLE
MARATHON CLINIC
SUNDAY MORNINGS
Aloha
ATHON
LINIC

51

Honolulu

More than a race, this is
a year-round fitness program

Mike Tymn

The Honolulu Marathon is just a few years old, but already it is being compared with the great granddaddy of them all in Boston. With the field growing in leaps and bounds each year, there is even talk of establishing a three-hour qualifying time as Boston has.

One big difference, however: the Honolulu qualifiers would be those *over* three hours. If competition is the name of the game at Boston, participation is the theme at Honolulu.

"Our course records are 2:17:24 at one end and 7:35:10 at the other. You are cordially invited to break either." This invitation, which was extended by race director John La Belle on the entry form for the Honolulu Marathon, perhaps reflects the philosophy of running in Hawaii.

An article by Ken Young in a 1976 issue of *Runner's World* indicates that, in at least one respect, Hawaii may be the running capital of the world. His research, based upon finishers in races of 15 kilometers and longer, shows 82.34 runners per 100,000 of population for Hawaii. (Far back in second place is Oregon at 19.85.) Considering the fact that Young's figures were to a large extent affected by the 703 finishers in the 1975 Honolulu Marathon and that 1452 finished in 1976, the spread is likely much larger now.

How does a state with a population of only three-quarters of a million, isolated from everyone else by a few thousand miles of ocean, draw a field of marathon runners nearly as large as that in the New York City Marathon? One might guess that it has something to do with the year-round warm climate and the recreational environment. However, these elements have been present for some time now, and it is only in the past three years that running has become popular in Hawaii.

Most of the credit has to go to a 41-year-old internist and cardiologist, Jack Scaff, Jr., who with his associates, Dr. John Wagner and Dr. Alfred Morris, formed the Honolulu Marathon Clinic in 1974.

Contrary to its name, the Clinic was not formed to foster marathon racing. In fact, competition is for the most part discouraged.

"Our objective is to get people running for exercise," Scaff says. "The marathon is just an excuse to keep them at it. It's an incentive. The average guy may be inclined to run only a mile or two a day or not at all. But if finishing the marathon is his goal, he'll get out there and put in an hour or more and be more regular at it.

"The marathon provides a more immediate and tangible reason to run. A guy may go home and tell his wife that he has to go out and run, and she asks him 'why?' If he says he's training for the marathon, it seems to make more sense than just to say that he's running for his health or his heart. It makes it more necessary, and women seem to prefer that type of explanation. Of course, we have quite a few women in the Clinic, so I guess it works the other way, too."

The dominant member and driving force in the Clinic and the official race organization, the Honolulu Marathon Association, Scaff emerges as something of a guru to many of the 1800 or so participants in the Sunday morning program. They listen intently as he lectures briefly on subjects ranging from diet to footwear before sending them off running in different directions. These 10-minute sermons have been referred to as "the gospel according to Dr. Jack." Few of his disciples deviate from the guidelines that he sets down.

Scaff became interested in running while training at Long Beach Memorial Hospital in 1967. "I was a typical sedentary overweight male with absolutely no interest in exercise when I got out of the Public Health Service in 1966," he says. "I became interested in stress testing while at Long Beach Memorial, and that led to an interest in exercise and running. I could find little in the various medical journals on the positive effects of exercise and that prompted me to dig into the subject more."

Convinced that a regular running program benefits the heart and health in general, Scaff started his own patients running and formed a cardiac rehabilitation program at a Honolulu YMCA for people who had suffered heart attacks or otherwise had heart problems. This program, which is still in existence, is closely monitored by Scaff, his associates and their nurses.

While running together on a Sunday morning in early 1974, Scaff and Wagner discussed the possibility of getting a group together—not just patients, but anyone interested in improving his health. They placed an announcement in the newspaper and about 80 people turned out for the first Sunday morning clinic. That was in April 1974. In addition to growing to more than 1800 registered participants, the Clinic has spread out to four different locations around Oahu, Hawaii's most populous island. It is now sponsored by the City of Honolulu Department of Parks and Recreation, which is under the direction of Tommy Kono, former Olympic weight lifting champion.

"I think that middle-aged men are sick and tired of being told they have to take it easy," Scaff comments in explaining the growth and success of the Honolulu Marathon Clinic. "Our program has given them the opportunity to engage in vigorous activity. It doesn't necessarily take a medical doctor to head up a program like ours, but people seem to feel safer knowing that a doctor is around. For the average uninformed and out-of-shape person, there are more risks in beginning a running or jogging program than in any other sport I know of except scuba diving."

The Clinic operates nine months a year, taking a break following the December marathon. However, even during the break period a large percentage of the participants continue to show up at the usual 8 a.m. starting time. When the formal program gets underway in March, new members are indoctrinated.

Following the brief lectures by Scaff and sometimes by Wagner, the runners take off from the park in which they meet in different directions. The "graduates" (those who have completed a marathon) usually run a 15-kilometer out and back course from the park, while the beginners circle the park under the watchful eyes of one or more of the doctors. Around September the intensity and duration of the runs increase in preparation for the marathon.

Scaff preaches long, slow distances—"recreational running" as he calls it. "I'm trying to train finishers, not racers," he says. "I really don't know that much about training racers, but I do know that a lot of speed work leads to injuries. They say that one of every three or four world-class runners is out with injuries at any one time, and we don't want that."

For health and fitness, Scaff recommends one hour of easy running every other day. For those planning to run the marathon, he recommends up to two hours every other day. He feels that the real training effect does not take place until a person has depleted his carbohydrates and switched to fat metabolism, and so runs of less than a half-hour do little good.

The typical Clinic participant is a business or professional person, the average age being somewhere around 35. While the exact figures are not available, there are several hundred participants over age 50 and more than 200 women.

"Unfortunately, we haven't been able to attract the younger people, especially the teenagers," says Jim Moberly, local AAU Chairman and another of the prime-movers in the Honolulu Marathon Association. "It seems to be mostly those people who have settled down in their careers and have found the need for more relaxation and recreation who have joined the program. Somehow we have to find a way to get to the young people before they develop all those bad habits, but it's going to be difficult."

Although the Honolulu Marathon Clinic contributes the great majority of runners to the annual marathon, the nucleus for the event was formed well before the Clinic came into existence. The Mid-Pacific Road Runners Club was organized in 1962 and sponsored the annual Norman K. Tamanaha Marathon on the island of Maui. The number of competitors in that race seldom exceeded 20.

Tamanaha, now 70, is called "the father of distance running in Hawaii." He was probably the only serious distance runner in the Islands in the post World War II years. Beginning in 1947, at the age of 40, he competed in the Boston Marathon six times. He finished fifth in 1952 at the age of 45 and turned in his best time of 2:38:30 in 1955 at age 48. Although he doesn't compete much these days, Tamanaha still puts in his daily mileage along the beach near his home.

Jim and Leah Ferris, Hawaii's foremost running couple, saw the need for a marathon on the island of Oahu, and in March 1973 they sponsored one that drew a field of nearly 100. A retired Army officer, Tom Ferguson, took over as president of the Mid-Pacific Road Runners Club later that year and was largely responsible for getting the first official Honolulu Marathon on the road. There were 157 finishers for that one. It was the first marathon in the world officially to sponsor a division for victims of cardiovascular disorders.

With the formation of the Honolulu Maraton Clinic in early 1974, a committee was formed to develop a bigger and better race, one that would attract some world-class runners from the mainland. There were 297 finishers in 1974, 703 in 1975, 1452 in 1976.

"In the footsteps of the Kings' Runners," is the official theme of the annual Honolulu Marathon. Unlike most marathons that are traditionally linked to ancient Greece, the Honolulu race can claim roots in its own Hawaiian culture.

Ancient Hawaii was a group of loosely knit fiefdoms whose communications were limited by the distance a man could run on foot or travel by boat. Trails consisting of small waterwashed stones line by curbstones through fields of lava were the roads of commerce and served as pathways designed to protect the barefooted slaves, warriors and professional runners (messengers) during their travels.

The most famous of these was "The King's Highway" (an eponym used for the first time by Mark Twain in his "Letters from the Sandwich Islands") during the reign of King Kamehameha I. Small stones from the highway are mounted on the trophies given to winners of the Honolulu Marathon.

History has not recorded how fast the ancient Hawaiian runners were, it is unlikely that there were any world-class distance runners among them. Polynesians are a people built more like weight lifters or wrestlers than distance runners. Modern-day Hawaii can, however, boast of a world class distance runner, even though his ancestors came from Scotland and not the South Seas. If Hawaiian Duncan Macdonald had lived in the early days of the monarchy, he probably would have been elevated to god status, as was Captain Cook.

When Captain Cook fell from grace with the Hawaiians, they killed him. Macdonald would probably have escaped similar fate as they wouldn't have been able to catch him. More than 1400 runners tried and failed in 1976.

52

Fukuoka

Next to the Olympics, the Japanese marathon is the Big One

Gary Tuttle

Fukuoka. In the words of Jerome Drayton, "This is the plum trip of marathoning." Drayton should know, since he is a major component of the history of the Japanese marathon. He has three victories there, and only Derek Clayton has run faster in this race than Drayton's 2:10:08 in 1975. Only one man has won more often at Fukuoka than Drayton—Frank Shorter.

Shorter has so dominated Fukuoka that the Japanese selection committee declined to invite him in 1976 in order to "get new faces at Fukuoka." I was one of those "new faces."

I spent six days finding out what makes Fukuoka so great, who pays the bills, who would become the next "world open marathon champion" and what makes the race so fast. In less than one week, I found the answers to all my questions.

Immediately upon leaving the customs area in the Tokyo airport, I was greeted by a local travel agent, Mr. Inuoe. He took me by taxi to my overnight room at the Imperial Hotel, one of Tokyo's finest, with dinner, breakfast and room all prepaid.

The next morning, I flew to Fukuoka, where I was whisked away to my first press interview. I was excited, but I couldn't help feeling that the interview was a trial run for the reporters who were eagerly awaiting Olympic gold medalist Waldemar Cierpinski's arrival on the next day.

Mr. Shibuya, the foreign-athlete liaison, dragged me from the airport lobby towards the waiting taxi. We made our exit while flash bulbs exploded in my face and applause rang in my ears. Marathoners are sports heroes in Japan. I could feel the pressure to run well beginning to grow.

As we finally drove away, I felt it was my turn to ask the question. I asked Mr. Shibuya, "Who is paying for my trip?" He explained that the race is sponsored by the Japan Amateur Athletic Federation and the Asahi Newspaper. I got the impression that the Federation did most of the legwork and the Asahi Newspaper paid most of the bills.

The *Asahi News* has a circulation of seven million, and apparently could afford the large sum. I never was able to find out the exact budget for Fukuoka, but my flight expense, six days of room, private interpreter, taxis and entertainment was right at $2000. In addition, there were four other foreign runners, plus two coaches, which brings the total to at least $10,000. This doesn't include one lunch for 400 policemen, who are needed on race day, cost of a massive awards ceremony which had free food and booze for around 300 dignitaries, or the free rooms for 42 Japanese runners who ran 2:20 or better in the last year. The final outlay probably was at least $20,000.

Some money was saved by the East German party of Cierpinski, Karl-Heinze Baumback (promising 19-year-old grooming for 1984?) and their coach. East Germany paid for their own airplane tickets, and Japan picked up on the in-country expenses. Therefore, Cierpinski was a nearly free commodity.

However, Ian Thompson of Great Britain cost the organizers double. In order to get Thompson, the Japanese also had to bring a team manager. (To my knowledge, Britain is the only "free world" country that requires a team manager for every trip.) When I asked Mr. Shibuya why a team manager accompanied Thompson, he said, "The English always send a team manager. The English system is run by the old. They protect their own self-interest. We always must bring a manager."

When I asked why I was invited to Fukuoka, he was very frank. He said, "We have a 10-11-man selection committee which decides who will be invited. We wanted (Lasse) Viren and (Shivnath) Singh from India, but they couldn't come. We then decided on an American, since they always run well here. Your AAU picked you, because you are a two-time American champion."

Now it was time to go through the two problems facing all runners in a new land. The first is the time change. A visitor wakes up several times at night and feels sluggish during the day's runs. Often, no matter how much one runs, his bowels never regain their early morning regularity, and nothing feels right until the final pre-race visit to the toilet.

The second problem is what to do in those pre-race days. A lot of time is spent watching television, and wishing it was in English. In between "Sesame Street' and "Switch" in Japanese, the race sponsor had scheduled a few excursions to ease the pain of waiting.

On Friday, we went to the Fukuoka Police Riot Academy to see its judo team, led by an Olympic champion. Of course, many pictures were taken of Cierpinski flipping the judo champs. Mr. Shibuya confessed that this visit was not so much for us as it was to keep the police cooperating. Apparently, in the early history of the marathon, the sponsors had to battle the police and local truckers to keep the roads blocked for two hours. Even now, any runner who is 15 minutes behind at the halfway point or 30 minutes behind the leader thereafter is pulled off the course.

On Saturday, the day before the race, we were bused to the civic center for the "citizens reception." We went through the token physical (Thompson never was able to urinate, but it didn't seem to matter), more press interviews and more gifts from the sponsor. (I came home with a wallet, Seiko battery shaver, four tie pins, two sets of cuff-links, serving tray, Christmas ornament, cosmetic case, 50 free picture postcards and more—all gifts.)

With the interviews over, we went to the auditorium for "further festivities." The first speaker made reference to the "disgraceful and dishonorable" performance of the Japanese marathoners at Montreal. He hoped for a better performance on Sunday against the foreigners. He said it was "embarassing that a Japanese runner has won only once in the 11-year history of Fukuoka," After finishing his speech and sitting down, he proceeded to fall asleep on stage, only to awaken to the sound of clapping at the end of another speech.

Upon later reflection, I began to soften on my criticism of the man. At first hearing his speech, the English-speaking runners were unanimous in their criticism. Drayton, in a speech of his own, even made a cutting reference to "the fine performance, not disgraceful history" of Japanese runners, and mentioned his outrage and embarrassment at hearing a poor speaking performance.

I don't appreciate the pressure to perform well which is applied to Japanese runners. In 1967, it caused top marathoner Kokichi Tsuburaya, to commit suicide over an achilles tendon injury. However, after seeing the culture and country, and reading the novel *Shogun,* I have a better understanding of the tremendous pride which causes the do-or-die effort found in Japan. Only Japan would find men proud enough to fly suicide planes, and that spirit lives on.

Finally, the festivities had ended, and it was just 16 hours until the race. Everyone turned to race preparations, contestants and officials alike. We were asked to prepare any special drinks we might require.

Cierpinski filled seven containers with black tea and sugar. Drayton prepared what Shorter uses, Coke which is defizzed and allowed to sit overnight. Thompson had a mineral-glucose package made in England. I decided to put out four containers of Body Punch and three containers of defizzed Coke—three Cokes and a half-gallon of Body Punch. "If I need all this, I know I'll be in trouble," I thought. (I drank it all, plus four cups of orange juice.)

All that was left now was the final evening meal of carbohydrates. So I headed to Shakey's Pizza Parlor for my third straight supper of pizza, salad and beer. There are not enough carbohydrates in octopus and raw fish. The three interpreters and I ate to the accompaniment of "Dixie" on the banjo.

Race time was noon on Sunday. At 10:30, we boarded a bus and traveled a mile to the Main Heiwadai Stadium. The sponsor had set aside a separate waiting room for us five foreigners. Thompson pretended to sleep, and Cierpinski and Baumbach talked in hushed voices. The boredom was relieved by a visit from Olympic marathon silver medalist in 1964 Games, Basil Heatley. Heatley was filming the race for a Japanese television station.

About a half-hour before race time, we entered the stadium and began our warmup. We had the field to ourselves as the Japanese runners were kept outside the stadium until 10 minutes before the start.

The start seemed more like they were launching a rocket than starting a race. The starter said "3—2—1" and the gun sounded. I immediately found myself chasing some 20 Japanese. I heard a "Bonzai!" and instinctively flinched. The last time I heard that, John Wayne was fighting 20 Japanese. I prefer running with them.

The streets were lined, six deep in strategic spots. The sponsor had passed out free plastic flags, and it seemed to be a waving sea of rising suns for the next two hours. If we had run within two feet of the curb, we would have been thoroughly thrashed.

At 14 kilometers, Drayton was leading the pack when all of a sudden there was a blur of jumping, dodging figures. Ian and I quickly divided to avoid falling on a Japanese runner and Drayton just rising from the ground. The Japanese, Kunimitsu Ito, said something in an apologetic tone. Drayton said "F---off," and they both stormed to the front again.

By 25 kilometers, Ito was behind and out of sight. We were fighting a head wind, and Thompson began to get a little worried. He said, "Tuck in behind me, mate, and I'll pull us up to the leaders."

We thrashed on for five more kilometers. However, this was the same five in which Drayton broke things apart. He had a 13-second lead on Cierpinski by 30 kilometers and was pulling away.

The next five-kilometer segment was decisive for Thompson and me. He picked off dying runners one by one (including Cierpinski), while I was doing some dying of my own.

Over the last eight kilometers, Drayton held his lead and finished in 2:12:35. Thompson was all alone in second in 2:12:54, happy to run his first good race in a couple of years. Cierpinski finished looking nothing close to an Olympic champion. His last 100 yards were a bug-eyed, staggering lunge for the finish as he ran 2:14:56.

I came in 30th, a bone-weary, cramp-ridden, fatigued beyond endurance American representative. The last eight miles took nearly an hour. I took a chance on a fast pace and completely destroyed myself. I never felt so bad in my life. I became so sugar depleted that I was a depressed paranoiac. I hated those flags, detested each step and was so sure everyone was laughing at me that I found myself mumbling uncomplementary nothings to the sea of faces.

In contrast, the first 10 finishers looked weary but pleased as they accepted the big silver cups at the stadium awards ceremony. I took one quick look, then searched out a beer and a blanket, and joined all the other losers under the stands.

The day and the race were over. However, we were treated that night to a free food and booze party with 300 guests. Immediately following this we foreign runners were packed into taxis and were taken to dinner. The sponsor again spared no expense. We had an entire small restaurant reserved for our group of 14. Not only was there free steak, and saki, but four pretty "club girls" were hired just to serve, dance and sing for us.

Suddenly, the trip was over, and I was on the plane back to Los Angeles. I understood why Drayton called it "the plum trip of marathoning." It had been a good week—except for a mere two hours and 26 minutes. Now if I could come back without having to run that damn race.

53

Fast Places to Race

Choosing a race that offers a good chance for a good time

Ray Hosler

In 1975, when Bill Rodgers ran 2:09:55 at the Boston Marathon, he not only established the American record for that distance but reconfirmed this course to be the country's fastest. Because it's the only US marathon with time qualifying standards, it's also one of the most competitive. In 1977, more than one-third of the field ran under three hours.

Rodgers's time at Boston was a mere 15 seconds better than his 2:10:10 at New York City one year later. Despite the insignificant time difference, Boston remains the official fastest course based on record time. Could Rodgers establish an even faster American time record in Eugene, Ore., on the Olympic Trials layout (history says no) or on some other equally fast course with fewer hills than at Boston? Based on his comments at the 1976 Maryland Marathon, it would seem so. Rodgers said his 2:14 at Maryland on some tough hills was comparable to the 2:10 effort at New York only two months earlier.

But there are so many other factors contributing to a fast course and time—hills being one of them—it's impossible to predict how well a runner will do from one course to the next. Competition, race organization, weather and the runner's mental and physical preparedness all play key roles in the final performance.

What is certain is that some courses are faster than others. For the average runner out to break three hours, it can mean the difference between achieving that goal and a 3:15.

Six of the 10 fastest marathon courses are on the East or West Coast. If you don't happen to live in one of these regions, you'll probably find yourself traveling hundreds, maybe thousands of miles to a very fast course. This logistical problem is enough to discourage many runners from taking advantage of the best courses.

Even if you have enough dedication to travel, don't expect miracles. For many runners, those great expectations wilt under a merciless sun, transform themselves into giant blisters or end with repeated trips to the nearest bathroom on marathon day.

SCOTTSDALE, ARIZONA (1977)

The year doesn't matter, nor the times; it would be my fastest marathon was all that mattered—the lucky seventh. The course was selected with the greatest of care, and my training had peaked at an all-time best for the big race. As race day neared, though, the inevitable doubt crept in. Had I trained enough?

Resting in a comfortable jet seat, downing an ice-cold beer far above the Arizona desert, I jotted down the reasons for a personal best in my favor. This list was impressive: carbohydrate-loading complete, injury-free, plenty of training and racing, familiar with the fast Fiesta Bowl course in Scottsdale and two years older than my last personal-best marathon. Twice before, I had run this seemingly charmed course to collect faster times.

Because of a gradual downhill layout, a drop of some 800 feet, this race has far greater potential than its good 2:14 record indicates.

I peered out the window and imagined myself battling defending champion Ed Mendoza to a sub-2:14 through the desert stillness below. Somehow another image, that of heat waves shimmering in the distance, brought me back to reality. What was the weather forecast? It can be hot in Phoenix, even in mid-winter. But the weather report called for temperatures in the mid-60s, with no wind. Mornings generally are cool and crisp. That kind of mild December sun warms participants just enough to make for comfortable running.

In the last six years, race organization had been good. The point-to-point course, with light traffic, cuts through scenic desert settings.

All this sounds pleasant, but catastrophes never announce their arrival. It was hot that day and by noon, when I was finishing with the other sub-three-hour-runners, the temperature was 80 degrees. A personal best melted under the pounding Arizona sun. Only the severe leg cramping would linger to haunt me.

How much of this disaster was just plain fate? Most of it. Never before had I been so well prepared, physically, and the Fiesta Bowl course had been kind. But unpredictable weather often leads to devastation; that's fate. So, this marathon goes down as the *Fiasco Bowl.* Once again, I search for the perfect wave, my ultimate marathon, which has drifted away to crash against the pavement of some other race course. Where do I start?

RESEARCHING THE RACE

Let's begin with the *Runner's World* special marathon issue (February 1978), listing most of the US and Canadian marathons. The survey describes course particulars like layout, time records and who holds them, certification status and highlights the previous year's race results. Each item gives clues to a course time potential.

There are 193 marathons you can choose. Marathons are in Maine, Alaska, Hawaii, even Wyoming. Which will carry me to the visionary personal best, or does it really matter where I run? Are the races all the same, differences mere illusions? Perhaps such intangibles as mood and race-day feelings determine the final time.

Realistically, at some places you'll never run great times. For example, the course record at the Alaska Equinox Marathon is a dismal 2:53. That's great, considering it was run on a mostly muddy, hilly trail. Save that race for a different kind of challenge, like an easy run to enjoy beautiful scenery.

How about the Summit County Marathon in Dillon, Colo.? First, look Dillon up on a map. Altitude is listed as 8600 feet, in the heart of the breath-taking Rocky Mountains. A great place for a picnic, but the race is a breath-taker in more ways than one. With a course record of 2:37, by a runner I know to be much faster, it looks like high-altitude marathons are out.

Skip the marathons scheduled for summer months. I can think of better ways to get a good suntan and no better way to get heat stroke. The only fast time you'll have at these races is the one you record sprinting for the nearest water fountain after its all over. Even Olympic runners suffer in the heat. Garry Bjorklund ran 2:21 at a June marathon in Minnesota with 80-degree temperatures. His best time improved six minutes in the 1977 New York Marathon four months later where it wasn't nearly so hot.

I'll also skip the lesser-known marathons with small turnouts. They may be well organized, but competition is probably absent.

Since I live on the West Coast, I've ruled out the Boston and other East Coast marathons. I'll also figure you're trying to break three hours for the first time. At Boston, you must qualify to run. This means breaking three hours in a marathon no more than one year previous to the Boston date (3:30 for men over 40 and women). But, if you should qualify, Boston is the "Indianapolis 500" of race courses. Even then, you have to hope Boston's notoriously unpredictable weather is on your side. It can be very hot or very cold.

Finally, I stop at the Nike Oregon Track Club Marathon. It's close, in Oregon. It's in September, where weather is usually mild that time of year. The course is listed as flat and certified. I don't want to run a short or long course. The race highlights are encouraging, too. In 1977, 35% of the runners were under three hours. That's probably a good field, but encouraging nonetheless. Now, if only I can get all those unpredictables out of my system, I might make it.

Obviously, certain conditions make for a fast marathon course. I've mentioned heat, altitude, competition and accurate distances. There are five other major features to consider when choosing a race for speed. They are:

• *Competition:* Without this, an elite runner, or any runner for that matter, probably won't run as hard. People tend to speed up when they have somebody to key on. How many times have you seen a top runner "coast" to victory? Rodgers consistently runs 2:11, or better, at the big-name marathons when he's running well. At the '77 Waynesboro Marathon in Virginia, he coasted to a 2:25 victory. There was nobody to push him.

• *Weather:* It's probably the most important factor and unfortunately, the most unpredictable. About all you can do is look for races in "fair weather" months and hope for the best. That means looking for races during winter months in the Southeast and Southwest; fall months in the Midwest, Rockies and Northeast and most any time but mid-summer on the West Coast. It also helps to check with a weather bureau to get an advance race-day forecast. According to running Dr. George Sheehan, 45 degrees is the ideal temperature for a marathon. Humidity is something to consider too. Runners accustomed to low humidity sometimes find breathing more difficult in humid conditions, and vice versa.

• *Terrain:* Obviously, the more hills the slower the time. Despite the severe Satyr Hill at about 18 miles in the Maryland Marathon, a course record 2:13 was set by Garry Bjorklund in 1977. Chalk that up to intense competition and a well-organized race. This kind of performance, though, is no measure of what to expect on the hills unless you excel at this kind of running terrain.

A new trend, in an attempt to create faster conditions and world-record times, is for downhill layouts with enormous elevation drops. If you're looking for a bad set of knees, these are the races for you. Two marathons in particular, both in the Rockies, boast their downhill advantage: the Pioneer, in Utah (from 5600 to 2745 feet) and the new Poudre River Canyon in Colorado (9500 to 6500 feet). Boston's course has a mild drop of 200 feet from start to finish, but still has several hills getting there. So, it would be wise to find out the exact course description before making any attempt on these super-downhill courses. It's also important to note that AAU standards in course certification allow no more than a 525-foot total elevation drop from start to finish.

• *Course Design:* You can run laps, point-to-point courses, out-and-back courses and many variations of these three. The out-and-back can offer advantages of easier traffic control and more aid stations. You'll probably find running a lot of laps boring and poorly located point-to-point courses develop traffic problems quickly. Traffic is becoming more of a headache and should be a major consideration in checking out a course. Running through smog reduces a body's ability to convert oxygen, which means you'll have a harder time breathing. Besides, your chances of "eating fender" go up markedly and that kind of distraction you don't want to worry about.

• *Race Organization:* A poorly-executed race quickly takes its time toll. The absent aid stations lead to dehydration. Poor traffic control leads to stopping for lights and cars. Unmarked turns and missing course officials lead to lost runners. Missing time splits along the way upsets pace plans. There are many poorly planned marathons to choose, only a few good ones. Check with a local running club where the race is held if you're planning an out-of-town journey. They can tell you the inside story about organization.

I've listed the all-time fastest marathon courses based on individual winning performance. Here's one more way to look for the best race. Why does Shorter or Rodgers run in a particular marathon? They probably go for the same reasons as somebody looking to run under three hours—the race is well-organized, the course is fast and the weather usually mild. That's after putting financial considerations aside.

A final but often misleading formula for finding the fast ones is to look at how many runners ran under three hours. Veteran marathon runner Ken Young, director of the National Running Data Center, cautions that these figures often are misleading: "The number of runners under a given time really reflects the constituency of the field. At a marathon with a large turnout such as New York, you'll find a lot of runners out for their first attempt and a resulting smaller percentage of fast times. Boston, with a qualifying time, displays the opposite effect, as a large percentage of runners finish under three hours."

In looking at the fast courses, Young continued, "Motor City is perhaps the fastest course, next to the Nike-Oregon TC. Look at the record by Jerome Drayton, a 2:12 back in 1969. Traditionally, the field is weak at Motor City, yet someone always wins in 2:18 or so.

Young contends that loop courses with several laps are the fastest. "It can be psychologically depressing to see a long straightaway in a race and realize you have to cover all that distance," Young notes. "However, a tailwind in a point-to-point race can be an important factor. "It happened at Boston when Rodgers ran his 2:09."

One final clue, Young says, is to check on how many age-group records a course has, to reveal something about it potential.

ALL-TIME FASTEST MARATHON COURSES

(based on course record times)

Race	Time	Person	Yr.	% sub-3:00*
1. Boston	2:09:55	Bill Rodgers	'75	37% **
2. New York	2:10:10	Bill Rodgers	'76	19%
3. Nike Oregon TC	2:11:51	Frank Shorter	'76	35%
4. Motor City	2:12:00	Jerome Drayton	'69	30%
5. Maryland	2:13:46	Garry Bjorklund	'77	19%
6. Fiesta Bowl	2:14:13	Ed Mendoza	'75	17%
7. Rice Festival	2:14:27	Neil Cusack	'74	8%
8. Trail's End	2:14:43	Brian Maxwell	'77	21%
9. White Rock	2:15:11	Jeff Wells	'76	22%
10. Western Hemisphere	2:15:21	Bill Scobey	'71	36%**

*—1977 race results; **—timing stopped at 4:00*

While the Nike Oregon TC course is not technically the fastest, it may very well gain that distinction. Already, it holds two American women's time records. The most recent set in 1977 by Kim Merritt with a 2:37:57. No doubt Shorter and Rodgers ran hard at the Trials, but certainly not as hard as they could have, had the stakes been more than just placing in the top three to qualify.

Other courses with good reputations for supplying fast times include: Mission Bay, Jersey Shore, Avenue of the Giants and Marine Corps Reserve. The list keeps growing.

MARATHON RACES IN THE UNITED STATES AND CANADA

These are races which were scheduled during 1978. Most are annual events, held at about the same time each year. Write to the listed race director for information. Included here are race name and city, date and contact, alphabetically by state.

Alabama

Rocket City (Huntsville)	Dec.	Harold Tinsley, 8811 Edgehill Dr., Huntsville 35802

Alaska

Equinox (Fairbanks)	Sept.	William Smith, University of Alaska, Fairbanks 99701
Midnight Sun (Anchorage)	June	Terry Martin, 3960 Reka Dr. B-6, Anchorage 99504
Resurrection Pass (Hope)	July	Lyla Richards, University of Alaska, Anchorage 99504
Sun Bear Midnight (Eielson AFB)	June	Wayne Grieme, 5179-B North St., Eielson AFB 99702

Arizona

Admissions Day (Tucson)	Feb.	J. McGee Evans, 400 N. 2nd Ave., Tucson 85705
Copper Valley (Globe)	Oct.	Chamber of Commerce, Box 2539, Globe 85501
Fiesta Bowl (Scottsdale)	Dec.	Fiesta Bowl, 3410 E. Van Buren, Phoenix 85008

Arkansas

Ground Hog Day (Little Rock)	Jan.	Gerald Hastings, 7 Hickory Lane, N. Little Rock 72118

California

Avenue of the Giants (Weott)	May	Dick Meyer, Rt. 1, Box 153-A, Eureka 95501
Bakersfield (Bakersfield)	Feb.	Bakersfield TC, Box 9391, Bakersfield 93309
Bidwell Classic (Chico)	Mar.	Walt Schafer, 1413 Salem St., Chico 95926
Hidden Valley (Newbury Park)	Feb.	Marathon, 180 Academy Dr., Newbury Park 91320
Livermore (Livermore)	Dec.	Livermore Jaycees, Box 524, Livermore 94450
Los Alamitos (Los Alamitos)	Mar.	Mitch Lansdell, 10911 Oak St., Los Alamitos 90720
Los Angeles (Los Angeles)	Mar.	Fred Honda, 3900 Chevy Chase Dr., Los Angeles 90039
Madera (Madera)	Dec.	Dee Dewitt, 200 S.L, Madera 93637

Race (Place)	Month	Contact
Mission Bay (San Diego)	Jan.	Marathon, 2691 Palace Dr., San Diego 92123
Mt. SAC Relays (Walnut)	Apr.	not available
Orange County (Orange County)	Apr.	Pete Dowrey, 9593 Pettswood Dr., Huntington Beach 92646
Orange Grove (Loma Linda)	Apr.	Loma Linda Lopers, Box 495, Loma Linda 92345
Palos Verdes (P.V. Peninsula)	June	Kiwanis Club, Box 153, Palos Verdes Estates
Paul Masson (Saratoga)	Jan.	Dan O'Keefe, 20032 Rodrigues Ave., Cupertino 95041
Rose Bowl (San Pedro)	Nov.	Pasadena YMCA, 235 Holly St., Pasadena 91101
Sacramento (Sacramento)	Oct.	John McIntosh, 4120 El Camino Ave., Sacramento 95821
San Francisco (San Francisco)	July	Jim Scannell, 365 24th Ave., No. 24, San Francisco 94121
Santa Barbara (Santa Barbara)	Oct.	John Brennand, 4476 Meadowlark Ln., Santa Barbara 93105
Senior Olympics (Irvine)	May	Warren Blaney, 5670 Wilshire, No. 360, Los Angeles 90036
Sonoma State (Rohnert Park)	Oct.	Bob Lynde, Sonoma State College, Rohnert Park 94928
Valley of Flowers (Lompoc)	June	Joe Sciame, 1305 N. Orchard St., Lompoc 93436
West Valley (San Mateo)	Feb.	West Valley TC, Box 1551, San Mateo 94401
Western Hemisphere (Culver City)	Dec.	Carl Porter, 4117 Overland Ave., Culver City 90230
World Masters (Orange)	Jan.	Bill Selvin, 2125 N. Tustin, No. 3, Orange 92665

Colorado

Race (Place)	Month	Contact
Denver YMCA (Denver)	Oct.	Phil Guries, 25 E. 16th Ave., Denver 80202
Pike's Peak (Minitou Springs)	Aug.	Rudy Fahl, 559-B Castle Rd., Colorado Springs 80904
Summit County (Dillon)	Aug.	Summit Visitors Service, Box 669, Dillon 80435
United Bank Mile-Hi (Denver)	May	Bill Michaels, 1035 Corona St., No. 6, Denver 80218

Connecticut

Race (Place)	Month	Contact
John W. English (Middletown)	Mar.	Parks and Rec. Dept., Box 141, Middletown 06457

District of Columbia

Race (Place)	Month	Contact
Marine Corps Reserve (D.C.)	Nov.	Marine Corps RESP, Washington, D.C. 20380

Florida

Race (Place)	Month	Contact
Florida (Ft. Myers)	Mar.	Lou Cappi, YMCA, Ft. Myers, 33901

Event	Month	Contact
Florida Relays (Gainesville)	Mar.	Paul Segersten, Box 14485, Gainesville 32604
Orange Bowl (Miami)	Dec.	Marathon Coordinator, Fla. Intl. Univ., Miami 33199
Space Coast (Melbourne)	Nov.	Bob Lawton, Box 94, Cocoa Beach 32931
Valentine Festival (Shalimar)	Feb.	Buford Potter, 136 Country Club, Shalimar 32579
Georgia		
Peach Bowl (Atlanta)	Jan.	Atlanta TC, Box 11556, Atlanta 30355
Stone Mountain (S.M. Park)	Feb.	Wayne Roach, 1736 N. Cliff Valley J-1, Atlanta 30307
Hawaii		
Big Island (Hilo)	July	Marathon, Box 1381, Hilo 96720
Garden Isle Lihue (Kauai)	Oct.	Greg Ogin, Box 711, Lihue, Kauai 96766
Honolulu (Honolulu)	Dec.	Marathon Assn., Box 27244/Chinatown, Honolulu 96827
Maui (Maui)	Mar.	Dave Wissmar, Box 888, Kihei, Maui 96753
Idaho		
Les Bois (Boise)	Nov.	Basil Dahlstrom, Box 9281, Boise 83707
Illinois		
Aurora (Aurora)	July	Alberto Meza, Waubonsee CC, Sugar Grove 60554
CCAP Southern Illinois (Flora)	Sept.	Rose Gill, Box 160, Flora 62839
DeKalb (DeKalb)	Apr.	Roy Carlson, 830 Edgebrook No. 229, DeKalb 60115
Freedom (Monticello)	Oct.	Illinois TC, Box 2976 Sta. A, Champaign 61820
Hinsdale (Hinsdale)	Nov.	Jim Hagel, 102 N. Quincy, Hinsdale 60521
Mayor Daley (Chicago)	Sept.	Ruth Ratney, 900 N. Michigan Ave., Chicago 60611
Indiana		
Marathon (Terre Haute)	June	Dave Phlegley, Ind. State University, Terre Haute 47809
Pizza Hut (Bloomington)	Nov.	Ray Vandersteen, 817 W. 17th St., Bloomington 47401
Three Rivers (Ft. Wayne)	July	Cal Mahlock, 2633 W. State Blvd., Ft. Wayne 46808
Windy (Carmel)	Mar.	Jack Beasley, 11040 Winding Brook, Indianapolis 46280

Iowa

Event	Month	Contact
Covered Bridge (Winterset)	Oct.	Jerrold Oliver, F&M Bank, Winterset 50273
Cyclone (Ames)	June	Dick Seagrave, 2500 Kellogg, Ames 50010
Drake Relays (Des Moines)	Apr.	Robert Ehrhart, Drake University, Des Moines 50311
Iowa City (Iowa City)	Nov.	Mike Kendall, Box 1925, Iowa City 52240
U. of Northern Iowa (Cedar Falls)	Apr.	Lynn King, UNI, Cedar Falls 50613

Kansas

Event	Month	Contact
Kansas Relays (Lawrence)	Apr.	Ed Elbel, University of Kansas, Lawrence 66045
Mel Voss Memorial (Topeka)	Dec.	Gene Johnson, 4330 Windsor Ct., Topeka 66604
USTFF (Wichita)	May	Herm Wilson, WSU Box 18, Wichita 67208

Kentucky

Event	Month	Contact
Kentucky Relays (Lexington)	Apr.	Jerry Stone, University of Kentucky, Lexington 40506

Louisiana

Event	Month	Contact
Christmas Festival (Natchitoches)	Dec.	Jerry Dyes, Northwestern State U., Natchitoches 71457
Intl. Rice Festival (Crowley)	Oct.	Charlie Atwood, 121 N. Ave. K, Crowley 70526
Mardi Gras (New Orleans)	Jan.	NOTC, Box 30491, New Orleans 70190

Maryland

Event	Month	Contact
Life and Health (Frederick)	Apr.	Marathon, 6856 Eastern Ave., N.W., Washington 20012
Maryland (Baltimore)	Dec.	Marathon, Box 11394, Baltimore 21239
Washington's Birthday (Beltsville)	Feb.	Bob Rothenberg, 6N Hillside Rd., Greenbelt 20070

Massachusetts

Event	Month	Contact
Boston AA (Boston)	Apr.	Will Cloney, 150 Causeway St., Boston 02114
Silver Lake (Newton)	Feb.	Fred Brown, 157 Walsh St., Medford 02155
VFW (Lowell)	Mar.	Fred Brown, 157 Walsh St., Medford 02155

Michigan

Event	Month	Contact
Breckenridge (Breckenridge)	July	Breckenridge TC, 8532 McClelland, Breckenridge 48615

Race (Location)	Month	Contact
Motor City (Detroit)	Oct.	Edward Kozloff, 10144 Lincoln, Huntington Woods 48070
NJCAA (Dowagiac)	June	Ronald Gunn, Southwestern Michigan College, Dowagiac
Oliver Hanton (Port Huron)	Sept.	John Hanchon, 2922 Pine Grove Ave., Port Huron 48060
Saginaw Bay (Saginaw)	May	Delta College HPER Dept., University Center 48710
West Bloomfield (W. Bloomfield)	Mar.	Parks and Rec., 6485 W. Maple Rd., West Bloomfield 48033
Minnesota		
City of Lakes (Minneapolis)	Oct.	Jeff Winter, 4900 Vallacher Ave., Minneapolis 55416
Mississippi		
Mississippi (Clinton)	Dec.	Walter Howell, Box 4006, Clinton 39058
Missouri		
Heart of America (Columbia)	Sept.	Joe Duncan, 4004 Defoe Dr., Columbia 65201
Third Olympiad Memorial (St. Louis)	Feb.	Jerry Kokesh, 13453 Chesterfield Plaza, Chesterfield
Montana		
Governor's Cup (Helena)	June	Mayo Ashley, 1530 Jerome Pl., Helena 59601
Jerry Anderson (Kalispell)	Oct.	Mike Lyngstad, 723 5th Ave. E., Kalispell 59901
Nebraska		
Omaha (Omaha)	Aug.	Sarah Carlos, 1620 Dodge, Omaha 68134
Tri-State (Falls City)	Oct.	Louis Fritz, R.R. 1 Box 21, Verdon 68457
Nevada		
Lake Tahoe (Incline Village)	June	Lake Tahoe TC, Box 5983, Incline Village 89450
Las Vegas (Las Vegas)	Feb.	Tommy Hodges, 6245 Hobart, Las Vegas 89107
Silver State (Reno)	Sept.	Martha Dow, 580 N. McCarran Blvd., Sparks 89431
New Hampshire		
Dartmouth Medical School (Hanover)	Oct.	Dartmouth Medical School, Hanover 03755
New Jersey		
Jersey Shore (Asbury Park)	Dec.	Convention Hall, Asbury Park 07712

New Mexico

Albuquerque (Albuquerque)	Oct.	Gil Duran, Box 4071, Albuquerque 87106
Clovis (Clovis)	Oct.	Bill Gaedke, 1720 Avondale, Clovis 88101

New York

Boston Qualifier (Ithaca)	Mar.	James Hartshorne, 108 Kay St., Ithaca 14850
Buffalo-Niagara (Buffalo)	Oct.	Frank Neal, 10 Beard Ave., Buffalo 14214
Champlain Valley (Plattsburgh)	May	YMCA, 13 Oak St., Plattsburgh 12901
Earth Day (Westbury)	Mar.	Paul Fetscher, 183 Maxine Ct., West Hempstead 11511
Finger Lakes (Ithaca)	Oct.	James Hartshorne, 108 Kay St., Ithaca 14850
First Trust (Liverpool)	May	Diana Peil, 406 Ruth Rd., North Syracuse 13212
Hudson-Mohawk (Albany)	Mar.	Burke Adams, 21 Chestnut Ct., Rensselaer 12144
Lake Placid (Lake Placid)	Sept.	R.A. Lopez, Sports Council, Lake Placid 12946
New York City (New York)	Oct.	Road Runners Club, Box 881, FDR, New York 10022
Rochester (Rochester)	Sept.	Eugene Osburn, 561 Van Voris Ave., Rochester 14617
Yonkers (Yonkers)	May	Mel Goldberg, Yonkers Raceway, Yonkers 10704

North Carolina

All-American (Ft. Bragg)	Nov.	82nd Division Recreation Officer, Ft. Bragg 28307
Charlotte Observer (Charlotte)	Dec.	Phidippides, 4400 Sharon Rd., Charlotte 28211
Greensboro (Greensboro)	Oct.	David MacKenzie, 1000 Fairmont, Greensboro 27401
International Masters (Raleigh)	May	Raiford Fulghum, Box 590, Raleigh 27602
North Carolina (Bethel)	Jan.	Clem Williams, Box 701, Bethel 27812

North Dakota

North Dakota (Grand Forks)	June	Dave Nieman, YMCA, Box 1317, Grand Forks 58201

Ohio

Athens (Athens)	Mar.	Ellsworth Holden, 26 Northwood, Athens 45701
Glass City (Toledo)	June	Arthur Johnson, 2520 Aldringham Rd., Toledo 43606

Heartwatchers (Toledo)	Mar.	Fred Fineske, 1707 Eastfield, Maumee 43537
Monroe (Monroe)	Oct.	Felix LeBlanc, 1013 Tralee Tr., Dayton 45430
Revco-Western Reserve (Cleveland)	May	John O'Neil, Case-Western Reserve Univ., Cleveland 44106
Oklahoma		
Oil Capital (Tulsa)	Mar.	Larry Aduddell, 6200 S. 221st E., Broken Bow 74012
Road Runner (Gage)	May	Peggy Ford, Box 428, Gage 73843
Oregon		
Nike-Oregon TC (Eugene)	Sept.	Geoff Hollister, 1172 Pearl St., Eugene 97401
Portland (Portland)	Nov.	Portland Jaycees, 824 S.W. 5th Ave., Portland 97204
Trail's End (Seaside)	Feb.	Chamber of Commerce, Box 7, Seaside 97138
Pennsylvania		
Boston Qualifier (North Park)	Mar.	Harvey Kucherer, 1321 Foxwood Dr., Monroeville 15146
God's Country (Potter County)	June	Ralph Wentz, Box 117, Ulysses 16948
Harrisburg National (Harrisburg)	Nov.	Park Barner, YMCA, Front and North Sts., Harrisburg
Johnstown YMCA (Johnstown)	Oct.	Thomas Loughrin, YMCA, Johnstown 15901
Nittany Valley (State College)	Feb.	Harry Groves, Penn State University, Univ. Park 16802
Penn Relays (Philadelphia)	Apr.	J.P. Tuppeny, University of Pennsylvania, Philadelphia
Prevention (Trexlertown)	Mar.	John Wachter, 1113 Broadway, Bethlehem 18015
Presque Isle (Erie)	Sept.	E.J. Whitman, 451 W. 9th St., Erie 16502
Provident-Bulletin (Philadelphia)	Oct.	Chris Tatreau, Memorial Hall, Philadelphia 19131
Rhode Island		
Ocean State (Newport)	Oct.	George Schobel, 61 Crowfield Dr., Warwick 02888
South Carolina		
Carolina (Columbia)	Feb.	Jim LaBonte, 2600 Bull St., Columbia 29205
South Dakota		
Longest Day (Brookings)	Nov.	Track Coach, SDSU, Brookings 57006

Tennessee

| First Tennessee (Chattanooga) | Nov. | Earl Marler, 701 Market St., Chattanooga 37402 |
| Smoky Mountain (Oak Ridge) | Feb. | Harold Canfield, 502 Alandale, Knoxville 37920 |

Texas

Houston (Houston)	Jan.	George L. Kleeman, 227 Faust Ln., Houston 77024
Las Colonias (San Antonio)	May	Diego Vacca, 903 N. St. Marys, San Antonio 78215
Palo Duro Canyon (Canyon)	Jan.	Bob Dunbar, 6526 Fulton, Amarillo 79109
Texas Relays (Austin)	Apr.	Hector Cisneros, Littlefield Building, Austin 78712
White Rock (Dallas)	Dec.	Sue Rhiddlehoover, 12100 Preston Rd., Dallas 75230

Utah

Deseret News (Salt Lake City)	July	Keith West, Box 1257, Salt Lake City 84110
Golden Spike (Brigham City)	May	John Ensign, Box 338, Brigham City 84302
Pioneer (St. George)	Oct.	Sherman Miller, 340 E. 200 S., St. George 84770

Vermont

| Green Mountain (South Hero) | Aug. | Leighton Walker, 2 Redwood Terrace, Essex Junction |

Virginia

Richmond Newspapers (Richmond)	Oct.	Robin Wood, 9301 Groundhog Dr., Richmond 23235
Rotary Shamrock (Va. Beach)	Mar.	Ed Kellam, Box 777, Virginia Beach 23451
Waynesboro (Waynesboro)	Oct.	Jan Miller, Box 965, Waynesboro 22980

Washington

Birch Bay (Blaine)	Apr.	James Pearson, 2509 Chuckanut Dr., Bellingham 98225
Cheney (Cheney)	Nov.	Ruth Van Kuren, 418 Cocolalla, Cheney 99004
Seattle (Seattle)	Nov.	Dean Ingram, 507 Cobb M.C., Seattle 98101
Spokane Heart (Spokane)	Sept.	Edward Rockwell, S. 11 Washington, Spokane 99204

West Virginia

| Hall of Fame (Huntington) | Mar. | Edward Canterbury, 714 Mary St., Huntington 25704 |

Wisconsin

Madison (Madison)	June	Dale Roe, 1517 Waunona Way, Madison 53713
Paavo Nurmi (Hurley)	Aug.	Chamber of Commerce, 10th Ave. N., Hurley 54534
Sugar River Trail (New Glarus)	Oct.	Marathon, Box 781, New Glarus 53574
Wisconsin Mayfair (Milwaukee)	May	C. Roger Bodart, 2500 N. Mayfair Rd., Milwaukee 53226

Wyoming

| Frontier Days (Cheyenne) | July | Cheyenne TC, Box 10154, Cheyenne 82001 |

Canada

Alberta (Calgary)	May	Bill Wylie, 2932 13th Ave. N.W., Calgary T2N 1M2
Golden Mile (Winnipeg)	May	Randy Longmuir, 136 Seven Oaks Ave., Winnipeg
Ile D'Orleans (Ile D'Orleans)	Oct.	Jean-Guy Cote, 26 rue Goudreault, St. Brigitte de Laval
Lion's Gate (Vancouver)	May	not available
Montreal (Montreal)	Mar.	Michel Rose, 12 232 Armand Bombardier, Montreal
National Capital (Ottawa)	May	Recreation, 111 Sussex Dr., Ottawa K1N 5A1
Newfoundland (St. Johns)	July	Joe Ryan, Newfoundland TYFA, St. Johns
Northern Lights (Espanola)	June	Norman Patenaude, Site 20, Box 25, Ft. 2, Sudbury

54

Going Beyond

The new frontier of running lies on the far side of 26 miles

Nick Marshall

Okay. So you've mastered the marathon. What's next?

You've probably heard vague tales about something wild called an ultra-marathon. I won't be so brash as to suggest you try such an event...but at least it's something to think about.

By definition, an ultra-marathon is any run longer than 26 miles, 385 yards (or 42.195 kilometers). The term is inclusive, and ultra-marathons are contested over a spectrum of long distances. Nonetheless, some "standard" events have achieved a modest but continuing degree of popularity. Presently in the United States, these standard events comprise a mix of English and metric measurements: 50 and 100 miles, and 50 and 100 kilometers. The most common of these is the 50-miler. It provides a good basis for comparison of individual performances in different sections of the country. Also, since 1966 it has been a national championship distance, the longest footrace with a US title at stake.

Although there were splashes of activity in super-long runs from time to time in the past, the modern era of this sport in the US coincides roughly with the growth of road running in general since the early 1960s. The concept first took root in the New York City area, with Olympian Ted Corbitt the driving force behind the idea. Throughout the decade, Corbitt made pilgrimages to the traditional London-Brighton double marathon held in England each fall. The rest of the time, he urged the institution of such races in America. There was initial resistance to the idea from some quarters, but eventually a series of races—mostly ranging from 30-45 miles—was added to the New York schedule. They attracted only a handful of participants but were a necessary first step. A small but hardy corps of ultra-distance enthusiasts grew from this program and spread the word further.

The northern California area joined the movement in the late '60s, and the two coasts were linked in 1970 when the first ultra was held in the Midwest. The corner had been turned, and by the following year Americans were attempting 100 miles and more for the first time in almost a half-century. Today, ultra-distance running stands where marathoning was 10 years ago. That is, the interest is limited and the fields involved are small, yet the opportunities to try these runs are steadily increasing.

In 1977, there were more than 30 ultra-marathons held in 15 different states. The majority of these had between 20 and 50 runners, while several had fewer than 10 starters and only one race had more than a hundred. So it remains a relatively obscure branch of running. At the same time, however, it is now firmly established as more than a novelty item. It seems fairly certain the incredible boom enjoyed by shorter distances will eventually flood over into the longer ones as well.

THE NEW ODDITIES

All very fascinating and awesome, you say, but it is something you could never do yourself? Well, think again.

After a runner's first mile comes his second, and then another and another. To their great surprise, some very unlikely candidates one day wind up as marathoners. A simple extension of this lengthening process is at work in the phenomenon of ultra-marathoning.*

Once, it was the people who went 26.2 miles who were thought odd or exotic. Now, with marathon mania rampant, that activity has reached respectability. The appellation of crazies can thus be pinned on those individuals who go beyond that: Why else would someone do such a thing?

In any endurance activity like distance running, there will always be a fringe group interested in pushing the limits further. It is the nature of the beast to seek new tests when the proportions of the old ones have lost their capacity to inspire awe. More specifically, in the context of running, there is no logical reason beyond tradition for the 26-mile mystique. To question why anyone would want to venture beyond that barrier is merely to rehash the perplexing and ultimately personal question of why we run in the first place. Why not?

---

* For purposes of this discussion, my references to ultra-marathoning will concern only runs of 50 miles or more. That's where the dilemma lies. Fifty kilometers (31.1 miles), while by definition an ultra, has more in common with the standard marathon than it does with these longer events. Unfortunately, there are currently no other inter-mediate steps on the way to 50 miles. Therefore, the aspiring ultra runner is typically confronted with a quantum leap from 26 to 50 miles.

The marathon barrier—the point where the large majority of distance runners say, "No more!"—is strictly a mental and artificial one. The numerical significance of 26 is man-made. It is invested with magical qualities, and the biggest roadblock to going beyond it is in simply shedding the myth. To do so can be an experiment in curiosity, as the runner is drawn ever outward into unexplored realms. But while events longer than a marathon can constitute a challenge and an adventure, there is little intrinsic difference in them. A six-mile run is an endurance event, even if people who go that far daily may tend to forget it. So it is with a 100-mile run. The difference is only in degree. The quantity may increase dramatically, but the qualities demanded remain similar. To truly accept this fact is necessary to your success in super-long runs.

HOW MUCH HURTING?

How can it be done?

Because of marathon mania, we hear constantly about "the wall" at 20 miles. With this emphasis on hitting the wall repeated again and again, many people have the mistaken belief the human body can tolerate only 20 miles or a little more before reaching a state of sheer depletion. Thus, runners feel they may be able to hang on past that crucial point and gut it out to the marathon distance, but anything more than that becomes inconceivable and almost scary to contemplate.

This overlooks the fact that the wall at 20 is inherent only in the nature of a marathon. An untrained athlete will crash well before that point. For the trained runner, depletion sets in there in a hard effort only because he is approaching the finish and has apportioned his energy accordingly.

Running is a ridiculously simple sport in its basics. Training one's body to best approach its potential can be a complicated proposition, yet the ingredients are few. They boil down to two: the speed and duration involved in any particular run. Assuming the runner is adquately conditioned beforehand, he simply has to pace himself to meet the task at hand. He can lose control with dire results in a mile or a marathon. The same applies to the ultra-marathon. If properly geared to it, the well-trained runner can plow on longer than he might expect.

What he needs to do is exercise his discipline and intelligence along with his heart, legs and lungs. Problems arise from the vast difference in volume one is faced with. The room for misjudgment increases greatly when you are running literally for hours on end. If you overestimate your capacities in a 440, say, this error can lead to extreme agony within seconds. However, the worst is over quickly. Once you get into trouble in an ultra, though, you are stuck with it for a prolonged period of time. The finish line may be a couple dozen miles away, and the runner must choose either to quit or suffer severe discomfort.

It is misleading to say ultra-marathons are necessarily filled with agony. Nevertheless, your body is put under extreme stress during the course of them, so it is similarly misleading to pretend they are a breeze. Clearly, they're not. But while the unpleasant aspects must be acknowledged, they should not dominate the issue. Ideally, they can be kept to a minimum. Just as boxers accept bloody noses as an occupational hazard, so ultra-marathoners know their endeavors will bring some disagreeable feelings. That is part of it all, yet it is certainly not the point of it all.

The point is to confront a difficult challenge and triumph over the situation. To do this, the beginner must approach his initial ultra attempt with a realistic attitude. The distance needn't be frightening but must be respected. The experience of others demonstrates that runs like these can be handled without super-natural abilities. However, it can't be done without fatigue. Everyone tires to differing extents after an extended time of non-stop running. This is where the fascination and challenge of these long runs sets in—much more so than in a marathon.

Understandably, since the idea isn't to inflict negative sensations on the body, caution is advisable for the novice. The cardinal rule is this: *Since fatigue cannot be avoided, it is imperative for the runner to postpone the inevitable onset of that fatigue for as long as possible.* To do otherwise is to invite disaster. Uncharted territory hides many shoals. Thus, the first-timer had better be conservative and save any bolder experiments for the future when the distances may seem less alien. There is no need to risk turning one's debut into a gruesome ordeal through the mistake of being too ambitious.

So a low-key mental preparation is essential. Know you'll be in action for a long time and know you'll become tired, but be ready to resist the weariness and conquer it in the end. I advise the novice to forget about time from the very beginning. For individuals with a history of serious racing at shorter distances, it may be tough to ignore the clock altogether. Of course, before it starts you will be wondering just how long it will last. Any worrying about time in the run itself, however, will most likely be counter-productive. The initial goal is merely to finish. That's enough. For once, you should enjoy the luxury of not being obsessed with time.

TAKE A WALK

The safest system of all is to include some pre-planned walking along the way. For example, run 25 minutes and walk five. Don't be afraid to rest. Walking breaks like this will make it much easier on the body, instill calm in the mind and not really penalize you as much as you'd think. It is a fact of ultra-marathoning that most entrants will slow considerably anyway, and many will have to walk at some time in the event. Voluntary walks are not a blow to the morale like ones forced upon you by a rebelling body. They keep you fresh.

The run-walk system, effective as it is, nonetheless goes violently against the grain of a runner. Few have the willingness or discipline to hold themselves back that much. They want to see how far they can run without having to stop. For this average contestant, then, whose hope is to run the whole way, the most tenable plan is to approach the project as an endurance jog. In other words, start out at the *slowest* normal pace at which you feel comfortable. Don't go so slow as to tire yourself with an unnatural pace, yet always remember that you want to minimize the stress and stave off fatigue for as long as possible.

Begin it like an easy jog and appreciate the early miles as a fun-run. It is most helpful if you can find someone to stride along with. Due to the small fields and massive lengths of these runs, the contestants can get spread far apart. Sometimes, I've gone more than 30 miles in such "races" without seeing another competitor. If you are lucky enough to fall in with someone else, it's a big psychological plus. As the day progresses and enthusiasm wanes, you can bolster each other when thoughts of quitting arise. A pair will often keep moving when a solo athlete would stop.

Aside from attitude, the nature of an ultra calls for some additional adjustments. Measures to prevent blisters and chafing must be applied even more rigorously than usual. What would be a minor annoyance in a short run can be magnified intolerably during a long one.

On the subject of shoes, opt for comfort and cushioning. The major cause of complaint will stem from the sheer accumulated shock of the tens of thousands of times each foot hits the ground. Sore soles and aching joints are almost guaranteed at some point, so once again the idea is to delay the consequences.

HANDLE WITH CARE

If at all possible, a handler should be enlisted to help you. This person's responsibility is to look after your personal needs, something that is very difficult for race organizers to do adequately in such a long race. The handler can either ride along beside you with a bike or meet you periodically with a car. Such a friend is necessary because there is so much time for something to go wrong. He provides things like medical aid, fresh shoes, and warm or dry clothes, depending on the situation. Most importantly, he keeps you supplied with drinks. Fluid replacement is crucial to avoid dehydration in an event requiring sustained effort for six hours or longer. Plan on drinking as much as you can.

Your handler can also assist with the mental aspect, by giving you encouragement to keep going. Mostly though, this motivation has to come from within. Will-power alone won't insure satisfactory results. The muscles still do the work. But unless they are backed by a strong will, they'll drain rapidly when fatigue hits. Momentary sags in morale are part of ultra-marathoning. Everyone is susceptible to them. Regardless of your high hopes prior to the race, there will be grave moments of doubt and weakness during it as the strain mounts. The battle is not to succumb, to weather the storm. Even in races I've won handily, I've considered quitting. There is just so darn much time to consider everything!

Understandably, one's resolve can waver as he becomes progressively more weary and an apparently pervasive exhaustion sets in. Still, at the slower paces involved in an ultra, there is more choice. You may literally ache all over, in places you've never been sore before. Despite this, the woes associated with super-long runs are generally of the dull, nagging variety. These are more amenable to management than the sharp stitches and cramping sometimes induced by faster running.

Therefore, ultras present a paradox. The runner has more time to dwell on the tough distance remaining. He can easily psych himself into an early defeat if he panics at the arrival of fatigue symptoms. On the other hand, he can take a more active role in the decision to continue. What he has to do is maintain control and plow on through the beginning signs of depletion. The entire process is a balancing act: Will I make it or will I crack? The balance swings side to side moment by moment. It can go either way. That is where the fascination lies. A surprising number make it.

TRAINING

You'll notice I have yet to mention any special training advice. Heading into an ultra-marathon, a major apprehension will concern whether or not you've trained hard enough beforehand. However, training requirements vary so much between individuals that general prescriptions aren't worth much. Obviously, the more your training increases your stamina, the better chance you have of success in going long. Beyond this guideline, the runner must be his own coach.

Fear of being undertrained is itself a danger. An obsession with training miles can suck one into trying too much, and getting run down instead of getting stronger. The body will dictate how much you can tolerate, and it is important not to exceed its dictates. So, to be best prepared, train as much as you can feel both mentally and physically comfortable in doing. What this translates to in numbers depends on your own judgment.

Meanwhile, speedwork can be dispensed with, except for purposes of play and variety. What helps is mental conditioning. One's total mileage should be weighted toward long runs. While it has been proven they aren't a physical necessity, it give one a big boost in confidence if he can get in at least one workout of four hours or more prior to race day. It doesn't matter how slow one goes in such a workout. The idea is just to gain practice in keeping "slogging." You thereby become attuned to the concept of long hours on the road and running while tired.

Because ultra-distance events are of somewhat mythic proportions, lots of crazy rumors and gross misconceptions crop up. Most of these concern training. People who know I compete regularly at 50 miles and above often form the mistaken notion I must therefore go that far in training as well. Not so at all. I know from experience I can race 50 miles and more, yet a 20-miler in training still counts as a long run. Occasionally, I'll go 25-35. That's what I can handle for now.

In my case, I log about 4400 miles in an average year. This ranges from about 50 miles a week in the "off" season and up to 110 weekly in heavy training. That does not come close to matching the legendary mileages achieved by a few ultra-marathoners, yet it is more than most of the breed does. The numbers aren't the important thing. You do what you can. If you presently train hard enough to enable you to survive marathons in good shape, probably the only change necessary in your program is an extension in your long workouts. Otherwise, with a modest start, a calm head and reasonable expectations, you're ready to go.

If this advice seems too glib, it can be that way because of the self-selecting phenomenon of ultra-marathoning. With the glamor and publicity surrounding marathons now, such events attract a lot of foolish joggers who have no business trying 26-milers on their limited backgrounds. But they see the fun and the masses involved, and jump into the fray unknowingly. Fifty-milers and 100-kilos are still obscure enough and awesome enough that this doesn't happen in ultras. They appeal to serious souls. People don't enter them on a lark. If one is assured enough to consider an ultra, this is a good sign he is at least somewhat ready for the test.

Conversely, if one dreads such a prospect, he should definitely stop before he starts. The first-timer should be respectful but eager in his attempt. After all, it's an adventure.

The curious people who embark on these journeys are generally men and women who already have wide experience at shorter distances. Novice ultra-marathoners are in no way novice runners. They tend to be veterans with extensive backgrounds involving years of running—dedicated individuals who are well-trained before they even consider an ultra, rather than the other way around. I've known many joggers who began training diligently in hopes of becoming a marathoner. I have yet to meet a runner who began with intentions of going into the ultra-distances. It is an afterthought which enters the mind only after the runner has already achieved a certain mastery of his art. These are the types who are in a long-term love affair with running. Ultras are a new place to go with their love. It is not a place for dilettantes!

SEX, AGE AND SPEED

The physical requirements are not restrictive. Stamina is the key, and stamina is available to anyone dedicated enough to work at developing it. Moreover, since stamina is less sex- and age-related than speed and more dependent on individual effort, the usual advantages held by young men in their prime are somewhat lessened. It's a wide-open field, and runners of both sexes and all ages can handle extremely long distances without ill-effects.

Although the average age of ultra-marathon starters is older than in other runs, youngsters can still do well if they have the patience of maturity. Ten-year-old Greg Hill finished fifth out of 28 runners in one 50-miler and Jose Cortez set the American road record for 100 miles at age 19 with a 12:54:31. Teenagers are a definite minority group, though. Due to the premium on experience, the ultra-distance scene is an area where the old coots can shine. Of the dozen fastest Americans at the breath-taking distance of 100 miles, four of them are Masters runners, and Ted Corbitt's national track record in the event was established when he was 49. Also included in this dauntless dozen is Natalie Cullimore, certainly a pioneer in dispelling the myth of female fragility.

Although the emphasis in ultra-marathons is on endurance rather than speed, it is a mistake to conclude that all ultra-marathoners are slow. In fact, the average field has a higher ability level than the normal shorter race, precisely because the beginning joggers are not in evidence. With fairly limited opportunities to try such events, runners will frequently have traveled a long way to take part in them, so even a small field of 20 may include entrants from four or five states. The racing in the front can be spirited competition.

Enough elite marathoners have stepped up to try ultras over the years that quality records have been established. The British are well ahead of their colonial counterparts on this score. Their fastest times are anything but slow. Cavin Woodward's 50-mile best of 4:58:53 is under 5:59 per mile pace, and Don Ritchie's 100-mile world mark of 11:30:51 is roughly equivalent to four three-hour marathons without a stop!

Thoughts about record performances can be put off until after you've sampled the waters for the first time. If your debut goes well and you complete it, you'll likely feel like a world-beater regardless of your time. It's something you never thought you could do.

But afterward, when you are flushed with pride over your achievement, can be a dangerous time. The only extended injury period of my career came on the heels of my first ultra. It had been a great experience as I finished second of seven men in a 100-kilo race. That was 30 miles farther than I'd ever gone before, and I was shocked when I didn't seem devastated by the after-effects. Within a week, I was back into heavy training and feeling invincible.

That lasted about two weeks, and then my legs went dead on me. I didn't run well again for over six months. It is a delayed reaction I've observed in other runners, too, when they take that first big leap upward. If no apparent problems surface at once, you may be fooled into underestimating the stress you've put your body through. Give it time to heal, so the latent effects won't be aggravated. Respect the distance.

Even though my first ultra helped lead me into a breakdown, I never had regrets about trying it, and eventually I roared back into the fray. Now, my running identity revolves closely around the challenge of the super-long runs. After becoming familiar with them, they lose some of their power to amaze. I've been amazed too often myself and by other runners. What the experience has brought home with convincing finality is that people are much stronger than they might ever dream or realize. Ultra-marathons reveal our strength by reducing us to a state of weakness and seeing what happens.

You'd be surprised.

Appendix

All-Time World Top 50 (Men)

Time	Name (Country)	Year
2:08:33	Derek Clayton (Aus)	1969
2:09:12	Ian Thompson (GB)	1974
2:09:28	Ron Hill (GB)	1970
2:09:55	Waldemar Cierpinski (EG)	1976
2:09:55	Bill Rodgers (US)	1975
2:10:08	Jerome Drayton (Can)	1975
2:10:20	David Chettle (Aus)	1975
2:10:30	Frank Shorter (US)	1972
2:10:37	Akio Usami (Japan)	1970
2:10:47	Bill Adcocks (GB)	1968
2:11:12	Eamon O'Reilly (US)	1970
2:11:12	John Farrington (Aus)	1973
2:11:12	Karel Lismont (Bel)	1976
2:11:15	Don Kardong (US)	1976
2:11:17	Seiichiro Sasaki (Japan)	1967
2:11:18	Jack Foster (NZ)	1974
2:11:35	Kenny Moore (US)	1970
2:11:45	Guiseppe Cindolo (It)	1975
2:11:54	Steve Hoag (US)	1975
2:12:00	Morio Shigematsu (Japan)	1965
2:12:02	Eckhard Lesse (EG)	1974
2:12:03	Hayami Tanimura (Japan)	1969
2:12:04	Jim Alder (GB)	1970
2:12:05	Tom Fleming (US)	1975
2:12:10	Pekka Paivarinta (Fin)	1974
2:12:11	Abebe Bikila (Eth)	1964
2:12:12	Yoshiaki Unetani (Japan)	1970
2:12:19	Don Faircloth (GB)	1970

2:12:19	Leonid Moisseyev (SU)	1976
2:12:25	David McKenzie (NZ)	1967
2:12:33	Gabashane Rakabaele (Les)	1976
2:12:40	Alexander Gozki (SU)	1976
2:12:47	Ferdie Le Grange (SA)	1974
2:12:50	Lutz Philipp (WG)	1974
2:12:52	Takeshi Sou (Japan)	1975
2:12:52	Pablo Garrido (Mexico)	1969
2:12:54	Franco Fava (It)	1976
2:12:54	Richard Mabuza (Swa)	1974
2:12:58	Yuriy Velikorodnych (SU)	1976
2:12:58	Terry Manners (NZ)	1974
2:13:04	Yasunori Hamada (Japan)	1974
2:13:05	Jerzy Gross (Pol)	1975
2:13:05	Massimo Magnani (It)	1976
2:13:06	Danny McDaid (Ire)	1976
2:13:06	Toshiharu Sasaki (Japan)	1969
2:13:10	Kenichi Ozawa (Japan)	1975
2:13:10	Lasse Viren (Fin)	1976
2:13:11	Chris Stewart (GB)	1974
2:13:13	Makoto Hattori (Japan)	1975
2:13:15	Kevin Ryan (NZ)	1975
2:13:15	Jeff Wells (US)	1977

Compiled by Antonin Hejda; marks through Jan. 1, 1978.

All-Time World Top 50 (Women)

Time	Name (Country)	Year
2:34:47	Christa Vahlensieck (WG)	1977
2:35:15	Chantal Langlace (Fr)	1977
2:37:57	Kim Merritt (US)	1977
2:38:09	Manuela Angenvoorth (WG)	1977
2:38:19	Jacqueline Hansen (US)	1975
2:39:11	Miki Gorman (US)	1976
2:42:24	Liane Winter (WG)	1975
2:45:32	Julie Brown (US)	1976
2:46:23	Diane Barrett (US)	1976
2:46:34	Leal-Ann Reinhart (US)	1977
2:46:54	Sue Kinsey (US)	1977
2:47:16	Beverly Shingles (NZ)	1977
2:47:20	Patricia LaTora (US)	1977
2:47:34	Doris Heritage (US)	1976
2:47:43	Gayle Barron (US)	1976
2:47:50	Claire Spauwen (Hol)	1976

2:48:07	Cindy Dalrymple (US)	1977
2:48:22	Sarolta Monspart (Hun)	1976
2:49:30	Marilyn Paul (US)	1976
2:49:40	Cheryl Bridges (US)	1971
2:50:22	Nina Kuscsik (US)	1977
2:50:26	Elisabeth Richards (Aus)	1976
2:50:36	Silvana Cruciata (It)	1976
2:50:40	Judy Leydig (US)	1977
2:50:47	Dorothy Doolittle (US)	1977
2:50:48	Lora Cartwright (US)	1976
2:50:48	Jill Hanson (US)	1977
2:50:55	Christine Readdy (GB)	1976
2:51:12	Marilyn Bevans (US)	1977
2:51:13	Lisa Lorrain (US)	1977
2:51:15	Joan Ullyot (US)	1976
2:51:37	Kathrine Switzer (US)	1975
2:51:38	Marjorie Kaput (US)	1974
2:51:41	Annick Loir (Fr)	1977
2:52:06	Tena Anex (US)	1977
2:52:32	Lauri Pedrinan (US)	1977
2:52:33	Irja Paukkonen (Fin)	1976
2:52:37	Phyllis Hines (US)	1977
2:53:09	D. Anderson (US)	1977
2:53:14	Vicki Bray (US)	1976
2:53:38	Susan Peterson (US)	1977
2:53:40	Teri Anderson (US)	1973
2:54:28	Judy Ikenberry (US)	1974
2:54:45	Magda Ilands (Bel)	1976
2:54:50	Christa Kloth (WG)	1976
2:55:03	Lisa Matovcik (US)	1977
2:55:09	Gisela Schneider (WG)	1977
2:55:12	Anita Ayers (US)	1977
2:55:22	Beth Bonner (US)	1971
2:55:24	Penny DeMoss (US)	1977

Compiled by Antonin Hejda; marks through Jan. 1, 1978.

All-Time U.S. Top 50 (Men)

Time	Name	Year
2:09:55	Bill Rodgers	1975
2:10:30	Frank Shorter	1972
2:11:12	Eamon O'Reilly	1970
2:11:15	Don Kardong	1976
2:11:35	Kenny Moore	1970

2:11:54	Steve Hoag	1975
2:12:05	Tom Fleming	1975
2:13:15	Jeff Wells	1977
2:13:46	Garry Bjorklund	1977
2:14:13	Ed Mendoza	1975
2:14:28	Leonard Edelen	1963
2:14:28	Amby Burfoot	1968
2:14:39	Chuck Smead	1977
2:14:46	John Bramley	1977
2:14:54	Jim Stanley	1975
2:14:58	Tony Sandoval	1976
2:15:04	Ron Wayne	1977
2:15:15	Gary Tuttle	1976
2:15:18	Dennis Williams	1974
2:15:21	Bill Scobey	1971
2:15:22	Russ Pate	1975
2:15:48	Doug Schmenk	1973
2:15:50	Bob Varsha	1976
2:15:51	Randy Thomas	1977
2:15:52	Norm Higgins	1971
2:15:52	Jon Anderson	1973
2:16:03	Kirk Pfeffer	1977
2:16:04	John Samore	1976
2:16:13	John Lodwick	1977
2:16:15	John Vitale	1973
2:16:20	Mike Hazilla	1971
2:16:43	Barry Brown	1975
2:16:48	Tom Laris	1967
2:16:51	Lee Fidler	1975
2:16:54	Bob Hensley	1977
2:17:05	Dave Harper	1977
2:17:07	Lionel Ortega	1977
2:17:23	Terry Ziegler	1975
2:17:26	Carl Hatfield	1976
2:17:23	Mike Pinnoci	1977
2:17:35	Steve Bolt	1977
2:17:38	Jack Bacheler	1972
2:17:43	Herb Lorenz	1975
2:17:48	Lou Castagnola	1967
2:17:49	George Christopher	1975
2:17:52	Dan Cloeter	1977
2:18:04	Bill Sieben	1977
2:18:06	Wayne Badgley	1975
2:18:06	Phil Camp	1976
2:18:11	Ed Schlegle	1977

Compiled by Ken Young; marks through Jan. 1, 1978.

All-Time U.S. Top 50 (Women)

Time	Name	Year
2:37:57	Kim Merritt	1977
2:38:19	Jacqueline Hansen	1975
2:39:11	Miki Gorman	1976
2:45:32	Julie Brown	1976
2:46:23	Diane Barrett	1976
2:46:34	Leal-Ann Reinhart	1977
2:46:54	Sue Kinsey	1977
2:47:20	Patricia LaTora	1977
2:47:34	Doris Heritage	1976
2:47:43	Gayle Barron	1976
2:48:07	Cindy Dalrymple	1977
2:49:30	Marilyn Paul	1976
2:49:40	Cheryl Bridges	1971
2:50:22	Nina Kuscsik	1977
2:50:40	Judy Leydig	1977
2:50:47	Dorothy Doolittle	1977
2:50:48	Lora Cartwright	1976
2:50:48	Jill Hanson	1977
2:51:12	Marilyn Bevans	1977
2:51:13	Lisa Lorrain	1977
2:51:15	Joan Ullyot	1976
2:51:37	Kathrine Switzer	1975
2:51:38	Marjorie Kaput	1974
2:52:09	Tena Anex	1977
2:52:32	Lauri Pedrinan	1977
2:52:37	Phyllis Hines	1977
2:53:09	D. Anderson	1977
2:53:14	Vicki Bray	1976
2:53:38	Sue Peterson	1977
2:53:40	Teri Anderson	1973
2:54:28	Judy Ikenberry	1974
2:54:34	Lisa Matovcik	1977
2:55:12	Anita Ayers	1977
2:55:22	Beth Bonner	1971
2:55:24	Penny DeMoss	1977
2:55:33	Karen McKeachie	1977
2:55:34	I. Griffith	1977
2:55:40	June Chun	1977
2:55:59	Ann Forshee	1977
2:56:07	Lili Ledbetter	1975
2:56:22	Jane Killion	1977
2:56:25	Susan Mallery	1976
2:56:40	Marie Albert	1977

2:56:55	Mary Pugh	1977
2:56:57	Merry Cushing	1975
2:57:02	Nancy Kent	1976
2:57:23	G. Anderson	1977
2:57:38	Kathy Gervasi	1976
2:57:41	Nicki Hobson	1976
2:57:44	Gillian Adams	1977

Compiled by Ken Young; marks through Jan. 1, 1978.

Progress of World Record (Men)

Time	Name (Country)	Year
2:55:18	John Hayes (US)	1908
2:42:31	Fred Barrett (Great Britain)	1909
2:36:55	Jim Corkery (Canada)	1912
2:36:06	Alex Ahlgren (Sweden)	1913
2:32:35	Hannes Kolehmainen (Finland)	1920
2:30:57	Harry Payne (Great Britain)	1929
2:29:20	Norio Suzuki (Japan)	1932
2:27:49	Fusashige Suzuki (Japan)	1935
2:26:44	Yasao Ikenaka (Japan)	1935
2:26:42	Kitei Son (Japan)	1935
2:25:39	Yun Bok Suh (Korea)	1947
2:20:42	Jim Peters (Great Britain)	1952
2:18:40	Jim Peters (Great Britain)	1953
2:18:34	Jim Peters (Great Britain)	1953
2:17:39	Jim Peters (Great Britain)	1954
2:15:17	Sergey Popov (USSR)	1958
2:15:16	Abebe Bikila (Ethiopia)	1960
2:14:28	Leonard Edelen (US)	1963
2:13:55	Basil Heatley (Great Britain)	1964
2:12:11	Abebe Bikila (Ethiopia)	1964
2:12:00	Morio Shigematsu (Japan)	1965
2:09:36	Derek Clayton (Australia)	1967
2:08:33	Derek Clayton (Australia)	1969[*]

current record as of early 1978.

Progress of World Record (Women)

Time	Name (Country)	Year
3:15:22	Maureen Wilton (Canada)	1967
3:07:26	Anni Peede (West Germany)	1967
3:02:53	Caroline Walker (US)	1970
3:01:42	Beth Bonner (US)	1971

2:55:22	Beth Bonner (US)	1971
2:49:40	Cheryl Bridges (US)	1971
2:46:36	Miki Gorman (US)	1973
2:46:24	Chantal Langlace (France)	1974
2:43:54	Jacqueline Hansen (US)	1974
2:42:24	Liane Winter (West Germany)	1975
2:40:15	Christa Vahlensieck (West Germany)	1975
2:38:19	Jacqueline Hansen (US)	1975
2:35:15	Chantal Langlace (France)	1977
2:34:47	Christa Vahlensieck (West Germany)	1977*

Record as of early 1978.

Progress of U.S. Record (Men)

Time	Name	Year
2:55:18	John Hayes	1908
2:41:30	J. Organ	1920
2:40:22	Clarence DeMar	1927
2:37:07	Clarence DeMar	1928
2:36:04	Joie Ray	1928
2:31:01	Leslie Pawson	1933
2:28:51	Ellison Brown	1939
2:27:29	Ellison Brown	1940
2:26:51	Joe Smith	1942
2:24:52	John J. Kelley	1956
2:20:05	John J. Kelley	1957
2:18:56	Leonard Edelen	1962
2:14:28	Leonard Edelen	1963
2:13:27	Kenny Moore	1969
2:11:12	Eamon O'Reilly	1970
2:10:30	Frank Shorter	1972
2:09:55	Bill Rodgers	1975*

Record as of early 1978.

Progress of U.S. Record (Women)

Time	Name	Year
3:02:53	Caroline Walker	1970
3:01:42	Beth Bonner	1971
2:55:22	Beth Bonner	1971
2:49:40	Cheryl Bridges	1971
2:46:36	Miki Gorman	1973

2:43:54	Jacqueline Hansen	1974
2:38:19	Jacqueline Hansen	1975
2:37:57	Kim Merritt	1977*

Record as of early 1978.

Olympic Marathon Winners

Time	Name (Country)	Year
2:58:50	Spiridon Louis (Greece)	1896
2:59:45	Michel Theato (France)	1900
3:28:53	Thomas Hicks (US)	1904
2:58:18	John Hayes (US)	1908
2:36:54	Kenneth McArthur (S. Africa)	1912
2:32:35	Hannes Kolehmainen (Finland)	1920
2:41:22	Albin Stenroos (Finland)	1924
2:32:57	Ahmed El Oufai (France)	1928
2:31:36	Juan C. Zabala (Argentina)	1932
2:29:19	Kitei Son (Japan)	1936
2:34:51	Delfo Carbrera (Argentina)	1948
2:23:03	Emil Zatopek (Czechoslovakia)	1952
2:25:00	Alain Mimoun (France)	1956
2:15:16	Abebe Bikila (Ethiopia)	1960
2:12:11	Abebe Bikila (Ethiopia)	1964
2:20:26	Mamo Wolde (Ethiopia)	1968
2:12:19	Frank Shorter (US)	1972
2:09:55*	Waldemar Cierpinski (E. Ger.)	1976

Olympic record through 1976 Games.

U.S. Olympic Marathoners

Listed are the site(s) of trials and results of US qualifiers in the years indicated; DNF-didn't finish; DNS-didn't start; DQ-disqualified; NT-no time; compiled by Brian Chapman.

1896—no trial

1900—no trial
   5. Albert Newton 4:03

1904—no trial
   1. Tom Hicks 3:28:53
   2. Albert Corey 3:34:04
   3. Albert Newton 3:47:33

Arthur Blake DNF

6. Dick Grant NT
7. John Cregan NT

11. F. Devlin NT
Bill Garcia DNF
Sam Mellor DNF
Mike Spring DNF

6. D. Kneeland NT   John Lorden DNF
7. H. Brawley NT   Frank Pierce DNF
8. Sidney Hatch NT   Fred Lorz DQ

1908—trials at Boston, St. Louis   9. Louis Tewanima 3:09:15
1. Johnny Hayes 2:55:18   14. Sidney Hatch 3:17:52
3. Joseph Forshaw 2:57:10   Mike Ryan DNF
4. Roy Welton 2:59:44   Tom Morrissey DNF

1912—trial at Boston   12. Clarence DeMar 2:50:46
3. Gaston Strobino 2:38:42   16. Louis Tewanima 2:52:41
4. Andrew Sockalexis 2:42:07   17. Harry Smith 2:52:53
7. John Gallagher 2:44:19   18. Tom Lilley 2:59:35
8. Joe Erxleben 2:45:47   Mike Ryan DNF
9. Richard Piggott 2:46:40   John Reynolds DNF
10. Joseph Forshaw 2:49:49

1920—trials at Brooklyn, Detroit,   12. Charles Mellor 2:45:30
Boston, New York   Arthur Roth DNF
7. Joe Organ 2:41:30   Frank Zuna DNF
11. Carl Linder 2:44:21   Jack Weber DNS

1924—trial at Boston   23. William Churchill 3:19:18
3. Clarence DeMar 2:48:14   25. Charles Mellor 3:24:07
16. Frank Wendling 3:05:09   Ralph Williams DNF
18. Frank Zuna 3:05:52   Carl Linder DNS

1928—trials at Boston, Long Beach,   27. Clarence DeMar 2:50:42
Baltimore   39. Jimmy Henigan 2:56:50
5. Joie Ray 2:36:04   41. Harvey Frick 2:57:24
9. Albert Michelsen 2:38:56   44. William Agee 2:58:50

1932—trials at Boston, Baltimore,   11. Hans Oldag 2:47:26
Los Angeles   Jimmy Henigan DNF
7. Albert Michelsen 2:39:58

1936—trials at Boston, Washington   Ellison Brown DNF
18. John A. Kelley 2:49:32   William McMahon DNF

1948—trials at Boston, Yonkers   21. John A. Kelley 2:51:56
14. Ted Vogel 2:45:27   24. Ollie Manninen 2:56:49

1952—trials at Yonkers, Boston   36. Tom Jones 2:42:50
13. Vic Dyrgall 2:32:52   44. Ted Corbitt 2:51:09

1956—trials at Boston, Yonkers   21. John J. Kelley 2:43:40
20. Nick Costes 2:42:20   Dean Thackeray DNF

1960—trials at Boston, Yonkers   30. A. Breckenridge 2:29:38
19. John J. Kelley 2:24:48   48. G. McKenzie 2:35:16

1964—trials at Yonkers, Culver City   14. Bill Mills 2:22:55
6. Leonard Edelen 2:18:12   23. Peter McArdle 2:26:24

1968—trial at Alamosa, Colo.
  14. Kenny Moore 2:29:49

1972—trials at Eugene
  1. Frank Shorter 2:12:19

1976—trial at Eugene
  2. Frank Shorter 2:10:45

16. George Young 2:31:15
22. Ron Daws 2:33:53
4. Kenny Moore 2:15:39
9. Jack Bacheler 2:17:38
4. Don Kardong 2:11:15
40. Bill Rodgers 2:25:14

European Games Winners

Time	Name (Country)	Year
2:52:29	Armas Toivonen (Finland)	1934
2:37:28	Vaino Muinonen (Finland)	1938
2:24:55	Mikko Hietanen (Finland)	1946
2:32:13	Jack Holden (Great Britain)	1950
2:24:51	Veikko Karvonen (Finland)	1954
2:15:17	Serey Popov (USSR)	1958
2:23:18	Brian Kilby (Great Britain)	1962
2:20:04	Jim Hogan (Great Britain)	1966
2:16:47	Ron Hill (Great Britain)	1969
2:13:09*	Karel Lismont (Belgium)	1971
2:13:18	Ian Thompson (Great Britain)	1974

European Championships record through 1974 Games.

Commonwealth Games Winners

Time	Name (Country)	Year
2:43:43	Duncan Wright (Scotland)	1930
2:40:36	Harold Webster (Canada)	1934
2:30:49	Johannes Coleman (S. Africa)	1938
2:32:57	Jack Holden (England)	1950
2:39:36	Joe McGhee (Scotland)	1954
2:22:45	Dave Power (Australia)	1958
2:21:17	Brian Kilby (England)	1962
2:22:07	Jim Alder (Scotland)	1966
2:09:28	Ron Hill (England)	1970
2:09:12*	Ian Thompson (England)	1974

Games record through 1974 race.

Pan-American Games Winners

Time	Name (Country)	Year
2:35:00	Delfo Carbrera (Argentina)	1951
2:59:09	Doroteo Flores (Guatemala)	1955
2:27:54	John J. Kelley (US)	1959
2:26:53	Fidel Negrete (Mexico)	1963
2:23:02	Andy Boychuk (Canada)	1967
2:22:40*	Frank Shorter (US)	1971
2:25:03	Carlos Mendoza (Cuba)	1975

Pan-American Games record through 1975 race.

International Women's Winners

Time	Name (Country)	Year
2:50:31	Liane Winter (West Germany)	1974
2:45:24*	Christa Vahlensieck (W. Ger.)	1976

Meet record through 1976 race.

A.A.U. Winners (Men)

Time	Name (Club/Country)	Year
2:33:00	Charles Mellor (Illinois AC)	1925
2:45:05	Clarence DeMar (Melrose Post)	1926
2:40:22	Clarence DeMar (Melrose Post)	1927
2:37:07	Clarence DeMar (Melrose Post)	1928
2:33:08	John Miles (Canada)	1929
2:25:21	Karl Koski (Finnish-American AC)	1930
2:32:38	William Agee (Baltimore)	1931
2:58:18	Clyde Martak (Baltimore)	1932
2:53:43	Dave Komonen (Finland/Canada)	1933
2:43:26	Dave Komonen (Finland/Canada)	1934
2:53:53	Pat Dengis (Stonewall Demo Club)	1935
2:38:14	William McMahon (Hibernians)	1936
2:44:22	Mel Porter (Millrose AA)	1937
2:39:38	Pat Dengis (Millrose AA)	1938
2:33:45	Pat Dengis (Baltimore)	1939
2:34:06	Gerard Cote (Canada)	1940
2:36:06	Joseph Smith (North Medford Club)	1941
2:37:54	Fred McGlone (Norfolk YMCA)	1942

2:38:35	Gerard Cote (Canada)	1943
2:40:48	Charles Robbins (US Navy)	1944
2:37:14	Charles Robbins (Norfolk Yard)	1945
2:47:53	Gerard Cote (Canada)	1946
2:40:11	Ted Vogel (Watertown, Mass.)	1947
2:48:32	John A. Kelley (Boston Edison)	1948
2:38:48	Victor Dyrgall (Millrose AA)	1949
2:45:55	John A. Kelley (Boston Edison)	1950
2:37:12	Jesse Van Zant (Boston AA)	1951
2:38:24	Victor Dyrgall (Millrose AA)	1952
2:48:12	Karl Leandersson (Sweden)	1953
2:46:13	Ted Corbitt (NY Pioneer Club)	1954
2:31:12	Nick Costes (Natick, Mass.)	1955
2:24:52	John J. Kelley (Boston AA)	1956
2:24:55	John J. Kelley (Boston AA)	1957
2:21:00	John J. Kelley (Boston AA)	1958
2:21:54	John J. Kelley (Boston AA)	1959
missing	John J. Kelley (Boston AA)	1960
2:26:53	John J. Kelley (Boston AA)	1961
2:27:39	John J. Kelley (Boston AA)	1962
2:20:17	John J. Kelley (Boston AA)	1963
2:24:15	Bud Edelen (Sioux Falls, S.D.)	1964
2:33:50	Gar Williams (Empire Harriers)	1965
2:22:50	Norm Higgins (Santa Monica AC)	1966
2:40:07	Ron Daws (Twin Cities TC)	1967
2:30:48	George Young (New Mexico)	1968
2:24:43	Tom Heinonen (San Diego TC)	1969
2:24:10	Robert Fitts (Millrose AA)	1970
2:16:48	Kenny Moore (Oregon TC)	1971
2:24:42	Edmund Norris (Boston AA)	1972
2:15:48	Doug Schmenk (E. Los Angeles AC)	1973
2:18:52	Ron Wayne (Oregon TC)	1974
2:17:27	Gary Tuttle (Beverly Hills Striders)	1975
2:15:15*	Gary Tuttle (Tobias Striders)	1976
2:17:49	Hakan Spik (Finland)	1977

Multiple winners: 8—John J. Kelley (1956-63); 3 each—Clarence DeMar (1926-28); Pat Dengis (1936, 38-39); Gerard Cote (1940, 43, 46); 2 each—Dave Komonen (1933-34); Charles Robbins (1944-45); John A. Kelley (1948, 51); Gary Tuttle (1975-76).

AAU meet record through 1977 race.

A.A.U. Winners (Women)

Time	Name (Club)	Year
2:55:17	Judy Ikenberry (Rialto RR)	1974
2:46:14	Kim Merritt (UW/Parkside)	1975
2:45:32*	Julie Brown (Los Angeles TC)	1976
2:46:34	Leal-Ann Reinhart (SFVTC)	1977

*AAU meet record through 1977 race.

Boston Marathon Winners (Men)

Time	Name (State/Country)	Year
2:55:10	John McDermott (New York)	1897
2:42:00	Ronald McDonald (Mass.)	1898
2:54:38	Lawrence Brignolia (Mass.)	1899
2:39:44	James Caffrey (Canada)	1900
2:29:23	James Caffrey (Canada)	1901
2:43:12	Sammy Mellor (New York)	1902
2:41:29	John Lorden (Massachusetts)	1903
2:38:04	Michael Spring (New York)	1904
2:38:25	Fred Lorz (New York)	1905
2:45:45	Timothy Ford (Massachusetts)	1906
2:24:24	Tom Longboat (Canada)	1907
2:25:43	Thomas Morrisey (New York)	1908
2:53:36	Henri Renaud (New Hampshire)	1909
2:28:52	Fred Cameron (Canada)	1910
2:21:39	Clarence DeMar (Massachusetts)	1911
2:21:18	Mike Ryan (New York)	1912
2:25:14	Fritz Carlson (Minnesota)	1913
2:25:01	James Duffy (Canada)	1914
2:31:41	Edouard Fabre (Canada)	1915
2:27:16	Arthur Roth (Massachusetts)	1916
2:28:37	Bill Kennedy (New York)	1917
	race not run	1918
2:29:13	Carl Lindner (Massachusetts)	1919
2:29:31	Peter Trivoulidas (Greece)	1920
2:18:57	Frank Zuna (New Jersey)	1921
2:18:10	Clarence DeMar (Massachusetts)	1922
2:23:37	Clarence DeMar (Massachusetts)	1923
2:29:40	Clarence DeMar (Massachusetts)	1924

2:33:00	Charles Mellor (Illinois)	1925
2:25:40	John Miles (Canada)	1926
2:40:22	Clarence DeMar (Massachusetts)	1927
2:37:07	Clarence DeMar (Massachusetts)	1928
2:33:08	John Miles (Canada)	1929
2:34:48	Clarence DeMar (Massachusetts)	1930
2:46:45	James Henigan (Massachusetts)	1931
2:33:36	Paul de Bruyn (Germany)	1932
2:31:01	Leslie Pawson (Rhode Island)	1933
2:32:53	Kave Komonen (Canada)	1934
2:32:07	John A. Kelley (Massachusetts)	1935
2:33:40	Ellison Brown (Rhode Island)	1936
2:33:20	Walter Young (Canada)	1937
2:35:34	Leslie Pawson (Rhode Island)	1938
2:28:51	Ellison Brown (Rhode Island)	1939
2:38:28	Gerard Cote (Canada)	1940
2:30:38	Leslie Pawson (Rhode Island)	1941
2:26:51	Joseph Smith (Massachusetts)	1942
2:28:25	Gerard Cote (Canada)	1943
2:31:50	Gerard Cote (Canada)	1944
2:30:40	John A. Kelley (Massachusetts)	1945
2:29:27	Stylianos Kyriakides (Greece)	1946
2:25:39	Yun Bok Suh (Korea)	1947
2:31:02	Gerard Cote (Canada)	1948
2:31:50	Gosta Leandersson (Sweden)	1949
2:32:39	Kee Yong Ham (Korea)	1950
2:27:45	Shigeki Tanaka (Japan)	1951
2:31:53	Doroteo Flores (Guatemala)	1952
2:18:59	Keizo Yamada (Japan)	1953
2:20:39	Veikko Karvonen (Finland)	1954
2:18:22	Hideo Hamamura (Japan)	1955
2:14:14	Antti Viskari (Finland)	1956
2:20:05	John J. Kelley (Connecticut)	1957
2:25:54	Franjo Mihalic (Yugoslavia)	1958
2:22:42	Eino Oksanen (Finland)	1959
2:20:54	Paavo Kotila (Finland)	1960
2:23:39	Eino Oksanen (Finland)	1961
2:23:48	Eino Oksanen (Finland)	1962
2:18:58	Aurele Vandendriessche (Belgium)	1963
2:19:59	Aurele Vandendriessche (Belgium)	1964
2:16:33	Morio Shigematsu (Japan)	1965
2:17:11	Kenji Kimihara (Japan)	1966
2:15:45	Dave McKenzie (New Zealand)	1967
2:22:17	Amby Burfoot (Connecticut)	1968
2:13:49	Yoshiaki Unetani (Japan)	1969

2:10:30	Ron Hill (Great Britain)	1970
2:18:45	Alvaro Mejia (Colombia)	1971
2:15:39	Olavi Suomalainen (Finland)	1972
2:16:03	Jon Anderson (Oregon)	1973
2:13:39	Neil Cusack (Ireland)	1974
2:09:55*	Bill Rodgers (Massachusetts)	1975
2:20:19	Jack Fultz	1976
2:14:46	Jerome Drayton (Canada)	1977

Meet record through 1977 race; race was less than full 26 miles 385 yards from 1897-1926 and 1953-56.

Multiple winners: 7—Clarence DeMar (1911, 1922-24, 1927-28, 1930); 4—Gerard Cote (1940, 1943-44, 1948); 3 each—Leslie Pawson (1933, 1938, 1941; Eino Oksanen (1959, 1961-62); 2 each—James Caffrey (1900-01); John Miles (1926, 1929); John A. Kelley (1935, 1945); Ellison Brown (1936, 1939); Aurelle Vandendriessche (1963-64).

Boston Marathon Winners (Women)

Time	Name (State/Country)	Year
3:10:26	Nina Kuscsik (New York)	1972
3:05:59	Jacqueline Hansen (California)	1973
2:47:11	Miki Gorman (California)	1974
2:42:24*	Liane Winter (W. Germany)	1975
2:47:10	Kim Merritt (Wisconsin)	1976
2:48:33	Miki Gorman (California)	1977

Meet record through 1977 race.

References

ORGANIZATIONS

Amateur Athletic Union (AAU). The AAU sponsors frequent local and regional events, and a full series of national championships from cross-country to ultra-marathons. Securing an AAU card (a testament of membership)—is a prerequisite to competing in an AAU event. It can be obtained at any AAU-sponsored race. It is, however, more practical to join before the race, since many events have entry deadlines and some have age or time restrictions. Yearly AAU dues generally are less than $5. The following are major AAU contacts:

● National Headquarters—AAU House, 3400 W. 86th St., Indianapolis, Ind. 46268.

● Long-Distance Running Committee Co-Chairmen—Bob Campbell, 39 Linnet St., West Roxbury, Mass. 02132; and Vince Chiappetta, 2 Washington Square Village, Apt. 9-D, New York, N.Y. 10012.

● Standard Committee (Course Certification)—Ted Corbitt, Apt. 8H, Sect. 4, 150 W. 225th St., New York, N.Y. 10463.

The national headquarters in Indianapolis can provide a list of its "associations"—the districts in which runners register. Association chairmen can give details on competition and clubs in an area.

Road Runners Club of America (RRCA). The RRCA chapters sponsor a variety of distance runs on a regular basis. These generally are less formal than AAU races and usually are less expensive to enter. The RRCA charges an annual membership fee similar to the AAU fee. The national president is Jeff Darman, 2737 Devonshire Pl., N.W., Washington, D.C. 20008. There are also five communications directors who can give regional information on competition and clubs:

● Ray Gordon, Route 2, Box 1037, Front Royal, Va. 22630.

● Nick Costes, Dept. of HPER, Troy State University, Troy, Ala. 36081.

● Bob Martin, 5834 Stoney Island Ave., Chicago, Ill. 60637.

● Steven Ryan, 9804 W. 12th St., Wichita, Kan. 67212.

● Herb Parsons, 170 Rosario Beach Rd., Anacortes, Wash. 98211.

PUBLICATIONS

A growing number of periodicals cover the booming sport of long-distance running. These range from international to local. The leading publishers:

● *Runner's World*, P.O. Box 366, Mountain View, Calif. 94042—publisher of *RW, The Runner, Marathoner* and the Runner's Book Series.

● *Track & Field News*, P.O. Box 296, Los Altos, Calif. 94022—publisher of *T&FN, Track Newsletter* and *Track Technique*.

● *Running*, P. O. Box 350, Salem, Ore. 97308.

● *Running Times*, 1816 Lamont St., N.W., Washington, D.C. 20010.

● *Runner's Gazette*, 102 W. Water St., Lansford, Pa. 18232.

● *Yankee Runner*, 19 Grove St., Merrimac, Mass. 01860.

● *NorCal Running Review*, P.O. Box 1551, San Mateo, Calif. 94401.

BOOKS/BOOKLETS

These publications relate closely to the material covered in *The Complete Marathoner*. All are available from World Publications, P.O. Box 366, Mountain View, Calif. 94042. Write for a book catalog.

● *Complete Diet Guide*, edited by Hal Higdon.

● *Exercises for Runners*, from the editors of *RW*.

● *Guide to Distance Running*, edited by Bob Anderson and Joe Henderson.

● *Interval Training*, by Nick Costes.

● *Jog, Run, Race*, by Joe Henderson.

● *New Views of Speed Training*, from the editors of *RW*.

● *Racing Techniques*, from the editors of *RW*.

● *Runner's Training Guide*, from the editors of *RW*.

● *Running with the Elements*, from the editors of *RW*.

● *The Complete Runner*, from the editors of *RW*.

● *The Running Body*, by E.C. Frederick.

● *The Running Foot Doctor*, by Steven I. Subotnick, D.P.M.

● *The Self-Made Olympian*, by Ron Daws.

● *Dr. Sheehan on Running*, by George Sheehan, M.D.

● *Training with Cerutty*, by Larry Myers.

● *Van Aaken Method*, by Ernst van Aaken, M.D.

● *Women's Running*, by Joan Ullyot, M.D.

Contributors

Thomas Bassler, M.D., practices in the Los Angeles area. As an officer with the American Medical Joggers Association, he has offered evidence to support his claim that marathoners develop an immunity to heart disease.

Ivan Berenyi, a resident of England, writes extensively on European athletics. This chapter originally appeared in *Athletics Weekly* and was adapted for *Runner's World*.

Gail Campbell of Los Gatos, Calif., authored *Marathon: The World of the Long-Distance Athlete,* a book covering many marathon-like activities.

Marshall Childs, a New York state marathoner, had several Bostons behind him when he wrote this chapter.

Alan Claremont, Ph.D., an exercise physiologist with the University of Wisconsin, also is one of the Midwest's leading long-distance runners.

Tom Clarke participated in the study he describes here while a student at the University of Florida. He now lives in Albany, N.Y.

Ted Corbitt was instrumental in establishing the course-measurement techniques recommended by the RRCA and AAU Standards Committees. He has headed the AAU committees for many years.

David Costill directs the Human Performance Laboratory at Ball State University, Muncie, Ind. He has written *What Research Tells the Coach about Distance Running.*

Ron Daws of St. Paul, Minn., made the 1967 Pan-American Games and '68 Olympic teams as a marathoner. He later authored *The Self-Made Olympian*, a book of training and racing advice.

Bob Fitts has both a wealth of marathon experience (including the Olympic Trials) and medical training. He runs and works in St. Louis.

E. C. Frederick and Jack Welch, both marathoners, are co-editors of the technical publication *Running*. Frederick also authored the booklet *The Running Body*.

Jack Galub is a free-lance writer working out of New York City, a runner and a frequent contributor to running publications.

Jacqueline Hansen of Los Angeles wrote of the race which resulted in a world women's record which stood for nearly two years.

Joe Henderson, editor of *Runner's World* from 1970-77 (and now the magazine's consulting editor), is a veteran of nearly 30 marathons.

Hal Higdon, *Runner's World* Editor at Large, has bests in the marathon of 2:21:55 as a 33-year-old youngster and 2:34:37 as a 46-year-old oldster. He doesn't recall his exact "very slow" time but suspects it to be around 3:30.

M. Dean Hill is a sportswriter for *The Daily Breeze*, a newspaper in the Los Angeles area where the Palos Verdes Marathon is conducted.

Ray Hosler, an experienced marathoner who did his early running in the Rocky Mountain area, now is a member of the *Runner's World* editorial staff.

Jerry Kanter is a computer scientist with the Honeywell company near Boston, the company which provides computerized scoring help for the Boston Marathon.

John A. Kelley is "Mr. Marathon" in the United States. He ran his first one 50 years ago, and has since won twice at Boston and qualified for three Olympic teams. Now in his 70s, he continues to compete and to work as an artist in his home at East Dennis, Mass.

Jim Lilliefors, author of *The Running Mind* (a study of the psychological aspects of the sport), is a member of the *Runner's World* editorial staff.

Ben Londeree, a seasoned marathoner, is an exercise physiologist with the Human Performance Laboratory, University of Missouri.

Nick Marshall of Camp Hill, Pa., is the third fastest 100-kilometer runner in US history, ultra-marathon statistician for the National Running Data Center and a staff writer for *Runner's Gazette* of Lansford, Pa.

Brian Maxwell, one of North America's best marathoners, finished third in the 1977 Boston race. He coaches distance runners at the University of California in Berkeley.

Dennis McBride, a marathoner from Milwaukee, interviewed Wisconsin runner Kim Merritt after the 1976 Boston Marathon.

Donald Monkerud of Watsonville, Calif., is a staff writer for *Runner's World* magazine. He frequently writes on diet-related subjects.

Jerry Nason, former sports editor of the *Boston Globe*, is acknowledged to be THE expert on the Boston Marathon. He has covered that race and its personalities for nearly 50 years.

Dr. Tim Noakes, a South African physician and long-distance runner, has studied and written extensively on the problems of hot-weather running. This chapter originally appeared in *Topsport*, a South African magazine.

Dave Prokop, a *Runner's World* staff member, edited the book *African Running Revolution.* Prokop is the Canadian record-holder for 50 miles.

George Sheehan, a medical doctor practicing in Red Bank, N.J., is medical editor of *Runner's World* magazine.

Paul Slovic worked as a statistician with the Oregon Research Institute in Eugene at the time he compiled this information.

Manfred Steffny edits the German running magazine *Spiridon.* He is a sub-2:20 marathoner who competed for West Germany in the 1968 and '72 Olympics.

Gary Tuttle of Ventura, Calif., won the AAU Marathon Championships in 1975 and '76. In addition, he holds several American long-distance track records.

Mike Tymn has been closely involved with the growth of marathoning in Hawaii, both as a promoter and runner. He ran 2:32 at age 40.

Joan Ullyot, a San Francisco medical doctor specializing in exercise physiology, competed in the 1974 and '76 International Women's Marathon Championships. A 2:51 marathoner, she also is the author of *Women's Running.*

Peter Van Handel is associated with the Human Performance Laboratory at Ball State University, Muncie, Ind. The lab, directed by Dr. David Costill, has done ground-breaking research on running physiology.

Len Wallach, a key official at a number of championship races, is the former National Chairman of AAU Masters Long-Distance Running. He wrote *The Human Race,* a book centering on the Bay to Breakers.

Dr. Young is associated with the Institute of Atmosphere Physics at the University of Arizona, Tucson. He has run a marathon in the mid-2:20s and held the indoor record for the distance.

Chapters without bylines were written by Joe Henderson.

Illustrations by Amy Schwartz.

The runner's bare essentials*

Your shoes, your shorts, *Runner's World* and off you go into the world of running.

Runner's World the nation's leading running publication, has been covering the jogging/running scene since 1966. Articles for the beginning jogger through the competitive racer appear monthly. Every issue of *Runner's World* is loaded with good practical advice on medical problems, technical tips, equipment reviews, interviews with leading coaches & runners, and much more.

Come run with friends. Each month 510,000 fellow enthusiasts are sharing the information in the pages of *Runner's World* The joy of running is explored and expanded with each information packed issue—it's your coach and trainer making a monthly visit.

Exciting articles monthly: Fun Running, Run Better on Less Mileage, The Basics of Jogging, First Aid for the Injured, Running and Mental Health, Beginning Racing. Monthly columns by Dr. George Sheehan on medical advice, Dr. Joan Ullyot on women's running, Arthur Lydiard on training and racing.

Subscribe now for trouble-free miles of running. Just send $9.50 for 12 months or call (415) 965-3240 and charge to Master Charge or BankAmericard/Visa.

*Possibly because of climatic conditions or modesty you might want to add a shirt.

Runner's World Box 2680, Dept. 5534, Boulder, CO 80322